Affordable Housing in Charlotte

Affordable Housing in Charlotte

What One City's History Tells Us
about America's Pressing Problem

Tom Hanchett

The University of North Carolina Press ■ Chapel Hill

This book was published with the assistance of the Luther H. Hodges Jr. and Luther H. Hodges Sr. Fund of the University of North Carolina Press.

© 2025 Tom Hanchett
All rights reserved

Designed by April Leidig
Set in Garamond and Alegreya Sans by Copperline Book Services, Inc.

Manufactured in the United States of America

Cover art: Booth Gardens, built in 1978 in Charlotte's Fourth Ward, exemplifies the trend away from large public housing projects to smaller "scattered" apartment complexes during the 1970s and '80s. Photo by Albert Dulin, 2020; used by permission.

Library of Congress Cataloging-in-Publication Data
Names: Hanchett, Thomas W., author.
Title: Affordable housing in Charlotte : what one city's history tells us about America's pressing problem / Tom Hanchett.
Description: Chapel Hill : The University of North Carolina Press, [2025] | Includes bibliographical references and index.
Identifiers: LCCN 2024060672 | ISBN 9781469686196 (cloth ; alk. paper) | ISBN 9781469686202 (paperback ; alk. paper) | ISBN 9781469683171 (epub) | ISBN 9781469687780 (pdf)
Subjects: LCSH: Housing—North Carolina—History. | Regional planning—North Carolina—History. | Housing—United States.
Classification: LCC HD7303.N8 H36 2025 | DDC 307.3/3609756— dc23/eng/20250307
LC record available at https://lccn.loc.gov/2024060672

For product safety concerns under the European Union's General Product Safety Regulation (EU GPSR), please contact gpsr@mare-nostrum.co.uk or write to the University of North Carolina Press and Mare Nostrum Group B.V., Mauritskade 21D, 1091 GC Amsterdam, The Netherlands.

CONTENTS

1 Introduction

11 **CHAPTER 1**
Before Government Got Involved
- NOAH and Market-Built Affordable Housing

25 **CHAPTER 2**
Federal Help for Better Housing
- FHA Apartments and Public Housing

47 **CHAPTER 3**
Subsidizing the "Free Market"
- FHA 608 Apartments

69 **CHAPTER 4**
Bathrooms, Building Codes, and "Slum Clearance"
- Minimum Housing Standards? Or "Urban Renewal"?

87 **CHAPTER 5**
Tax Shelters and Investor-Built Low-Rent Housing
- Accelerated Depreciation
- FHA 221(d)(3), FHA 236, and the Turnkey Programs

115 **CHAPTER 6**
Dispersing Subsidized Housing throughout the City
- Scattered-Site
- Section 8 Project-Based

143 **CHAPTER 7**
1980s Housing Revolution:
Inventing the Low-Income Housing Tax Credit Era
- Low-Income Housing Tax Credit
- North Carolina Housing Finance Agency and North Carolina Housing Trust Fund
- Charlotte's Innovative Housing Fund (Today Charlotte Housing Trust Fund)
- Section 8 Vouchers

169 **CHAPTER 8**
Remix:
Rediscovering Mixed-Income Housing,
1990s and Beyond
- Federal HOPE VI
- Local Nonprofit Charlotte–Mecklenburg Housing Partnership

197 **CHAPTER 9**
The Tumultuous 2010s
- RAD, Inlivian, and Business-Driven Public Housing
- Cheap Money, K-Shaped Recovery, Gentrification, and Loss of NOAH
- Local Push for Affordable Projects—While Falling Further Behind

227 **EPILOGUE**
After a Whole Book about Affordable Housing, Where Are We?
- Affordable Housing in the COVID Years
- Lessons of History
- A Way Forward

237 A Few Words about Methods and Sources
241 Acknowledgments
243 Notes
303 Bibliography
317 Index

Affordable Housing in Charlotte

Introduction

Most books about the history of affordable housing in America are Washington-centric. They trace the factions and philosophies that have clashed over time to produce US housing policy.

This book explores what happens in the real world after policy is made.

A dizzying array of variables shape low-income housing, far more than can be addressed in one book. This study focuses on the role of government and how that has changed from the 1930s to today. I touch on other issues—architecture, race, the lived experience of tenants. But to make this a manageable project, I'm mostly trying to document what got built and to puzzle out why that changed from decade to decade.

Charlotte, North Carolina, provides the case study. It's a fast-growing midsize city that's zoomed from 100,000 people in 1940, roughly when public housing began in the United States, to nearly 900,000 in the early 2020s, when this book ends. Today, like most of America's growth hotspots, it's experiencing rapid gentrification in older, once-affordable neighborhoods. There is a serious shortage of housing for low-income residents.

That has produced intense and widely felt frustration. Why doesn't someone do something? That was my question when I started this research. What I found surprised me.

Six Myths, Three Hard Truths, Two Surprising Ironies

Six Myths

"Charlotte never does anything about affordable housing." UNTRUE. Government bodies, nonprofits, and other organizations have developed projects in every decade from the 1930s to the 2020s. More than 150 exist today in Charlotte–Mecklenburg, supplying nearly 14,000 units of housing to people at every level of need.

"Whatever's been done about affordable housing, it's been a failure." UNTRUE. There indeed have been projects that did badly over time, because of either the way they were planned or the way they were maintained. Many more have succeeded—so well, indeed, that neighbors are often unaware of them.

"Build affordable housing in my neighborhood and my property values will collapse." UNTRUE. In developments near elite SouthPark Mall, in First Ward and Third Ward and Fourth Ward in the center city, at Brightwalk north of downtown, and on Providence Road to the south, low-income units mix with market-rate housing. Value of the market-rate dwellings in those places is going up rapidly, typically doubling—or more—in less than ten years.

"Charlotte has a booming economy. People don't need 'affordable housing'—they just need to get a job. If they'd work, their housing problems would disappear." UNTRUE. In Charlotte's homeless shelters right now, over half the people have jobs—and in fact are working full-time.

"Affordable housing efforts make people rent rather than help them buy and build equity (wealth)." UNTRUE. While some initiatives indeed have aimed at helping renters (the focus of this book), many others have aimed at helping people buy. Charlotte's Habitat for Humanity, to name just one effort, has assisted over 1,500 low-income Charlotteans in becoming owners of new houses throughout the city.

"Affordable—for whom? So-called affordable housing doesn't help those who really need it." UNTRUE. Charlotte has over 4,000 apartments built to serve people making 30 percent or less of area median income (an official measure of extremely low-income). That said, many more units are needed. Charlotte has shortages of housing at every level from median income down. Shortages are most acute in the lowest-wealth range. More housing is needed over all ranges.

Three Hard Truths

Build wealth AND stay affordable? We want real estate to build equity (rise in value over time)—but also to stay affordable over the decades. *It is impossible to do both* (though Habitat for Humanity comes close—see chapter 7).

"The private market can do it better" OR *"Government can do it better"*? Americans have moved back and forth in their thinking. The reality? *History shows that neither is the magic bullet.*

If we just (insert new magic bullet here), can we solve the housing problem once and for all? Not likely. The real estate market is fast-changing, especially in this fast-growing city. The residents who need affordable housing, the investors, the developers, the governments and organizations—all have ever-changing situations and desires over time. *History shows that no ONE solution has worked in the past—but Charlotte does possess a range of approaches that have worked and are working, offering multiple models for how to move forward.*

Two Surprising Ironies

Irony 1: The subsidies in "subsidized housing" do make that housing affordable for poor people who could not otherwise afford it—*but the actual subsidy dollars mostly go to rich people.* This book will trace the history of how that came to be.

Irony 2: As you ponder that, consider this reality, as well: *You live in subsidized housing. Yes, you do.* From the federal loan guarantees of the Federal Housing Administration (FHA) to obscure aids such as federal grants underwriting the extension of suburban water lines, Washington assistance has greatly shaped our built environment. You benefit, whether you're a renter or an owner. For instance, the mortgage interest deduction on our federal income tax, just by itself, gives homeowners a subsidy that runs roughly five times larger each year than the US government's direct spending for low-income housing.[1]

What's the Story?

The chapters ahead will trace the interplay of two themes. One has to do with how affordable housing has been financed over time, the other with changing notions about how such housing should fit into the city at large.

As we explore, the main focus will be on multifamily rental apartments. Watch for sidebars that add info on single-family and owner-occupied housing.

Finance Phase 1, 1930s–1980s:
Get Government Involved? If So, How?

Before the late 1930s, nearly all rental housing for low-income people was what's now called **NOAH: naturally occurring affordable housing**.

But reliance on unregulated capitalism didn't work well—not only for tenants stuck in unheated ramshackle dwellings without toilets but also for upscale neighbors who slowly realized that squalor meant health risks for the city as a whole.

Why Read a Book about Charlotte?

In most scholarly fields, the "case study" is a powerful tool. Carefully documenting how forces play out in a particular situation gives insights that are often not visible when looking only at the big picture.

That's seldom been done in histories of affordable housing.

Digging into Charlotte's experience over the entire eighty-plus years since the start of public housing offers clues about how Washington policies actually worked on the ground—*not just in Charlotte, but in your city as well.*

A Few Things to Know about the Queen City

- Named for England's Queen Charlotte, it was founded in 1768 but remained small until it became the trading hub for America's main textile mill region after 1900. Charlotte banks, begun with textile money, led the way in inventing interstate banking starting in the 1980s. That fueled a growth spiral that made Charlotte the nation's fifteenth largest city and second biggest banking center by 2020.* Banks will be major players in this book, especially Bank of America (and its predecessors NCNB and NationsBank), whose world headquarters is the tallest tower on Charlotte's skyline.
- Social groups here are a bit different from those in cities outside the South. This region got few immigrants in the decades around 1900; until recently Charlotte's population was roughly two-thirds native-born white, one-third native-born African American. Charlotte's prosperity began attracting immigrants during the 1990s, and today the population is about 15 percent foreign-born.
- Charlotte's borders have grown with the population. Unlike many US cities that are hemmed in by politically separate suburbs, Charlotte has been able to annex most of its surrounding area until recently.
- That may have helped Charlotte enjoy relatively good government over time. Without separate suburbs to run away to, Charlotteans have often worked together to tackle problems. In 1971, for instance, the US Supreme Court

(continued)

---

*Charlotte is a good example of an urban growth machine, as defined by John Logan and Harvey Molotch. Land use and land values are central concerns in most political debates in Charlotte. Logan and Molotch, *Urban Fortunes*. On the interplay of racial dynamics, growth concerns, and political regime theory in Charlotte, see S. Smith, *Boom for Whom?*

But housing advocates—not just anti-poverty activists but also real estate developers—rose up in protest.

So Congress created two new mechanisms, Section 8 vouchers and the Low-Income Housing Tax Credit. The vouchers gave rent supplements to low-income households, which helped them to rent existing for-profit apartments. LIHTC (pronounced "lie-tek," rhyming with "high tech") granted substantial tax breaks to private investors who put dollars into constructing apartment projects for the not-well-to-do.

Scholars, by the way, often point to this as evidence of a new era of "neoliberalism," sweeping away a previous commitment to government-provided public housing. But in reality, the drive to minimize Washington's role and instead to subsidize "private" developers had been underway since FHA 608 in the 1940s. The 1980s legislation differed in specifics but not in general thrust.

Section 8 worked pretty well (though there's a nagging problem with landlords who refuse to accept the vouchers), and it's still going strong today.

LIHTC worked even better. Apartments got built. Investors generally did adequate maintenance over time. And they became advocates for the program—which helped it continue with minimal changes for four decades, to the present day.

However, in the long term, LIHTC had serious flaws. It defined "low-income" as households earning 60 percent of the local area's median income, ignoring the many people who made less than that. Also, credits from the LIHTC program are sharply limited. Washington never has enough to fund all the good projects that apply. Those flaws have meant that our supply of affordable housing is falling further and further behind our need.

Where to Build? From Set-Apart, to Scattered-Site, to Mixed-In

Our second theme, interwoven with the financial story, is a shift in the ideal of what makes good urban housing. NOAH had been mixed throughout the city (as we shall see in chapter 1), to an extent that is now surprising. As reformers worked to eliminate bad housing, they initially thought that new low-income apartments should be built in big projects, set apart on their own.

The error of that thinking became painfully apparent. By the 1960s, barely twenty-five years after construction of the first public housing, such projects were widely regarded as hellholes. Some cities dynamited derelict high-rises, most notoriously the Pruitt-Igoe complex in St. Louis, demolished in the 1970s. Housing advocates urged a new "scattered-site" approach to low-income housing. Smaller projects should be inserted among other developments in many parts of the city. In Charlotte, an interracial cohort of activists, both in the community and in government, made this city a national leader in scattered-site construction by the 1980s.

What if such housing was even more integrated in the city? What if multiple incomes mingled in the same development? What if housing and other types of uses coexisted in the same walkable area? Since the late 1990s, most of Charlotte's low-income housing has followed this newest philosophy—part of a wider shift toward mixed-use in every aspect of urban design.

The shift from **set-apart** to **scattered-site** to **mixed-income** has produced noticeably better housing. Residents report feeling less isolated and unsafe. Neighbors are often only vaguely aware that affordable housing is nearby.

Another big measure of success: not one low-income housing site developed in Charlotte since the dawn of the scattered-site era has been abandoned. Even when new construction on the land brings more units, the neighbors have not risen in opposition. And that comfort level has increased since mixed-income developments began in the late 1990s.

For all the uproar that often transpires when a fresh site is announced, in reality low-income housing is generally a good neighbor.

Today and Tomorrow

Even with all of the effort through a span of eight decades, Charlotte still woefully lacks housing for its poorest residents. Reported the *Charlotte Observer* in 2021: "An average one-bedroom apartment in Charlotte … is $1152 per month, but households at 30% AMI can only afford $405. … There is a dire lack of housing for those at or below 30% AMI, which is $17,700 for an individual or $25,250 household income for a family of four. … There are roughly 5,000 Housing Choice (more commonly known as Section Eight) vouchers in circulation locally, but a waiting list of 6,000 individuals, Inlivian [Charlotte's housing authority] officials have said."[2]

Some percentage (10 percent? 20 percent?) of Charlotteans will always need housing assistance. As a society we've begun to recognize that reality. Since the mid-2010s, Charlotte has dramatically ramped up its aid to affordable housing construction. The city's Housing Trust Fund announced seventeen new apartment complexes in 2020 alone, adding 1,786 new units.[3]

But estimates put Charlotte's shortfall at anywhere from 23,000 to 34,000 units.

Current programs, no matter how energetically administered, can come nowhere near supplying that number.

In the final section of this book, I'll suggest one approach, rooted in history, that could help close the gap and keep it closed.

Some Definitions

What's "Affordable"?

Your residence is affordable if it costs not more than 30 percent of your income.

The phrase "affordable housing" came into use in the 1970s.* Other common terms over the years have included "low-rent housing," "low-income housing," and "low- and moderate-income housing."

Washington defines "affordable housing" at three levels pegged to area median income (AMI):

- Households earning 80 percent or less of AMI = "low-income"
- Households earning 50 percent or less of AMI = "very low-income"
- Households earning 30 percent or less of AMI = "extremely low-income"†

That covers a wide array of people, many of whom you almost certainly rely on in your own life. Most nurses, most teachers, and some first responders fall in the first category. Food service workers, maintenance workers, and childcare providers are often in the second category. Many combine several part-time jobs, laboring more than forty hours per week. People in the bottom category include retirees who depend on Social Security (which pays only about $1,000 per month—desperately inadequate when rent alone is $1,000+).‡

Who Owns Affordable Housing?

"Public housing" makes up only a small fraction of low-income housing.

(continued)

---

* The term "affordable housing" was not used in the United States before the mid-1970s. HUD chief Patricia Harris helped popularize it: "An adequate supply of affordable housing continues to be our greatest challenge." "Free Enterprise?," *Chicago News Journal*, June 23, 1977. While "affordable housing" has referred mainly to rental units for low-income tenants, Ken Szymanski of the Charlotte Apartment Association observed in 2018 that an overheated housing market was making it difficult for even middle-income Charlotteans to find affordable homes—as I will document in chapter 9. Szymanski, "Can We Revive Real Meaning of 'Affordable Housing'?"

† Anderson with assistance from Butts, *Charlotte–Mecklenburg*, 28.

‡ Popkin et al., *Decade of HOPE VI*, 44–45; Baker et al., "Grandparents Raising Grandchildren."

Public Housing

Public housing is built, owned, and operated by government. It is funded in part by the federal government and operated by the local tax-funded housing authority (in this case, the Charlotte Housing Authority, renamed Inlivian in 2019).

Examples in Charlotte have ranged from big Southside Homes to mixed-income First Ward Place.

Affordable Housing Built and Operated by Nonprofits

Charlotte has a very active housing nonprofit, the Charlotte–Mecklenburg Housing Partnership, founded in 1988 (renamed DreamKey Partners in 2021). Among its dozens of projects is mixed-income Brightwalk on Statesville Avenue. Other nonprofits that have developed apartments include the Salvation Army (Booth Gardens in Fourth Ward) and the YWCA (townhouses on the Y's campus on Park Road).

Investor-Owned Low-Rent Housing

Did you know that nearly one-third of the housing that's been purpose-built for low-income tenants is owned by private investors? The current subsidy is the Low-Income Housing Tax Credit, introduced in 1986. I was surprised to discover earlier tools—the obscurely named FHA 608, FHA 221(d)(3), Section 236, Turnkey I, and Section 8 Project-Based—all of which produced low-income housing that continues to function as an important part of our city today.

Section 8 Housing

This term usually refers to housing choice vouchers, introduced in the 1980s, which give low-income renters a supplement that they can use to rent existing, privately owned apartments. A Section 8 tenant thus can be anywhere in the city (though, in practice, some landlords refuse to participate).

There are some other variations, such as Section 8 Project-Based, which I'll define in chapter 6.

NOAH

NOAH stands for "naturally occurring affordable housing." That means privately owned apartments, usually located in areas where housing stock has aged and lost some value, pushing rents down into the affordable range.

Traditionally, NOAH is the biggest source of low-rent housing—though that is in jeopardy today.

CHAPTER 1

Before Government Got Involved

- NOAH and Market-Built Affordable Housing

When housing advocates talk about NOAH, they aren't discussing the guy who led his followers through the biblical flood. But there are some similarities.

NOAH stands for "naturally occurring affordable housing"—which is the way that nearly all low-income people have been housed throughout our history. The various efforts to intentionally create affordable housing that will be discussed in this book are a small drop in the bucket compared to the housing that's traditionally been available through NOAH.

That's especially important to understand today in Charlotte. As in many other cities across America, NOAH is disappearing rapidly. During the decades since about 2000, for reasons no one fully understands, urbanites with money and choice started moving inward toward the central neighborhoods of US cities.

That's a huge reversal from the pattern of the previous couple hundred years. Traditionally, Americans with the cash to do it moved outward—to new streetcar suburbs in the 1890s, to "ranch house" (note the romantically rural terminology) subdivisions in the 1950s, and so on. As they left older areas, those neighborhoods "filtered down," becoming less expensive and thus more affordable to low-income residents. For folks struggling to keep their heads above water economically (that's the parallel with biblical boat-building Noah), the old dwellings were a godsend.

Filtering down is not happening now but instead the opposite. Today, every neighborhood within five miles of Charlotte's center city is seeing prices rise, worn-but-serviceable older houses and apartments torn down, and big new single-family dwellings, townhouses, and mid-rise apartment structures built. Between 2010 and 2017, some 28,000 units of rental housing in apartment complexes dating from the 1950s to the 1970s disappeared; investors bought them up, did renovations and added granite countertops, and doubled the rent.

NOAH rentals aren't gone completely. But that segment of the housing market—which society has relied upon so heavily, often without realizing it—is no longer something that we can take for granted.

In this chapter we'll look back at NOAH during the early twentieth century, exploring how and where it was created—in the center city, in early suburbia, and in African American neighborhoods. Then be watching throughout the subsequent chapters for ways that NOAH has expanded or contracted.

From NOAH to Parking Lot

To begin to get a sense of how NOAH has traditionally functioned, let's look at a couple of blocks in Charlotte's center city. Today the two-story red-brick William Treloar House is a forlorn landmark, presiding over two blocks of parking lots adjacent to Imaginon, Charlotte's children's theater and library. A century and a half ago, this was prime residential real estate—but it also held dwellings of some of Charlotte's least wealthy citizens.

That mixing of incomes surprises us today, but it was typical of American cities in the nineteenth century. It persisted as these blocks aged. Well into the 1930s, as we'll see, homeowners such as the Treloar family lived alongside renters. The mixing including more than just different incomes. A grocery store did business on one corner. And the blocks held Black residents as well as whites—a pattern that existed for many decades.

■ ■ ■ ■ ■

William Treloar built his house in 1887.[1] It's actually a pair of townhouses, a form common in Philadelphia where Treloar had previously lived. He had come to Charlotte as a young entrepreneur, got involved in gold mining, and then owned the Central Hotel and a string of store buildings. He was a wealthy man when he erected his two-story home just a short walk from the heart of the city. North Brevard Street was then filling up with spacious two-story residences of business leaders.

The national Sanborn Map Company drew maps of the block in the decades after 1900. They show Treloar's double-house at bottom left (see fig. 1.2). Five other big two-story houses marched down Brevard Street, and houses nearly as large stood along Seventh and Sixth Street.

So, it's an upper-income block, right? Well, not exactly. Look closely and you'll see a mix of buildings that seems remarkable by today's standards.

Figure 1.1. *A*: William Treloar's double house, 328 N. Brevard Street. It is the only survivor today from a block of Victorian-era dwellings in Charlotte's center city. Albert Dulin photo, 2024. *B*: Treloar house and neighbors as they may have looked circa 1890s. Drawing by David Woodley.

- At least four of the big houses have tiny houses behind them, each with its own street number.
- The house next to Treloar's is labeled "Board'g"—a house in which rooms were rented to people who also were provided with meals ("room and board").
- The dwelling (labeled "D") at the upper left of the map has a one-story grocery store ("Gro.") attached to it.
- Turn the corner onto Caldwell Street and the dwellings get smaller, most of them duplexes. And note that all three buildings are on a single parcel of land, likely all rental units owned by the same landlord.

Who lived on this block? To get a sense of that, let's look at the 1930 US Census, in which the census taker walked down each street, talked to residents, and made a careful list showing every occupant.

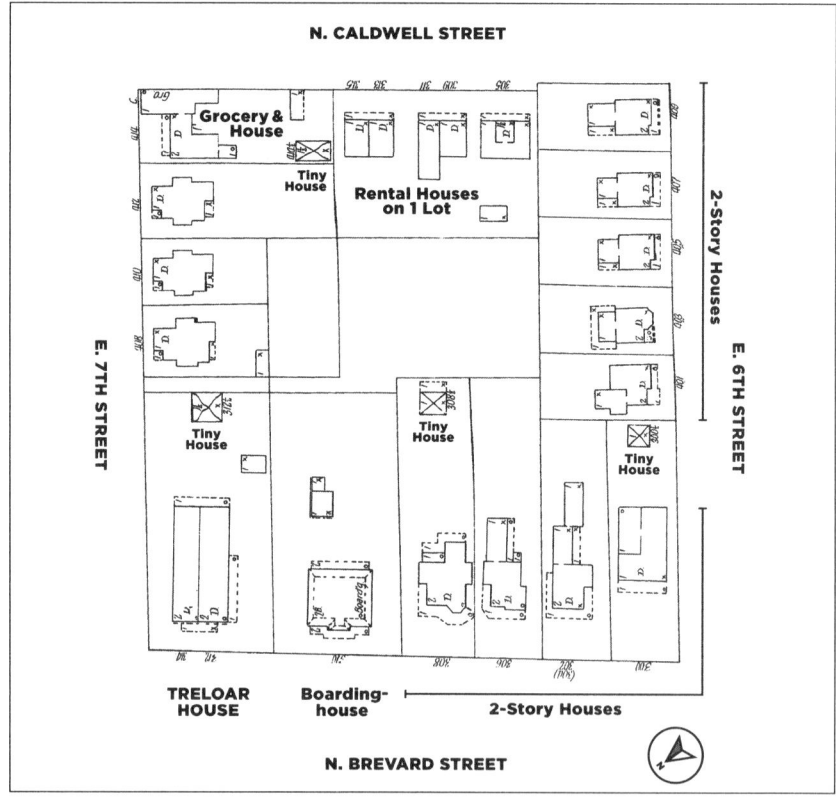

Figure 1.2. The Treloar house and surrounding buildings on its block. Base map: Sanborn insurance map, 1911, courtesy of Library of Congress.

Nearly every house held not just a nuclear family (father, mother, children) but usually additional relatives. And nearly every dwelling also held lodgers: unrelated individuals or couples who rented rooms by the week.

At 300 North Brevard Street, for instance—the corner property at the lower right—in 1930 there lived Fannie Morris with her son, sister, and niece plus ten lodgers. Mrs. Morris worked full-time running the lodging house, her son was unemployed, her sister was an inspector at a manufacturing plant, and the niece was a department store clerk. The lodgers included a shipping clerk, a house carpenter, a gas station attendant, a store clerk, a sheet metal worker, and two electricians.

One house, fourteen residents! We can't literally calculate their wealth in terms of area median income, the metric used today. But many of the jobs were similar to those held now by "working poor" who qualify for affordable housing. Many—though not all. Note the two electricians, likely pretty well paid.

This boardinghouse phenomenon was commonplace in older neighborhoods near America's downtowns. Thomas Wolfe's novel *Look Homeward, Angel* recalled life in his mother's boardinghouse in Asheville, North Carolina, during the early 1910s. Carson McCullers, who boarded on Central Avenue and on East Boulevard in Charlotte during 1937–38, made a boardinghouse the setting for her 1940 classic novel, *The Heart Is a Lonely Hunter*.

A block with boardinghouses typically also held single-family dwellings. The 1930 census counted twenty residences on our Charlotte sample block. Five were single-family homes. It would not be until the late 1940s that Charlotte adopted the new idea of "zoning" (see chapter 4), which would designate neighborhoods as either all single-family or all multifamily.

Indeed, William Treloar and his family enthusiastically embraced the mixture of owners and renters. In 1887 he published a newspaper ad seeking a tenant for the other half of his new home: "handsome dwelling, eleven well-ventilated rooms with every convenience a man could desire. The ladies are especially invited to examine. The owner will occupy the Seventh Street side of said house in a few days."[2] When William passed away, his married daughter and her husband continued to live on one side and rent out the other into their old age in the 1930s—five decades of comfortable coexistence of owners and renters.

▪ ▪ ▪ ▪ ▪

Even more surprising, our block was racially mixed. Whites lived on the Brevard, Seventh, and Eighth Street sides of the block. Along Caldwell Street, however, the 1930 census showed that all residents were African American. That interracial pattern, seldom seen in our own lifetime, actually was not unusual in southern cities during the first half of the twentieth century. My history book about Charlotte's urban development, *Sorting Out the New South City*, describes racial geography as a "quilt" during these decades. A few blocks might hold African Americans and then give way to a few blocks of whites.

African Americans lived on this particular part of Caldwell Street and blocks just to the east for half a century—from the first decade of the 1900s through the mid-1950s (when Charlotte's city directories stopped showing race). It was a stable pattern, not just some momentary transition. In 1930, the African Americans in the duplexes along Caldwell Street included a "runner" for a bank, a butler, a hotel bellhop, three maids, a laundry worker, a "common laborer," a cook in a private home, and a cook in a café. Again, it was an economic mix that included working folk who today often qualify for affordable housing assistance.

■ ■ ■ ■ ■

So, what are we seeing here? Looking at one typical block of the center city, we're finding an impressive array of naturally occurring affordable housing. It welcomed people low on the economic ladder—though very few of them were jobless. Rental and single-family housing was intermingled. Most residents could likely walk to work, not needing to own a car—an additional boon to household budgets. Black and white areas had some separation, but it was minimal. Everyone was in close proximity to each other and to employment opportunities.

If this pattern held across all of the center city (which it largely did), the area that is now inside today's Interstate 277 beltway—roughly 150 blocks—had perhaps 22,500 units of NOAH during the first half of the twentieth century.

Today, it's entirely gone. Some purpose-built low-income housing does exist: nine apartment complexes holding about 900 units. That's probably more than you are aware of (see chapters 6 and 8). And it's a commendable achievement. But the contrast between 22,500 units and 900 units is stark.

■ ■ ■ ■ ■

Later in this chapter, we'll venture out to the new "streetcar suburbs" of early twentieth-century Charlotte, where we'll find interesting variations on the theme of mixture. But before we leave the Treloar block, let's peek at how its history unfolded from the 1910s into the 1960s.

The Sanborn map drawn in 1911 documented the density and variety we've been discussing. A subsequent Sanborn visit in 1951, forty years later, showed the same thing with only tiny differences (see fig. 1.3). After 1951, however, things

Before Government Got Involved ■ 17

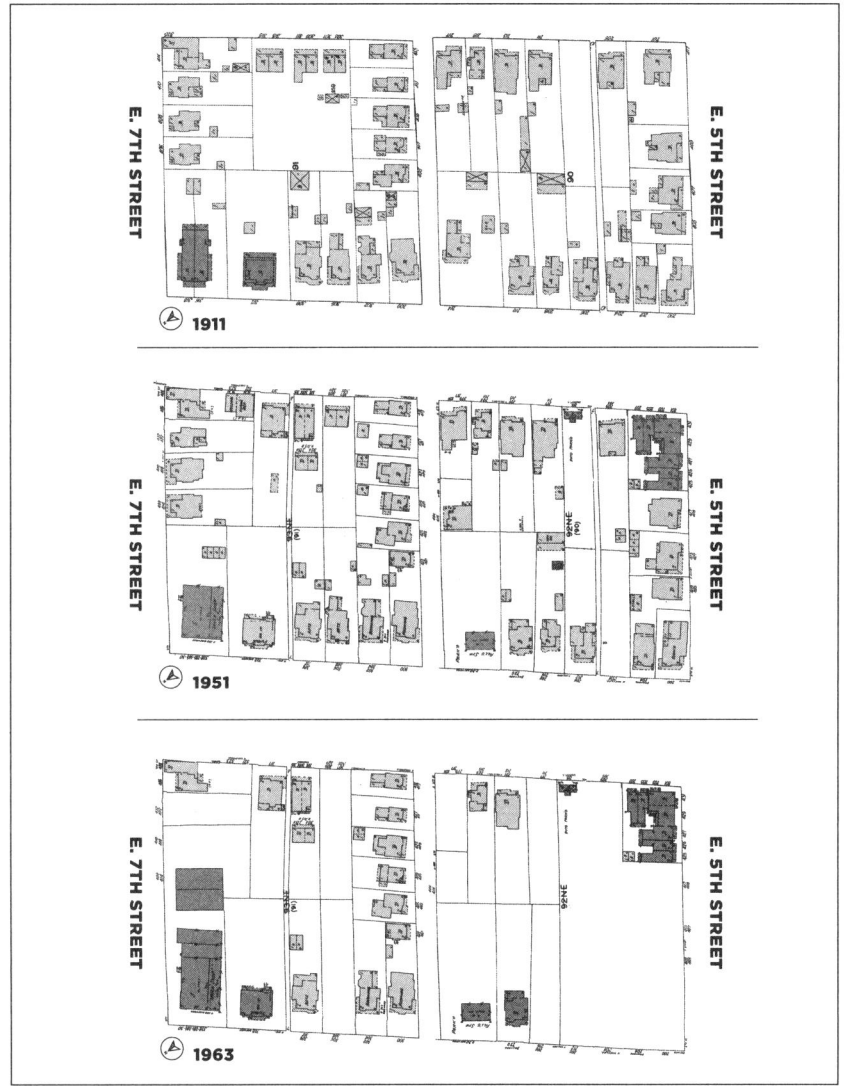

Figure 1.3. Sanborn maps showed much continuity in our sample blocks in 1911 and 1951; then came rapid change. Sanborn insurance maps, 1911, 1951, and 1963, courtesy of Library of Congress.

changed dramatically. Compare the 1951 map with the 1963 map, and you see a growing emptiness. Density was eroding sharply. On the Treloar block, six houses disappeared. On the adjacent block, a dozen more were gone. The land sat vacant—temporary parking lots awaiting some future development.

What's going on here? As we'll see in chapter 2 of this book, part of the story will be new government incentives for development in the suburbs, courtesy of the Federal Housing Administration. FHA aid after World War II enabled rapid construction of single-family homes and apartment complexes, pulling middle-income—and below-middle-income—folks out to the city's edge. Another part of the story will be a mindset: mixture is bad, separation is good. FHA planning assistance and the rise of zoning encouraged that way of thinking, as we shall see. Eventually, Washington offered money to cities that demolished low-income residential areas (see chapter 4). But even before that so-called urban renewal program, NOAH was slipping away.

Suburban Rental Housing for the Middle Class and the Elite

Well into the early twentieth century, most Charlotteans lived in rental housing. Until the introduction of federal mortgage insurance and the long-term twenty-year or thirty-year mortgage in the 1930s, the obstacles to homeownership were daunting. You had to make a cash down payment of half the purchase price or more. Then you had to pay the balance in two to five years. Only about one-third of American families owned their own home, compared with about two-thirds today.

Every neighborhood included rental housing mixed in with owner-occupied dwellings. To live in rental housing carried little stigma. Neither did living next to rental housing. Indeed, just the opposite held true. The range of investment possibilities we take for granted today—easy access to the stock market, certificates of deposit, mutual funds, money market accounts, and the like—did not exist. So, a prosperous middle- or upper-income family with surplus cash often bought a house-lot next door or nearby and erected a residence to rent.

The mixing existed even in the most upscale neighborhoods. Myers Park, the wealthiest suburb of the streetcar era, included among its stately single-family homes a number of multifamily buildings. Some were duplexes, designed to closely resemble single-family homes: one unit entered from the front, the other from a side porch. Others were frankly multifamily in architecture. The 1924 Hunter Apartments, owned by Mrs. J. D. Hunter, who lived around the corner, was among Myers Park's largest at eight rental units.

Rental units in suburbia were not deeply affordable, initially. When built, they cost too much for very-low-income households. But they did broaden the neighborhood's availability to newlywed couples, single senior citizens, and others who couldn't buy a big one-family dwelling. And over time the rents would drop. My first home as a young newcomer to Charlotte in the 1980s was on a block in the Elizabeth neighborhood with several duplexes; neighbors included

Figure 1.4. Multifamily dwellings in elite Myers Park. *Top photo and 1924* Charlotte Observer *ad*, Hunter Apartments alongside a single-family residence. *Bottom photo*, discrete duplex on Henley Place. Hanchett photos, 2022.

a donut-shop waitress, a maintenance man at a furniture rental company, and a retired construction worker and his wife.

Also unlike what we saw in the center city, the suburban rentals were not racially mixed. Starting in 1900, nearly all of Charlotte's new subdivisions carried restrictive covenants that explicitly barred African Americans.

Those caveats aside, the apartments that dotted the early suburbs did make those neighborhoods much more mixed-income than we take for granted today. At the start of the 2020s, Charlotte debated a Unified Development Ordinance that rewrote zoning to allow small rental units in formerly single-family-only areas.[3] Opponents charged that it would bring ruination. Proponents pointed to Myers Park, Elizabeth, and other vintage neighborhoods. Renters and owners had once mingled happily. So perhaps they could again.

For-Profit Investors and Market-Rate Affordable Housing

What would happen if we relied on "the market" to build low-income housing, unfettered by government aid or regulation? The "Negro dwellings" constructed by absentee investors in early twentieth-century Charlotte provide a historical example.

Dating back to slavery times, small houses for African Americans were scattered throughout the city, seldom more than two or three together. We saw that mingling on the Treloar block. But as the twentieth century dawned, the new streetcar suburbs that ringed the city forbade that practice. "This property shall be used only for members of the Caucasian race," for a residence costing not less than $4,000 (an upscale house), read one of the first restrictive deed covenants, in what is now the Elizabeth neighborhood.[4]

With African Americans explicitly barred from the suburbs, parts of the center city became increasingly Black. African Americans who had risen into the middle class built homes and business structures for themselves. Physician and political leader J. T. Williams, for instance, constructed a gracious two-story residence and helped found the nearby Grace AME Zion Church and the Mecklenburg Investment Company office/retail building on South Brevard Street, heart of an emerging Black neighborhood known as Brooklyn (see fig. 4.1a in chapter 4). Most African Americans—barely a generation out of slavery—could not afford to buy or build, however.

Real estate investors realized they had a ready market. They threw up rows of rental dwellings on vacant lots anywhere they could find them. A dozen or more dwellings, each usually two rooms with a front porch, would be packed tightly together side by side. "Excellent Property Investment" headlined one 1920s advertisement for "a block of negro houses" (see fig. 1.5). The ad boasted that the units were fully rented, with a long waiting list. "This is a valuable piece of property and is good for 15 per cent or more on investment."[5]

Fifteen percent, then or now, represented a lucrative return. Landlords could make even more if they tightly limited expenses. "Water and sewerage to every house," this ad noted, emphasizing features that were unusual in Charlotte's rental stock. Until well into the 1940s, this city had no effective building code that mandated toilets and running water. Most investors cut costs by skipping such amenities.

Cost-saving continued throughout the life of the building. Photographs of rental rows in the 1960s show buildings that seem never to have been painted (see fig. 1.6). Look closely and you'll see no investment in sidewalks either. Children

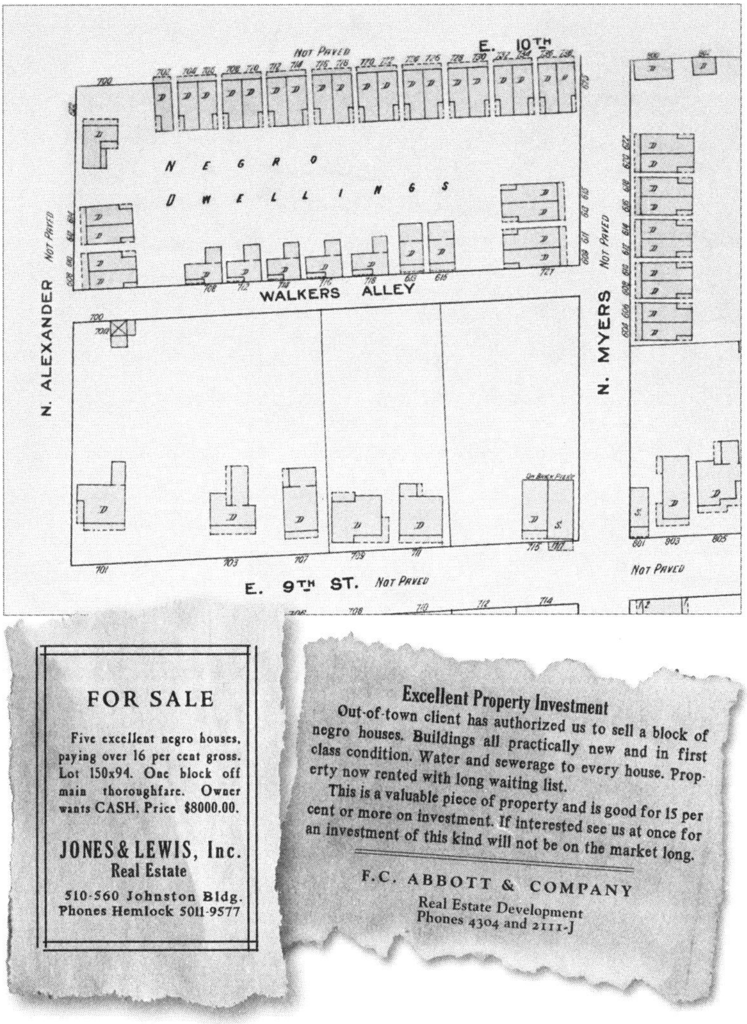

Figure 1.5. "Negro dwellings." Map adapted from Sanborn 1911 map; ads adapted from the *Charlotte Observer*, 1920.

play in the mud by their front porch. The street is muddy, too, since landlords wished to avoid being charged by the city for paving work.

Absentee owners felt no attachment to the neighborhood. White landlords in Charlotte's Brooklyn community blithely rented to prostitutes, most of them white. Rose Leary Love, daughter of Charlotte's first Black attorney, recalled her family's frustration and powerlessness:

Figure 1.6. Rental houses in Second Ward, early 1960s. Courtesy of the Robinson-Spangler Carolina Room, Charlotte Mecklenburg Library.

One of my strangest and saddest remembrances of Brooklyn was the fact that Spring Alley, a red-light district, once existed there.

When my mother and other homeowners came to . . . live in their modest homes, such a notorious section was not there. I have often asked myself these questions: Why was it planned to be in this area of colored homeowners? . . . .

When I hear the notoriousness of Brooklyn being discussed and written, I always remember these dens of sin being placed among decent colored people.[6]

■ ■ ■ ■ ■

Run-down housing existed because it was profitable, often extremely profitable, for those who owned it. That's still true today, by the way.[7] But as the twentieth century wore on, a growing segment of Charlotte—including wealthy leaders—began to recognize that the harm caused was not limited to the unfortunate tenants.

In the chapters ahead we'll trace how reformers started to call for government to get involved with housing. What form should that take? Building codes? Zoning? Government-owned housing? Or should it do nothing at all? In America's biggest cities, those debates had been swirling ever since urbanization ramped up in the late nineteenth century. It would require a national crisis—two, actually: the Great Depression in the 1930s and a polio epidemic in the 1940s—to bring those debates to Charlotte and cause real change on the ground.

CHAPTER 2

Federal Help for Better Housing

- FHA Apartments and Public Housing

The hard times of the Great Depression forced Americans to confront the fact that naturally occurring affordable housing fell short of society's needs. In this chapter, we'll explore the creation of Charlotte's first public housing developments. Fairview Homes and Piedmont Courts opened in 1940, and two other projects followed during the 1950s.

But the US government's housing aid did not begin with public housing. In the mid-1930s, President Franklin Roosevelt's new Federal Housing Administration began offering financing and planning assistance to developers of for-profit apartment complexes. The FHA underwrote long-term amortized mortgages—a revolutionary innovation, as we shall see—and also provided architectural consultants who fostered state-of-the-art designs. The aid was very similar to the subsequent public housing program, but it helped middle- and upper-income Americans.

Together, the precedents set during the 1930s and 1940s by the FHA and Washington's public housing officials would shape all multifamily housing in Charlotte and across America well into the 1970s.

More generally, the tendency to aim new government aid at middle- and upper-income people first, and only later extend it to low-income people, will become a recurring theme in this book.

Great Depression as a Lesson: Government Can Help

The Great Depression hurt nearly everybody in America. That opened the door for major changes in US society. Government pensions to provide social security for the elderly and unemployed, a minimum wage and an eight-hour workday, federal support for massive infrastructure projects such as school and highway construction or rural electrification—all of these ideas had been swirling for a generation or more. But they had seemed too radical, too big to be funded, and too focused on particular groups to be politically possible. By the time that President Franklin Delano Roosevelt took office in 1933, however, so many people had experienced unemployment, lost their homes, and watched businesses collapse that sweeping action from Washington seemed entirely reasonable. The private market had failed. Might government do better?

Roosevelt's New Deal programs brought forth an economic system marked by extensive federal involvement and the social safety net that we now take for granted. But FDR stopped short of full-blown radicalism.[1] When it came to aiding the very poorest and least politically powerful Americans, FDR never did as much as advocates hoped. And he took care to extend benefits to the middle class and to not overly disrupt the lives of the very wealthy. That built support among middle- and upper-income voters for the expansion of government.

Before we explore how that pattern played out in housing, here's a quick glimpse of it in two other FDR signature programs, Social Security and the Fair Labor Standards Act.

- Social Security created a system in which the federal government used its taxing power to help citizens of all ages contribute to a pool of money, which paid out basic income stipends for the elderly and disabled. It was truly a huge change, still derided as "socialism" by some critics today.

    But it did not apply to all Americans. Farmworkers and service workers (such as maids and butlers to the wealthy) weren't made part of the system initially. Most middle-income citizens, in contrast, were included, and they felt great gratitude toward FDR when checks started arriving to help out with care for Grandma and Grandpa. That gratitude meant support as Washington gradually enlarged the safety net over the coming decades.

- The Fair Labor Standards Act, likewise, instituted reforms that so-called radicals had long sought, particularly a minimum wage and the eight-hour workday. Roosevelt envisioned a nation in which that applied to everyone: "No business which depends for existence on paying less than living wages to its workers has any right to continue in this country. By 'business' I mean the whole of commerce as well as the whole of industry; by workers I mean all workers, the white-collar class as well as the men in overalls; and by living wages I mean more than a bare subsistence level—I mean the wages of decent living."[2]

    But by the time that the 1938 Fair Labor Standards Act got through Congress, it failed to cover farm and service laborers. Millions of middle-class office workers, conversely, now enjoyed having a standard workday that ended at five o'clock.

Such successes, partial though they were, could be powerfully persuasive. People's lives got better when government stepped in. Voters reelected Roosevelt in 1936—with an unheard-of 61 percent of the popular vote—and elected him again for an unprecedented third term in 1940. A "New Deal consensus" about the positive value of big government would be embraced by both Republicans and Democrats for the next four decades.

Housing Bubble Collapses—What to Do?

When the Great Depression pushed the American housing market into collapse, Roosevelt stepped in to find ways government could help. During the Roaring Twenties, a "bubble" of real estate optimism had generated America's largest-ever wave of overbuilding, with street after street of wood-shingled bungalows and red-brick Colonials springing up around every American city. The go-go era came to a screeching halt with the stock market crash of 1929. The housing bubble popped. Unemployed people—25 percent of the population—faced eviction if they were renters or lost their homes if they could not pay their mortgage. Tent cities of the newly poor and displaced huddled at the edge of every city. People called them Hoovervilles, a derisive epithet flung at Roosevelt's predecessor President Herbert Hoover for his refusal to do much to help. No matter what citizens' status had been, you now knew housing insecurity yourself or on the part of someone close to you.

■ ■ ■ ■ ■

As cities had swelled with workers during the Industrial Revolution of the nineteenth century, urban landowners found they could cram renters together tightly for profit. That brought hardship not just for the renters themselves but also for community well-being at large. Doctors, just beginning to grasp the realities of infectious disease, warned that bad housing set up conditions for the spread of sickness throughout the city. Experts in the new field of "social work," such as Jane Addams in Chicago, showed that such neighborhoods could stunt children's physical and social development.

Could governments or other public-spirited entities get involved? That was a radical notion in an era when government was much smaller than it is today and when few nonprofit organizations existed. Men and women who called themselves progressives explored an array of new possibilities to tackle urban housing problems.

Water and Sewer Systems, Building Codes

Reformers urged city governments to construct and operate sewers and water systems, connected to all homes. Today we take that for granted, but Charlotte did not get into the water business until 1896, when it bought out a private company that failed to provide reliable service. City-owned sewers appeared at about the same time, but only in the most densely settled blocks at the heart of town.

National reform advocates also proposed a new kind of government regulation of private property. Building codes should be instituted to require landlords to provide habitable and safe dwellings. Minimal codes did exist in big cities but seldom went beyond mandating brick construction for fire safety. New York City led the way with its 1901 Tenement Law. The word "tenement" referred to multifamily rental housing, any building with three or more apartments. The Tenement Law required that such rental structures have adequate ventilation and fire exits—and especially, it insisted on a bathroom in each apartment.[3] Similar laws spread very gradually to other major cities. It would be many years before smaller towns such as Charlotte (see chapter 4) embraced such regulation.

Garden City New Towns

Some reformers imagined housing possibilities that went beyond building codes. In England, where the "dark satanic mills" of the Industrial Revolution deeply scarred English cities, urban activist Ebenezer Howard led a garden city movement. Could civic-minded developers leave the existing crowded urban realm and go out to the countryside to construct entire new towns? Howard's 1902 book, *Garden Cities of Tomorrow*, called for carefully planned housing set amid parkland, creating walkable communities infused with the goodness of nature.[4]

Limited-Dividend Experiments—Long-Term Financing

In New York and Chicago, a few rich progressive philanthropists experimented with "limited-dividend" multifamily apartment blocks. What if they set up a pool of capital and committed to only a slim 5 percent return over a period of several decades—could they "do things right" in terms of solid construction, indoor plumbing, a window in each room for light and ventilation, and so on? Fabulously wealthy railroad tycoon Cornelius Vanderbilt contributed to one early effort, the Improved Dwellings Association in New York City in 1880. It constructed an entire city block of up-to-date apartments around a central courtyard—a rare bit of greenspace in overcrowded Manhattan.[5]

The big aha moment of the limited-dividend experiments: a relatively small payout over a long time could be attractive to investors. Today we take that for granted, but then it was audacious. Banks in that era usually required that loans be repaid in five years or less. Anything beyond that seemed too risky. In a limited-dividend company, conversely, funders turned their back on quick profit but instead banked on careful planning to generate a predictable stream of rents over the long haul.

Only a few wealthy folks had such deep pockets and such patience, however. Might there be a way to decrease the risk? Perhaps some type of insurance that would guarantee that a mortgage would be repaid? If that could happen, it might convince banks to make long-term home loans (at 5 or 6 percent interest over twenty or thirty years) to any qualified borrower. That idea would become a linchpin of New Deal housing efforts.

■ ■ ■ ■ ■

During the first decades of the twentieth century, a handful of projects combined garden city ideals with limited-dividend financing. Forest Hills Gardens in Queens on the outskirts of New York City called into existence an entire neighborhood of picturesque brick low-rise townhouse apartments and single-family homes intertwined with greenspace, dedicated in 1908. Planned by the renowned Olmsted landscape firm and financed by the Russell Sage Foundation (the philanthropy of the widow of another railroad tycoon), it remains a highly desirable area today.[6]

Another New York City bedroom community, Radburn, underwritten by a limited-dividend company headed by a wealthy New York City realtor in 1929, took the greenspace idea further. Planners Clarence Stein and Henry Wright cut very few roads through the site, instead arranging the low-rise apartments into pods called "superblocks."[7] The arrangement gave everyone in a pod a shared communal greenspace, intended to promote socializing and children's play.

In Chicago, big-hearted philanthropist Julius Rosenwald opened Michigan Boulevard Garden Apartments the same year.[8] He had built Sears Roebuck into America's first large-scale catalog retailer, equivalent to today's Amazon, and then used a substantial part of his fortune to make matching grants for rural African American schools across the South. In his housing venture, Rosenwald set moderate rents and welcomed Black working-class families. The 454 units, in five-story brick walk-up buildings, surrounded a large grassy interior park where children could play without the danger of street traffic—similar to Radburn's superblocks. Residents loved it, among them rising jazz singer Nat King Cole, Olympic athlete Jesse Owens, and young musician Quincy Jones.

Model developments such as Forest Hills, Radburn, and Rosenwald's Chicago

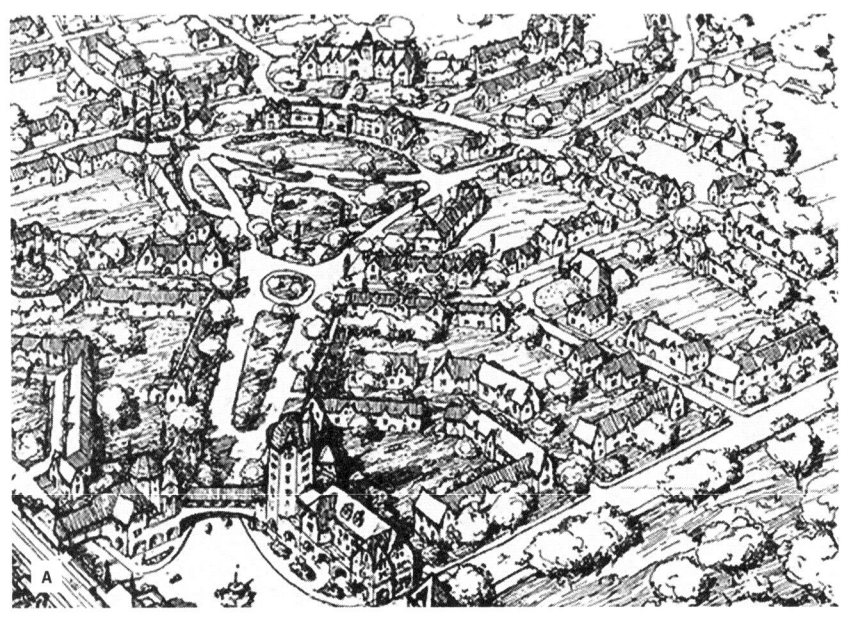

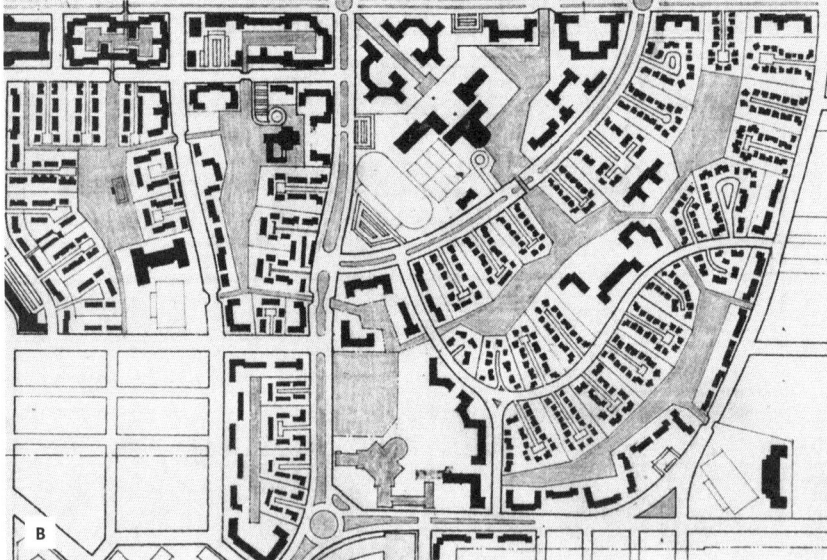

Figure 2.1. *A*: Forest Hills Gardens, 1909 limited-dividend project planned by Frederick Law Olmsted. Drawing courtesy of Forest Hills Gardens Foundation. *B*: Radburn. Planned by Clarence Stein and Henry Wright, Radburn created "superblocks" with greenspaces winding between buildings. Image from Adams, *Regional Plan*, 2:134.

Federal Help for Better Housing ■ 31

Figure 2.2. A grassy courtyard was the central feature of Michigan Boulevard Garden Apartments, today Rosenwald Homes, on Chicago's South Side, 1929. Chris Moe photo, 2017.

apartments indeed showed the value of enlightened planning, but they barely scratched the surface of actual need in the United States. The philanthropic developers intended the projects to be models, literally—emulated by others far and wide.[9] But out in the real world, hardly anybody possessed investment cash at that scale. There just weren't enough Vanderbilts and Rosenwalds to meet the nation's low-income housing needs.

Might government get involved? There was a precedent. Back during World War I, for the first time ever, the United States had arranged for construction of housing for wartime workers. In Wilmington, Delaware, for instance, Garden City disciple John Nolen planned Union Park Gardens for shipyard employees, with townhouse apartments set in abundant greenspace.[10] To finance, Washington tried two methods. At shipyards, the feds gave "loans to realty companies incorporated by shipbuilding companies," noted an official report.[11] At other defense plants, Washington set up a new government agency, the US Housing Corporation, and gave it federal cash directly to build and manage apartment projects. Both techniques—loan help for private developers and direct government ownership—would be used in New Deal housing.

All of which brings us back to the early 1930s. The US housing market was in turmoil amid the Great Depression. Models existed for creating better housing. What would the newly elected President Roosevelt do?

Inventing the Federal Housing Administration

Housing had played a big part in the downward economic spiral of the Great Depression. With the crash of 1929, banks stopped lending to home buyers and apartment builders, often "calling" the loans—demanding immediate repayment. Not only did millions of people face eviction, but construction jobs disappeared, further hollowing out the economy. Immediately upon taking office, FDR made housing a top priority.

First, the president moved to halt the free fall of the mortgage market. He had Congress establish a new entity, the Home Owners' Loan Corporation, and give it $3 billion of federal funds to directly refinance the mortgages of 1 million homeowners. This represented an unprecedented expansion of the federal government. Nothing like that had ever been done. It worked; home prices stopped falling. But it stimulated no new construction.

FDR considered, but discarded, proposals that Washington launch its own housing construction program, similar to the New Deal's famous infrastructure construction projects (the Civilian Conservation Corps; the Public Works Administration and its successor, the Works Progress Administration). Instead, he went with something less radical. "Roosevelt's growing unease with budget deficits led him back to a plan involving little direct spending," writes historian Gail Radford. "This became the National Housing Act of 1934"—creating the Federal Housing Administration.[12]

The FHA started by helping owners of single-family homes. This was a decidedly upper-middle-income population. Under free-market conditions, in order to get a home loan you'd had to make a hefty down payment—half the purchase price or more. Then you'd had to pay the entire balance in two to five years. Long-term mortgages did not exist.

Now the FHA transformed that playing field. It told banks that it would insure mortgages, guaranteeing payback. Freed from risk, banks recognized that they no longer needed a huge down payment. More importantly, they could offer a long-term payback of twenty years (later extended to thirty years, still the standard today), which meant smaller monthly payments. The payments would be "amortized," calculated so that each equal payment included a bit of the principal and a bit of the interest—yet another innovation that we take for granted today.

The long-term amortized mortgage was revolutionary. It took the idea of creating a steady and predictable payout to the lender—seen in the earlier limited-dividend experiments—and made it part of everyday home finance. Thanks to the FHA's guarantee, relatively small down payments and similarly reasonable monthly payments became standard. The FHA thus put homeownership within reach of millions of Americans. In the 1920s, roughly one-third of Americans had owned their own home. By the 1940s, two-thirds did.

Commendable as it was, none of this helped folks at the bottom of the economic ladder.

Redlining

The policies of the FHA and its sister agency the Home Owners' Loan Corporation (HOLC) often shortchanged working-class Americans, both white and Black.

The HOLC, as part of its efforts to stimulate the national mortgage market, instituted a program of credit-mapping—which became notorious as "redlining." In 1937 it sent staff out to nearly every large and midsize US city to meet with local real estate leaders and develop maps showing the "good credit risk" neighborhoods. That sounds innocuous, but the maps routinely gave the highest grades ("A" mapped in green, "B" mapped in blue) to upscale white single-family neighborhoods. Low grades ("C" in yellow, "D" in red) went to working-class areas. On Charlotte's map, for instance, the green/blue zones included the upscale Myers Park and Elizabeth and Dilworth neighborhoods. In contrast, North Charlotte (today known as NoDa, then a white working-class area of textile laborers who were mostly renters) was red and yellow. The African American neighborhood of Brooklyn, even the blocks where prosperous business families lived, was entirely red.*

HOLC ratings also punished any kind of mixing, whether of races, of incomes, or of owners and renters. In First Ward (including the Treloar House block discussed in chapter 1), the rating sheet called out the presence of both "small cheap negro houses" and "large type single houses used as boarding and rooming houses." Part of Fourth Ward earned a similar red "Hazardous" rating: "Area composed of negroes and white people." The Belmont neighborhood just north of First Ward got an undesirable yellow rating because of its "mixture of population type," which ranged from "clerical" (office workers) to low-grade "laborers." Complained the HOLC official: "Properties are not uniform, containing many small houses and also quite a few larger old type houses."†

(continued)

---

* Charlotte's HOLC map, with its neighborhood evaluations, is on the University of Richmond website Mapping Inequality: Redlining in New Deal America; see Nelson et al., "Charlotte."
† Nelson et al., "Charlotte," HOLC map.

The HOLC maps became a self-fulfilling prophecy. In green and blue areas (such as Charlotte's Myers Park and Elizabeth neighborhood), residents enjoyed well-maintained owner-occupied homes. Real estate values rose. In red and yellow areas (such as mill village NoDa or the Black district of Brooklyn), it was difficult to get a loan to become a homeowner. So absentee landlords predominated. Real estate values fell.

The maps were secret. Most people, seeing the diverging property values, put the blame on the residents. Bad character must be at fault. Lesson: Avoid any kind of mixing. Keep Blacks and low-income whites and renters of any race as far away from your neighborhood as possible.

FHA loans magnified those biases. If you wanted an FHA-insured loan, you had to convince the bank that your desired home was in a financially strong part of town. By that logic, areas colored blue and green on the HOLC map had the inside track.

The FHA did not completely freeze out African Americans, contrary to what is suggested in the recent influential book *The Color of Law: A Forgotten History of How Our Government Segregated America*. Studies of Charlotte's post–World War II Black neighborhoods of Oaklawn Park and McCrorey Heights show that African Americans—both white collar and blue collar—did get loans insured by the FHA and by the affiliated VA program offered to veterans.‡ But the numbers fell far below those for whites, writes national historian Andrew Wiese: "Contemporary estimates suggested that less than two percent of FHA-insured loans and three percent of VA-guaranteed loans" would go to non-whites during the 1950s, despite the fact that they made up 11 percent of the US population.**

---

‡ Rothstein, *Color of Law*, 50, 67, gives the impression that African Americans were entirely barred from FHA and VA lending programs. This overstates the reality. Though Blacks did receive much less than whites, FHA/VA mortgages still improved hundreds of thousands of lives. "As much as 40 percent of new housing occupied by African Americans" was FHA/VA-assisted during the 1950s. Wiese, *Places of Their Own*, 140.
** Wiese, *Places of Their Own*, 140; Woods, "Almost 'No Negro Veteran.'"

FHA Aid to Apartment Investors

While the FHA's involvement in single-family homes is well known, the 1934 act also called for the agency to offer planning assistance and mortgage insurance to multifamily construction. As first written, FHA Section 207 was supposed to produce apartments for "persons of low income."[13] But developers showed no enthusiasm. So, during 1937 the section was rewritten to extend mortgage insurance to projects aimed at any and all tenants.[14]

Under the revised Section 207, the FHA told banks it would insure loans of up to 80 percent of the cost of a multifamily project. Interest was a low 4.5 percent amortized over many years; FHA backing made it risk-free. The Radburn/Rosenwald type of project, previously possible only for a limited-dividend company backed by a super-wealthy and patient philanthropist, suddenly was in reach of local developers in places such as Charlotte.

The FHA went further than just setting favorable loan terms. In the spirit of using "the power of the federal government to establish the conditions under which private initiative could feed itself and multiply its own benefits," FHA experts oversaw every aspect of the apartment ventures it insured. "The private mortgagors were regulated by FHA as to rents or sales, charges, capital structure, rate of return, and methods of operation in such manner as to provide reasonable rentals and a reasonable return on the investment," a federal report explained. "The project covered by the mortgage had to be found economically sound."[15]

The hands-on involvement by FHA staff meant that developers who met the requirements could do bigger deals than they had ever imagined on their own. Instead of scrambling to find 100 percent of the money needed for a venture and then facing investors impatient for a quick return, now developers had to come up with only 20 percent of their own cash and Uncle Sam set the decades-long timetable for loan repayment. FHA administrators very much encouraged the shift to big projects. Weeding out small-time players created a more efficient market and better housing, they believed. "The long-term mortgage, the provisions for amortization, the limitation as to dividends and the requirements laid down as to scale, etc., tend only to make large-scale rental properties attractive investments over a long period of time," FHA official Miles Colean said with pride.[16]

* * * * *

Before we look at Charlotte's initial FHA apartments, it's worth noting how New Deal officials regarded their intervention in housing finance.

Treasury official Marriner Eccles, who drafted the 1934 legislation that created the Federal Housing Administration, wrote proudly that the FHA's approach "avoided any direct encroachment of the federal government into the domain of private business." Instead, it "used the power of the federal government to establish the conditions under which private initiative could feed itself and multiply its own benefits."[17]

That wasn't true, really. The US government *was* providing what now would be called consultant services, the type of expertise that today commands big bucks in the private market. This was a direct benefit to business, a taxpayer-funded subsidy—but it came in the form of planning and organization by Washington. That made it harder to see, tougher to criticize, more in keeping with America's capitalist self-image. Yet it was a subsidy, nonetheless.

The tax dollars invested by the FHA would be multiplied many times over, Eccles promised, as private profit-makers brought their own expertise and dollars to the game. That public-private strategy likely sounds familiar. Variations on it have informed US housing policy—and indeed much of American government—from Roosevelt right through Ronald Reagan and on to our own day.

Charlotte's First Big Garden Apartment Projects

In Charlotte, savvy investors seized upon FHA subsidies to create the city's first large-scale garden apartment developments in 1938 and 1939. Each covered nearly a city block, and each catered to wealthy renters. The Myrtle Apartments went up in Dilworth, the city's first streetcar suburb. Alson Court followed soon afterward in Eastover, then and now Charlotte's most exclusive residential district.[18]

■ ■ ■ ■ ■

Typical of the big developers that the FHA favored, Joe L. Blythe, who headed up the Myrtle project, ranked among Charlotte's most well-connected construction contractors. He had led the Public Works Committee of Charlotte's Chamber of Commerce, where he sought out New Deal opportunities for Charlotte. In 1936 he took charge of publicity for Franklin Roosevelt's campaign visit to the Queen City, where the president gave his Green Pastures speech touting New Deal accomplishments.[19] During World War II, Blythe Brothers Construction would use Joe's Washington connections to become one of the South's largest defense contractors, constructing military bases and airfields from Puerto Rico to Africa.[20]

With much hands-on help from FHA officials, Blythe and his team drew up a proposal for the Myrtle that attracted serious out-of-town investment: Prudential Life Insurance.[21] It would be the biggest building effort of any kind in Charlotte since the downtown Wilder Building skyscraper was built before the 1929 crash. Charlotte architect Charles W. Connelly made the Myrtle a showplace of up-to-the-minute apartment design, inspired by the garden city projects previously seen only in bigger cities. His blueprints showed suave Art Moderne buildings containing seventy-two apartments ranging from two-room to five-room units. Each had an electric range and refrigerator and a modern tile bathroom.

In keeping with FHA advice, Connelly arranged the structures on a three-acre site in a "U" to create a large central courtyard, much like that seen in Julius Rosenwald's 1929 development in Chicago. Units set amid generous greenspace would become a hallmark of FHA-sanctioned apartments into the 1950s. The FHA continued its help right up to the opening. Regulations required "that an FHA inspector be on the scene of construction for the entire building period," reported the *Charlotte Observer*.[22] When the complex debuted in August 1938, both the *Observer* and the *Charlotte News* celebrated with multipage special coverage.[23]

The following year, work began on FHA-insured Alson Court, located in even more posh Eastover. Its details differed from the Myrtle, but the process and the product were essentially similar. Rather than Art Moderne architecture, it featured stately colonial-style brickwork with slate-covered gable roofs. The sixty units were wrapped around a pair of courtyards to create the garden apartment ambience that the FHA favored. Charlotte-based developer Alson Lloyd Goode and his two Washington, DC–based partners were the type of large-scale players that FHA officials liked. In fact, Goode's team was simultaneously working with the FHA on apartment complexes in Richmond, Norfolk, and Newport News, Virginia, as well as in Mobile, Alabama, and Jacksonville, Tennessee.[24]

With the completion of the Myrtle and the Alson, patterns were set in Charlotte that would continue up through the present day. Nearly every multifamily project in the mid-twentieth century went through FHA review and reaped the benefits of FHA mortgage insurance (the program continues on a smaller scale today).[25] Thanks to federal intervention, large garden apartments would become ubiquitous in every community across the United States. The duplexes, quadraplexes, and other small apartments of the 1920s (see chapter 1) would become rare.

Public Housing Begins in Charlotte

US voters signaled strong approval for FDR's New Deal by overwhelmingly re-electing him in 1936. With his second term assured, Roosevelt felt able to do more to help Americans at the bottom of the economic ladder. His second inaugural speech set the tone: "I see one-third of a nation ill-housed, ill-clad, ill-nourished. ... The test of our progress is not whether we add more to the abundance of those

Figure 2.3. *A:* Myrtle Apartments and courtyard. Google aerial, 2019. *B:* Alson Court. The buildings were arranged in an S to create a front courtyard and a rear courtyard. 1939 postcard courtesy of Alson Court Condominiums.

who have much; it is whether we provide enough for those who have too little."[26] In the housing arena, that meant at last getting around to helping people below the middle class.

At FDR's urging, Congress passed the Wagner–Steagall Act of 1937, Washington's first meaningful investment in public housing.[27] It created a sister agency to the FHA, the United States Housing Authority (USHA), which would focus on public housing, and it encouraged cities to create their own Public Housing Authorities. The USHA would not attempt to pull in private financing (that hadn't succeeded with Section 207, you'll recall). Instead, the USHA would use federal dollars, doled out in the form of long-term loans to Public Housing Authorities. The loans covered 90 percent of the cost of constructing a public housing development, leaving the city government to contribute just 10 percent. The USHA loans ran for sixty years at 5 percent interest (very similar to the terms that had been pioneered by limited-dividend companies). Once the apartments were built, rents from tenants would cover half of the payback, one-third would come from small annual federal grants, and one-sixth would be contributed by the locality out of local tax dollars.[28]

Charlotte mayor Ben Douglas, who had a sharp eye out for New Deal opportunities, perked up at the offer of federal dollars for public housing. Imagine the profits to be made by local real estate and construction firms! Imagine the wages to be earned by rank-and-file laborers—in a time when Depression-era unemployment still ran high. And nearly all the cash would come from Washington. First, however, Douglas needed to court local business leaders and Charlotte voters.

The city's Business and Professional Women's Club had already made housing conditions a topic of study, and what the clubwomen found horrified them. Cora A. Harris led the charge, a teacher who had come face-to-face with neighborhood realities when she visited parents of her students. Her interest deepened when the FHA employed her to help administer home modernization grants. "I made a very close study of these houses," she told the *Observer*, "and found unspeakable conditions" affecting "approximately 30 percent of our citizenry." Among them: "Groups of houses served by one or two broken down toilets, which means that men, women and children had to trudge from seventy-five feet to 150 feet to improper sanitation [that is, use an outdoor privy] and to get a bucket of water." There were "houses with portions of the roof completely gone" and windowless interiors "where kerosene lamps shed a dismal glow during sunny days." And lest her listeners dismiss these problems as affecting only African Americans, and thus find them easy to ignore, she pointedly told of finding "eleven white persons living in three rooms."[29]

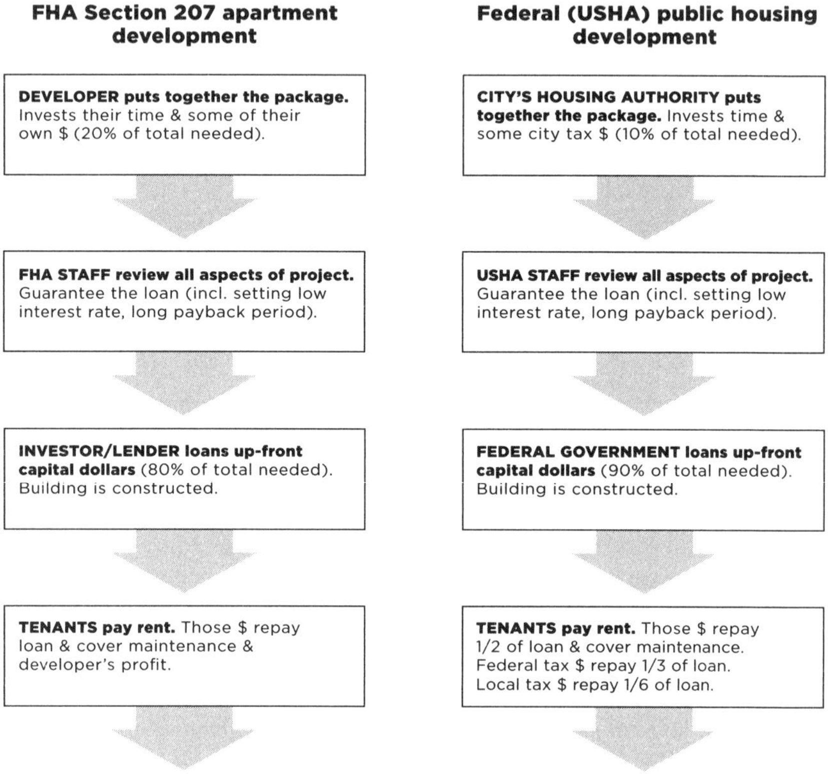

FHA Section 207 apartment development

DEVELOPER puts together the package. Invests their time & some of their own $ (20% of total needed).

⬇

FHA STAFF review all aspects of project. Guarantee the loan (incl. setting low interest rate, long payback period).

⬇

INVESTOR/LENDER loans up-front capital dollars (80% of total needed). Building is constructed.

⬇

TENANTS pay rent. Those $ repay loan & cover maintenance & developer's profit.

Federal (USHA) public housing development

CITY'S HOUSING AUTHORITY puts together the package. Invests time & some city tax $ (10% of total needed).

⬇

USHA STAFF review all aspects of project. Guarantee the loan (incl. setting low interest rate, long payback period).

⬇

FEDERAL GOVERNMENT loans up-front capital dollars (90% of total needed). Building is constructed.

⬇

TENANTS pay rent. Those $ repay 1/2 of loan & cover maintenance. Federal tax $ repay 1/3 of loan. Local tax $ repay 1/6 of loan.

Figure 2.4. Financing for public housing closely echoed the FHA's earlier apartment program. Both featured long-term amortized loans guaranteed by Washington. Both supplied federal consultants to shape the architecture, land design, and financial planning.

The clubwomen succeeded in getting City Council to fund a study, completed in 1938. It counted "5,044 [dwellings that] have no indoor flush toilets, 4,317 have no running water, 4,389 have neither electric nor gas lighting, . . . 6,616 are in need of major repairs or are unfit for use." All told, "28 percent of the white and 83 percent of the negro dwelling units in the city are substandard," it concluded: "5,098 white and 7,063 negro families are living in substandard homes."[30] A follow-up survey by the WPA in 1939 confirmed the deficiencies.[31]

Should Charlotte institute a strict building code? Should it construct public housing? Real estate leaders lobbied hard against the building code proposal. "Many of the owners of cheap property are improving that property," they asserted, and besides that, "slums are far fewer than one would suppose." They adamantly opposed public housing, too; it would "lessen the value of present construction."[32]

The possibility of $3 million in federal aid proved persuasive, however. Charlotte officials took no steps to institute a building code (we'll return to the building code fight in chapter 4), but they moved decisively to get public housing dollars. Mayor Ben Douglas chartered a Charlotte Housing Authority and appointed Edwin L. Jones to lead it. Jones, who would chair the CHA board into the 1960s, had strong ties to real estate men. He helmed his family's J. A. Jones Construction, which built major Charlotte projects, and also did New Deal and military work: warehouses in the Panama Canal Zone; hospitals for the Veterans Administration in Columbia, South Carolina, and Jacksonville, Florida; and a new city hall and courts complex in Nashville hailed as the largest WPA project in the South.[33] Notably, J. A. Jones Construction had recently handled construction of Techwood Homes in Atlanta, the very first public housing project underwritten by the federal government.[34]

Edwin Jones and his fellow CHA board members—all male and white—possessed no particular expertise in issues of poverty or social uplift, but they did know real estate economics. "Charlotte might as well participate in the USHA program and receive some of the benefits," Jones told a reporter, "because the people of Charlotte, through [federal] taxes, will pay their proportionate part of the total cost of the nation-wide program whether we have our . . . projects or not."[35]

Work began in 1939, first on Fairview Homes for African American tenants and then on Piedmont Courts for whites a few months later. Separate teams of local architects developed the two designs: M. R. Marsh and Charles Connelly for Fairview (Connelly had recently completed the Myrtle Apartments); Martin Boyer and J. N. Pease for Piedmont Courts.[36] The layouts used the superblock idea, as seen in the 1920s in Radburn, creating as few streets as possible so as to maximize greenspace. The arrangement would create "a great deal of open play area for children and grownups," the *Observer* pointed out.[37] Each complex included a community building that held administrative offices, recreation facilities, and space for classes.[38]

Fairview Homes had 452 units, making it one of the city's largest-ever multifamily developments. Plans for white Piedmont Courts initially called for 258 units, but when additional federal dollars became available, more were added, finally totaling 368 apartments. Martin Boyer lobbied successfully for pitched roofs at Piedmont Courts, homier—but also more expensive—than the flat-roofed International Style design at Fairview Homes.[39]

In both complexes, units ranged from one to three bedrooms. Each included a living room, a modern bathroom, and a kitchen with "coal/wood burning stove,

Figure 2.5. A: Fairview Homes, 1968. J. Murrey Atkins Library Special Collections and University Archives, University of North Carolina, Charlotte. B: Piedmont Courts, 1992. Courtesy of the Robinson-Spangler Carolina Room, Charlotte Mecklenburg Library.

... combination sink and laundry tub, and built-in-cabinets," said the *Observer*. Every apartment had a refrigerator, not yet a common appliance in many Charlotte homes. "The purpose of these two low-cost housing projects was to provide ... modern housing," the article explained. Refrigerators should not be considered a luxury but rather a money-saving investment enabling "low-cost and efficient preservation of food."[40]

The openings of the two projects in 1940 brought enthusiastic multipage newspaper coverage. Photographs showed furnished model apartments and exterior views. Contractors purchased display ads boasting of their work. Home economics students at the city's high schools added handmade curtains and other accessories. When Fairview debuted on Sunday, June 23, 1940, all of Charlotte's African American churches joined in celebrating Housing Day.[41] That December, members of the Business and Professional Women's Club volunteered as hostesses during a weeklong public open house at Piedmont Courts.[42]

Who were the initial tenants in the two public housing complexes? Louise W. Frye handled the tenant selection.[43] A former regional director of the American Red Cross, she already knew Charlotte's low-income families well from a stint dispensing aid as the city's New Deal relief supervisor. She operated under guidelines from the US Housing Authority. "Occupancy will be limited to natural families or cohesive family groups who have been living in the city at least three months prior to the time of making application. No roomers or boarders will be allowed," a press release advised. "Preference will be given to families living under housing conditions most injurious to health, safety and morality, having the lowest family income, and having children under 16 years of age."[44] And finally, tenants had to be under a maximum-income limit. "Families making more than five times the rental asked cannot be accepted."[45]

A look at the 1942 city directory, the first to include both complexes, suggests the tenants were "working poor." The first three households listed at Fairview Homes were janitor William Edwards and his wife, Mabel; laborer James Blair with wife Eva; and Ada and Walter Taylor, he a porter at Ivey's Department store. The initial three listings at white Piedmont Courts were Mrs. Mabel Taylor, a stenographer; James A. Murray, a machine operator at the Whitin textile machinery installation and repair company, with wife Rachel; and Annie Taylor, a cake icer at a commercial bakery, who lived with Addie Taylor, no occupation given, who may have been her elderly mother.

Pluses and Minuses of Charlotte's First Public Housing

Though Piedmont Courts and Fairview Homes were equivalent, they were not equal. The greatest disparity was in location. Piedmont Courts, at Seigle Avenue and Tenth Street just east of the center city, put white workers near the heart of Charlotte, an easy walk to downtown employers or to jobs along the Southern Railway industrial corridor, which extended through the cluster of textile mills in the area that is today called NoDa. In contrast, Fairview Homes put its Black tenants out at Charlotte's far rim on Oaklawn Avenue off Statesville

Avenue—near the army's huge quartermaster depot (today Camp North End) but not much else. In terms of dollar investment, Piedmont Courts' construction cost came in at $912,000, compared with $1,050,000 for Fairview. Per apartment, that worked out to $2,478 a unit for whites and $2,323 a unit for African Americans.[46]

Advocates envisioned public housing as a replacement for substandard housing, but Charlotte fell short. As part of the deal for USHA money from Washington, cities had to agree to eliminate one existing run-down unit for every new unit built with federal aid. In Charlotte that meant 820 dwellings, which local officials discovered was easier said than done. City staff identified bad houses one by one and sent a letter to each owner requiring improvement or demolition. By mid-1941, officials had dealt with about 400 units, about half being demolished and the rest improved (which allowed landlords to charge more rent).[47] But there, things stalled. "City Facing Difficulties in Keeping Housing Terms," the *Observer* headlined in late 1942, bluntly calling the city's progress "turtle-like." "Building inspectors, unequipped with any binding legal authority, tried to substitute persuasive powers to bring about repair of substandard dwellings," the newspaper explained.[48] Charlotte still had no effective building code.

A more subtle but more devasting reality of public housing was what it did to the fabric of daily life of its residents. The planners of public housing—like nearly all forward thinkers of their era—believed in a sorted-out city. They disdained the messy intermingling of land uses found in old, unplanned urban areas. In the bright future they dreamed of, there should be "a place for everything and everything in its place." So Fairview Homes and Piedmont Courts held only housing. That monoculture might work for FHA projects such as the Myrtle Apartments or Alson Court, where many middle-class tenants owned automobiles—though Myrtle residents could walk one block to a large Colonial Supermarket as well as to other small shops. For low-income folks at Fairview, sited so pristinely at the city's edge, the meeting of daily needs—and the socializing that went along with that—no longer happened within the neighborhood.

To gauge the scale of this change, compare Fairview with Charlotte's Brooklyn district. When Brooklyn was cleared by "urban renewal" in the 1960s, the bulldozers would displace not merely 1,004 families but also 200 small businesses. Those corner stores and doctor's offices and tailors and day-care homes and unlicensed liquor houses and sellers of firewood and on and on not only provided the sustenance of daily life conveniently at hand but also provided jobs and routes to advancement, even if limited under Jim Crow. Fairview housed nearly half the number of families—with exactly zero small businesses.

Further, public housing sorted out social groups. Only low-income people lived there, those who had been most battered by the economic system. In Brooklyn, you lived around the corner from physician and retired diplomat J. T. Williams, saw up-close the success of funeral home entrepreneur Zech Alexander and his son Kelly (future North Carolina NAACP president), witnessed the printing press operators and editorial executives on their way to and from work at the AME Zion Publishing House, and so much more. In Fairview Homes or Piedmont Courts, by contrast, children grew up mostly with role models who had not excelled in the attempt to climb the economic ladder. That did not mean that they were bad people or that they could not climb; some public housing residents did rise to success. Within public housing, as scholar Mindy Fullilove and others have shown, vibrant networks developed that fostered social engagement and mutual aid.[49] People who grew up there remember that you always knew neighbors who would help run an errand, watch a child, or offer food in time of need. But how much more robust such networks could be in an economically diverse neighborhood! Eventually, by the 1980s, the socioeconomic isolation of public housing would come to be seen as a major problem. But in the 1940s, the immediate blessings of a weathertight home with indoor plumbing at reasonable rent represented a vast advance from the status quo.

1940s–1950s: Build More Public Housing?

The 820 apartments that opened in 1940—452 at Fairview Homes and 368 at Piedmont Courts—were a commendable first step. But they were a drop in the bucket when measured against the 12,000 families that the 1938 study had found living in substandard dwellings. What would Charlotte do next?

One answer came in the form of a pair of unexpected short-term gifts from the federal government. When the United States entered World War II, Congress got back into the business of building military housing. In Charlotte that meant massive temporary barracks for soldiers at Morris Field, an airbase that eventually became part of today's Charlotte Douglas International Airport. After the war, Washington gave the 404-unit development to the Charlotte Housing Authority.[50] Morris Field Homes served as public housing for whites, many of them veterans, until the wooden structures wore out and met the bulldozer in 1955. The wartime housing push also resulted in Stonewall Jackson Homes, a sturdier apartment project of 85 units for military officers in 1941.[51] After the war, the federal government leased it to the CHA for use as public housing for veterans. The tenants organized to purchase the complex in 1949.[52] In the early 2020s the brick buildings still stood off West Boulevard near Morris Field Drive.

In terms of race, with the addition of Stonewall Jackson Homes and Morris

Table 2.1. Public Housing in Charlotte: The First 25 Years, 1940–1965

Development	Opened	Funding	Units	Race	2022 status
Fairview Homes 1026 Oaklawn Av 28206	1940	US public housing loan	452	Black	replaced by Park at Oaklawn
Piedmont Courts 831 Seigle Av 28204	1940	US public housing loan	368	white	replaced by Seigle Point
Stonewall Jackson Homes 5751 Airport Dr 28208	1941	Lanham Act, WWII	85	white	sold to tenants in 1949
Morris Field Homes Airport Dr 28208	1946	Lanham Act, WWII	404	white	demolished 1955
Southside Homes 2950 S Tryon St 28203	1952	US public housing loan	400	Black	still public housing
Belvedere Homes Rozelles Ferry Rd 28208	1953	US public housing loan	200	white	Greenway Business Center
Total complexes: 6			Total units: 1,909		

Source: Table excerpted from Tom Hanchett, "Master List of Low-Income Multifamily Housing Constructed in Charlotte, 1940–2019," in the data collection of J. Murrey Atkins Library, University of North Carolina at Charlotte, https://doi.org/10.15139/S3/XQBOFW.

Field Homes, Charlotte now had many more white units than Black units of public housing. Back in 1938, Charlotte's housing study had shown that African Americans far outnumbered whites in substandard housing. Public housing—as salutary as it might be for those lucky enough to get in—did nothing to improve that imbalance.

Charlotte would see fit to construct only one more round of public housing before the 1960s. Southside Homes for African Americans opened in 1952 at the southern edge of the city along South Tryon Street.[53] Belvedere Homes for whites, on Rozelles Ferry Road to the northwest, followed in 1953.[54] Both resulted from new appropriations by Congress under the 1949 Housing Act pushed by FDR's successor, President Harry Truman.[55]

Charlotte leaders were willing to go after public housing dollars when Washington offered them. But they weren't ready to consider initiating any other types of projects. Poor people, by themselves, were not a compelling political constituency. But what if the feds came up with a housing program that cut private developers in for a piece of the action? An initiative from Washington called FHA 608 would do exactly that.

CHAPTER 3

Subsidizing the "Free Market"

- FHA 608 Apartments

In its short existence, the FHA 608 program became perhaps the most effective producer of low-income multifamily housing that the United States has ever seen. Charlotte's experience confirms that impact. In just four years, 1948–51, construction crews built 1,948 low-rent apartments in seven Charlotte complexes—more than during the entire first twenty-five years of federally funded public housing. A trio of those complexes remain in use today in the 2020s, Brookhill Village on South Tryon Street, Plaza Terrace Apartments on the Plaza, and Weyland Homes off Wilkinson Boulevard.

During those same four years, the exact same program also subsidized middle- and upper-income apartments. Indeed, some of Charlotte's wealthiest young families lived in Scotland Colony, Selwyn Village, and other high-end garden complexes. One such resident, whose father developed Charlotte's biggest FHA 608 projects, would become North Carolina's richest billionaire.

The Federal Housing Administration wrote the Section 608 regulations very intentionally.[1] It designed the program to alleviate a nationwide housing shortage after World War II. The FHA gave developers sweetheart deals, made even sweeter by a technique called "mortgaging out." Ultimately Congress decided that the FHA had gone too far, and it abruptly shut the program down.

But the hope that well-placed federal stimuli—incentives to developers, rather than direct federal expenditures—might solve affordable housing problems, that hope never went away.

Section 608 and the Wonders of "Mortgaging Out"

As the end of World War II neared, the Federal Housing Administration ratcheted into overdrive. Officials remembered the unrest that had swept the nation after World War I during the "Red Summer" of 1919. Veterans had returned from battle to find shortages of jobs and housing. Riots had rocked American cities,

Figure 3.1. Plaza Terrace for whites and Double Oaks for Blacks were both "low-rent" apartments built in 1949–50 under FHA 608. Note the grassy courtyards and similar architecture. A: Plaza Terrace. Albert Dulin photo, 2020. B: Double Oaks. 1950s photo, courtesy of the Robinson-Spangler Carolina Room, Charlotte Mecklenburg Library.

some directed at African Americans, some allied with the Communist Party, but all linked directly or indirectly to an unmanaged economy. This time things would be different, vowed President Franklin Roosevelt.

Well before peace was achieved, Roosevelt's Office of Price Administration, which had taken control of all building materials early in the war, began releasing some construction supplies to private homebuilders. In tandem, the FHA resumed insuring single-family home mortgages. FHA chief Abner Ferguson personally visited Charlotte in January 1945 to stir up North Carolina bankers and other lenders. "All over the United States there is a shortage of housing," he explained. "The shortage which accumulated during the Depression never was overcome. And then came the war period and conditions that strictly curtailed building construction." Now, in contrast, he promised, building materials would be plentiful. Even more importantly, "Everyone interested in housing construction can be assured there will be plenty of money available for housing loans."[2]

New single-family subdivisions blossomed throughout 1945. "FHA Approves Builders' Plans for 235 New Houses," trumpeted an *Observer* banner headline, one of several during the spring and summer.[3] But that barely made a dent in the demand. In January 1946, Roosevelt's successor, President Harry Truman, appointed a "housing expediter" and declared that 50 percent of the nation's building materials would go to construction of low-cost small homes for veterans.[4] Shortages continued to persist. "Damp basements, cold warehouses, chicken houses—actually chicken houses—are serving as makeshift homes," the *Charlotte Observer* discovered in late 1946, estimating that over 1,200 local veterans needed housing.[5]

So, Washington ramped up loans to apartment builders. "Most families in need of housing want apartments, rather than homes of their own," FHA surveys showed.[6] Back in 1942 a small program had been initiated to help private builders construct rental housing near defense plants. Located in Section VI, subsection 8, of the FHA enabling legislation, it became known as "Section 608" or "FHA 608." Now Congress poured in fresh cash, dramatically increasing its loan insurance program. "FHA Allots Billion for Rental Homes," headlined the *New York Times* on April 15, 1947. A billion dollars in 1947 represented a huge amount of money. "Currently about a third of the mortgages insured by FHA are for rental housing . . . ," said the *Times*, "but the volume is expected to rise to more than half."[7]

In a series of regional conferences, FHA officials brought the news about the Section 608 apartment program directly to "builders, architects, material dealers, realtors and mortgage lenders." A visiting FHA administrator spoke at Charlotte's Chamber of Commerce, promising "financing up to 90 percent of actual

FHA Single-Family Aid and the US Postwar Suburban Boom

Along with its FHA 608 program, Washington also enthusiastically encouraged single-family home construction in the wake of World War II.* Long-term mortgages, subsidized by FHA insurance, enabled homeownership for millions of Americans. For veterans, the "GI Bill of Rights" guaranteed bank loans covering 100 percent of a dwelling's purchase price: no down payment!† If you were not a veteran, other FHA programs offered financing that was nearly as spectacular. In 1947, FHA 603 (the single-family cousin of FHA 608) encouraged lenders to make twenty-five-year loans at 4 percent interest, with just 10 percent down.‡ In 1948, a revision of the FHA's Section 203 program dropped the down payment to 5 percent.**

(continued)

---

* FHA loan assistance for single-family homes has had much attention from historians. Jackson, *Crabgrass Frontier*, chapter 11; Wright, *Building the Dream*, chapter 13.
† Katznelson, *When Affirmative Action Was White*. For a list of housing programs introduced by Washington in the mid- and late 1940s: Milgram, *Chronology of Housing Legislation*.
‡ "Meeting Held in Charlotte: FHA Financing Program Explained at Conference," *Charlotte Observer*, February 7, 1947; Mason, *History of Housing*, 50–51.
** "New FHA Rules Are Explained," *Charlotte Observer*, September 23, 1948. "On a house which can be built for $6,300, the owner can borrow $6,000, which means that he can finance the house for five percent, or $300 down." On other FHA single-family aid: "New Home Building Plan Announced by Loan Body," *Raleigh News and Observer*, November 2, 1946; "Holland Is Leaving FHA Post for Private Venture," *Charlotte Observer*, June 25, 1950.

---

costs of production, 4 percent money, and a period of 32 years and seven months to pay the debt." Tenants did not have to be veterans, but that was certainly a robust market: "Of all veterans who seek living accommodations approximately 86 percent prefer to rent rather than buy or build a home."[8] The FHA guaranteed investors at least a 6½ percent profit. The actual number ran closer to 9 percent, officials reported happily, and could hit twice that amount if there were no vacancies.

It worked. "FHA Mortgages Bring Boom in Rental Field," headlined an Associated Press story in late 1947. In the New York City area, "60 percent of all new dwelling units under [FHA] jurisdiction are now going forward in the rental

Streets of newly built small homes sprang up all around Charlotte's suburban rim.

Nationally, the FHA 603 subsidy boosted the rise of many of the era's biggest names in real estate. William Levitt developed portions of his famed Levittown suburbs outside New York City under FHA 603.†† Angus G. Wynne, who became a premier builder in Dallas, constructed both FHA 603 single-family and FHA 608 multifamily dwellings in his vast Wynnewood community of 2,200 houses and 1,000 apartments.‡‡ The same financing combination also fueled Park Forest just south of Chicago, "a complete new city of 11,000 population"—later the focus of sociologist William Whyte's classic study *The Organization Man*.***

---

†† "Housing: Profits vs. Shortage," *Time*, July 26, 1954.
‡‡ Mason, *History of Housing*, 51.
*** "FHA Impact on the Financing and Design of Apartments," *Architectural Forum*, January 1950, 97–108, https://usmodernist.org/AF/AF-1950-01.PDF; Mason, *History of Housing*, 48; Carruth, "Big Move to Small Towns," *Fortune*, 1971, reprinted in the *Congressional Record* S41417 (November 16, 1971); "Park Forest Moves into '52," *House and Home*, March 1952, 114–21, https://usmodernist.org/HH/HH-1952-03.pdf.

---

field and only 40 percent in the single-family house classification."⁹ By the end of September 1947, a whopping 533 projects were underway across the United States.

One cause of the frenzy: with a bit of creative accounting, the FHA loan could actually cover not just 90 percent but 100 percent of costs. "One of the most unorthodox features of the set-up is the possibility of 'mortgaging out,'" marveled the Associated Press reporter: "Theoretically a builder, architect, lawyer and land-owner can get together and float a small project without investing any cash. The builder can take his profit in stock, the architect and lawyer [take] their fees [likewise,] while the land-owner, who may have bought at a bargain, can mark up his land to a reasonable up-to-date value."¹⁰

"Mortgaging out" constituted an amazing subsidy. It meant that developers put up only their time in creating a project—no cash at all—and then reaped a share of the rental income each month for decades.¹¹ Rents paid by tenants covered all of the landlord's expenses—monthly loan repayments, maintenance costs—and produced a handsome profit. An FHA 608 project became a money machine for its owner.

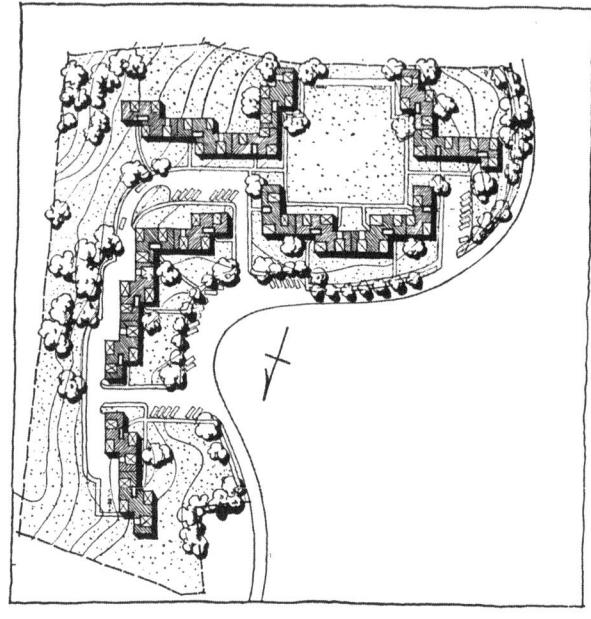

Figure 3.2. The 1947 FHA plan book encouraged buildings to be grouped to create courtyards. FHA, *Planning Rental Housing Projects*, 50.

To understand what a windfall "mortgaging out" was, imagine yourself in this scenario. Someone hands you $1 million. They coach you to build an apartment project that will provide you with an ongoing profit stream—and that will pay back the entire $1 million loan. All of your expenses are covered, you draw out a profit each year, and you get to keep the project when it's paid off. Sweet deal, right?

Men who would become Charlotte's real estate leaders of the 1950s through the 1980s—C. D. Spangler, Charles Ervin, M. R. Marsh, John Crosland, and others—got big assists early in their careers from FHA 608 and its companion program FHA 603, which underwrote single-family construction on the same generous terms.

■ ■ ■ ■ ■

As part of the FHA's careful coaching, officials in Washington developed an architectural template for the Section 608 apartment complexes. The FHA reissued its multifamily plan book, created earlier for Section 207.[12] The images of low-rise buildings grouped amid greenspace did much to shape Americans' notion of how multifamily housing should look.

In some parts of the United States, FHA 608 aided mid- and high-rise "elevator buildings," but not in North Carolina. James McRae at the FHA's Carolina regional office in Greensboro refused to fund them. "Tall apartment buildings are suitable in large cities where there is great density of population and there is an extremely high value put upon the suitable land close to the business districts. That situation doesn't exist in North Carolina's cities," wrote the *Observer*. "McRae and his staff . . . have let developers know they wouldn't approve those tall buildings."[13]

Nationwide, much of the FHA's help went to low-rise suburban complexes: "Although almost any style of rental housing can be built under Section 608, one of the most popular now going forward is the low garden apartment type," said a 1947 FHA publication. "These structures, spread out over acreage, take advantage of lower land costs in outlying sections [of suburbia] and meet tenant preferences for private entrances, two-story layouts resembling row houses, and ample grounds with parking and play spaces."[14]

Thanks to FHA 608, the dream designs prototyped at Radburn during the 1920s and in the initial FHA-underwritten apartments such as the Myrtle in Charlotte during the 1930s were now replicated by the hundreds, becoming commonplace in every American city.

FHA 608 Starts in Charlotte: Scotland Colony

The first FHA 608 project out of the gate in Charlotte was—you'll notice a recurring pattern here—aimed at the well-to-do. Developer W. Marshall Moore, who had cut his teeth building FHA-backed single-family subdivisions, announced a big new apartment initiative to be called Scotland Colony.[15] The name signaled its location on upscale Scotland Avenue and Colony Avenue at the southern edge of posh Myers Park. Moore was already building single-family residences there, at $25,000 apiece, a top-bracket price in this era when an FHA-assisted home for a returning veteran typically cost $5,000 to $6,000.

Moore hired architect Charles W. Connelly, who by now had extensive experience meeting federal guidelines thanks to his designs for Myrtle Apartments and also Fairview Homes. At Scotland Colony, Connelly chose red-brick Williamsburg-style architecture.[16] He arranged eighty-six two-bedroom "large size family units" in a series of separate buildings, each holding between two and six apartments. The buildings were scattered on large blocks to allow green space with playgrounds and an internal network of concrete sidewalks. Tenants

Figure 3.3. Scotland Colony, funded via FHA 608, was Charlotte's first big post–World War II apartment project. Hanchett photo, 2023.

parked in spaces notched along the street edge or behind the units. FHA officials personally inspected the gently rolling hillside site and pronounced it "the most beautiful land they have seen for a project of the type planned," Moore bragged to the *Observer*.[17] He announced the project at the end of 1947, and tenants were moving in by the end of 1948.

Scotland Colony set the standard locally for what a suburban apartment complex would be. Well into the 1970s, multifamily housing would consist of multiple low-rise buildings scattered on superblock sites. That held true no matter what the price point. To upscale a project, give the buildings a brick veneer. To make it more affordable, clad them in wooden clapboards or maybe the newest materials: asbestos shingles in the 1950s, aluminum siding in the 1970s. If desired, mix some two-story buildings among the one-story ones. Assume that your tenants will have automobiles. The idea of walking from your apartment to shops and gathering places would remain out of fashion until well into the twenty-first century.[18]

Savvy Finance and Assembly-Line Construction: C. D. Spangler

Upscale renters were the target audience for all Charlotte FHA 608 projects that first year—with one noteworthy exception. Two high-rent complexes went

Subsidizing the "Free Market" ■ 55

up near Myers Park Country Club, two others in the top-drawer suburbs of Dilworth and Elizabeth, and another in middle-class Sedgefield.[19] The only Charlotte complex that bucked the upscale focus was Tryon Hills, in an industrial corridor along North Tryon Street. "The apartments are planned for families needing places to live but unable to pay the high rental costs often charged," explained owner C. D. Spangler.[20]

Clemmie Dickson Spangler grew up on a farm in rural Cleveland County, came to Charlotte to enroll in Kings Business College, and then found employment in the office of Edward Dilworth Latta. Latta had developed the Dilworth suburb back in the 1890s, and he encouraged Spangler to build houses on the last few vacant lots. By the late 1930s, Spangler accumulated enough capital to go out on his own, offering homes with the new FHA mortgages insured by Washington.[21] During the 1940s, Spangler grew wealthy with government contracts—barracks for World War II soldiers at Camp Lejeune in Jacksonville, North Carolina, and then postwar military housing in Georgia, Virginia, and beyond. To arrange financing, he helped start the Bank of North Carolina in Jacksonville—which later would become part of mammoth Bank of America and make the Spangler family the single biggest stockholder in the nation's first coast-to-coast bank.[22]

Spangler took a contrarian approach to the FHA 608 game. Rather than aiming for the high end of the market, he focused on low-income tenants. In March 1948 he announced construction of Tryon Hills, 250 apartments for working-class whites to be located off North Tryon Street.[23] Later that year he also began preparations for Double Oaks near Statesville Avenue, with 506 units to serve African Americans.[24] Eventually Spangler would develop more FHA 608 projects than anyone else in Charlotte, five in total, with all but one at the low end of the rental scale.

Nothing in Spangler's background seems to have made him particularly sympathetic to low-income renters, but as a smart businessman he recognized a surprising truth. Thanks to the FHA's profit guarantee, he could make exactly the same return on investment no matter what the rental price point. In fact, low-income projects may have been slightly more lucrative. Land constituted the biggest up-front expense that an FHA developer typically faced. Land cost more in upscale neighborhoods, less in blue-collar areas. If a developer could avoid paying much for land, he more likely could reach the financial nirvana of "mortgaging out."

For Tryon Hills, Spangler picked a site off North Tryon Street near the Southern Railway industrial corridor. Being within walking distance of the warehouses and small factories that lined the railroad meant access to jobs for Tryon Hills' blue-collar tenants. It also meant low land costs for Spangler. That helped him set rents at forty to fifty-five dollars per month, affordable "for families of moderate means who cannot pay large rentals."[25] Scotland Colony, in contrast, rented for about ninety dollars monthly.[26]

To further reduce costs, Spangler pioneered "assembly-line" construction at Tryon Hills. The basic layout and design were by now familiar: "duplex and triplex buildings... grouped in an attractive manner around courts... designed by the land-planning division of the FHA in Atlanta," reported the *Observer*.[27] The innovation came in the workflow on the jobsite. "With Assembly-Line Housing, Charlotte Builder Is Making History" the newspaper marveled.[28] The building process was split into "25 to 30 operations" with a team for each. Survey engineers staked out the front corners of a building, and then "their place at first is taken by the layout men who put in the stobs for digging. Next come those who dig the foundations, and then the brickmasons.... Another group comes to put in the sills and floor joists and subflooring. When this has been done, a big truck drives up with the [wall] sections, already built [at another station on the jobsite], which are put up. Then other workmen prepare for the inside walls and ceiling joists. The rafters are put on, then the sheetings and the roof." Additional teams finished out the plumbing, painting, and other details.

Reported the *Observer*, "'It's like chasing a fox,' said Mr. Spangler. 'We always have a group in front being chased by the next group and on down the line until the last piece of wall-paper has been put on and the last inch of the floor has been polished.'"[29]

The tenants who rented at Tryon Hills seem mostly to have been couples with two jobs, often in Charlotte's warehouse sector—not poor, but not wealthy either.[30] Louis A. Wintzer, one of the earliest to be listed in the city directory, was an order clerk at the Allison-Erwin appliance parts warehouse, while his wife, Hazel, worked as a clerk at Southern Bearings & Parts. Their neighbor Robert R. Harwell was a "paper handler" at the *Charlotte News*, his wife, Evelyn, a telephone operator at Southern Bell. Tryon Hills was often mentioned in marriage announcements as a home for newlyweds. A 1949 newspaper piece on the wedding of Mary Beth Wall to Benton Long Jr. at Myers Park Methodist Church noted that both had attended college. He worked at Crane, a plumbing parts wholesaler, and she at Goodyear Tire and Rubber.[31]

■ ■ ■ ■ ■

With Tryon Hills underway, Spangler got a nudge from Black leader Fred D. Alexander. In that era of segregation, African Americans had no chance at living in a white complex, but Alexander believed that a Black project might be possible.

His alliance with Spangler would produce Double Oaks (including an extension called Newland Homes) and Brookhill Village, two of the largest low-income housing initiatives in North Carolina. Much later, Alexander would become the first Black person on Charlotte's City Council in the twentieth century.[32]

The Alexander family possessed deep credentials in building, in business, and in community betterment. Fred's father, Zechariah Alexander, started off installing wooden lath for plasterers, served as a bookkeeper for Black brick manufacturer/contractor William Houser, became district manager for big Black-owned North Carolina Mutual Insurance, and then launched Alexander Funeral Home.[33] It served Black clients, a steady source of income unbeholden to whites, which allowed Zech and his sons to take active leadership in civil rights. The family formed Charlotte's chapter of the NAACP in the 1940s, and Fred's brother Kelly became longtime president of the statewide NAACP. Fred focused on finance. In the mid-1930s, he joined Southern Fidelity Mutual Insurance, which sold automobile and health insurance, dealt in long-term loans, and refinanced mortgages.[34] He also emerged as a community figure, active in the AME Zion Church, officer in the Masons, and chair of the Negro Division of the Community Chest.[35] In 1939 Fred volunteered as secretary for the WPA housing study (see chapter 2) that set the stage for Fairview Homes public housing.[36]

When FHA 608 became available, Fred Alexander quickly understood its potential—and began working his connections. A biographer later wrote, "After World War II there were few places in Charlotte for returning veterans to live. A white contractor, C. D. Spangler, became interested in building an apartment complex for blacks—and Fred Alexander had the ear of Mayor Victor Shaw. After a series of talks some land was made available . . . and so Double Oaks was hatched . . . under the new Government Provision 608."[37]

The land that Alexander helped Spangler obtain was next to Fairview Homes public housing along Statesville Avenue. The property included the former city dump (which would trigger brownfield cleanup issues decades later). Cost was low, $1,440 a year in a fifty-year lease, with an option (which Spangler exercised) to buy for even less: $36,000.[38]

Architects Lyles, Bissett, Carlisle and Wolff of Columbia, South Carolina, the South's busiest designers of FHA-sanctioned apartments, drew up the blueprints. The architecture emphasized simplicity of horizontal line with big picture windows in each living room—foreshadowing the "ranch-style" houses that would shortly become popular in Charlotte and across the United States. Asbestos siding, a newly developed material, covered the exterior walls, tinted in buff, green, white, or blue to differentiate the buildings.[39]

Spangler hired Alexander as Double Oaks' property manager, tasked with selecting the tenants. One-bedroom units rented at $7.75 a week, two-bedroom at

$9.25.⁴⁰ (That worked out to $31 and $37 monthly, compared with $40 and $55 at Tryon Hills.) Interestingly, where white apartments always rented by the month, African American housing rented by the week—perhaps an indication of how precarious it could be for most Black southerners to stay employed in that era.

A September 1949 *Observer* story showed Fred Alexander handing over keys to the first tenant, Mrs. J. C. Clemmons, while Spangler, local dignitaries, and FHA officials looked on.⁴¹ Alexander carefully handpicked the Clemmons family, hardworking and well-connected in Black Charlotte. Mrs. Clemmons taught at Biddleville Elementary, a mile away up Oaklawn Avenue. She had served as an officer in the city's Black Classroom Teachers Association and would soon be elected vice president of the local Pan-Hellenic Council, an organization of Black college graduates.⁴² Mr. Clemmons was similarly well educated, a graduate of Johnson C. Smith University, where he had starred on the basketball team.⁴³ He made his living as a mail carrier for the post office, served as vice president of the young men's club at the McCrorey YMCA, and was a lay leader at St. Paul Baptist Church.⁴⁴

Double Oaks was Charlotte's largest-ever building project as of 1949 and was also said to be the largest housing development up to that time for African Americans anywhere in North Carolina.⁴⁵ "Mr. Spangler has pioneered the program for providing adequate modern housing for Negroes in this state. The projects he has built in Charlotte have served as examples for builders in a number of other cities, who have visited them and gone home and built similar developments. This is true of cities in other states as well as of several in North Carolina," said the *Observer* in 1950.⁴⁶ "The Federal Housing Administration, through which financing of the job was arranged, considers it a model."⁴⁷

Double Oaks expanded in 1950, a project known as Newland Road Apartments. It added 178 more apartments in 57 buildings along Newland Road, just north of the original development.⁴⁸ Spangler donated a site there for a city-owned swimming pool and sold land to the school system for a state-of-the-art elementary school between Double Oaks and Fairview Homes.⁴⁹ The area was still isolated, however, when compared with bustling in-town Black neighborhoods such as Brooklyn. Only a few scattered shops and social spaces took root along Oaklawn Avenue and Statesville Avenue across from the massive housing projects.

■ ■ ■ ■ ■

C. D. Spangler's other FHA 608 development for African Americans went up at the far south edge of Charlotte in 1950–51. Brookhill Village on South Tryon Street held 418 apartments.⁵⁰ It stood next to the Southside Homes public

DOUBLE OAKS OPENING Charlotte's huge new residential development for Negroes, Double Oaks, off Statesville road near the city limits, is accepting tenants. Yesterday the formal opening was observed, with (left to right), Mayor Victor Shaw; City Manager Henry Yancey; Mrs. J. C. Plemmons, the tenant; Fred Alexander, project manager; Jerry Jerome of Greensboro, North Carolina chief underwriter of the FHA; Builder C. D. Spangler; and Charles Rich of the Wachovia Bank and Trust company, along with other representatives of various groups in the city, present. (Observer Staff photo—Houston.)

Figure 3.4. Double Oaks opening. In the 2010s it would be replaced by mixed-income Brightwalk (see chapter 8). *Charlotte Observer,* September 28, 1949.

housing then being developed. Two new African American schools were adjacent, York Road High and Marie G. Davis Elementary.[51] Architects Lyles, Bissett, Carlisle and Wolff drew plans that included a handful of shops and a small supermarket facing busy South Tryon, the major highway into Charlotte from the south, but otherwise the site was again an isolated island.

Learning from his success at using low-cost land at Double Oaks, Spangler came up with a subtle twist at Brookhill. He created an entity called Brookhill Village, Inc. to apply for the FHA 608 funds and develop the property—but he held onto the land separately under his own name. Brookhill Village, Inc. leased the land from Spangler for ninety-nine years.[52]

The separation was only on paper. Spangler owned both entities. But it accomplished two things. First, the Brookhill project would pay Spangler every year for the use of the land; that fee could be set higher than the 6½ percent that FHA allowed for return on capital investment.

Second, it gave Spangler a no-risk position if the project happened to fail. "[General US] law, of course, says that whoever has the land-lease in case of default on a mortgage owns the property. In other words, [the FHA] cannot repossess without purchasing his land or making a deal." Those words came from a US Senate investigation of FHA 608 abuses, which we will discuss below.[53]

The separate land-lease would become a devilish complication decades later (see the sidebar "A Problem Called Brookhill" in chapter 9). Brookhill still stands in the early 2020s, in poor repair. Spangler descendants continue to control the land.[54]

FHA 608 Shifts toward "Lower Rent"— with Some Exceptions

Once Spangler proved how profitable low-rent apartments could be, other Charlotte developers got interested. During the first eighteen months of FHA 608—from announcement of Scotland Colony in December 1947 through June 1949—seven FHA 608 multifamily complexes had been completed. Every one of them was in the upper-income range except for Tryon Hills and Double Oaks. During the next nine months, however, up to the program's termination in March 1950, developers dove into downscale projects.

The FHA encouraged the shift. Administrators put out word in November 1949 that the "'terrific' boom in higher-rent apartments is dealing a heavy blow to that phase of the housing shortage." They cautioned that "in the upper-rental brackets ... the apartment market [is] close to saturation in a number of areas."[55] Section 608 subsidies remained available, officials advised, "but in most areas only the builders of lower-rent apartment developments need apply."[56]

Charlotte developers took heed. Paul Younts, who had earlier created the Younts Apartments at Selwyn and Croydon Avenues near the Myers Park Country Club, now developed Plaza Terrace. Aimed at white working-class tenants, it stood within walking distance of the textile mill villages along Thirty-Sixth Street (the area today known as NoDa). Its one-story shingle-clad buildings looked much like Double Oaks. Rents on 158 four-room units ran $53.50 per month.[57]

Lex Marsh, whose earlier Oakcrest Apartments in Sedgefield rented at $72.50, now created Weyland Homes off Wilkinson Boulevard on the city's more workaday west side.[58] The land cost less, and Weyland's buildings used cheaper brick and wooden clapboard exteriors, in contrast to all-brick Oakcrest. The 168 Weyland units rented for $55.00 per month. C. D. Spangler, in addition to Tryon Hills ($40 and $55 monthly), Double Oaks ($31 and $37 monthly), and Brookhill Village ($34 to $42 monthly) now built whites-only Westwood Apartments off West Morehead Street with rents ranging from $37.50 for a one-bedroom to $52.50 for a three-bedroom.[59]

The FHA also approved two new middle- to high-end developments: Morningside Apartments and Selwyn Village. At Morningside, Charlotte real estate man Dwight Phillips chose full brick exteriors for his two-story buildings on relatively expensive land in the desirable Plaza Midwood vicinity. Rents were $78 per four-room unit. That was high for FHA-assisted complexes, but FHA officials rationalized that their assistance put top-notch design within reach of a wider market—"compared with $85–$90 that such apartments are bringing elsewhere in the city." Said the *Observer*, "The FHA feels this will be a step in the direction of less costly housing."[60]

Selwyn Village opened in early 1950 south of elite Myers Park, renting for $62.50–$75.00. C. D. Spangler initially sold the land to a young developer named Wriston Thompson. Spangler managed the finished project and then became owner when Thompson decided to sell.[61] Lyles, Bissett, Carlisle and Wolff again did the architectural design, mostly two-bedroom units geared to families with small children. The 234 apartments, arranged in forty-five two-story brick buildings, were set in landscaping by Charlotte's A. V. Blankenship, which included park space and a playground.[62]

Shutting Down FHA 608—and Accusations of Scandal

When Congress funded FHA 608 in 1947, it set the program to expire at the end of June 1949.[63] Real estate interests lobbied hard for an extension, so Washington pushed the termination into the following March and authorized an extra half-billion dollars of loan guarantees.[64] Applications flooded in as the clock ticked away.[65] FHA 608 shut down completely at midnight on March 1, 1950, three years after its initial announcement. Construction continued on the approved projects, most wrapping up by 1951.

Washington's reasons for the shutdown lie beyond the scope of this book, but overbuilding was one large worry. In Florida, in particular, the FHA was beginning to experience defaults. Builders of "luxurious, expensive Florida resort apartments" had overestimated the high-end market, a Tampa newspaper reported. Developers simply walked away from vacancy-troubled projects and left the FHA holding the bag.[66]

Remembering Selwyn Village

Young families flocked to FHA 608–subsidized Selwyn Village in the 1950s, many at the start of prosperous careers. Nationwide, a post–World War II "baby boom" occurred as couples who had delayed marriage and parenthood made up for lost time. Many got a career boost thanks to the GI Bill, which put college financially in reach of millions of Americans. "So many couples started families at Selwyn Village that it was nicknamed 'Fertile Valley,'" chuckled the *Charlotte Observer*.* Selwyn Village had a no-nonsense rental manager named Clyde Daves, a counterpart to Fred Alexander at Double Oaks. "He set the tone of that community," one tenant remembered. "He insisted on meeting both Mr. and Mrs. If he didn't care for the way you talked or dressed, you didn't get in, waiting list or no. It was considered a real coup to get in." Single men were prohibited, recalled another tenant, who went on to be mayor of the Charlotte suburb of Mint Hill: "The exception was if you said you and Sally were getting married in 60 days. They'd take you, but you'd better be sure you and Sally *did* get married." For couples starting out, having so many similar neighbors created an instant social life. "Nobody had any money," one woman recalled. "If one person bought a children's wading pool, nobody else in that building bought one. It was a sharing environment."

People who passed through Selwyn Village, typically staying two or three years until children outgrew the apartments, went on to become a who's who of Charlotte. John Crosland Jr., who would take leadership from his father of one of the South's top real estate firms (see chapters 6–8), lived there. So did future Charlotte mayor Eddie Knox; Fred Bryant, who became Charlotte's chief city planner; Jerry Shinn, who was later the *Charlotte Observer*'s lead editorial writer; and Stuart Dickson, whose family nurtured Harris Teeter supermarkets into a South-wide brand. At least one neighbor became a national household name: journalist Charles Kuralt rented at Selwyn Village during his years as a local newspaper reporter, before television stardom at CBS.

Three other tenants made big impacts on US financial history. The story began with "a billion-dollar touch-football game. Although nobody knew that at the time," wrote Charlotte columnist Tommy Tomlinson. "In the 1950s, three young men started socializing in the Selwyn Village apartments, home to a lot of Charlotte's young up-and-comers. Hugh McColl, Dick Spangler and Ed Crutchfield all lived there. Back then, at Selwyn Village, a lot of the men got together on

Saturdays to throw the football around. 'It was supposed to be touch football,' McColl says. 'But it got kind of rough.'"†

The games built a camaraderie. The trio had similarly privileged backgrounds that put them on rapid upward paths. McColl, son of a big South Carolina cotton farmer, had arrived in Charlotte as an executive trainee being groomed for the highest echelons of what was soon to be called North Carolina National Bank. C. D. Spangler Jr. was about to step into leadership of his father's real estate firm and would also take charge of the family-founded Bank of North Carolina. Crutchfield, son of a North Carolina judge, was rising quickly at First Union Bank.‡ Over the next five decades, their paths would often intertwine. McColl built the country's first coast-to-coast bank, Bank of America, headquartered in Charlotte. Asked how he did it, he credited a rivalry with Crutchfield's First Union and also nodded to the importance of an early merger with the Spangler family bank—which made C. D. Spangler Jr. the largest stockholder in Bank of America, personally worth over $2 billion.** Locally, the three men supported each other in civic work, as McColl, for instance, lured NFL football to Charlotte, as Crutchfield raised millions to put Johnson C. Smith University on a firm footing, and as Spangler became president of the University of North Carolina system statewide.††

The Selwyn Village history upends stereotypes about government-subsidized housing. Such living spaces can be highly desirable. And being a tenant there does not necessarily sap one's will to work hard in the capitalist system.

---

*Except as noted, all quotations in this sidebar are from "Selwyn Village Spawned City's Leaders," *Charlotte Observer*, November 21, 1981.
† "From a Small Town to the Big Time: How Decades of Bold Moves Have Positioned Charlotte on the International Stage," *Charlotte Observer*, February 20, 2011.
‡ "Edward Crutchfield," North Carolina Business Hall of Fame, accessed November 6, 2024, https://www.historync.org/laureate%20-%20Ed%20Crutchfield.htm.
** Late in life, Spangler was often the highest-ranked North Carolinian on *Fortune* magazine's annual roster of US billionaires. "Charlotte's C. D. Spangler Makes Fortune's Billionaire List," *Charlotte Business Journal*, March 5, 2013.
†† Schexnider, *Saving Black Colleges*.

That overbuilding never hit Charlotte, but default still could be a problem. When the Forest Apartments developed structural flaws due to a new all-concrete construction technology, builder V. P. Loftis quickly defaulted and put the complex into the FHA's hands.[67] With little cash personally invested, getting out was nearly painless. Surprisingly, the FHA seems to have experienced very few defaults. According to a 1951 report, "FHA Commissioner Franklin D. Richards said his agency has had to take ownership of 66 projects across the country, out of 6,684 approved since 1942"—a notably low failure rate.[68]

More than the defaults, the fact that so much of the federal aid went to upscale apartments rankled some observers. "Section 608 was designed to stimulate multifamily housing for . . . veterans," chided the *Tampa Tribune*. "In Florida, at least, the program went far afield from the law's intent."[69]

Accusations of cheating began to surface in mid-1950. Initial barbs came from the American Federation of Labor. It alleged that numerous FHA 608 developers had not abided by federal minimum wage laws as they paid construction workers. An ensuing US Senate investigation specifically pointed to Charlotte's Double Oaks, Plaza Terrace, Oakcrest, Morningside, and Selwyn Village as underpayment culprits. The investigation petered out with no resolution.[70]

In 1954—four years after the program's end—a full-blown FHA 608 scandal hit national headlines. Congress took a careful look back at FHA 608's "mortgaging out" feature. Not merely had developers found ways to arrange loans for the entire cost of a project, thus contributing no capital of their own, charged the congressional committee, but many developers had gotten loans for more than 100 percent of project cost. That provided "windfall profits" that they simply pocketed. No need to pay back the money, since rents from tenants had already been set to cover all loan payments.

Weeks of hearings in Washington splashed across newspapers nationwide.[71] Among the developers questioned was Fred C. Trump of New York City. He had set up his 1,860-unit Beach Haven project to generate $3 million in extra profit, investigators calculated. Trump put the windfall into a bank account that launched the careers of his children, notably future US president Donald Trump.[72]

In Charlotte, the FHA 608 windfall scandal focused on C. D. Spangler.[73] At Double Oaks, Spangler had apparently taken the land sold to him by the city for $36,000 and leased it to his Double Oaks development corporation for $10,000 a year, folding the inflated cost into the rents. He did a similar switch when paying the architects. His development corporation gave them stock with a face value of $219,401. Spangler bought it back from them with $16,570 out of his own pocket—the actual cash value of the designers' work. But again, he was able to fold $219,401 into the "expenses" of Double Oaks and boost the rents accordingly.

Lawyers fought for years over whether such actions were in fact illegal under the FHA law as written. Ultimately the battle moved into tax court, where Spangler was charged with underpayment to the IRS. He ended up paying additional tax for the years in question.

Newspaper stories made no mention, however, of any effort to recalculate rents for Double Oaks' residents. They evidently continued to pay the inflated rates that Spangler had set.[74]

Looking Back at FHA 608

FHA 608 worked extraordinarily well at stimulating housing production, the task it was created for. Americans hungered for rental apartments, and FHA 608 got developers to supply that need. It did so with minimal federal outlay. It has not been possible to determine exactly how much the FHA spent on its planning office, which directly cocreated site plans and architectural designs, and on its underwriting experts, who worked with developers and banks to craft loan-ready packages, nor how much the FHA spent to cover defaults. But it was surely a tiny fraction of the money that the developers brought to the table. The FHA reported that it insured over $6.5 billion in Section 608 mortgages during the program's three years—at a time when the entire federal budget ran only $37 billion annually.[75]

The program brought the garden apartment concept to nearly every city and most sizable towns. The FHA reported eighty-six projects across North Carolina containing 9,107 units.[76] Cameron Village in Raleigh, which included a suburban shopping center and single-family homes as well as Section 608 apartments, gave that city's northeast suburbs a glow of desirability that has never faded. In Chapel Hill, the Glen Lennox FHA 608 development became a beloved stepping-stone for recent University of North Carolina graduates, including future NFL star Charlie "Choo-Choo" Justice and basketball coach Roy Williams.[77] In Winston-Salem, Cloverdale Apartments, Ardmore Terrace, and Miller Park Apartments form an integral part of the Ardmore Historic District.[78] Likewise, some who developed FHA 608 projects went far beyond the real estate arena: J. Willie York (Cameron Village and Washington Apartments in Raleigh) saw his son Smedes York become two-term mayor of Raleigh; Charles Bennett Deane (Oakwood Courts in Rockingham) served five terms in the US House of Representatives.[79]

After FHA 608 ended, its design ideas continued to be standard across

Table 3.1. FHA 608 Apartment Complexes Built in Charlotte, 1948–1951

Development	Opened	Developer	Units	Race	2022 status
Scotland Colony 1931 Lynnwood Dr 28209	1948	Marshall Moore	86	white	condos
Younts Apartments Selwyn Av & Croydon Rd 28207	1948	Paul Younts	16	white	demolished
Selwyn-Queens 2337 Selwyn Av 28207	1948	Walter Revis	16	white	condos
Forest Apartments 2421 Vail Av 28207	1948	VP Loftis	88	white	condos
Berkmore 1125 E Morehead St 28204	1948	VP Loftis	19	white	offices
Oakcrest 2700 Oakcrest Pl 28209	1948	Lex Marsh	76	white	being demolished
*Tryon Hills 26th St & N Tryon 28206	1948	CD Spangler	250	white	demolished
*Double Oaks 2623 Double Oaks Av 28206	1949	CD Spangler	506	Black	replaced by Brightwalk
*Newland Road expands Double Oaks	1950	CD Spangler	178	Black	demolished
Morningside 1218 Hanover St 28205	1950	Dwight Phillips	216	white	replaced by Village at Commonwealth

America. In Charlotte, Cotswold Village took shape in 1952 with courtyard apartments around a shopping plaza. Seward Mott, who had just stepped down as chief planner at the FHA, created the design.[80] Thousands of other projects nationwide throughout the 1950s, 1960s, and 1970s, no matter who the designer, followed the FHA 608 pattern. Low-rise buildings scattered on greenspace, occupying large tracts of land and rigorously limited to rental housing (without corner grocery stores, dry cleaners, taverns, or other uses)—that model became the American norm.

In today's affordable housing parlance, the low-rent FHA 608 projects such as Plaza Terrace and Double Oaks might be called "workforce housing." The renters—such as nurses, teachers, food service workers, and maintenance

Table 3.1. (*continued*)

Development	Opened	Developer	Units	Race	2022 status
*Plaza Terrace 1327 Murdock Rd 28205	1950	Paul Younts	158	white	still apartments
Selwyn Village 127 Wakefield Dr 28209	1950	Thompson/ Spangler	234	white	condos
*Westwood Apartments 1864 Fleetwood Dr 28208	1950	CD Spangler	270	white	demolished
*Weyland Homes 2814 Marlowe Av 28208	1951	Lex Marsh	168	white	still apartments
*Brookhill Village 2506 S Tryon St 28203	1951	CD Spangler	418	Black	being demolished
Total FHA 608 complexes, all rent levels: 15			Total FHA 608 units, all rent levels: 2,699		
Total FHA 608 complexes, low-rent: 7			Total FHA 608 units, low-rent: 1,948		

* "Low-rent" project

Source: Table excerpted from Tom Hanchett, "Master List of Low-Income Multifamily Housing Constructed in Charlotte, 1940–2019," in the data collection of J. Murrey Atkins Library, University of North Carolina at Charlotte, https://doi.org/10.15139/S3/XQBOFW.

workers—hold jobs that do not pay especially well.[81] Over time, as the complexes aged, they did come to house society's poorest members. As built, however, they served not the poorest of the poor but rather helped people on the next rungs of the economic ladder.

Was that a good thing? Harold Dillehay, who made affordable housing his career as longtime chief of the Charlotte Housing Authority, believed that FHA 608 filled a definite need. But it was no replacement for government-owned public housing. A 1949 *Observer* story quoted him speaking bluntly: "Private industry has not done the job . . . and it cannot do the job for the lowest-income families." The *Observer* continued: "Mr. Dillehay congratulated local builders, and C. D. Spangler in particular, for recent efforts to build low-rental housing projects but said that public housing is designed for families who don't make enough to pay even the lowest rental in such privately constructed dwellings."[82]

Charlotte still needed at least 1,000 additional units of public housing, Dillehay asserted, even as the new FHA 608 projects were welcoming tenants. To be a healthy city, Charlotte required *both* types of subsidized housing— *government-owned* public housing and *government-assisted* private developments.

That is a lesson that we struggle to relearn in every generation. Since the late 1980s, most low-rent housing has been built through the federal Low-Income Housing Tax Credit (see chapters 7–9). LIHTC works differently than FHA 608, but at its heart it relies on the same underlying premise: sweeten housing deals to give private investors a profit when they put their money into affordable housing.

Today, America is rediscovering what Harold Dillehay realized back in the FHA 608 era: subsidies to private developers can go only so far in meeting society's needs.

■■■■■■■■■■■■■■■■■■■■■■■■■■■■■■■ **CHAPTER 4**

Bathrooms, Building Codes, and "Slum Clearance"

■ Minimum Housing Standards? Or "Urban Renewal"?

At first glance, this chapter may seem out of place in this book. Why look at local building codes in a study of affordable housing? Why delve into the 1950s–1960s federal demolition program popularly known as "slum clearance" or "urban renewal"? And why put the two subjects in the same chapter?

Of the two, Washington-aided slum clearance/urban renewal might seem more logical to discuss since it began as part of the Federal Housing Act of 1949.[1] But in actuality, as we will learn, the act destroyed many hundreds of homes in Charlotte, creating a housing shortage that lasted for years.[2]

Building codes, on the other hand, turn out to be deeply connected with affordable housing. The private market has always provided low-cost living units. That type of investment is often very profitable. Most of our affordable housing supply, in fact, is not government subsidized but market-rate—which includes both older properties that are converted to low-cost rentals (see the discussion of NOAH in chapter 1) and purpose-built units. That market-rate housing has ranged from adequate to terrible, however. For decades, Americans debated whether government might get involved.

Should landlords be required to provide every residential unit with running water and a working indoor toilet? Today we expect that answer to be "yes." But it took over thirty years of struggle before Charlotte created and enforced an effective building code in the late 1940s.[3]

The terms of the debate shifted abruptly in 1949. The new Housing Act from Washington gave aid to cities to wipe out slums. Charlotteans had been using the term "slum clearance" when they talked about code enforcement. Making landlords add plumbing and fix up substandard dwellings—that would clear away Charlotte's slum *conditions*. But when local leaders read the fine print in the 1949 Housing Act, they realized that Washington was offering something bigger. Federal dollars could be used to knock down entire neighborhoods—and the land then could be used for *anything*. This bulldozer approach to "slum clearance" would become known, with unintended irony, as "urban renewal."

Building Codes: A Thirty-Year Battle, 1910s–1940s

"Can any of you state with any degree of certainty where the fly that dashed through your screendoor and lighted on the baby's oatmeal, had his previous meal?"[4] So spoke V. S. Woodward, head of Charlotte's private Associated Charities in an address to a local women's club in 1916.[5] The technology of indoor plumbing had been in existence for decades, but it remained largely a luxury for the wealthy.[6] Poor folk used the old-fashioned outhouse, also called a privy—a pit dug in the ground with a wooden seat above it. Woodward described more than fifty alleys and crowded courts with "not a bathroom, a toilet, or even running water in any of them; not a vestige of paint on the exterior." He wanted his white-collar listeners to understand that disease could travel swiftly from open sewage pits to the finest dining room.

Woodward's point got corroboration from the US government the next year. In 1917, Charlotte leaders invested thousands of dollars assembling land to host a military training facility for World War I soldiers. During its two-year existence, Camp Greene housed a total of more than 20,000 soldiers on-site. As the project got underway, health inspectors from Washington visited to see if sanitary conditions in a five-mile radius around the camp (encompassing most of Charlotte) were ready for the warm spring and summer ahead, when fly-born typhoid typically spread quickly. Instead, they found 2,600 "surface closets"—outhouses.

Local leaders, worried that their Camp Greene investment might be in jeopardy, quickly hired a public health officer, apparently the city's first. Dr. C. C. Hudson was a medical doctor with extensive training in public health who had previously headed the health department in Danville, Virginia.[7] Dr. Hudson and Camp Greene medical officer Maj. F. W. Brown convened a series of public meetings to explain why all Charlotte residents should hook up to water and sewer lines. Not only did flies carry disease from pit toilets, but as many as 15,000 Charlotteans got their water from open, shallow wells that were easily fouled by nearby outhouses.[8] Said Brown: "You can't have health on the boulevard and contamination in the slums."[9]

But nothing happened. "Installation of a new sewerage system that would connect all houses . . . would entail an expense of several thousand dollars," the *Observer* explained. Rather than spend substantial tax dollars, the city vaguely promised to institute inspections "whereby the closets will be kept in strictly sanitary conditions at all times."[10]

Dr. Hudson soon departed Charlotte, replaced by another health officer and then another. In 1930, Dr. W. A. McPhaul won what seemed to be a major advance. He convinced elected officials to pass an extensive health code. A lengthy section required that in every dwelling within 200 feet of a sewer line, the owner must "make sewer and water connections . . . installing one commode and one sink in each residence." The wording sounded strict. But the ordinance contained no punishments for those who violated it.[11]

Housing advocates mobilized again in the late 1930s, inspired by creation of the New Deal's Federal Housing Administration. The FHA's new mortgage underwriting and public housing programs stood ready to spark "construction of new housing facilities with funds to be borrowed from local banks," the *Charlotte News* reported excitedly.[12] First, however, the FHA wanted a survey of existing housing conditions. Charlotte's Business and Professional Women's Club, at the instigation of Cora Harris (as mentioned in chapter 2), brought the matter before City Council. Under leadership of Mayor J. H. Wearn, a building materials dealer who would likely benefit from a surge in construction, City Council jumped to make a $500 appropriation toward a survey of slum conditions.

In an era when no women served on any elected body, the women's club movement offered an important avenue for women to have some voice in civic advancement.[13] Modern urban government was coming into existence in US cities. Old traditions of limited government were inadequate to handle problems brought on by the fast-growing, densely settled concentrations of population. Could new rules help people live together more safely? Women often took the lead in issues of health and neighborhood planning, since those seemed to be natural extensions of the Victorian adage "a woman's place is in the home." Charlotte's clubwomen devoted great care and energy to their task of surveying the city's housing.

Both the *Charlotte Observer* and the *Charlotte News* gave the Business and Professional Women's anti-slum activism big coverage. Slums were not in any one part of town, the report documented, and occupants were both Black and white. Photographs, a new thing in the local media, showed alarmingly substandard dwellings "niched in . . . wabbly lanes on streets that begin respectably and end in rattleboard confusion."[14] Running water was the exception rather than the rule. "When water is piped to houses of this kind, it emerges from a spigot on the porch. . . . The kitchens do not have sinks. The housewife sets a tub under the back-porch spigot." Outhouse privies were "spaced one to every two or three houses." And the toilets froze solid whenever temperatures dropped.[15] "It is common knowledge that owners of slum properties enjoy large percentages of profit from them, as high sometimes as 20 percent. They should be forced," said a *News* interviewee, "to provide sanitation which would not only protect residents of these houses but other residents, as well."[16]

Charlotte's City Council, however, felt little of the Business and Professional Women's urgency. Not only were council members all male, but all were white, wealthy, and well insulated from poverty. They did use the 1938 study—supplemented by a 1939 follow-up prepared by the WPA—to apply for federal grants to build Fairview Homes and Piedmont Courts public housing.[17] But the council took no action on the much wider task of addressing slum conditions elsewhere throughout the city.

In 1940 the *Charlotte News* picked up the issue again. An exposé pointed out Charlotte's lack of code enforcement. Dr. G. L. Rae, the most recent city health officer, oversaw a staff of just two people. He focused on new construction, making no effort to police existing substandard dwellings. "Dr. Rae readily admits that the laws requiring sinks and toilets in [existing] houses are not being enforced, and he gave humanitarianism as the greatest reason for this," said the *News*. Quoth Rea: "We can't force people to get out ... they would have no other place to go."[18]

Was there any way to change real estate investors' minds about implementing a strong building code? Help came from an unexpected direction: Washington. In the mid-1940s, federal agencies began to increase aid to localities, hoping to bolster a smooth transition to peacetime. To qualify, a city needed to show smart planning. Mayor Herbert Baxter—another building materials dealer—energetically positioned Charlotte to drink deeply from the federal spigot. The 1944 Highway Act offered roadbuilding aid; Baxter got the city to draw up a Thoroughfare Plan, which won federal dollars to build the city's first crosstown expressway, Independence Boulevard. As the FHA began releasing construction materials from wartime rationing, it favored cities that embraced planning and zoning. Charlotte created its first Planning Commission in 1944 and would publish its first zoning map in 1947.[19] FHA administrators let it be known that they liked building codes, as well. With the carrot of FHA mortgages dangling, Charlotte's real estate leaders suddenly became advocates for a strong code.

In early 1945 they proposed a Realtors' Standard House Ordinance—an update to the building regulations that they had so long resisted.[20] Their proposal represented "private capital's solution to the problem of ever-worsening slums," said the real estate men, much preferable to the "threat of more 'socialized housing' [that] hangs over the city." Substandard dwellings were no fault of property owners, they blithely explained. "Slum conditions were caused by a lack of planning in the past. . . . Developers laid out . . . narrow streets because they were allowed to do so by the city at the time.... Houses were built that met the requirements of the code that was then in force."[21] Now, the Real Estate Board demanded, regulations must "force the installation of electric lights, bath or shower" and set other specifics such as "ample living space and ample clearance between houses."[22]

Thanks to the Realtors' turnabout, the Standard House Ordinance won swift adoption in late 1945. By unanimous vote, City Council mandated that "all houses in the city area be equipped with inside running water, kitchen sink, tub or shower, electric lights, enclosed water closet (toilet), adequate heating facilities and screens over doors and windows. It [the ordinance] includes certain other restrictions concerning structural safety and minimum floor space."[23]

That sounded so impressive, just what FHA officials recommended. But in actuality, the city held off on enforcement yet again, this time citing scarcity of building materials as wartime shortages slowly eased.[24]

In 1948, two things put the Standard House Ordinance back on the table. One was a nationwide polio epidemic, which hit severely in North Carolina. The United States saw a record 2,140 deaths from polio in 1948, with many more instances of paralysis and breathing issues that crippled victims for years or for life. North Carolina became the nation's hotspot, rivaled only by South Dakota.[25] Greensboro, North Carolina, to cite one example, reported 249 cases that year, most of them children.[26] Across the state, frightened local authorities shut down most public gatherings in the spring and summer, even curtailing church Sunday school. Scientists were eventually able to confirm that polio was a virus and that it often spread via water contaminated with human waste.[27] Suddenly, bathrooms for every household seemed imperative.

The other spur to code enforcement in 1948 came from Washington, indirectly. The US Housing Authority announced a second round of public housing aid. Charlotte real estate interests hated the idea of public housing. So, the local Real Estate Board dusted off its Standard House Ordinance and offered a bargain. Realtors would support active code enforcement, they proposed, if Charlotte would solve its slum problem via "private initiative and capital rather than government."[28]

The Realtors' Standard House Ordinance strategy represented a masterpiece of messaging. It gave real estate men something to wave around as an alternative to public housing—even as many owners of rental units continued to resist the actual implementation of a strict building code. At a 1948 hearing, one property owner called the proposed law "unnecessary and unreasonable," described it as "socialistic and un-American," and said, "If it is enforced it will provoke a real crisis in housing." Another claimed that poor people did not want such luxuries:

"You know how much it would cost to do what this law requires? And they don't want it; they don't want bathtubs and they couldn't pay for them."[29] Some landlords threatened to demolish unfit buildings and turn as many as 1,000 families out into the pre-Christmas cold. That rhetoric was a bargaining chip: "If the bath requirement is relaxed for a while, they expressed their belief that no more than 100 to 200 houses will be destroyed."[30]

Ultimately, however, the polio scare plus the Real Estate Board's official endorsement of code enforcement plus the lure of US Housing Authority construction dollars did finally convince City Council to take meaningful action in 1948. Charlotte hired additional building inspectors, who began a crackdown on substandard apartments. And it also accepted federal public housing aid to build Southside Homes and Belvedere Homes (see chapter 2).[31] "There may be a few houses demolished by owners, rather than have the necessary improvements made," said CHA board chair Edwin Jones, calling the landlords' bluff. Generally, though, "property owners will readily comply with the housing code and begin soon to install toilets, wiring, running water, and other improvements needed. And the costs won't be so great that the owners will be unable to amortize them."[32]

In other words, these long-sought basics would be folded into developers' normal cost of doing business—as they should have been, all along. The Real Estate Board did briefly float the possibility that government might set up some kind of grant program, particularly for small-time landlords, but no funds existed for anything like that in city budgets of the 1940s.[33] And City Council was well aware of the substantial profit margins on investor-owned housing.

Council did still meekly defer to the real estate men, however, when it came to instituting the full Standard House Ordinance. Elected officials in late 1948 "struck out requirements for non-freezing plumbing," made existing dwellings exempt from the minimum room size provision, and put off the mandate for bathtubs for three years.[34]

A sink and a commode, however, had finally become an accepted part of every rental dwelling.

■ ■ ■ ■ ■

We could keep going, but I think you get the picture by this point. Skirmish by skirmish, progress was made until we did come to expect that indoor plumbing should be required in all living units. The struggle for decent low-income housing would never completely end. In 1962, Washington would require that Charlotte pass a housing code to supplement the building code; it attempted to spur the city to continue enforcement after a new structure initially met the building code.[35] In the 1970s, housing activist Ted Fillette would still be fighting for a state law to mandate that landlords provide "habitable accommodations" (see the sidebar "'So Much Dilapidated, Terrible Housing'" in chapter 6).[36] And the issue has recently come up again in the 2020s. At Lake Arbor Apartments, tenants struggled with nonworking plumbing, mold, and leaky roofs, sparking community outcry—while local government responded that it lacked legal tools to remedy the issues.[37]

Analysis: Code Enforcement as a Strategy for Affordable Housing

Before we explore how building code–based "slum clearance" transitioned into demolition-based "urban renewal," let's pause to point out some valuable aspects of Charlotte's 1948 code enforcement strategy.

Today, scholars and advocates for the poor have a much more sophisticated understanding of what constitutes a good living situation than they did in the 1940s and 1950s. Dwelling units should be weathertight and sanitary, for sure. But we now also recognize that low-income tenants are part of communities, both with their immediate neighbors and with the city as whole.

With that in mind, we can now see that energetic code enforcement was a smart strategy in at least three ways: it allowed low-income workers to continue to reside throughout the city, within walking distance of jobs; it did not disrupt "helping networks" that already existed between neighbors; and it uplifted many thousands of dwelling units, exponentially more than could be produced by direct investment in public housing. Let's consider each of those three aspects in turn.

Affordable Housing Dispersed

As we saw in chapter 1, and as the newspaper exposés of slum conditions always pointed out, affordable housing existed in many parts of the city. In chapter 1 we saw the pattern around the Treloar House, where well-to-do whites (including the Treloar family) shared the block with both blue-collar whites and African Americans. A few areas, such as the Brooklyn neighborhood, held concentrations of low-income rental housing, but those were exceptions to the general scattered pattern. Today we recognize that geographical dispersal can be a very good thing. It gives opportunities for working-class people to live close to jobs and allows youngsters to see a range of role models as they grow up.

Intermingling persisted well into the mid-twentieth century. To use today's language of market-driven capitalism, we might say that the market "wanted" affordable housing to be dispersed. Only with government intervention, zoning, would that natural pattern be disrupted. Fixing up existing houses respected, rather than disrupted, the naturally occurring market-driven geography.

The code enforcement approach also held sociological benefits for low-income residents. Scholars in recent years have documented the "helping networks" that low-income people forge with neighbors, aiding each other with childcare, checking in with seniors, sharing food when a job falls through, and so on.[38] Code enforcement, which made houses better without wholesale displacement of tenants, kept those networks intact.

10,000 Dwellings Improved

When Edwin Jones of the Charlotte Housing Authority talked with the *Charlotte Observer* in 1948 about his hopes for the new code enforcement initiative, he envisioned a two-tier approach:

1. His Charlotte Housing Authority would provide 2,000 or so units of government-funded public housing for Charlotteans at the very bottom of the economic ladder.
2. Private enterprise would provide the rest. The bulk of the city's needs for affordable housing would be met as the existing substandard dwellings came up to code. Jones expected a couple hundred houses to be demolished, but the net number of decent and affordable dwellings might total as high as 10,000 units.

The approach took advantage of the fact that affordable housing was being created all the time. The prospect of a 20 percent return on investment attracted investors who put in capital up front, buying and converting big old houses into apartments or purpose-building new small houses and duplexes for rent. Likewise, landlords were always doing maintenance on existing rental housing. If the city enacted strict building codes, and if it actually made landlords obey the law, the costs of meeting the code would become part of those normal ongoing expenditures—tiny when spread out over the life of the building. Because the standards applied to all, no investor needed to worry about being at a competitive disadvantage.

Indeed, during the five years after the city finally got serious about code enforcement in 1948, landlords brought 9,625 dwellings up to standard.[39] Only about a thousand were demolished. The city's Standard House Ordinance and the progress it brought during the late 1940s and early 1950s won national attention, including mentions in *Architectural Forum* and the *Saturday Evening Post*.[40] The *Post* waxed rhapsodic, pointing to Charlotte and Baltimore as cities at the forefront of a Realtor-led "national slum-rehabilitation movement that doesn't cost taxpayers a cent."

For all that success, Charlotte's commitment to code enforcement had a lot of holes. The *Saturday Evening Post* reporter documented a decidedly chummy relationship between code enforcement staff—once again, only two people—and landlords. Charlotte's chief inspector, wrote the *Post*, was an individual of "easy-going and even temperament ... who pushed nobody around" and "cheerfully granted time extensions and other concessions, so long as the property owner, in the end, got the job done." By 1952, nearly every rental unit in the city at last possessed indoor plumbing, but under "Charlotte's easygoing enforcement method" the installation of tubs and showers was still only half complete.[41] And in some parts of Charlotte, notably the blocks of ramshackle "Negro housing" in Brooklyn, conditions remained terrible.

"Slum Clearance" Comes to Mean Demolition

It is possible to pinpoint the exact moment in 1950 at which "slum clearance" ceased to be about helping the poor.

In late 1949, the *Charlotte Observer*'s Washington correspondent had reported on the new federal Housing Act: "Charlotte and other communities throughout the country are being informed that the Federal government is ready for the first steps in a program of slum clearance and urban redevelopment." Under the act, "Congress has authorized $500 million in capital grants and $1 billion in loans."[42] Details became clearer the following spring: "The program permits the Federal government to grant funds to local redevelopment commissions.... After the 'master plan' is adopted, the local group may borrow Federal money to acquire the blighted land, clear it, and offer it to sale to private investors who will agree to develop the area according to the plan. Any loss in the overall transaction is borne by the Federal and local governments on a two-thirds and one-third share arrangement."[43]

Significantly, the aid did not have to be used to construct new dwellings. Wrote the American Institute of Planners in a report to its members: "A residential slum can be acquired for housing OR for business or industrial use."[44]

On March 22, 1950, City Council voted 6–1 to apply for funds "to wipe out slum dwellings and make the 'blighted' areas available for other uses."[45] Better low-income housing was no longer a goal.

Officials knew exactly which "blighted" land they wanted to turn to "other uses." Brooklyn, the Black city-within-the-city in Charlotte's Second Ward, had long inspired white envy. "The Second Ward is already populated by [Black people], many owning comfortable homes," noted the *Charlotte Observer* way back in 1912, but "farsighted men believe that eventually this section, because of its proximity to the center of the city, must sooner or later be utilized by the white population."[46]

As part of its 1950 application to Washington, Charlotte set up a Redevelopment Commission—which made no pretense of improving housing. "'The public mind has been more or less confused' about urban redevelopment," city manager Henry Yancey told the *Charlotte Observer*. "[It] is not, he declared, aimed primarily at building of more low-rental public housing. Additional housing of any kind may not enter the picture, he explained. The program is one offered by the Federal government to assist cities in the clearance and the redevelopment of undesirable slum areas in reclaiming the land for more beneficial use."[47]

But Brooklyn wasn't a slum, City Council was aggravated to discover. North Carolina law prohibited governments from demolishing buildings that were in good shape. Condemnation could not take place unless 100 percent of properties in an area were substandard.[48] Brooklyn had too many homeowners and successful businesses to qualify.

By one estimate, 7 percent of Brooklyn residents owned their own property, a much lower percentage than in the city as a whole, but still significant.[49] Surviving photographs show the Black business district along Second Street and Brevard Street, home to the Lincoln movie theater and the three-story Afro-American Mutual Insurance building, where doctors and other Black professionals had offices (see fig. 4.1a–b). Around the corner on Brevard Street stood other multistory commercial buildings, including the offices of the printing house for the nationwide AME Zion religious denomination. There were a dozen large brick churches, intermingled among well-kept owner-occupied one-story and two-story houses. Rental houses for working-class families filled out the district, most owned by absentee investors and seldom well maintained.

Many of the rental rows looked pretty bad by the 1950s. That was due not only to their genesis as absentee-owned "Negro housing" but also to three government actions that actively promoted disinvestment: redlining, zoning, and highway construction.

- In 1937, to encourage banks to make home loans in the midst of the Great Depression, the federal Home Owners' Loan Corporation created maps of every American city to show lenders the "good credit risk" neighborhoods (see the sidebar "Redlining" in chapter 2).[50] The maps marked undesirable areas in red (hence the nickname "redlining"). The presence of African Americans automatically meant an area was colored red—making it nearly

Figure 4.1. A: Brooklyn's South Brevard Street. The home of physician and US diplomat J. T. Williams is on the left, with Grace AME Zion Church and the Mecklenburg Investment Company in the distance. B: East Second Street business district. Black architect W. W. Smith designed the tall Afro-American Mutual Insurance building (*left center*), which held offices of doctors and attorneys. Under the tree in the distance, facing Brevard Street, stood the first Black public library in North Carolina. Photos circa 1960, courtesy of the Robinson-Spangler Carolina Room, Charlotte Mecklenburg Library.

impossible for even the most qualified buyer to get a home loan. Not surprisingly, all of Brooklyn was red.
- In 1947, Charlotte adopted zoning.[51] The new law promised to "protect" single-family neighborhoods, which in practice meant white suburban areas at the city's south and east. Conversely, "industrial" zoning allowed any type of land use. Brooklyn, despite its businesses and homeowners, was zoned entirely industrial. Investors who looked at the zoning map could see little reason to do much maintenance of their rental dwellings; the map predicted that higher and better uses were coming soon.
- Starting in the late 1940s, the city took new federal dollars available via the Highway Act of 1944 and built Independence Boulevard. The four-lane highway plowed across the city. Its first segment in 1949 sliced through the heart of Brooklyn along Stonewall Street.[52]

After much lobbying—including a newspaper campaign that played upon fears of crime, showing photos of "switch-blade territory" at the city's "business doorway"—local leaders convinced Raleigh to rewrite the urban renewal–enabling legislation in 1958.[53] The revised law allowed demolition of good structures along with the bad if an *area* was deemed blighted. City officials quickly drew up an *area* map, as required. No surprise: "The Brooklyn slum area behind City Hall has been repeatedly mentioned, almost to the exclusion of any other locale, as having priority in any redevelopment plans."[54]

Bulldozers would begin to roll in 1962, the start of a demolition process that would take six years and in which 1,004 families were displaced and 200 businesses closed, most never to reopen. A dozen churches were kicked out. Not one new housing unit went up on the cleared land.

NAACP: An Alternative Vision

Actually, a vision did exist for housing in Brooklyn. Beginning in 1950 and continuing for fully twenty years, Black leaders in Charlotte put forward proposals that would have built upon the district's strengths, keeping the businesses and homes that were in good shape and adding public housing to replace the worst of the absentee-owned shacks. Kelly Alexander led the early efforts. A Brooklyn businessman whose family ran Alexander Funeral Home (see chapter 3), he reactivated Charlotte's NAACP chapter in the 1940s and rose to lead the NAACP statewide. His brother Fred Alexander would take over the fight for Brooklyn housing in 1965 when he won election as Charlotte's first African American on City Council in the twentieth century.

Charlotte's Brooklyn Doomed By Progress?

Jonas Says He'll Accept Renomination

Mrs. Evans' Name Enters Speculation Among Democrats

By KAYS GARY
Observer Staff Writer

Rep. Charles R. Jonas said Wednesday he will accept renomination by 10th District Republicans if it is offered to him.

Neither issue has been in doubt. Jonas had told intimates he wanted "at least another term" and party leaders wouldn't turn a winner loose, anyway.

He'll get the nomination at the party's district convention in Lincolnton March 9.

Meanwhile, Democrats of the district stirred themselves on the heels of The Observer's Wednesday story that either Attorney Paul Ervin or Ben E. Douglas, recent state director of Conservation and Development, would file Saturday afternoon.

MADE STATEMENT

It was Ervin who made the statement following a Tuesday afternoon conference with Gov. Hodges.

It was indicated that only one would announce as a candidate.

Political ringmasters believe it will be Douglas, although he had pledged to support Ervin if the attorney should choose to run. This is the prediction despite the feeling that Ervin, long undecided, seemed to become suddenly eager this week.

The situation brought a third name into the speculation, that of City Councilwoman Martha Evans.

"At the moment," she said Wednesday evening, "I have one positive thought about the congressional race — I think there should be more than one candidate in the Democratic primary so the people may choose their strongest candidate."

It was true, she said, that she had received telephone calls, mostly from women's organizations, all day Wednesday urging her to consider making the race if only one Democratic candidate appeared.

Third Street May Be Key To Commerce

End Predicted To Crime-Ridden, Crowded Section

By HOKE MAY
Observer Staff Writer

The bell is tolling for Charlotte's Brooklyn.

Its death knell may yet ring weakly.

But men who peer into the city's future say it chimed boldly this week.

One day—perhaps sooner than many believe — it will sound an end to the crowded, crime-ridden 24 square blocks which have squatted a lifetime at Charlotte's eastern business doorway.

The bell is progress and Southern Railway struck it a mighty blow Monday.

By clearing a path for opening Third Street to Brevard, planners believe, the railroad may have unlocked the commercial gateway into Brooklyn.

PARKING LOT

Southern enhanced the step by deciding to establish and operate a huge parking lot at the site of its fire-gutted freight terminal.

These two moves, planners predict, may change the whole complexion of uptown Charlotte — from Brevard to McDowell Street and from Fourth to Independence.

Beginning at College, a drab companion to bustling Tryon Street, a sweeping surge of commercial development may lie ahead.

Not overnight. Not next week nor a year from now. But in the foreseeable future.

Gradually, the narrow, alleylike streets and dingy houses may give way to stores, shops and offices until the city's business district marches in a solid line between Fourth and Independence.

FIRST INROADS

Progress has made its first probing inroads.

Independence Boulevard sliced Brooklyn in half and new enterprise sprang up along the broadened thoroughfare.

A widened McDowell severed the section from north to south and business has infiltered there.

Largely, Brooklyn is what it has been as long as Charlotte's oldest

Ax May Hit This Switch-blade Territory (Observer Photo—Kelly)

Figure 4.2. Local media hammered away at Brooklyn as a place of depravity: "switch-blade territory." Contrast this front-page article with the figure 4.1 photos. *Charlotte Observer*, February 23, 1956.

A 'New Brooklyn'—It'll Pay Dividends

Figure 4.3. A: Brooklyn, looking north across Morehead Street. *Charlotte Observer*, January 10, 1960. B: Postcard showing emptiness after urban renewal, mid-1970s. The view looks west, at ninety degrees from the 1960 view, but covers almost exactly the same land. Courtesy of Joe W. Joseph.

The Alexanders' first salvo came in 1950. Kelly Alexander and the NAACP put forth a ten-point program for African American advancement in the post–World War II era. It called for educational opportunity: a Black representative on the school board and construction of a vocational high school for Black students. It urged a loosening of segregation: "gradual elimination" of "white" and "colored" signs on buses and at water fountains and also a request that Black businesses be allowed to operate in every part of the city, not just in Black neighborhoods. And it addressed municipal disinvestment, asking for "street improvements in Negro areas, where, said Alexander, 'in many places there are no sidewalks.'"[55]

At the top of Kelly Alexander's list: demolish the worst housing in Brooklyn and replace it with "a low-cost housing project for low-income Negroes." He commended C. D. Spangler's Double Oaks apartment complex newly constructed at the city's northwest edge under the FHA 608 program (see chapter 3). But, said Alexander, "the number of [low-rent] units recently approved is not enough to meet the needs of the low-income people—white or black." Implicit in the NAACP report was a vision of a healthier Brooklyn, building on its existing strengths. Government investment could surgically remove the worst of the absentee-owned slum housing, thus helping the current homeowners and businesses to flourish in the heart of the city.

Such carefully focused renewal, however, held no appeal for Charlotte leaders, excited by the dream of big federal dollars. Again and again, African Americans called for new public housing in Brooklyn as Charlotte officials moved ahead with "urban renewal." Again and again, the requests were denied.

In 1960, when the Redevelopment Commission held a federally required public hearing before beginning land acquisition, Kelly Alexander and the NAACP gave written testimony. The city should safeguard Brooklyn businesses, churches, and other institutional buildings, Alexander advised, and also keep the decent existing housing. Brooklyn's problems were not of its own making, the letter stressed: "The advancing age of the structures coupled with the lack of maintenance by indifferent and greedy absentee owners, who knew it was not necessary to maintain the properties to hold tenants when the shortage was so acute, was the primary cause of the slum conditions—the dwellers were not."[56]

Alexander warned that unless the plan retained Brooklyn's good dwellings and added more, Charlotte would face housing shortages: "Average monthly income of 1,923 Brooklyn families is only $161.48 and the private housing market can't provide them with adequate dwellings."[57]

Redevelopment officials countered that they "respectfully disagreed" but offered no supporting data. City staff had made no survey of Charlotte's low-income housing stock, Redevelopment Commission chief Vernon Sawyer blithely admitted.⁵⁸ Paul Guthrey, representing the Board of Realtors, "stated they were unalterably opposed to additional public housing."⁵⁹ He pointed to the 1948 code enforcement program ("the second one in the nation and . . . used as a model throughout the country") as a reason why public housing was not needed.

The NAACP asserted its points again at public hearings in 1961 and again faced a wall of white indifference.⁶⁰ "Plea Made to Council: Public Housing Sought for Negroes," headlined the *Observer*.⁶¹ In response, officials blandly insisted that the private real estate market would have no trouble supplying good homes to displaced Brooklynites. "This is a dream. This is a farce. It can't be done," exclaimed the normally staid Kelly Alexander. "Decent housing for low-income families at moderate prices is more scarce than deer in Freedom Park."⁶²

Indeed, the short-term effect of "urban renewal" was to worsen the housing situation—even before demolition actually began. Following on the heels of redlining in 1937 and zoning in 1947, the years of urban renewal planning during the 1950s and early 1960s convinced absentee investors that there was no point in doing any maintenance. Houses and business buildings deteriorated, becoming uninhabitable. A fire swept through the empty Black business district in the summer of 1963, destroying the once-proud Lincoln Theater and the Afro-American Mutual Insurance building, among others.⁶³ When the bulldozers finally began to roll, the newspapers belatedly took notice of a citywide housing shortage. "Slum Clearance, Expressway Plans Create Hazardous, Empty Homes," reported the *Observer* in 1963.⁶⁴

Federal officials at last started to pay attention. During 1962 and 1963—with bulldozers already grinding through Brooklyn—Washington put pressure on the Redevelopment Commission to build at least some public housing somewhere. "Federal urban renewal officials have all but told Charlotte that new low-rent public housing must be built before any more money for Brooklyn slum clearance is approved," reported the *Observer*.⁶⁵

Grudgingly the commission condemned several blocks of First Ward not far from Brooklyn and hurriedly constructed a public housing complex called Earle Village, opened in 1967.⁶⁶ Black minister Coleman Kerry derided its rows of boxy brick low-rises as "just one big blob."⁶⁷ "A pre-fabricated slum . . . an ugly thing to do to people," said white civic leader Jack Pentes.⁶⁸ The *Charlotte Observer* declared the project "20 years behind the times" and said it was "appalled by the lack of imagination in the layout and design."⁶⁹

Most damning, Earle Village's 409 apartments were actually fewer than the 514 units that were torn down to create it.⁷⁰ It did nothing to ease the housing shortage.

Also in 1967 and 1968, the Charlotte Housing Authority began construction of two public housing high-rises for senior citizens, Edwin Towers in Fourth

Ward and Strawn Apartments in the Dilworth neighborhood. Both involved the demolition of existing housing. They did provide better conditions for their elderly residents—but again did little to meet the needs of the hundreds of families pushed out of Brooklyn.

The commission never relented on its prohibition of housing in Brooklyn—even when few buyers materialized for the cleared land. It turned out, ironically, that no one particularly wanted the acres emptied by urban renewal, not in Charlotte nor in most cities nationwide. On one hand, federal aid to suburbia had helped spur a rush outward. New malls and office parks set amid miles of fresh-built "ranch houses" pulled commerce away from America's downtowns. And on the other hand, planners were surprised to discover, the value of land near the center city depended on the fact that multiple uses were crowded together there. If you cleaned away that mixture, urban activity ceased—and value evaporated along with it. In Charlotte, few bidders showed interest in the Brooklyn parcels. In a 1971 auction, only one plot on McDowell Street attracted competitive bids. "There was no competition for the five other tracts in the same area, with one bid received for each," the *Observer* reported. "It is no secret that many city leaders had been disappointed with the previous failure of the Brooklyn project to attract private development."[71]

As the city struggled to sell Brooklyn parcels, Fred Alexander—Kelly Alexander's brother, now the sole Black member of City Council—made a motion that housing be added to the list of approved uses. This would be market-rate housing, created by developers, rather than public housing. Nonetheless, City Council treated the idea with derision, as it had since 1950. No other council member even condescended to second Alexander's motion.[72]

Chapter Conclusion

To understand Charlotte leaders' true priorities, it is instructive to contrast how they moved on four strategies for improving low-income housing: building codes, urban renewal, public housing, and FHA 608.

In each, government took action, involving itself in modifying the "forces of the market." Looking back from today's perspective, you might expect that the fewer the tax dollars involved and the less that Washington played a role, the faster that Charlotte would embrace the program. You would be wrong.

- The building code required the least government expenditure, relying mostly on the private market to build and operate affordable housing. Only local tax dollars were used, nothing from Washington. Once local government implemented and enforced the building code, landowners came to regard

- toilets and running water as a basic cost of doing business. So, the approach resulted in many thousands of affordable housing units. But it came only after decades of resistance.
- Federally funded public housing, in contrast, won rapid—though small-scale—adoption. As described in chapter 2, Charlotte officials accepted federal grants within months after Washington announced availability. Real estate interests whined and objected, but the lure of cash from Washington spoke louder.
- While local business leaders had mixed feelings about public housing, they positively loved FHA 608 housing (see chapter 3). Washington's aid to developers sparked construction of fifteen apartment complexes, seven of them low-income. All went up almost instantly and resulted in no objections. Businessmen made big profits. Low-rental housing got built.
- Compare the federal dollars spent on public housing and FHA 608 with the much more massive outlay for urban renewal. Demolition of Brooklyn required condemning hundreds of acres of private land, a huge government intrusion in the real estate market. But business and political leaders rallied around the program. It was "free" cash from Washington. As quick as they could, Charlotte officials set the bulldozers rolling.

All four approaches promised to wipe away the scourge of bad housing. The test of a program, however, was not how much it helped poor Charlotteans. If an approach put government dollars into the pockets of the business community, it won much quicker implementation than an approach (such as building codes) that did not.

CHAPTER 5

Tax Shelters and Investor-Built Low-Rent Housing

- Accelerated Depreciation
- FHA 221(d)(3), FHA 236, and the Turnkey Programs

One of the biggest ongoing government subsidies ever created for real estate development came about with a little-noticed tweak to the US tax code written in 1954 and still in effect today. Called "accelerated depreciation," it made construction of every new apartment complex, shopping center, and office park into a "tax shelter" for private investors. As developers discovered the provision and learned to manipulate it during the 1950s and 1960s, waves of apartment construction remade the American landscape.

Once again, like we've seen with the initial FHA assistance to apartment developers in the 1930s and with much of the FHA 608 program after World War II, these federal benefits went to for-profit developments with market-rate rents. Most renters were middle- and upper-income.

As accelerated depreciation took hold, affordable housing activists wondered if it could be harnessed to produce lower-income apartments. What if government crafted some extra incentives to lure for-profit developers? Programs with hard-to-remember names—FHA Section 221(d)(3), FHA Section 236, HUD Turnkey I, Turnkey Leased Housing—spilled out of Washington during the 1960s. Each used different mechanisms to sweeten deals, but all rested on the ability of private developers to profit from depreciation tax breaks.[1]

Such projects *had* to be privately built. Why? Local governments (and their public housing authorities) don't pay federal income tax. So, in order to get the lucrative tax shelter, a low-income apartment complex had to be in nongovernmental hands, at least initially. A project could become publicly owned after it opened, but a private entity had to own it up front.

These public-private initiatives proved effective in spurring construction—but turned out to be deeply flawed in what they produced. In Charlotte, some thirteen affordable housing complexes sprang up under the programs between 1968 and 1977 (far more than under conventional public housing). They included several of Charlotte's least loved projects, notably Boulevard Homes and Dalton Village on West Boulevard. In more than one instance, promoters delivered apartments that were literally uninhabitable. Business-minded developers, it turned out, held no magic key to creating good housing.

We'll see in subsequent chapters how the ideas that emerged during the 1950s through the 1970s—tax shelters, public-private partnerships—eventually came of age in the 1980s. A tax shelter called the Low-Income Housing Tax Credit would become the backbone of nearly all affordable apartment development in the United States from 1986 to the present. But before we explore that in chapter 7, it's valuable to trace the journey that got us there.

Accelerated Depreciation—Sounds Dull, but What an Impact!

A tax break for "depreciation" of big investments, especially factories and heavy machinery, had existed ever since federal income tax began in 1913. The idea was that such items wear out over time and need to be replaced. As they depreciate (lose value), the owner might want to set aside a bit of cash each year to cover the eventual replacement. The tax code allowed that amount to be subtracted from the business's taxable income over a period of years, roughly the useful life of the item. Sounds reasonable, right?

In 1954, as the United States struggled with a momentary economic recession that has long since been forgotten, Congress put in place an accelerated timetable for depreciation.[2] It permitted much of the deduction to be taken in the first years. That by itself reduced taxes in those years. But the deal got sweeter. First, the break could be taken on any "new income-producing property"—which meant not just factories and machinery but a large array of real estate ventures, including apartment complexes. Second, there was no requirement that cash actually be set aside for replacement. Third, in the real world, the value of buildings often went up over time, not down. And fourth, if the paper losses were greater than the income from the property itself, they could be applied against the owner's other unrelated taxable income. That made commercial real estate into a "tax shelter."[3]

If you are still with me at this point, you are to be applauded. Hang in there; we've got another page of it. When most folks hear this stuff—unless they themselves have business income to shelter from the IRS—they lose interest. That makes tax shelter laws an ideal thing for politicians to tinker with. Since 1954, Congress has tightened and loosened depreciation laws numerous times, sometimes striving to increase tax yield to the US Treasury, sometimes seeking to aid a particular business constituency, sometimes intending to produce some greater social good.

- A 1960 IRS regulation, for instance, made the depreciation tax shelter especially lucrative for doctors, lawyers, and other professionals, encouraging them to set up limited partnerships and build new offices for themselves.[4]

    Initially, that may have been intended to stimulate modernization of America's medical infrastructure, but it also stimulated hundreds of thousands of accountants to look for other tax shelter partnerships for their clients. Not just doctors and lawyers but all types of investors now began to sniff the air for tax-favored real estate projects.

- America's housing sector recognized an opportunity. Into the Housing Acts of 1961 and 1964, legislators inserted language that allowed partnerships (any partnerships, not just doctors and lawyers) to own and operate FHA-sponsored rental housing—"opening the way for limited-partnership tax shelters," in the words of a federal report.[5]

    A limited partnership, set up specifically to construct one project, became a hugely attractive investment tool. A wealthy person could buy into a limited partnership and get depreciation benefits without any responsibilities or entanglements that might be involved in being part of a wider real estate company. Most multifamily housing in America was FHA-sponsored, as we have seen in chapter 3. Investors' dollars now began to flow into FHA-assisted limited partnerships to construct apartments.

- Some zealous journalists in the mid-1960s wrote exposés of the tax shelter racket, as they called it, which led to calls to limit the break.

    That prompted Democratic president Lyndon Johnson to experiment briefly in 1967 with curtailing accelerated depreciation for nearly everything—except multifamily housing, which he deemed a social good that should be promoted as part of his Great Society. The sixteen-month suspension of the tax breaks on industrial and commercial buildings would have the effect of "releasing more money for needed housing," LBJ told Congress.[6]

- Republican Richard Nixon won the 1968 election, but he initially chose to continue on the same path when it came to housing and tax shelters. In 1969, Nixon OK'd legislation that boosted depreciation write-offs during a building's first months. Rather that deducting equal amounts each year, called a "straight line" rate, the revised rules doubled the initial shelter—specifically for apartment projects.[7]

Criticizing Accelerated Depreciation

Real estate investors loved depreciation tax shelters, but government officials who administered them sometimes had a different perspective.

Assistant Treasury Secretary Stanley S. Surrey, 1968

"It is familiar fact that income tax laws now provide preferential treatment in the housing field which subsidizes rental real estate operators," said Treasury official Stanley S. Surrey in 1968.* "Acceleration of depreciation for buildings in 1954 appears to have been a happenstance, coming along as an inadvertent appendage to the liberalization directed at machinery and equipment. No conscious decision was made to adopt the present system as a useful device to stimulate building or to provide us with more or better housing, let alone lower-income housing. The present tax system for buildings just happened."

Surrey suggested that depreciation policies actually decreased the amount of well-maintained "used" housing (today called NOAH: naturally occurring affordable housing). Because accelerated depreciation put the biggest tax shelter benefit in the first years of ownership, owners often quickly sold out to other buyers, who could start the depreciation cycle anew. Thus, there was little reason for an owner to build (or maintain) for the ages. US tax policy "aids new construction more than improvement or remodeling," Surrey asserted. "The present treatment seems to create a tax environment favorable to frequent turn-over which discourages long-range stewardship."

For certain, the tax laws enriched the already wealthy. "Sample tax returns," he noted, "showed some tax-payers should more aptly be termed 'non-taxpayers.' One group of 13 individual returns . . . all of whom had very substantial gross incomes . . . showed depreciation 'losses' [that] reduced the federal tax liability of nine of them to zero and of two others to less than $25." Emphasized Surrey, "Tax incentives have the potential for making tax-free millionaires."

(continued)

---

* All quotes by Surrey in this sidebar are from Surrey, "Tax Assistance for Housing." See also Surrey, *Pathways to Tax Reform*.

Congressional Budget Office, 1977

"Tax shelters provide a 10- to 20-year stream of tax savings which the builder/developer can sell to wealthy outside investors.... Only about half of what the tax shelter costs the government in lost revenue ... ever reaches builders and developers. The remainder goes ... to the outside investors ... [and] to the syndicators, lawyers and accountants who are needed to put together and sell the tax shelter package....

"Real estate tax shelters will provide an estimated $1.3 billion in subsidies for past and current real estate construction in fiscal year 1978.... 35 percent of this subsidy goes to assist the construction of commercial buildings—office buildings, shopping centers, and the like. Another 54 percent goes to assist the construction of middle- and upper-income rental housing, mostly apartment buildings. Only about 11 percent of the total goes to assist low-income rental housing."[†]

[†] Congressional Budget Office, "Real Estate Tax Shelter Subsidies and Direct Subsidy Alternatives," May 1977, pp. xiv, 37, www.cbo.gov/sites/default/files/95th-congress-1977-1978/reports/1977_05_shelter.pdf. The Tax Reform Act of 1976 trimmed tax shelters for everything except low- and moderate-income housing, which were exempted from changes until 1982. Verdier, *Real Estate Tax Shelter Subsidies*, xiv, 37.

During the late 1960s and early 1970s, in short, apartment construction became the nation's top real estate tax shelter. The flow of investment dollars became a gushing flood.

To see the impact of Johnson's and Nixon's depreciation tax laws in Charlotte, compare permits issued each year for single-family versus multifamily construction. During the early 1960s, about 2,000 houses went up each year but only 1,000 apartments. Numbers started to shift in 1965, running neck and neck. Then in 1969–70, multifamily construction exploded. "Apartment Permits Zip Ahead of Houses at Two-to-One Rate," marveled the *Charlotte Observer*. "The apartment phenomenon is something new to Charlotte," the newspaper explained. "When the Tax Reform Act of 1969 closed many tax loopholes, one that was intentionally left open was ownership of apartment complexes.... The tax

Graph 5.1 (*top*). Changes in depreciation laws sparked an apartment boom, late 1960s–early 1970s. Adapted from *Charlotte Observer*, 1972. Figure 5.1 (*bottom*). Crosland's Vista Villa was typical of Charlotte's circa-1970 apartment construction. Albert Dulin photo, 2020.

laws allow a limited partnership to benefit from depreciation, which is a paper expense . . . used to shelter other income."[8]

For wealthy investors in the topmost "50 percent tax bracket, the yield in cash and tax avoidance is more than 25 percent . . . for the first year," noted the *Observer* in 1972.[9] Suddenly, every developer wanted to build multifamily. "Making Jump into Apartment Field," read a headline about Charlotte's leading suburban builder John Crosland, whose company "for almost 30 years has confined itself almost exclusively to the single-family home business."[10]

Vista Villa by Crosland, Part of Charlotte's East Side Apartment Boom

John Crosland Jr., previously purely a single-family homebuilder, entered apartment construction in 1970. His initial project, Vista Villa, stood just off Plaza Road Extension at Charlotte's fast-growing eastern edge. The 132-unit garden-style complex of two-story buildings featured architectural trim recalling "the beauty of old Spain," advertising proclaimed.*

What made the project possible was much less visible: tax shelter syndication. The *Charlotte Observer*'s business columnist explained the new technique: "The syndicate, which calls itself Vista Villa Associates, has John Crosland Jr. (developer of Vista Villa) as the general partner, and the other 13 partners seem to have bought 22 shares at $10,000 a share. The biggest single purchaser is James Cannon [whose family owned the massive Cannon Mills textile empire], with four shares."† Three weeks later, the newspaper reported, "The heart of the syndicate's appeal is tax loss, caused by depreciation. An apartment complex, say, can show a tremendous paper loss (because of the depreciation) while producing a sizable cash flow. ... If you're in a high enough income bracket, the tax loss is equivalent to income. ... If the deal is structured well and the partners' tax bracket is high enough, the return from the actual cash inflow and the property's paper deficit can produce a yield on investment well over 20 percent."‡

Driven by racial and economic factors, Charlotte's east side felt the greatest impact of the circa 1970 apartment boom. South Charlotte, well-to-do and white, had higher land costs. The west and north sides included both white and African American areas—regarded as risky by real estate developers who were almost entirely white and had come of age in the era of federal redlining. That left the east: white and middle-class. Former farm lanes—Sharon Amity Road, Albemarle Road, Central Avenue, Idlewild Road—now blossomed with apartments.**

---

*"Have a Fling at Life, Spanish Style," *Charlotte Observer*, May 9, 1971.
† "Syndicate Buys Vista Villa," *Charlotte Observer*, May 1, 1971. Newspaper stories often did not differentiate between John Crosland the company and John Crosland the man. I will refer to them interchangeably in this book.
‡ "Real Estate Syndicates Growing in Popularity," *Charlotte Observer*, May 22, 1971.
** "Apartments" map, *Charlotte Observer*, March 11, 1973.

It wasn't just Charlotte. Halfway across the United States in Minneapolis–St. Paul, economic geographer William Sperbeck documented a multifamily boom just like Charlotte's. A rapidly expanding "suburban ring of apartments constructed in the 1968–1973 period" was leading to abnormally high vacancy rates. The cause? "Federal tax policies on income derived from multifamily real estate appear to have generated excessive apartment construction."[11]

By 1973, analysts were raising alarms about overbuilding. But construction did not slow. "Builders Fight for Renters," cautioned the *Observer*. As developers competed to attract tenants, they added amenities. "Pretty soon, apartment dwellers were boasting about the central heating, the air conditioning, the swimming pools, the tennis courts."[12] All those innovations—today regarded as standard in US apartments—qualified for depreciation tax write-offs.

The side effects of the depreciation laws extended beyond the new amenity packages. Tax considerations helped determine where apartments got built. Accelerated depreciation applied only to what was erected on a parcel of land, not to the cost of the land itself (since land does not wear out). So, developers discovered that they got the best deductions for projects where land cost was minimized. That usually meant the very edge of town, where former farmland was available cheaply. In an earlier era, apartment complexes sometimes had been built as part of neighborhoods—the Myrtle in Dilworth, for instance (see chapter 2). New projects from the 1960s onward, in contrast, nearly always sprang up as self-contained pods at the suburban periphery.

How much difference did the tax breaks make in the Charlotte area's overall urban development? In Mecklenburg County (including Charlotte), apartment construction surged 400 percent from 1962 to 1972, while single-family construction held steady. Only a small part of that increase could be attributed to rising demand; Mecklenburg's population grew by 30 percent in those years.[13] Clearly the intervention by Washington brought a large benefit to developers.

* * * * *

We could continue this thread, looking at tax law changes in 1976, 1978, 1981, 1986, and beyond—but instead let's turn back to our affordable housing story. One way this tax-fueled history plays into the low-income housing narrative is that those overbuilt apartment complexes have themselves become affordable. The vast stock of apartments constructed in the late 1960s and 1970s have mellowed into old age and are now a major source of naturally occurring affordable housing. Activists today are striving to safeguard those complexes, keeping them affordable and well-maintained (see chapter 9).[14]

The tax environment of the 1960s and early 1970s also reshaped low-income housing production more directly. Developers (and their tax shelter–savvy accountants) had all this expertise building apartment complexes now, right? Could some small additional incentives entice them to produce low-rent projects? Might America even get government out of the business of constructing public housing, some advocates asked, and put that work into the hands of the "private market"?

Let's Put Businesspeople in Charge: FHA 221(d)(3) and Its Offspring

"New Tax Loophole: Big Profits Possible in Low-Cost Housing." Sylvia Porter was breathless with excitement in her January 1970 financial advice column, featured in newspapers across the nation. "There are unparalleled opportunities for profit awaiting you, the investor, in low-cost housing in the 1970s—as a result of the meshing of giant new housing and tax laws." In particular, the "newly liberalized Section 236" from FHA "will then permit you to get extraordinarily attractive depreciation," she explained. These were "'some of the hottest real estate breaks' in history," making real estate "'a top-payoff investment,'" Porter quoted a housing expert as saying. "[It's] 'the opportunity of a lifetime to pyramid a small investment into a real estate fortune.'"[15]

The FHA's Section 236, along with three related programs—Section 221(d)(3), Turnkey 1, and Turnkey Leased Housing—indeed transformed low-income housing into a bonanza for developers. We'll trace the programs' rise and fall in Charlotte. A larger number of affordable apartment complexes would be built under the new subsidies by 1977 than had been built with conventional federal public housing dollars. Ultimately, we'll see, serious problems with all four programs forced Washington to pull back.

■ ■ ■ ■ ■

The story starts with FHA Section 221(d)(3). Introduced in 1961, it "provide[d] for 100 percent loans at below-the-market interest rates to non-profit corporations, co-operatives and public agencies" for construction of apartment projects "for low to moderate income families." That's what today is known as "workforce" housing (80 percent to 120 percent AMI). The *Observer* described it as "the so-called 'no-man's land of public housing,' those families whose incomes are too high to permit them to live in public housing projects but too low to enable them to acquire standard accommodations in the private market."[16]

Initially, Section 221(d)(3) was pretty much a failure. Few nonprofits had the

Tax-Shelter Bonanza

Sylvia Porter, a New York–based writer whose financial columns ran in numerous newspapers throughout the United States, alerted investors to the lucrative combination of FHA loans and depreciation tax breaks—a primer worth reproducing at length here:

New Tax Loophole: Big Profits Possible in Low-Cost Housing

By Sylvia Porter
Charlotte Observer, January 24, 1970

There are unparalleled opportunities for profit awaiting you, the investor, in low-cost housing in the 1970s—as a result of the meshing of giant new housing and tax laws.

In fact, "some of the hottest real estate breaks" in history are opening up and "the tax law has re-established real estate as a top-payoff investment," says Eli Warach, . . . nationally recognized authority on housing. Washington is eager to see you take advantage of the tax breaks in order to stimulate the flow of money into the construction and rehabilitation of low-cost housing. . . . The newly liberalized Section 236 of the National Housing Law is specifically designed to pull private enterprise (as opposed to the federal government) into low-cost housing. . . .

- the interest on your mortgage is a mere one percent!
- The government will pay the mortgage lender the difference between the 1 percent you pay and the mortgage's actual cost.
- The new tax law will then permit you to get extraordinarily attractive depreciation treatment. . . .

"Watch the profits pile up," says Warach. . . .

[For example, imagine a small apartment house financed under Section 236.] You borrow $150,000 on a 40-year mortgage at 8½ percent. . . . The first year, the government pays the lender $9,390 on your mortgage (at the 8½ percent rate) and it continues to pay year after year. You pay only the amortization costs of a mortgage at one percent interest.

(continued)

> The first year, you deduct $30,000 (one-fifth of $150,000) in depreciation. This is much more than you're out of pocket. During the next four years—while your out-of-pocket costs remain minor—you deduct $30,000 a year.
> You use these big deductions to offset your other highly taxed income.
> . . .
> Again, to quote Warach: it's "the opportunity of a lifetime to pyramid a small investment into a real estate fortune."

expertise to assemble such a project. Five years into the program, only three apartment proposals in all of North Carolina made it through the red tape.[17]

So, the US Housing Act of 1964 rewrote Section 221(d)(3) to include commercial developers. They could create projects on their own. Or they could partner with a nonprofit; the for-profit company would take out the mortgage loan and build the project and then sell it at cost to the nonprofit.[18]

Why the partnership arrangement? Tax shelter considerations. The for-profit developer could get a tax shelter, which a nonprofit did not qualify for. And by selling the project quickly, the for-profit company got its investment back almost instantly, with no long-term management responsibilities.

That's important to understand and worth restating. The tax breaks really sweetened a deal—"the rate of return under a Section 221(d)(3) property arises primarily because of the depreciation advantages for real estate built into present law," noted a US Treasury report—but the breaks could go only to private owners.[19] That's because private owners pay US income tax. Nonprofits and local government agencies do not. So, the efforts I am describing in this chapter all shared a basic principle: the need for a for-profit entity to initially own the property.

The revised Section 221(d)(3) stimulated at least four Charlotte projects between 1968 and 1971.[20] They demonstrated the variety of paths available under the new rules.

- *A local real estate man*, Dwight Phillips, built Roseland (today called Pressley South End).[21] Phillips had cut his teeth in multifamily construction with Morningside Apartments, financed via FHA 608. Roseland, off Clanton Road near West Boulevard, opened in 1968 with 252 apartments—one-, two-, and three-bedroom—for "low-to-moderate income families." A second 221(d)(3) loan enabled it to double to 504 units in 1971. Phillips would continue as owner for decades.

- *A national developer*, Connecticut-based Jack Cooper and Associates, initiated University Gardens off Beatties Ford Road in a Black area near West Charlotte High School.[22] The forty-year mortgage financed 133 two- and three-bedroom units in twenty-two two-story brick buildings. Cooper seems to have had no previous ties to Charlotte. The property remains privately owned today.
- *A Charlotte civil rights leader*, dentist Dr. Reginald Hawkins, put together a limited partnership to construct Parker Heights Apartments. The FHA provided a forty-year mortgage at 3 percent.[23] More than forty African Americans bought shares, including architect and future mayor Harvey Gantt. The project produced 101 apartments, half of them subsidized, half market-rate, on Remount Road off West Boulevard. It remains in private hands today.
- *A for-profit/nonprofit partnership* between the national Westinghouse Corporation and Charlotte's Little Rock AME Zion Church constructed Little Rock Homes on West Boulevard.[24] Westinghouse had just established a subsidiary to develop low-rent housing: Urban Systems Development Corporation.[25] Civil rights activist Rev. George Leake, a bishop in the AME Zion denomination, led the effort locally.[26] Westinghouse built the complex, and then after reaping the first year's accelerated depreciation tax break, it sold it to Leake's nonprofit.[27] Little Rock accepted tenants at both market-rate rent and also with subsidies. Of the 240 units, "150 will be under the rent supplement program which pays the difference between what the tenants can afford and the established market rent," mentioned the *Observer*.[28] The AME Zion church struggled to manage the property, selling in 1978 to for-profit out-of-state investors, who eventually sold to the Charlotte Housing Authority, which now operates it as public housing.[29]

▪ ▪ ▪ ▪ ▪

Department of Housing and Urban Development (HUD) officials in Washington liked the results of Section 221(d)(3)—but could the incentives be improved to attract even more developers? The Housing and Urban Development Act of 1968 introduced an entire suite of programs: Section 236, Turnkey Leasing, and Turnkey I, plus a new federal mortgage bank called "Ginnie Mae." (The legislation also included Section 235 and Turnkey III for single-family development—outside the scope of this book.) What all had in common was their aim to

Low- and Moderate-Income Housing

Section 221(d)(3) and Section 236 projects were built to house tenants of "low- and moderate-income." What did that mean?

- Households could earn no more than 80 percent of area median income (AMI). Today that's termed "workforce housing."* Then it was called "moderate-income housing."
- "The federal government gave additional, deeper rent subsidies to a limited number of low-income households," writes housing policy historian Alex F. Schwartz. "These tenants were provided with 'rent supplements' to cover the difference between . . . their income . . . and the basic rent."† (See discussion of Little Rock Homes in this chapter.)

In encouraging a mixture of incomes, these programs were ahead of their time. The benefits of mixed-income housing would become clearer in the years after 2000 and would become a major thrust in national and local housing policy.

The circa 1970 projects described in this chapter, however, kicked up such a firestorm of opposition for other reasons that the income-mixing received little attention. Most Americans heard the "low-income" language, saw the problems, and forever associated the two.

---

* "The Almost-Poor Getting Housing," *Charlotte Observer*, August 22, 1968. "The so-called 'no-man's land of public housing'" is described as "those families whose incomes are too high to permit them to live in public housing projects but too low to enable them to acquire standard accommodations in the private market." "N.C. Fund Aims to Untie Housing Red Tape," *Charlotte Observer*, July 15, 1966. Schwartz, *Housing Policy*, 179–80; "Section 221(d)(3) below Market Interest Rate (BMIR)" and "Section 236," National Housing Preservation Database, accessed November 7, 2024, https://preservation database.org/documentation/program-descriptions/.

† Schwartz, *Housing Policy*, 179–80.

---

produce low-income housing by harnessing the abilities of businesspeople, with tax shelters as the carrot. "Important provisions of the Housing Act of 1968 relating to the construction of low- and middle-income multifamily," explained Assistant Treasury Secretary for Tax Policy Edwin S. Cohen at a how-to seminar for developers, "were built on existing tax incentives."[30]

Section 236 replaced Section 221(d)(3). It gave developers and banks an even nicer deal on mortgage financing. Under the old law, the FHA had provided direct loans at 3 percent interest. Section 236 bettered the rate and changed the tool for achieving it. Instead of the FHA making the loans itself (which showed up as a big expense in the federal budget, not a popular situation), the agency now offered yearly subsidies to lenders. The subsidy gave lenders a profit, enabling them to cut the interest rate for borrowers to an amazingly low 1 percent.[31]

At the same time, Washington made such mortgages risk-free for banks. A provision in the 1968 Housing Act created "Ginnie Mae," the Government National Mortgage Association. As soon as a bank wrote a mortgage for subsidized housing, the bank could turn around and sell the mortgage to Ginnie Mae, which would take over the work of collecting payments. Not only did the bank thus shed any risk of loss, but it also avoided the hassle of servicing the mortgage over many years. And the bank had its capital back instantly, ready to invest in the next project.[32]

Investors—the passive partners who put up capital in exchange for tax shelter—also loved Section 236 once they did the math. On one hand, Section 236 capped the profit that an investor could reap at 6 percent annually—well below the rate achieved by market-rate projects. But on the other hand, the Section 236 loans required only a 10 percent down payment rather than the 25 percent that was standard for market-rate apartments. Investors thus got less cash flow from rents—but they got more of a tax shelter for each dollar that they invested. According to analysis by the US Comptroller's office, "By using tax shelters, Section 236 investors can obtain, after tax, returns of 15 to 25 percent on their initial investment, compared with 14 percent indicated as the median average rate for all investors in multifamily projects."[33]

Write-offs were heavily weighted to the start of a project. "During the construction period, the owner of the project may deduct . . . interest payments on the construction loan, real estate taxes and certain other fees . . . thus sheltering the [owner's] other income," noted a federal analysis of FHA 236.[34] Once the apartments opened, the owner-developer could sell almost immediately—but still claim a full year's worth of accelerated depreciation, ruled the Supreme Court.[35] Putting together a deal paid handsomely, wrote tax lawyer Perry Rowan Smith: "It is usually the profit-motivated forces of . . . the attorney, the consultant, the architect, the realtor, the builder and the manager who . . . instigate and pursue the development of a project to reality."[36]

All the various incentives made Section 236 very attractive to banks that lent the initial capital, to investors who co-owned the property over the long haul, and especially to the developers who conceived and packaged the project. By 1971, Section 236 already had helped spark "an unprecedented building boom,"

Cheap Money

Low interest rates are a powerful tool to stimulate development. Real estate projects run on borrowed money. Interest payments are a big part of a developer's expense. If those payments are reduced, then profits shoot up, and developers get excited to start new projects.

Real estate people have a name for it: "cheap money."

Section 236 offered a 1 percent interest rate—a great stimulus. By comparison, the standard mortgage rate during the 1970s ranged from 7 percent at the start of the decade to nearly 13 percent by the end.

How did the Department of Housing and Urban Development make that low rate happen? It gave subsidies to lenders to "write down" the interest rate they charged. With Washington dollars in hand, the lenders could drop the rates and still make a profit.

More generally, special low interest rates form a recurring theme throughout this book, starting with the public housing and FHA apartment programs back in the 1930s. When we get to the 2010s, we'll watch as ultra-low-interest policies of the Federal Reserve drastically reshape the entire US housing market.

wrote the Associated Press.[37] The program officially ended in 1973 (projects in the pipeline continued to completion). All told, it funded over 500,000 apartments, including five new complexes in Charlotte.[38] Section 236 "far outdistanced the traditional public housing program," said the US comptroller general. "Only once before did housing production under Federal housing programs even approach this scale"—FHA 608 after World War II.[39]

In Charlotte, profit-minded real estate people who had sat on the fence in the 1960s during Section 221(d)(3) now jumped into the low-rent game. Charles Ervin, one of the nation's biggest suburban single-family developers from his base in Charlotte, set up a subsidiary called Kingston and developed 101-unit Barrington Oaks (today called Timber Ridge) off Milton Road in east Charlotte, opening in 1973.[40] The same year, John Crosland (whose market-rate Vista Villa Apartments we saw earlier) completed 152-unit low-rent Woodland Hollow at the city's northeast rim. Crosland would soon emerge as North Carolina's dominant builder of affordable apartments, as we will discover in subsequent sections of this book.

The Westinghouse subsidiary, Urban Development Systems Corporation, also successfully pursued Section 236 funding, first for an expansion of Little Rock Homes and then for Village Town Houses (1974) off Beatties Ford Road.[41] At Village Town Houses, the Urban Development Systems Corporation once again partnered with a nonprofit. The Foundation for Cooperative Housing, based in Washington, DC, and still active in the 2020s, had a long track record of projects both in the United States and abroad.[42]

The federal officials who oversaw Section 236 liked projects that involved nonprofits. Such partnerships could help groups long frozen out of real estate development to gain a place at the table, developing skills and forging networks. Not everyone appreciated that effort, though. Wrote the Associated Press, "[Section 236] attracts two major types of sponsors—the non-profit corporation, often formed by a church or civic group, and the limited entrepreneur. Housing professionals sneer at the non-profit corporations. 'A half-dozen bewildered Negro preachers and a sharp-shooting lawyer,' is how one described the nonprofits."[43]

In Charlotte, a nonprofit called MOTION, Inc. (Model Cities Organization to Improve Our Neighborhoods) achieved success in developing two Section 236 apartment projects, Orchard Park in then run-down Fourth Ward and Greenhaven in an urban renewal area called Greenville. MOTION began in 1971, a local offshoot of the federal Model Cities program that encouraged grassroots efforts to revitalize neighborhoods, "working on the premise that ordinary people can do something about slums." MOTION initially undertook small-scale rehab of existing dwellings.[44]

Two idealistic young men, one Black, one white, led MOTION into apartment construction. Charlotte native Ernest Alford had been a social worker and then tried selling houses—and discovered that his people skills were a perfect fit.[45] His white counterpart, Paul Leonard, had also experienced a career realignment. A junior minister at a swank south Charlotte church, he left to start his own interracial congregation—a courageous commitment to civil rights. His flock needed housing, so he helped them develop a cluster of affordable ranch houses called Clawson Village off Park Road under FHA 235.[46] Project management fit his temperament, which led him to take charge of MOTION's two-person office. Somewhere along the way, MOTION crossed paths with John Crosland, mega-homebuilder just then getting into apartments. Would MOTION like to partner on a Section 236 application or two?

"Because of what I'd learned in doing Clawson Village, I got to know a lot of the people in the Planning Department, a lot of people at HUD in Greensboro," Leonard remembered in 2020. Those connections brought swift approval of the two Crosland/MOTION applications: Orchard Park Apartments with

Figure 5.2. One of the nine buildings at MOTION's 1977 Greenhaven Apartments. Built with Section 236, it resembled other HUD-aided projects in Charlotte during the 1970s: two-story, mixing brick and siding, with gable roofs. Hanchett photo, 2023.

forty-two units off West Fifth Street in the center city, and Greenhaven with forty-nine units out in the cleared land of old Greenville. But no sooner had HUD given the nod than President Nixon froze all affordable housing appropriations (discussed later in this chapter). It would not be until 1976, with Alford at MOTION's helm, that Orchard Park came to fruition, Greenhaven not until 1977.[47]

The delay frustrated Paul Leonard. So, he left MOTION and went to work for Crosland, where he soon headed up all multifamily market-rate construction. As we shall see in chapter 6, he would become pivotal in making Charlotte a national leader in scattered-site housing—and would eventually go on to head Habitat for Humanity International.

∎ ∎ ∎ ∎ ∎

Alongside Section 236, the Housing Act of 1968 also included something called "Turnkey." Under 221(d)(3) and 236, apartments stayed in the hands of their private owners, who screened tenants for eligibility, collected rents, did maintenance, and so on. Under HUD's Turnkey program, in contrast, developers acquired land and built complexes—but then sold them to the local Public Housing Authority (or the Public Housing Authority might buy a fifteen-year lease).[48]

Explained a HUD official at a seminar for prospective builders, the arrangement would "give the builders the opportunity for early profits in depreciation."[49]

The public-private partnership seemed extremely promising. The local housing authority would avoid most or all of the painful work of asking for public input, since private developers were under no requirement to seek community comment. New complexes would arise swiftly, harnessing the expertise and profit motive of builders who knew how to bring a project to market quickly. Developers, too, would benefit, able to recoup their entire investment and get tax shelter advantages, while turning over the ongoing day-to-day management to government bureaucrats who were used to working with low-income clients.

What could possibly go wrong?

Robert C. Weaver, secretary of the newly created US Department of Housing and Urban Development, regarded public-private partnership as America's great hope.[50] His Turnkey initiative for affordable housing included three main subsections: Turnkey I for constructing apartment complexes, Turnkey II for contracting out the management of public housing complexes to private firms, and Turnkey III, under which developers constructed single-family homes and duplexes for low-income buyers.[51] We'll look only at Turnkey I, in keeping with this book's focus on multifamily construction. We'll also get a glimpse of a lesser-known adjunct to Turnkey I, called Turnkey Leased Housing.

The first Charlotte project initiated under the Turnkey heading, Pitts Drive Apartments, showed that private enterprise could definitely move quickly.[52] A developer named Richard H. Wright III out of Durham, North Carolina, put together the deal. Grandson of a tobacco tycoon, Wright pursued various real estate ventures often in partnership with his brother Thomas.[53] In Charlotte, the pair incorporated as TomRich and bought acreage in Washington Heights, an African American "streetcar suburb" begun in the 1910s and named for national leader Booker T. Washington. TomRich announced construction in January 1969, and by early summer the tenants were moving in—dramatically faster than the two to three years normally required for government-built projects.

As prearranged, the Charlotte Housing Authority took charge of the property in a fifteen-year lease. Pitts Drive was built under the Turnkey Leased Housing program, newly authorized by HUD in 1968. Back in 1965, legislation had enabled local housing authorities to contract with existing apartment complexes; the housing authority could lease units and then re-rent them at subsidized rates to low-income tenants. In 1968, HUD tweaked this to include new apartment complexes purpose-built for lease to local housing authorities.[54] The developer continued to own the property for tax purposes, while the housing authority handled day-to-day management and paid the developer a guaranteed fifteen-year income stream—as well as the "opportunity for early profits in depreciation."[55] For the wealthy investor, Turnkey Leased Housing combined "net long-term income" from rents with "what he can gain from tax shelter."[56]

Faith in the efficacy of private business blinded HUD to a major shortcoming built into the Turnkey Leased Housing program, however. With a guaranteed fifteen-year lease in their pockets, developers had little incentive to take care in construction.

Problems surfaced almost immediately at Pitts Drive Apartments: "poorly-hung doors, bathroom sinks that fall off the walls, steps varying in height from three inches to nine and one-half inches, and grassless, poorly landscaped grounds," reported the *Observer*.[57] An open drainage ditch flooded into several units after any sizable rain. "Every time I go out there it makes me sick," said CHA board chair Pat Hall.[58]

The CHA battled TomRich for years, with tenants bearing the brunt. "They're finally fixing the hole in the outside wall of Anna Honeycutt's apartment," wrote the *Observer* nearly seven years after the project opened. "She's hoping that means no more $100 a month electric bills."[59] A few months later the City of Charlotte took ownership of the property, doing substantial renovations and renaming it Mayfield Terrace.[60] In 2004 it would be demolished with Hope VI funding and replaced with a better-constructed apartment community called Nia Point.

Site Selection by Private Developers—West Boulevard Fireworks

Malfeasance by developers was not the only landmine hidden in the Turnkey strategy. The regulations absolved housing authorities of the difficult work of site selection, where discomforted neighbors could make things messy and slow, and instead put it in the hands of businesspeople. Surely this would be a boon to all, commentators predicted. But avoiding community input turned out to produce deeply flawed site decisions—which generated an unprecedented level of anger, not just from neighbors but also from elected officials.

Three Charlotte projects went up with funding under Washington's Turnkey I program—similar to Turnkey Leasing but with the completed project being sold rather than leased to the local housing authority. Boulevard Homes and Dalton Village opened in 1970, and Dillehay Courts followed in 1974. All three, you will not be surprised to learn, experienced construction woes. The CHA withheld $100,000 payment from Boulevard Homes' developer over exterior construction deficiencies.[61] At Dillehay Courts, the CHA ordered work to cease as it attempted to pressure the developer "to bring the eleven buildings already under construction up to standards."[62] Eventually the developer quit the project, selling the half-finished apartments to the CHA.[63]

Those were minor problems compared with the fireworks set off by the announcement that Boulevard Homes and Dalton Village were being planned for sites on West Boulevard. The outcry would change the course of Charlotte's urban geography—and would push city leaders to rethink affordable housing policies in the city.

Ever since the 1940s, low-income apartments had been grouped in clusters. Hardly anyone complained when C. D. Spangler put his 1949 Double Oaks FHA 608 project adjacent to the Fairview Homes public housing, or when Brookhill Village went up next to Southside Homes, or when Earle Village got built just up the hill from Piedmont Courts. In that same spirit, Dillehay Courts occasioned little discussion when its site was announced next to the big Tryon Hills FHA 608 apartments off North Tryon Street. No problem: that was already a blue-collar part of the city.

West Boulevard was a different sort of place. A minor farm lane until recently, West Boulevard in the 1960s was becoming a busy spoke in the "wagon wheel" of major arteries that converged on downtown. Back in rural days, an important Black church named Moore's Sanctuary AME Zion and its affiliated Plato Price School had acted as a magnet attracting African Americans. Ross Reid, an African American landowner, platted Reid Park in the 1940s, the first of a series of developments where Black families built humble semirural homes. Street names often honored Black leaders: Dr. Carver Drive for the Tuskegee University scientist; Amay James Avenue for a local educator. Then during the 1950s and early 1960s, Charlotte's widening wave of white suburbanization washed over the area. Middle-income ranch houses lined new streets such as Barringer Drive and Clanton Road. Even when a few middle-income African Americans, displaced from downtown neighborhoods by "urban renewal," began buying homes, most white people stayed. By the late 1960s, many observers held hope that West Boulevard might thrive as a racially diverse sector of Charlotte.

To local real estate broker E. L. Vinson, however, West Boulevard was simply a blank slate awaiting sale and development. He assembled an inventory of former farmland and went looking for buyers.[64] It was Vinson who in 1967 helped bring together Westinghouse Corporation's Urban Systems Development Corporation and AME Zion bishop George Leake to create the 240-unit Little Rock Homes, using FHA Section 221(d)(3) and FHA Section 236, as we have seen. Vinson knew the tax quirk that made cheap "raw" land highly attractive to tax shelter investors. As explained earlier in this chapter, the cost of land was not depreciable—so the less a project spent on land, the better the tax shelter.

Indeed, the incentive to seek cheap land had the effect of skewing low-income apartment locations nationwide: "Despite the need for housing in the nation's inner cities, only 28 percent of projects built so far under the Section 236 subsidy program are located there," the *Boston Globe* reported in 1971. "Instead, the projects tend to be located in fringe areas (61 percent) where the risks are minimal and land is cheaper."[65]

When Vinson heard about the HUD Turnkey I program, he jumped at the opportunity to make more big sales. Young developer D. Cam Summers Jr., son of a Charlotte stockbroker, bought thirty-six acres from Vinson and drew up plans for a 300-unit Turnkey public housing project to be called Dalton Village.[66] At the same time, Vinson connected with Henry L. Coble of Greensboro, who had a strong track record developing FHA-approved subdivisions there. Coble agreed to buy forty-one acres along West Boulevard at Clanton Road, constructing 300 units of Turnkey public housing for the CHA to be called Boulevard Homes.[67]

In barely four years, the 2.5-mile heart of the West Boulevard corridor went from being a mostly single-family area to the locus of five big low-income apartment complexes: Dr. Reginald Hawkins's Parker Heights (101 units, 1969), Dwight Phillips's Roseland (504 units, 1968), Rev. George Leake's Little Rock Homes (240 units, 1971), Cam Summers's Dalton Village (300 units, 1970), and H. L. Coble's Boulevard Homes (300 units, 1970).

■ ■ ■ ■ ■

Racial issues complicated the situation—thought not always in ways you might expect. The West Boulevard complexes were officially racially "integrated," which ironically meant nearly entirely Black. The Charlotte Housing Authority had ended racial segregation policies in 1964, and almost immediately—due to the great need of people being displaced by Brooklyn urban renewal—African Americans moved into every available CHA apartment. Wrote the *Charlotte News* in 1969, "It is a fact that low-income housing rapidly becomes predominantly black housing."[68]

On West Boulevard, white homeowners spoke out against the proposed projects. So did Black homeowners, as we shall see. Local government officials took up the call, attempting to halt the developments. All three groups, to their great consternation, found themselves completely powerless in the face of HUD's policies.

Firm Offers Turnkey Job On Public Housing Unit

County Sets Up New Arm

By TOM SESLAR
News Staff Writer

The Board of County Commissioners today unanimously approved creation of the County Department of Public Works and Utilities.

Replacing the engineering department, the new government arm includes an inspections unit which will enforce building, electrical, plumbing, mechanical, heating, air conditioning and zoning restrictions in rural areas outside the Charlotte zoning perimeter.

The inspections unit will start operating April 1 and was established in lieu of long-

Architect's Rendering Of The Townhouse Apartments To Be Proposed For Public Housing

West Blvd. Location Proposed

By KAY REIMLER
News Staff Writer

A Charlotte developer today said he plans to submit a proposal to the Charlotte Housing Authority to build a 230-unit public housing project on West Blvd. and sell it to the Housing Authority when completed.

If approved, he said, more will follow.

This would be a departure from the standard procedure used by the housing authority in constructing projects.

In the past, the authority has hired architects, bought land and awarded construction contracts.

D. Cam Summers of Summers Development Co. said he

Observer Photo by Joe

B Boulevard Homes Off West Boulevard Near The Airport
... Sprawling Public Housing Project Will House 300 Fan

Figure 5.3. A: Announcing Dalton Village on West Boulevard. *Charlotte News*, February 19, 1968.
B: Boulevard Homes. Note the wooded, rural surroundings of the development, an isolated pod at Charlotte's far edge. *Charlotte Observer*, January 15, 1970.

As announcements of the projects followed one another in quick succession during 1967, 1968, 1969, and 1970, white middle-income residents mobilized in opposition at every step. Stories peppered the newspapers: "Zoning Battle Blocks Low-Income Housing," "City Seeks Temporary Housing Project Delay," "Suit Filed to Block Little Rock Project," "Westside Group to Fight at Polls," "Westside Units OK'd over Protest."[69]

Charlotte's Black residents mobilized, too. That surprised most whites. Weren't African American leaders such as Fred Alexander calling loudly for more low-income housing? Yes, but they did not want it concentrated out at one edge of town, far from jobs and shopping. "Our great concern is not with low-income housing," Clanton Park resident Jimmy Hackett explained in an article under the headline "Negroes Oppose Apartments." "Our purpose is to force the city to realize they are not distributing this housing throughout the city."[70]

Despite collecting 10,000 signatures on petitions, the protesters discovered they had no voice. Remarkably, neither did political leaders. Mayor Stan Brookshire and fellow elected officials tried every action they could think of—including cornering US congressman Charles Jonas as he boarded a flight at the Charlotte airport—to no avail. At a 1969 City Council meeting, Charlotte's city manager laid out the realities:

> Under the Turnkey and Leased Housing Programs, the private developer makes the site selection. The local Housing Authority must approve the selected site but does not make the selection. . . .
>
> The local Housing Authority has no role in any aspects of the several FHA low-income housing programs. The only opportunity for local government to influence the site-selection process . . . is through local zoning regulations.
>
> The private developers may locate all FHA housing and . . . turnkey and leased housing at any location appropriately zoned for multifamily housing.[71]

In short, local government and its citizens discovered they were helpless in the face of the badly conceived national housing laws.

The frustrations sparked a civil rights court case. The law firm of nationally known African American attorney Julius Chambers filed suit in 1970 on behalf of a West Boulevard corridor resident named America McKnight and other Black citizens. *McKnight v. Romney* charged that government had acted willfully to "perpetuate and intensify" segregation by locating "public housing to perpetuate racially segregated residential districts."[72]

McKnight would spur dramatic changes in Charlotte's affordable housing policies, causing a shift to a "scattered-site" philosophy—as we'll see in the next chapter.

■ ■ ■ ■ ■

Along West Boulevard, white middle-income families gave up the fight and departed. The concentration of low-income housing branded West Boulevard as a corridor of poverty in the minds of many decision-makers. Despite the fact that a sizable population of middle-income homeowners remained, the corridor never succeeded in attracting a major grocery store. Even after Dalton Village and Boulevard Homes, barely thirty years old, were bulldozed during the first decade of the 2000s and replaced with handsome mixed-income neighborhoods called Arbor Glen and Renaissance West (see chapter 8), the stigma lingered. In the early 2020s, West Boulevard remained a "food desert" without a supermarket.

Outcry over bad low-income housing decisions was becoming a rising roar all across urban America during the early 1970s, a force that Washington could not ignore. And as flawed as multifamily programs were (our focus in this book), problems in federally subsidized single-family housing were much worse. The Turnkey III program, in which private developers built single-family homes and duplexes to sell to low-income families, witnessed the same abuses by contractors that characterized Turnkey I apartments. In Charlotte, a development called Windsong on the city's east side and Pine Valley off South Boulevard made headlines for years due to shoddy construction.[73] Exponentially worse scandals resulted from Section 235, the single-family counterpart to Section 236. Section 235 sounded great: to help low-income people buy homes, HUD would underwrite mortgages at just 1 percent interest. But HUD, with its blind faith in business, failed to imagine that real estate speculators might artificially inflate home prices and also foist barely habitable structures on unsuspecting first-time buyers.[74]

Finally in 1973, an exasperated President Richard Nixon took the extraordinary step of declaring an eighteen-month moratorium on all US low-income housing subsidies.[75] Projects underway in every American city were frozen in mid-construction. New projects would not be approved until HUD and Congress rewrote housing regulations.

Over the next few months in 1973 and 1974, the history of low-income housing would take a sharp turn—both in Charlotte and in the United States.

Table 5.1. Investor-Developed Low-Rent Housing in Charlotte, 1968–1977 Funded through Section 221(d)(3), Section 236, Turnkey Leased, and Turnkey I

Development	Opened	Funding	Developer	Units
Roseland (2 phases) 1210 Pressley Rd 28217	1968 & 1971	221(d)(3)	Dwight Phillips	504
University Gardens 3115 Southwest Blvd 28216	1969	221(d)(3)	Cooper & Assoc.	133
Parker Heights Remount Rd at Parker Dr 28208	1969	221(d)(3)	Reginald Hawkins et al.	101
Pitts Dr Apts 2618 Pitts Dr 28216	1969	Turnkey Leased	TomRich	50
Boulevard Homes West Blvd 28208	1970	Turnkey I	H. L. Coble	300
Dalton Village off West Blvd 28208	1970	Turnkey I	Summers Development	300
Little Rock Homes West Blvd 28208	1971	221(d)(3), 236	Urban Systems/ AME Zion Church	240
Woodland Hollow 6205 Dove Tree Ln 28213	1973	236	Crosland	152
Barrington Oaks 7123 Barrington Dr 28215	1973	236	Ervin (Kingston division)	101
Dillehay Courts Matheson Av 28206	1974	Turnkey I	Vector Corp.	136
Village Town Houses 1801 Griers Grove 28216	1974	236	Foundation for Cooperative Housing	99

Table 5.1. (*continued*)

Development	Opened	Funding	Developer	Units
Orchard Park Apartments 845 Cates St 28202	1976	236	MOTION/ Crosland	42
Greenhaven Apartments 1407 Spring St 28206	1977	236	MOTION/ Crosland	49
Total complexes: 13				Total units: 2,207

Note: Data in all tables were gathered project-by-project from newspaper articles in those years. I have found no official list, either in public records or in the media. I suspect that there were other small projects not covered by news media, such as Keyway Apartments and Coronet Way Apartments; see note 52 in this chapter.

Source: Table excerpted from Tom Hanchett, "Master List of Low-Income Multifamily Housing Constructed in Charlotte, 1940–2019," in the data collection of J. Murrey Atkins Library, University of North Carolina at Charlotte, https://doi.org/10.15139/S3/XQBOFW.

Table 5.2. Public Housing Developed by Charlotte Housing Authority, 1967–1977

Development	Opened	Funding	Units
Edwin Towers 201 W 10th St 28202	1967	Section 202	175
Earle Village 426 N Caldwell St 20202	1967	HUD loan	409
Strawn Apartments 1301 S Blvd 28203	1971	Section 202	316
Addison Apartments 831 E Morehead St 28202	1974	purchased with local funds	77
Charlottetown Terrace 1000 Baxter St 28204	1976	Section 8 Project-Based	180
Park Towne Terrace 5800 Fairview Rd 28209	1977	Section 8 Project-Based	163
Total complexes: 6			Total units: 1,320

Source: Table excerpted from Tom Hanchett, "Master List of Low-Income Multifamily Housing Constructed in Charlotte, 1940–2019," in the data collection of J. Murrey Atkins Library, University of North Carolina at Charlotte, https://doi.org/10.15139/S3/XQBOFW.

In the Investor-Built Era, What Was the Charlotte Housing Authority's Role?

By the definitions of this book, the investor-built projects discussed in this chapter were not **constructed** as "public housing" (they were developed by private entities rather than by the Charlotte Housing Authority). But about half ended up **becoming** public housing under the ownership of the CHA:

- Dalton Village and Boulevard Homes were sold to the CHA soon after construction was complete—as intended under the Turnkey program.
- Orchard Park and Greenhaven, co-developed by the city's MOTION nonprofit, became wholly owned by the CHA at some point fairly early in their existence.
- Pitts Drive Apartments and Dillehay Courts were sold to the CHA when their developers proved unable to produce livable apartments.
- The Little Rock Homes development was sold to a California-based limited partnership in 1979. In 2002, Mecklenburg County issued bonds that raised funds to purchase it for the CHA.*

The other six projects discussed in this chapter still seem to be in private hands in 2022. It is not known whether they continue to be low-rent or have become market-rate.

■ ■ ■ ■ ■

Meanwhile, the Charlotte Housing Authority constructed just a handful of projects on its own during these years.

One was 409-unit Earle Village on Seventh Street near downtown (discussed previously in chapter 4).

Two others were high-rises for senior citizens that utilized HUD's Section 202 program. Instituted in 1959, it gave low-interest loans to localities specifically

(continued)

---

*"No One Takes the Blame for Crumbling Complex," *Charlotte News*, April 19, 1979. The for-profit buyer was National Investment Development Corporation of Los Angeles. "Little Rock Apartments to Be Rebuilt with Grant," *Charlotte News*, July 29, 1980; "Notice of Public Hearing on Proposed Multifamily Housing Revenue Bonds," *Charlotte Observer*, September 9, 2002; deed book 14503, p. 143, Mecklenburg County Register of Deeds, Charlotte, NC.

to build senior apartments.† Edwin Towers in Fourth Ward, 1967, was the first public housing high-rise in North Carolina purpose-built for senior citizens.‡ Strawn Apartments in Dilworth, 1971, featured a seven-story tower plus one-story units scattered on a grassy superblock.** Both have been recently renovated and remain in use.

Three additional projects for seniors pulled funds from other sources. Charlottetown Terrace and Park Towne Terrace used Section 8 Project-Based funding, discussed in the next chapter. Local tax dollars paid for the purchase and rehab of the Addison Apartments, which had been constructed as an upscale high-rise on the edge of Dilworth in the 1920s.

To compare: 2,207 units were created by investor-driven projects, 1968–77. In contrast, conventional public housing programs produced only 1,320 units.

---

† "The Section 202 Program was established under the Housing Act of 1959 and is administered by HUD.... The program has evolved over the years, but has either provided direct loans or capital advances from the federal government for the development of housing for low income seniors. From 1959 to 1990 the program provided below market-rate direct loans (usually at a 3% interest rate for up to 50 years) to nonprofit organizations. Between 1974 and 1990 these loans were subsidized further by Project-Based Section 8 contracts. In 1990, the funding transitioned from these below market-rate direct loans to capital advances." "Section 202 Direct Loans," National Housing Preservation Database, accessed November 6, 2024, https://preservationdatabase.org/documentation/program-descriptions/.

‡ "Towers Will Be a First," *Charlotte News*, May 18, 1967; "Elderly Units: Bids on 13-Story Building Approved," *Charlotte Observer*, July 23, 1965; "Elderly Gain More Housing," *Charlotte Observer*, October 8, 1978.

** "New Units Will Cater to Elderly," *Charlotte Observer*, September 1, 1968. For profiles of three initial tenants, all white women: "Strawn Apartments: 'It's Too Good to Be True,'" *Charlotte News*, November 12, 1971.

CHAPTER 6

Dispersing Subsidized Housing throughout the City

- Scattered-Site
- Section 8 Project-Based

The 1970s saw the start of a big change in ideas about land use in US cities. From the early twentieth century into the 1960s, separation had been the watchword. Mixture seemed so old-fashioned, so random and messy. "Exclusive" upscale-only neighborhoods, retail-only shopping centers, and the legal tool called "zoning" came into existence. By the same logic, Charlotte had neatly set off its early low-income housing projects from the rest of the city.

But now that faith began to waver. For one thing, big public housing complexes were not aging well. Neither residents nor neighbors seemed to hold any love for them, and housing authorities let them slide into disrepair. Officials in St. Louis used dynamite in 1972 to demolish Pruitt-Igoe, a project less than twenty years old.

The civil rights movement also spurred new thinking. In 1954, the US Supreme Court declared that racially separate schools were "inherently unequal." The ruling rippled across American society. What other kinds of separation, created intentionally to marginalize Black people and poor people, needed to be dismantled? The 1955–56 Montgomery bus boycott led by Rosa Parks and Rev. Martin Luther King Jr. and the 1960 lunch counter sit-ins organized by college students showed that local people could come together to change the system. You didn't have to wait for Washington.

The questioning of the status quo extended to low-income housing. Activists now began to talk about a "scattered-site" approach. Smaller developments, dispersed in every part of the city, could begin to break down separation.[1]

Charlotte took the new philosophy to heart. A trio of lawsuits filed by equality-minded attorneys, including civil rights leader Julius Chambers, resulted in a

1973 "consent decree" in which the city agreed to transform its housing policy. Using local tax dollars plus a Washington innovation called revenue sharing, Charlotte would become a US leader in scattered-site housing. By the mid-1980s, nearly every part of town would have at least one freshly completed city-owned complex, twenty-one in total.

At the same time, a different Washington program encouraged local developers to do their own scattered projects. Known as Section 8 Project-Based, it did not resemble today's familiar Section 8. Instead of providing vouchers for renters, it helped developers construct low-rent buildings. Its rules encouraged projects to be geographically scattered. In Charlotte, about thirteen complexes opened with Section 8 funding during the late 1970s and early 1980s, dispersed throughout the city.

The Scattered-Site Idea

When President Lyndon Johnson created the Department of Housing and Urban Development in 1965, he called for America to "break the pattern of central city ghettos by providing low- and moderate-income housing in suburban areas."[2] But LBJ's "plea for 'scattered-site' public housing," as one newspaper dismissively termed it, gained little traction. It would take Rev. Martin Luther King to get the ball rolling.[3]

In the last great campaign before his assassination, King made Chicago the focus of protests against systemic racism outside the South. He moved into a rundown westside apartment to dramatize housing shortcomings. In July 1966, King's aide Jesse Jackson co-led a massive march to city hall to present a list of "Demands for Open Housing." The twelve-page document targeted interlocking issues of redlining, Realtor actions, bank lending policies, and government policies, especially those of the Chicago Housing Authority. Demanded King:

> [The Authority must initiate] no more public housing construction in the ghetto until a substantial number of units are started outside the ghetto; [And the Authority must launch] a program to vastly increase the supply of low-cost housing on a scattered basis. The program should provide for both low- and middle-income families.[4]

King's allies backed him up by filing a court case. *Gautreaux v. Chicago Housing Authority* charged that government had used public housing intentionally to increase racial segregation.[5] That violated Title VI of the 1964 Civil Rights Act. *Gautreaux* would reach the US Supreme Court in 1976, which ordered the Chicago Housing Authority to scatter its public housing across the Chicago metro area. But even before that, as similar suits sprang up in other cities, HUD began to push housing officials nationwide to rethink segregationist practices.

Then on April 4, 1968, an assassin's bullet ended Reverend King's life. On April 5, President Lyndon Johnson went before Congress to urge passage of the Fair Housing Act as a memorial. Previously stalled on Capitol Hill, it prohibited discrimination in the sale, rental, and financing of housing based on race, religion, or national origin, and it required HUD to actively prosecute violations. On April 11, LBJ signed the Fair Housing Act into law.[6]

A hopeful moment, but would it have a real-world impact?

Three Charlotte Lawsuits and a Consent Decree

In Charlotte, a cohort of idealistic young people—white and Black, most in their late twenties or early thirties—took up Reverend King's call for fair housing. Three pairs of attorneys led the way, filing a trio of lawsuits inspired by *Gautreaux*. They would find allies in government, in the press, and among neighborhood activists.

Attorney Julius Chambers was already well known by 1970—but not yet as nationally famous as he would become. With support from the national NAACP Legal Defense Fund, he moved to Charlotte as a civil rights lawyer in 1964. The next year he filed what would be a landmark case. Charlotte had done next to nothing to desegregate its school system, he charged in *Swann v. Charlotte-Mecklenburg Schools*. Charlotte-based US judge James McMillan ruled in Chambers's favor in 1969. Government had helped cause school segregation through years of actions—including the siting of public housing west of Tryon Street in the mostly Black west side of town. Thus, said McMillan, government now must act assertively to mix pupils. The US Supreme Court would agree in 1971—one of its most historic civil rights decisions. *Swann* would make busing for racial balance a central feature of education policy nationwide.

As *Swann* moved up the court ladder, Chambers's law partner James A. Lanning saw an opportunity to tackle housing issues. If Judge McMillan was willing to rule that government actions had warped educational opportunity, might he do the same for housing?

Jim Lanning knew about low-income housing firsthand.[7] His father had been a prisoner of war during World War II, and young Lanning and his mother wound up in public housing. He later recalled seeing people digging through trash for food and asking his mother why. He went to the University of North Carolina at Chapel Hill for law school, where he interned with Black civil rights activist Floyd McKissick, a highly unusual choice for a white person. After graduating, Lanning moved to Charlotte in 1967 at age twenty-seven to join the just-established Legal Aid office. But he grew frustrated within a year, hungry to work for systemic change. Julius Chambers was looking to add a fourth attorney to his bold little law firm. Lanning jumped at the job offer.

Together Chambers and Lanning filed *America McKnight v. George Romney, Secretary of Housing and Urban Development* in July 1970. Lanning was lead attorney, on behalf of a West Boulevard corridor resident named America McKnight and eight neighbors, all African American.[8] Lanning's suit, to be heard by Judge McMillan, targeted as defendants the City of Charlotte, the Charlotte Housing Authority, the Redevelopment Commission, the Planning Commission, and HUD. It charged that their actions in

- locating and constructing public housing,
- assigning tenants to public housing on the basis of race,
- allowing private owners and brokers to discriminate in sale and financing of housing,
- instituting zoning that kept Blacks out of white areas and that put industrial land uses near Black areas, and
- locating "parks, schools, hospitals and other public facilities to deny Black citizens the equal enjoyment of them"

had all worked together to foster a "pervasive community-wide custom" of racial discrimination in which "Black residents are compelled to reside in a defined area of the city."[9]

Charlotte newspapers gave *McKnight* front-page headlines. Might it, like *Swann*, also go to the Supreme Court and set national precedent? Chambers and Lanning surely had that possibility in mind. But their basic hope was to disrupt the interlocked networks that stymied Black opportunity in Charlotte. "What we were saying," Chambers later explained, "was that schools were not the only players contributing to the segregated community and the segregated schools."[10]

■ ■ ■ ■ ■

As *McKnight* attacked housing policy broadly, a second lawsuit specifically addressed the situation on West Boulevard (see previous chapter). Lawyers Tom Ray and Hugh Casey filed suit on behalf of fifteen Black homeowners, seeking to stop Rev. George Leake from expanding his low-income Little Rock Homes. Members of the homeowner group, led by Black Baptist minister Rev. Richard A. Macon, feared that their dream of middle-class racially integrated suburbia was slipping away.[11] They sued Reverend Leake and his funders at HUD: enlarging

Civil Rights Linkages between Schools and Housing

Judge James McMillan believed that the courts had the obligation to redress racial inequality. He saw *Swann* as not narrowly about schools and busing but as part of a wider movement toward an America with liberty and justice for all. According to Don Carroll, a McMillan law clerk 1972–74:

> Those [housing] lawsuits that overlapped with *Swann* were really all about trying to undo generations of racial segregation....
>
> [Judge McMillan] was looking at it from the perspective of how do you minimize the impact of busing to have desegregated schools? He was seeing both of them [school issues and housing issues] through the same lens.
>
> He understood that, fundamentally, the more scattered-site housing you could have, the less of a transportation impact desegregation would have. He was OK with kids riding the school bus—if that was the only way to do it. But he would have preferred anything else but that.*

When Charlotte officials debated scattered-site housing during the 1970s and 1980s, effects on school desegregation were always top-of-mind. "Scattered Sites to Ease Busing," read a typical headline.† As one resident put it in a newspaper story: "If people could live wherever the hell they want to, the neighborhoods would be integrated and you wouldn't have to bus."‡

Carroll agreed: "If you solve your housing problem, you solve just so many other problems. You solve the school busing problem. You solve code enforcement problems. The maintenance of housing problems. All these different social issues that need to be addressed are intertwined with housing, its quality and location. It all gets to be, at some point, how to make it a livable city for everybody. A more humane city for everybody."**

---

*Don Carroll, interview by Tom Hanchett, July 13, 2021.
† "Scattered Sites to Ease Busing," *Charlotte Observer*, November 15, 1979. Other examples: "Charlotte May Be Ahead on Schools, Housing," *Charlotte Observer*, May 6, 1973; "Archdale: Someone Must Take the First Step," *Charlotte News*, July 14, 1975; "A Start on Schools and Housing," *Charlotte News*, January 17, 1978; "Housing Plan Jeopardizes Pupil Ratios," *Charlotte News*, November 11, 1981.
‡ "Scattered Site Project Alive in Charlotte," *Charlotte Observer*, October 20, 1979.
** Carroll interview.

Little Rock would "'perpetuate racial segregation' in violation of federal law and the US Constitution."[12]

The lawsuit's racial politics were complicated—an indication that housing issues refused to follow a simple "Black versus white" narrative. On one hand, Martin Luther King's vision and the Fair Housing Act both aimed for integrated neighborhoods. Reverend Macon's suit would advance that goal. And the legal team—Black plaintiffs served by white attorneys Ray and Casey—also embodied the interracial ideal. But on the other hand, Reverend Leake was himself Black and an outspoken civil rights advocate with a large following in Charlotte and beyond.[13] His Little Rock Homes, with its 240 new apartments, constituted a huge achievement not just in serving needy Black people but also in terms of Black economic empowerment; the church would own the apartments once they were completed.

A third lawsuit, also filed in 1970, added to the pressure. Margaret Green Harris had been displaced during urban renewal demolition of Charlotte's Greenville neighborhood along Statesville Road. George Daly, a white attorney with a sympathy for underdogs, took on the case, later joined by another attorney-activist named Ted Fillette.[14] The *Harris* suit took aim at Charlotte's relocation policies and lack of replacement housing—a serious shortfall that Fred and Kelly Alexander of the NAACP had been pointing out for years. This violated the new US civil rights laws, Daly now charged. Until Charlotte fixed the housing shortage, Daly demanded, the court must forbid HUD from funding *any* of the city's redevelopment projects.[15]

■ ■ ■ ■ ■

All of that got leaders' attention, both at the city and at HUD. What action could Charlotte take that would make the lawsuits go away?

HUD officials, facing *Gautreaux*, *McKnight*, and other suits nationwide, now strongly urged scattered-site initiatives. HUD "told housing authorities across the country that they should select public housing sites that give 'members of minority groups an opportunity to locate outside of areas of concentration of their own minority group,'" reported the *Charlotte News* in 1971.[16] Charlotte must "recognize the need to proceed" with new low-income construction, said HUD, and "do it in such a way that you are not going to be subject to the injunctive process." In other words, quit doing the stuff that's gotten you sued.[17]

Until Charlotte came up with a new housing plan, HUD threatened, the feds would freeze all redevelopment projects—even the glistening new Convention Center then under construction in the heart of downtown.

The turning point arrived when the Charlotte Housing Authority appointed Attorney Tom Ray to its board in 1972.[18] The officials may have hoped to co-opt Ray and stop his West Boulevard lawsuit. But the forces of change now had a man "on the inside." Ray was passionate about the public interest, and his law background—honed at the University of North Carolina law school and Cambridge University in England—made him a savvy strategist. With input from colleges, architects, and housing activists, he wrote a seventy-four-page report that set forth a believable vision of small apartment complexes "dispersed throughout the City and County." Ray pointedly listed court cases that were striking down old-style public housing. Don't fight that losing battle, he implied. Scattered-site apartments could be an "integral part of the total housing inventory of a neighborhood, reducing the stigma upon residents . . . [and] setting a tone of acceptance of racially and economically mixed neighborhoods."[19]

The *Charlotte Observer* summed up what transpired:

The Housing Authority saw the writing on the wall.

Housing guidelines from Washington were shifting toward small, scattered projects. Chairman [of the CHA] Pat Hall commissioned Tom Ray to study the feasibility of scattered housing in Charlotte. Mr. Ray conducted the study in early 1972, just as two lawsuits against city housing policies were coming to a head in Judge James B. McMillan's U.S. District Court.

Mayor Belk and Housing Chairman Hall moved to settle those suits out of court. They had experienced the turmoil caused by Charlotte-Mecklenburg schools' protracted court fights. They knew the costs, both in money and in community discord, and they wanted none of that. Citing Mr. Ray's findings, they met quietly over several weeks with members of the Planning Commission, the Redevelopment Commission, the Housing Authority and the City Council and hammered out [an] agreement on a settlement: The city would pledge to place no more public housing in black-impacted neighborhoods.[20]

On April 30, 1973, McMillan officially approved a consent decree, also referred to as a memorandum of understanding—an out-of-court settlement signed by all parties in the *McKnight* lawsuit. It committed the city to build public housing, in developments of no more than fifty units, located outside of areas that were more than 40 percent Black ("racially impacted") or that were mostly low-income ("blighted").

The consent decree became the basis for a series of three-year Housing Assistance Plans, which would shape policies into the late 1980s. CHA attorney Bob Sink summed up the 1975 plan.

The Authority declared as its scattered site policy a commitment to build:

- east of Tryon Street
- outside blighted and racially impacted areas
- less than 50-unit projects
- no closer than ½ mile from other projects.[21]

Reverend Macon's lawsuit also was settled in 1973.[22] It allowed Leake's expansion of Little Rock Homes to proceed, but future public housing had to be dispersed. The third lawsuit, *Harris v. HUD*, would not conclude until 1985—which kept Charlotte housing under the watchful eye of Judge McMillan, as we shall see in the following pages.

New Revenue and a New City Council: Scattered-Site Housing Gets Built

Declaring policy is one thing. Finding the dollars and the political will to turn words into reality—that's something else.

Revenue sharing helped provide the cash. Launched by President Nixon in 1972, it reinvented how Washington funded urban needs.[23] People of every background—Democrats and Republicans, national leaders and local officials, grassroots residents of all races—had become fed up with heavy-handed Washington-run urban renewal and horrified at the unresponsiveness and mismanagement evident in federal housing programs such as Section 235 and 236 (see chapter 5). What if Washington gave money to localities and let them utilize it as they saw best? The IRS would continue to use its well-oiled tax collection machinery, but a chunk of the cash would go back to city governments.[24] That fit well with the conservative doctrine that small local government was preferable to big federal initiatives. For too long, Nixon said, "power and responsibility have flowed to Washington—and Washington has taken for its own the best sources of revenue. We intend to reverse that tide."[25]

Community Development Block Grants, begun in 1974, extended the revenue sharing idea. Washington shut down seven previous programs, including the notorious urban renewal program, and instead gave money to cities to use as they wished for urban improvement.[26] At first, the shift seemed mostly semantic. In Charlotte, the Redevelopment Commission changed its name to the Office of Community Development. Vernon Sawyer, who had sent urban renewal bulldozers to flatten Brooklyn with no plan for replacement housing, remained in charge.[27] But Community Development Block Grant and revenue sharing rules gave decision-making power to local elected officials—a big change.

Once revenue sharing became available, City Council allocated funds to the Charlotte Housing Authority to buy land for scattered-site housing.[28] The CHA didn't move with particular speed, but by 1975 it had four parcels. "A Bold Step: Scattered Site Plan Off to a Good Start," commended a *Charlotte News* editorial.[29]

Charlotte's newspapers played an active role in drumming up popular support, especially the lead editorial writer for the *Observer*, Jack Claiborne. In his reporting career, he had covered both business and civil rights, winning trust among a wide array of readers. "Scattered Site Concept Can Work," he had written as early as 1971.[30] An *Observer* survey the next year "showed a majority of residents favoring a low-unit scattered-site policy for future public housing."[31] Now with land acquired, Claiborne cheered: "[This acquisition] firmly established a long-sought city policy of placing small units of public housing in predominantly white, middle-class neighborhoods, in a non-disruptive way."[32]

Bids were let in 1976 for construction of the first two projects.[33] Both were located in white south Charlotte, though in the middle-income South Boulevard corridor rather than the most elite Providence Road corridor.

- Leafcrest on Archdale Drive, forty-eight units completed in 1979
- Cedar Knoll off Nation's Ford Road, forty-nine units completed in 1979

Two more got underway the following year, both in white middle-class east Charlotte:

- Meadow Oaks, off Rama Road in the Independence Boulevard corridor, thirty-two units completed in 1980
- Sunridge, on Milton Road at Sharon Amity, forty-four units completed in 1980[34]

Each scattered-site project had fifty or fewer apartments. That was part of the consent decree, and it was also now a policy of HUD (which had oversight power on housing funded through revenue sharing). The fifty-unit cap didn't apply to senior citizen complexes; most 1970s and 1980s apartments for the elderly in Charlotte would have 100–150 units. But in all other projects, the *Charlotte Observer* explained, the CHA must not "violate a federal rule that no more than fifty units of subsidized housing can be built on one site, and one site can't be within a half-mile of another."[35]

■ ■ ■ ■ ■

Scattered-site construction might have continued to just putter along, if not for a political revolution in Charlotte.

Figure 6.1. Meadow Oaks scattered-site housing, located off Rama Road in southeast Charlotte. Albert Dulin photo, 2021.

For decades, City Council had been elected at-large, representing the city as a whole rather than any particular neighborhood.[36] That sounded fine, but in reality it meant that only candidates with pockets deep enough to mount a big campaign could run and win. Nearly all elected officials hailed from upscale south Charlotte—wealthy, white, and male.

During the 1970s, as conflicts over civil rights, school busing, and public housing stirred anger in neighborhoods across the city, a rebellion grew. Neighborhood groups organized to collect 5,000 signatures and force a referendum. It ushered in a new, mixed system: seven representatives elected from districts, four elected at-large. Headlined the *Observer*: "Districting Ends Era of Clout for Affluent Southeast Charlotte."[37]

In the first election under the new system, neighborhood-based progressives swept the field, all sympathetic to low-income housing. Top vote-getters at-large in 1977 were a woman, Betty Chafin, and an African American, Harvey Gantt.[38] Both would soon move to Fourth Ward, a center-city neighborhood where young people were renovating abandoned Victorian houses alongside Edwin Towers and Booth Gardens low-income housing. Most of the seven district reps were neighborhood movement insurgents, as well. Don Carroll, for instance, was a former law clerk for Judge McMillan and had helped organize the Elizabeth Neighborhood Association, a group that included renters in NOAH as well as homeowners. Overall, women held 36 percent of City Council seats, African

Dispersing Subsidized Housing throughout the City ■ 125

Figure 6.2. *Charlotte Observer*, November 9, 1977.

Americans held 27 percent (matching their percentage in the city's population), and council's median age lowered to thirty-five years old.[39]

Almost as soon as they took office, the new council members allocated $2 million annually—a large sum in that day—for public housing construction.[40] Gantt, Chafin, and Carroll often led those discussions, all firmly favoring scattered-siting.

Harvey Gantt emerged as a particularly strong advocate. He brought several kinds of expertise to the table. A practicing architect, he co-led Gantt-Huberman

Associates, a busy interracial architectural firm whose work connected him with banks, finance, and government agencies. His training included not just the design of buildings but also the planning of cities, thanks to a master's degree in urban planning from MIT. "Gantt's power of persuasion and leadership ability," said the *Charlotte News*, made him a consensus-builder on City Council and in the community.[41] In 1983, Gantt would win election as Charlotte's first Black mayor—one of the first African Americans to lead a majority-white major US city.

Grassroots Pressure—Backed Up by Judge McMillan

Gantt and colleagues, for all of their official City Council clout, wouldn't have accomplished much without pressure brought by outsiders. Public interest attorney Ted Fillette and grassroots Black activists in low-wealth neighborhoods such as Phyllis Lynch, Louise Sellers, and Luciel McNeel—all backed up by the ever-present threat of action by Judge James McMillan—played large roles in forging Charlotte's political will to act.

"I had probably the single most life-changing event on November 13, 1964," Fillette recalled in an interview. A white southerner born in Alabama, Fillette was an undergraduate at Duke University. "I cut my geology lab and went to hear Dr. King speak at the auditorium on the campus. And that's where I learned what was going on in my home state."[42] King's words inspired him to try community organizing, then law school at Boston University. "[I] saw what urban poverty was like, you know, close up . . . and was exposed to various civil rights lawyers and Legal Aid people up there, in a state that had modern, progressive housing laws, even in the early 1970s. They had everything that North Carolina did not have."

Returning to North Carolina, Fillette interned with George Daly, who was still pursuing the *Harris* lawsuit—now joined with another and renamed *Harris and Kannon v. HUD and City of Charlotte*, but still charging that HUD and local officials had egregiously failed to help people displaced by urban renewal. Fillette found a job with Legal Aid but kept working on *Harris* through numerous twists and turns. His Legal Aid cases often dealt with displacement issues, which in turn added weight to the arguments in *Harris*. He got to know well the federal laws on civil rights and urban displacement.

"When a municipality is using federal money for either urban renewal, transportation projects—like interstate highways, things like that—or community development work, which displaced people from their homes," Fillette explained in his interview, "they were required to provide suitable alternative, affordable housing."⁴³ Charlotte had failed miserably at that during the massive demolition of Brooklyn. As highway construction, code enforcement, and the urban renewal bulldozing of Greenville continued during the 1970s, the city fell further and further behind. "So, we had to get Judge McMillan to *make* them not displace people until they had a place that was affordable," Fillette continued.

One day in 1977, residents of the low-income Black neighborhood of Cherry, led by outspoken thirty-one-year-old Phyllis Lynch, showed up at Fillette's Legal Aid office.⁴⁴ The city was planning large-scale demolition of substandard absentee-owned houses—which would put inhabitants out in the cold. Could Legal Aid help?

"Well, it was 1977, the watershed year when we had district representatives on City Council. . . . And the representative for District 1 [including Cherry] was Don Carroll, former law clerk to Judge McMillan," recalled Fillette, a note of glee in his voice. With Carroll in the lead, Cherry allies rounded up support from Betty Chafin, Harvey Gantt, and other pro-neighborhood members of City Council. They voted to use Community Development Block Grant and revenue sharing money to

> buy out all the absentee landlords, save all the rental housing that was physically sound enough to be worthwhile, demolish the units that were totally unfeasible, and replace those with new *public* housing that the housing authority would build in Cherry, which became Tall Oaks. And, have the city pay the Cherry Community Organization to be the property manager of those rental units that were bought out by the city. Homeowners got to stay, and if they needed rehab money, they could get that. It was the complete opposite approach from what had been urban renewal.⁴⁵

It would take several years, but Tall Oaks opened in the early 1980s, adding fifty units to Charlotte's growing roster of scattered-site public housing.⁴⁶

Cherry's success inspired other neighborhoods. Community leader Louise Sellers in Biddleville, a Black area adjacent to Johnson C. Smith University where absentee landlords owned much of the property, asked Legal Aid to help block a massive demolition plan by the city. "She became my primary client for a year," said Fillette:

> Did you ever see the movie *Norma Rae* [in which Sally Field played a charismatic textile union organizer]? She was our Norma Rae. She would go get in the face of tenants until they agreed they were going to get on the bus and they were going to go to the City Council chambers. She could get a busload to City Council and razz them and fill the chambers and show up

with signs. We never even had to file a lawsuit. It was all about community solidarity."[47]

The city used Community Development Block Grant funds to renovate homes and buy out the worst of the landlords' properties. The CHA constructed Tarlton Hills, a fifty-unit scattered-site public housing development that remains attractive today. "And that's why Biddleville was preserved for forty years, until this recent wave of gentrification," said Fillette in 2019. "That's why there was still a community there."[48]

■ ■ ■ ■ ■

Activists turned the pressure up another notch in 1981. Fillette argued before Judge McMillan that the city was dragging its feet remedying *Harris and Kannon*; the court should appoint a monitor to watch and prod.[49] Years later, Fillette smiled as he recalled, "We made the city pay for an attorney's time to oversee the relocation. That was Fred Hicks. The City Council never realized that Hicks was the law clerk who'd [worked for Judge McMillan on] the *Swann* busing decision!"[50] With Fred Hicks acting as a sheepdog nipping at the city's heels, City Council and the CHA funded twenty-nine-unit West Downs in the Biddleville neighborhood, thirty-two-unit North Clarkson Street Apartments (later renamed Victoria Square) in the Third Ward area near downtown, and fifty-unit Coliseum Drive Apartments off Independence Boulevard.[51]

At the same time, City Council continued to allocate revenue sharing dollars every year for other scattered-site construction. Live Oaks opened about 1981 in the heart of south Charlotte, located on Sharon Road a few steps from elite SouthPark Mall.[52] Savanna Woods debuted the same year off Marsh Road, bringing low-income apartments to south Charlotte's Park Road corridor.[53] Mallard Ridge Apartments opened in the Starmount neighborhood, adding another scattered-site project to the South Boulevard corridor.[54] These followed the rules about siting east of Tryon Street and outside Black or poor existing areas—rules that were sometimes bent in other situations where Black activists specifically requested housing in their own neighborhoods.

■ ■ ■ ■ ■

The most contentious scattered-site success was Gladedale. CHA planned it for a spot right on Providence Road, the spine of south Charlotte's wealthiest corridor. All up and down the ten-mile boulevard, residents erupted in fury.

"I went to that meeting, the neighborhood meeting," Fillette remembered:

There were 500 angry white people there, and they were using the N-word, and "those people," and "We're going to have crime, and we're going to have rapes" and things like that.

And Luciel McNeel was there with me, listening to all of this. . . . In fact, Luciel McNeel had been a domestic servant and used to travel out to Providence Road to clean people's houses.[55] And . . . these people were talking about, "This is a terrible site. Black people will never be able to get into town because there's no bus that comes out to Providence Road, and it'll be inconvenient for them."

She jumped up on her chair and said, "I see you. I used to have to come out to clean your house. You weren't so concerned about how I was going to get to your house, and now you don't want me to have a good house because you're worried about whether I can get a bus ride." And it was hilarious. It was amazing.[56]

Fillette and Leslie Winner at Legal Aid immediately "filed a suit in Federal Court in front of Judge McMillan, claiming that the refusal to rezone the property was based on racial animus from the opposing neighbors and that the city's acquiescence in that was effectively a violation of the Fair Housing Act," Fillette continued.

City Council had no desire to be entangled in yet another court case. The CHA found an alternate site, also prominently located on Providence Road at Old Providence Road, and council quickly rezoned it.

Gladedale opened in 1983.[57] Fillette recalled:

White people on Providence Road saw what it looked like and their children were not raped at the bus stop, their houses were not burglarized, and then they started going to school with the kids that were going there . . . and they would be on the same athletic teams. And the neighborhood didn't disappear. Nobody sold out. There was not even a blockbuster's attempt to terrify the neighbors; it didn't happen.

So that became the case example that subsidized housing can coexist with suburban single-family housing and not ruin the neighborhood.

Subsidizing Investors: Section 8 Project-Based

In the same years that Charlotte launched its own scattered-site initiative, the new Section 8 program from HUD helped fund some thirteen other low-income apartment developments. Four of them were created by the Charlotte Housing Authority, the rest by private companies, sometimes in partnership with local

Figure 6.3. Gladedale, scattered-site success on Providence Road, 1983. Albert Dulin photo, 2020.

nonprofits. Some were new construction, others were renovations of existing buildings under a HUD subprogram called Section 8 Substantial Rehabilitation. All featured intentionally small numbers of units, located on sites geographically dispersed around the city—closely resembling Charlotte's scattered-site projects.

When you say "Section 8," most people think of rental assistance vouchers given to low-income tenants.[58] That is indeed the longest-lasting and most impactful part of Section 8 of the 1974 Housing and Community Development Act, and we'll get to it later in this book. But initially the act's primary thrust was "project-based."[59]

Here's how Section 8 Project-Based worked. If the developer of an apartment project promised to rent to low-income tenants, HUD would guarantee a rent supplement. Tenants would pay no more than 25 percent (later increased to 30 percent) of their income as rent; HUD would send the building's owner a check each month to make up the difference between that and "fair market rent." That helped tenants—but the actual subsidy was "attached to the building," unlike later vouchers that would "follow the tenant." The deal could run forty years or more (rules varied as the program evolved, and HUD also gladly renewed contracts). It gave a low-income apartment building a guaranteed income stream, year in and year out—a golden situation for an owner.[60]

Once Section 8 was up and running, HUD drastically cut back on its other types of construction assistance, especially its grants to local housing authorities.

Washington approved only 37,000 new units of public housing nationally during 1975–79, compared with 275,000 units of Section 8 construction.[61]

Initially, however, Section 8 Project-Based was a tough sell. Local developers showed scant interest in mastering its complexities. HUD officials held a public meeting in Charlotte in late 1975 and placed "request for proposal" ads in the *Observer*, to no avail.[62]

So, HUD shifted gears and reached out to local governments. "Charlotte Housing Authority, along with fourteen other housing authorities in North Carolina, has been invited by HUD to develop 800 units of housing for the elderly and handicapped under the new construction phase of the federally subsidized Section Eight program," reported the *Observer*.[63] The CHA accepted the invitation. It erected Charlottetown Terrace, a 180-unit high-rise for the elderly on urban renewal land overlooking the center city's Pearl Street Park, and Park Towne Terrace, a 163-unit mid-rise for senior citizens near the new SouthPark Mall.[64] The CHA also acquired and renovated two old center-city hotels under Section 8 Substantial Rehabilitation. The former Red Carpet Inn on East Morehead Street and the twelve-story Cavalier Inn (initially built as the Barringer Hotel) on North Tryon Street reopened as low-income apartments in 1978 and 1983.[65]

To finally lure for-profit developers into the game, Washington set up a multibillion-dollar fund to aid Section 8 Project-Based mortgages. "The Section Eight program floundered for the first two years of its existence, according to a HUD official, because there wasn't any long-term financing available. The program became more attractive to private developers when Congress appropriated more than $5 billion for low-cost long-term financing for these projects," explained the *Observer*.[66]

Hang in with me here—this is arcane stuff, but it's an important behind-the-scenes part of how affordable housing gets built still today.

The new dollars went to Ginnie Mae (Government National Mortgage Association, created in 1968; see previous chapter) to buy Section 8 mortgages from the banks that originated them. That reduced the banks' risk. Less risk meant lower interest rates and a longer payback period—thus cheaper monthly payments by the building's owner—which in turn meant lower rent for tenants. "The $5 billion was used to provide 7½ percent, 40-year mortgage financing for multifamily construction," said the *Observer*.[67] The Ginnie Mae fund, said a federal loan officer, "has been the thing that has made the program take off."[68]

Two companies did most of the Section 8 Project-Based work in Charlotte. Westminster was the home-building division of the national wood products giant Weyerhaeuser, then getting into market-rate apartment construction.[69] With a staff of experienced accountants already at work, Section 8 apartments seemed an easy next step. Among Westminster's four local projects was Hillcrest Apartments (1982) on Arnold Drive in east Charlotte with forty-eight units.[70]

The other Section 8 builder was Crosland, on its way to becoming Charlotte's biggest multifamily developer. Crosland was growing adept at navigating the new world of tax shelters and HUD grants, and it had a passion for low-income projects. The company had recruited Paul Leonard, the former Presbyterian minister whom we met in chapter 5, from the nonprofit MOTION, where he'd collaborated with Crosland to put together Section 236 low-rent Orchard Park and Greenhaven Apartments.[71]

Leonard saw Section 8 projects as a natural part of the portfolio that also included high-end developments adjacent to the elite Country Day School and Quail Hollow Country Club. Wrote the *Observer*:

> All are set up the same way, Leonard said. After the Crosland company plans and develops a project, a partnership [LLC] is formed with either the company, President John Crosland, Jr., or the Crosland family as general partner. Interest is then sold to investors, who become limited partners.
>
> Leonard said investors must be in a 50 percent tax bracket [the highest bracket at that time] so the full tax-shelter aspects of apartment ownership, added to the cash flow, give them a healthy return on their investment.[72]

For low-income projects, Leonard then layered the Section 8 incentives on top of the tax-shelter breaks—a legally permissible "double dip" at the federal feed trough.

> "It might blow the mind of someone starting out," Leonard said, "because of the rules and regulations and delays, but if you allow enough lead time and deal with the people who handle the processing... you can make the programs work."
>
> One benefit of patience in dealing with FHA [the HUD division that oversaw Section 8 Project-Based], Leonard said, is the availability of lower 7½ percent, 40-year loans—permitting a lower rent structure and enabling Crosland to borrow more of the construction costs.
>
> Does his background as a minister interested in low-income families reflect itself in the various low-income apartment projects Crosland has built? Leonard leaned back, thought a minute and said, "It reflects more of an area of business where we can make a profit and also perform some service. Because of the subsidy programs, we can do some things where nothing else will work."[73]

Under Leonard's leadership, Crosland completed Hollis House (1978) off South Boulevard, a fifty-unit low-rent complex very much like the CHA's scattered-site projects.[74] Fairmarket Plaza, 120 units for low-income elderly, opened on Plaza Road in 1979.[75] Crosland also used Section 8 Substantial Rehabilitation aid to acquire and renovate three of C. D. Spangler's circa-1950 FHA 608 projects (see chapter 3): Double Oaks, Tryon Hills, and Westwood.[76]

Analysis: Looking Back at Scattered-Site Housing

Thanks to the city's scattered-site program and HUD's Section 8 Project-Based developments—all done in the same spirit—Charlotte decentralized its low-income housing much more dramatically than most US cities during the 1970s and 1980s.

When New York City's suburb of Yonkers made national headlines for blocking scattered-site housing in 1988, Tom Ray—now on County Commission—pointed out that "Charlotte is light years ahead of Yonkers. Instead of choosing resistance and procrastination to the point of defiance, Charlotte successfully began scattering its public housing some fifteen years ago."[77] *New York Times* columnist Tom Wicker echoed Ray: "Yonkers: Learn from Charlotte."[78]

In Chicago, where the US Supreme Court had required scattered-site public housing under its landmark 1976 *Gautreaux* decision, only 358 apartment units had been built by 1987 across a metro area of more than 7 million people.[79] By contrast, Charlotte could boast of 770 apartments by that time, serving a much smaller metro of less than half a million.

A national study of seventy-four US metro regions, looking at changes in housing and other indicators during the 1980s, found Charlotte in the top five in "relative improvements in equity" and "residential integration of the poor," thanks in large part to City Council's scattered-site policy.[80]

How had that happened? It may have helped that Charlotte did not have well-organized suburbs. North Carolina law gave cities the power to annex any adjacent built-up area. Where New York City and Chicago faced off against suburban governments, Charlotte's prosperous and predominantly white areas at the edges of the city did not possess strong local governments of their own.[81] In other metro areas, suburban governments effectively blocked scattered-site housing; that did not occur in Charlotte.

Political will played perhaps a larger part. That intangible is often mentioned in political analysis—but it is seldom clear how it comes about. The appetite for scattered-site housing in Charlotte resulted from much effort by many people over more than two decades. Fred Alexander had laid groundwork back in the early 1960s with his persistent calls for public housing. President Johnson's leadership played a role, pushing Washington to embrace Reverend King's vision of integration—manifest in the 1968 Fair Housing Act, in policy shifts at HUD, and in the Supreme Court's endorsement of Judge McMillan's 1969 *Swann* decision. At the local level, Charlotte could thank the courageous activism of attorneys Chambers and Lanning, Ray and Casey, and Daly and Fillette, as well as the political leadership of Gantt, Chafin, Carroll, and others inside government, bolstered by Louise Sellers, Jack Claiborne, Paul Leonard, and others working from out in the community.

■ ■ ■ ■ ■

The policy of scattering low-income housing was not perfect—something we will explore in the next chapters—but compared with previous affordable housing strategies, scattered-site represented a definite improvement.

A 1983 survey asked Charlotte public housing residents how they felt about living in the eight scattered-site housing authority projects then available. People responded with

> markedly high levels of general neighborhood satisfaction—only 13.7 percent of the respondents were "dissatisfied" or "very dissatisfied." . . .
>
> [Looking at specific factors,] satisfaction ranged from a low of 50 percent for easy access to public transportation (a result, perhaps, of the fact that only 42 percent of the households owned an automobile) to 97 percent who were either "satisfied" or "very satisfied" with the size of the project.
>
> Residents were generally highly satisfied with the neighborhood and with their neighbors. For example, 94 percent considered their neighbors "good" people . . . ; 93 percent were satisfied with the apartment unit; and 68 percent appraised the neighborhood as "much better" than where they previously lived.[82]

Likewise, scattered-site projects did not hurt surrounding neighborhoods, another careful study showed. A University of North Carolina at Charlotte researcher charted house prices over ten years around scattered-site complexes and then compared them with neighborhoods elsewhere in the city. House prices went up everywhere—"from 84 percent to 127 percent over the study period."[83] And if house prices already were going up in a neighborhood before public housing got built, the prices continued on exactly the same trajectory afterward.

When HUD commissioned political scientist James B. Hogan to examine scattered-site policies nationwide in 1996, his review of three dozen studies cor-

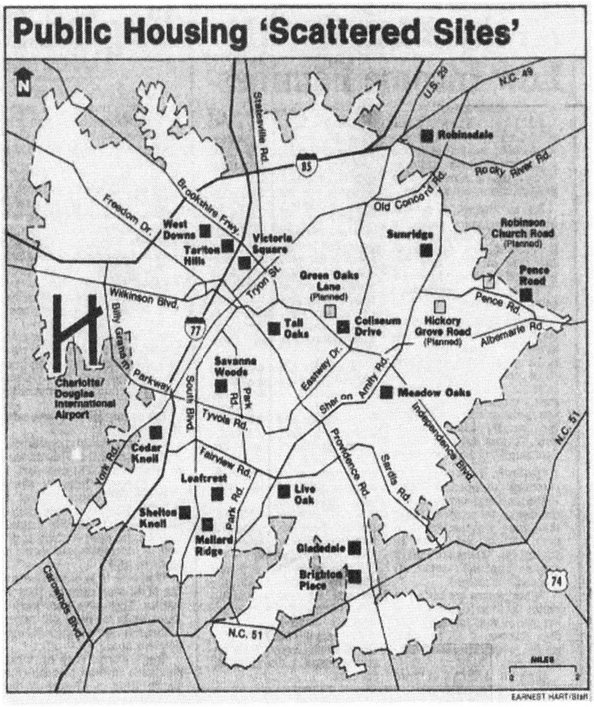

Public Housing 'Scattered Sites'

Figure 6.4. Charlotte's scattered-site program wrapped up in 1987. Most complexes were located in majority-white and relatively wealthy south/southeast Charlotte. *Charlotte Observer*, October 19, 1987.

roborated the Charlotte findings. Living out in the suburbs pleased tenants, despite "significant dissatisfaction with [access to] public transportation." Hogan's study singled out Charlotte for its "high levels of tenant satisfaction."[84]

And the scattered-site developments caused no decline in property values. Wrote Hogan: "No causal connection exists between [scattered public housing] facilities and the loss of value in neighborhood homes."

■ ■ ■ ■ ■

Those realities, sadly, had little impact on housing debates within Charlotte. No matter how well the developments fit into suburban neighborhoods, each new proposal ignited intense opposition.

By the late 1980s, scattered-site public housing could be found at nearly every point of the compass in Charlotte. Twenty-one Charlotte-initiated projects plus thirteen Section 8 Project-Based complexes coexisted peacefully with suburban neighbors, who often were not even aware that low-income folks lived nearby.

Decades later, Harvey Gantt still relished the accomplishment:

> Years ago, I used to do this: take people into those neighborhoods where we built those . . . scattered-site units. Drive them by and see the rest of the neighborhood and say: "You saw some public housing." They'd say: "Where?" I'd say: "See, you didn't even notice it."
>
> You didn't notice it. But those people who live over here have an advantage of shopping at nicer grocery stores and maybe their kids will get to go to a school that's better resourced.[85]

But nonetheless, Gantt mused sadly in 2021, "those policies were fought tooth and nail by neighborhoods and others. There was a lot of resistance . . . not only on the part of the politicians elected by those [neighborhoods], but by the developers, vehemently."[86]

Scattered-site housing was especially vulnerable to opposition, ironically. The fifty-unit cap, which was good for both tenants and neighbors, meant that many, many projects would be needed to meet Charlotte's needs. The twenty-one scattered-site projects discussed above created only 946 living units in total—about the same number as Charlotte's two initial public housing projects back in 1940.

Proponents hoped that opposition would slacken as people realized how much better the new way was. But it never did. Resistance would continue, decade after decade, soaking up the time and resources of affordable housing advocates.

Table 6.1. Scattered-Site Housing Built in Charlotte, 1979–1989 Developed by the Charlotte Housing Authority (renamed Inlivian in 2019)

Development	Opened	Units	Status in 2022
Leafcrest 6513 Leafcrest Ln off Archdale Dr 28210	1979	48	owned by Inlivian
Cedar Knoll 304 Green Needles Ct off Nations Ford 29217	1979	49	owned by Inlivian
Meadow Oaks 6011 Florence Av off Rama Rd (Independence Blvd corridor) 28212	1980	32	owned by Inlivian
Sunridge 4005 Sunridge Ln on Milton Rd (Plaza Road corridor) 28215	1980	44	owned by Inlivian
Live Oaks on Sharon Rd (near SouthPark Mall) 28210	1981	32	replaced by Ashley Square, mixed-income, by Inlivian
Savanna Woods 3124 Leaside Ln (off Marsh Rd) 28209	1981	49	owned by Inlivian
Mallard Ridge 1428 Axminster Ct (Starmount off South Blvd) (originally Muddy Pond Ln) 28203	1981	35	owned by Inlivian
Gladedale 5805 Old Providence Rd 28226	1983	49	owned by Inlivian
Wallace Woods 7120 Wallace Rd (near E Meck High) 28212	1980s	48	owned by Inlivian
N Clarkson St Apts (renamed Victoria Sq) 225 N Clarkson (3rd Ward)	1984	32	owned by Inlivian
Coliseum Dr Apts (renamed Claremont Apts) Coliseum Dr (off Independence Blvd)	1984	50	owned by Inlivian
Tall Oaks 201 Baldwin Av (Cherry)	1984	50	redeveloped by Inlivian

Table 6.1. (*continued*)

Development	Opened	Units	Status in 2022
Tarlton Hills 201 Frazier Av (Biddleville)	1984	50	owned by Inlivian
Robinsdale 10001 Margie Ann Dr (off Old Concord Rd)	1985	30	owned by Inlivian
West Downs I & II 325 Mattoon St (Biddleville)	1983 & 1986	29	owned by DreamKey Partners
Shelton Knoll 516 Arrowhawk Dr (Old Pineville Rd off Arrowood)	1986	49	owned by DreamKey Partners
Brighton Pl Apts 3412 Hilldale Way (off Swan Run, Arboretum)	1986	49	owned by DreamKey Partners
Pleasant View Apts 8225 Pence Rd (JH Gunn area)	1987	85	owned by DreamKey Partners
Oak Valley 2700 Oak Valley Ln (off Green Oaks Ln near Central Av)	1988	50	owned by Inlivian
Valley View 5117 Hickory Valley Ct (off Hickory Grove Rd near Shamrock)	1988	50	owned by Inlivian
Grove Place 6059 WT Harris (near Robinson Church Rd)	1989	36	owned by Inlivian
Total complexes: 21		Total units: 946	

Source: Table excerpted from Tom Hanchett, "Master List of Low-Income Multifamily Housing Constructed in Charlotte, 1940–2019," in the data collection of J. Murrey Atkins Library, University of North Carolina at Charlotte, https://doi.org/10.15139/S3/XQBOFW.

Table 6.2. Section 8 Project-Based Housing Built in Charlotte, 1976–1986

Development	Opened	Developer	Units
Booth Gardens (senior) 423 N Poplar St (4th Ward)	1976	Salvation Army/Crosland	130
Charlottetown Terrace (senior) 1000 Baxter St	1976	Charlotte Housing Authority	180
Park Towne Terrace (senior) 5800 Park Rd (now Fairview Rd)	1977	Charlotte Housing Authority	163
*Red Carpet Inn 605 E Morehead St (center city)	1978	Charlotte Housing Authority	150
Fairmarket Plaza 6427 Plaza Road Extension	1979	Crosland	120
Farm Lane Apartments 5500 Farm Pond Ln (off Albemarle Rd)	1979	Westminster	120
Hollis House 3423 Weston St (near Sedgefield off S Blvd)	1979	Crosland	50
Midland Commons 2457 Midland Av (off Wilkinson)	1980	Fred D. Godley Jr.	60
Woodstone Apartments 4826 Woodstone Dr (Derita)	1980	Westminster (with MOTION)	50
Hillcrest Apartments 2603 Arnold Dr (off Central Av)	1982	Westminster	48
Victoria Townhouses W 4th St (3rd Ward)	1982	Westminster (with MOTION)	31
*Cavalier Inn (Barringer Hotel) 426 N Tryon (center city)	1983	Charlotte Housing Authority	190
Grier Park Apartments 3424 Arbor Ln (Grier Heights)	1983	Westminster	50
Total Section 8 complexes: 13			Total units: 1,342

*Renovated under the Section 8 Substantial Rehabilitation program.

Note: In addition, Double Oaks, Tryon Hills, and Westwood (existing low-income complexes built by C. D. Spangler via FHA 608 circa 1950) were renovated by Crosland in 1981 under the Section 8 Substantial Rehabilitation program.

Source: Table excerpted from Tom Hanchett, "Master List of Low-Income Multifamily Housing Constructed in Charlotte, 1940–2019," in the data collection of J. Murrey Atkins Library, University of North Carolina at Charlotte, https://doi.org/10.15139/S3/XQBOFW.

"So Much Dilapidated, Terrible Housing"
Tackling Systemic Problems in NOAH

As important as Ted Fillette's work was in spurring construction of new scattered-site public housing, his deeper passion lay in addressing systemic issues that plagued Charlotte's supply of naturally occurring affordable housing (NOAH). Fillette knew that public housing filled only a tiny fraction of the need for low-income rentals. Ten times as much came in the form of old houses and existing apartments where rents dropped as buildings aged.

Keeping those properties in good condition required vigilance by code enforcement officials. But the city had slacked off. Back in the late 1940s and early 1950s, the Realtors' Standard House Ordinance and aggressive enforcement of its requirements (see chapter 4) had pushed landlords to supply indoor plumbing, electrical systems, and such in their low-rent apartments. But then, from the early 1950s into the 1960s, the federal urban renewal program took the city's eye off the ball. Wholesale demolition seemed so much sexier than code enforcement.

Federal urban renewal officials noticed. During the 1960s they began to press the city to get serious about addressing run-down conditions, threatening to withhold urban renewal dollars if the situation did not improve. Charlotte instituted a housing code in 1962, requiring property owners to provide decent accommodations and keep them in good repair. (Unlike the earlier building code, which focused on new construction, the housing code explicitly covered existing structures.)* But in practice the city typically demolished the dwellings that inspectors found to be substandard—which resulted in the housing shortages that Fillette, Harvey Gantt, Betty Chafin, Louise Sellers, and others battled against during the 1970s and 1980s.

In a 2019 interview, Fillette explained the systemic legal context:

> There was no mystery about why there was so much dilapidated, terrible housing.... It's because the landlords were able to provide the most minimal structures, including shotgun houses with no operable heat, ... and there was no prohibition against that.... There had never been any legal right, for 200 years, for any tenant to have any repairs. The whole rental inventory of housing was in terrible shape....
>
> *(continued)*

---

*Ted Fillette, written communication to Tom Hanchett, March 25, 2022. "The Charlotte Housing Code," said Fillette, now "has 144 subsections and covers structure, wiring, plumbing HVACs, roof, flooring, walls, drainage, rodents, insects, locks, etc."

>The entire legal system was oriented towards maintaining the status quo with respect to economic conditions and housing and employment relationships.... The housing law, which was governed mostly by common law, essentially worked like this: landlords had no duty to provide fit and habitable housing to their tenant unless they gratuitously agreed to do that.... Leases could be written or oral; they could be for any amount of time. Most low-income people's leases in 1973 were oral and on a week-to-week basis. And under North Carolina law, a week-to-week lease could be terminated by giving two days' notice to the tenant.[†]

Tenants learned not to request repairs or to contact building inspectors, for fear of being evicted.

Ted Fillette and other housing activists struggled to find ways to put some legal weight behind building code enforcement. If a local government fell short, could tenants sue it in court? Not as the laws were written in 1973, the housing advocates discovered.

So Fillette and allies worked to get a "habitable housing" requirement added to state law. It was an uphill battle, since many North Carolina elected officials were themselves investors in rental property—"a legislature that was dominated by landlords who would not vote for the public interest against their personal business interest." The effort took years of lobbying, culminating in "passage of the N.C. Residential Rental Agreements Act sponsored by Rep. Henry Frye in the 1977 session."[‡]

In 1979 Fillette's team also convinced Mecklenburg's state legislator Parks Helms to push through a state law forbidding "retaliatory evictions."[**] Says Fillette, "The people that helped us convince him to sponsor it were Betty Chafin, Don Carroll, and Harvey Gantt. And the main argument they used—they were on the City Council—was that the city could not do effective code enforcement because the tenants were terrified." Fearing retaliatory evictions, tenants would not allow code inspectors to enter their dwellings.

(continued)

[†] All quotations in this sidebar, except as noted, are from Ted Fillette, interview by Tom Hanchett, May 12, 2019.

[‡] For more on the legislation: "Poor Renters Need a Break," *Charlotte Observer*, May 20, 1977; "Facing Winter in the Chill—at Home," *Charlotte Observer*, December 23, 1977; Fillette, "North Carolina Residential Rental Agreements Act"; NC Gen. Stat. 42–38 et seq.

[**] NC Gen. Stat. 42–37.1 et seq.

The successes of the 1970s improved affordable housing in Charlotte and statewide. But still today, maintenance by landlords and diligent code enforcement by city officials is not a "done deal." Ted Fillette retired from the Charlotte office of Legal Aid of North Carolina (one of two legal advocacy organizations that evolved from the original Legal Aid Society of Mecklenburg County) in 2018, but its team of lawyers continues to work extensively with tenants who struggle to have decent housing.

CHAPTER 7

1980s Housing Revolution
Inventing the Low-Income Housing Tax Credit Era

- Low-Income Housing Tax Credit
- North Carolina Housing Finance Agency and North Carolina Housing Trust Fund
- Charlotte's Innovative Housing Fund (Today Charlotte Housing Trust Fund)
- Section 8 Vouchers

President Ronald Reagan's election in 1980 ushered in a sweeping reorganization of America's multifamily affordable housing efforts. Eager to cut government programs, Congress terminated Section 8 Project-Based subsidies in 1983. For the first time since the early 1960s, Washington offered no aid for low-income apartment construction.

Housing advocates—not only anti-poverty activists but also real estate developers—scrambled to come up with alternatives. Charlotte people, notably developer John Crosland Jr. and civic leader Betty Chafin Rash, played key roles locally and statewide. The resulting toolkit was not planned in advance but sprang up piecemeal during the years 1983–88:

- The **Low-Income Housing Tax Credit** (LIHTC, pronounced "lie-tek," rhyming with "high tech") from Washington gave a tax shelter to wealthy investors who put up cash to construct affordable apartments.[1]
- A new type of **Section 8**—the vouchers we know today—helped low-income people to rent anywhere (at least that's the theory) in the city.
- The **North Carolina Housing Finance Agency** (NCHFA) selected which proposals would receive the very scarce LIHTC aid. The NCHFA also launched a **North Carolina Housing Trust Fund** to give out small grants to "help make the numbers work" in LIHTC projects.

- The City of Charlotte's Innovative Housing Fund (later reconfigured as today's **Charlotte Housing Trust Fund**) helped close financing gaps, getting deals to happen.
- Navigating this system required **highly specialized experts**. That could be a for-profit developer, such as the Crosland firm (its successor today is Laurel Street Residential). Or it could be a nonprofit, such as the new Charlotte–Mecklenburg Housing Partnership (now DreamKey Partners). Or it could be the old-line Charlotte Housing Authority (today Inlivian), which eventually cultivated this new expertise.
- At the same time, **all of the existing, previously constructed affordable housing** (more than sixty apartment complexes in Charlotte) still required management, maintenance, tenant screening, and the like. So, all of the entities that had developed/owned those projects, discussed in previous chapters, remained players in Charlotte's housing scene.

Today four decades later, this system—with its interplay of government assistance and business profit—remains the way that America builds low-income housing.

Thinking about Housing in the Era of Ronald Reagan

Q: What are the nine most terrifying words in the English language?
A: "I'm from the government and I'm here to help."

President Reagan told that joke with a genial smile, but he was completely serious.[2] Government was the problem, he asserted, not a solution to problems.[3] Reagan's election marked a turning point in America's general attitude about how to approach societal challenges. Ever since President Franklin Roosevelt's New Deal helped ease the suffering wrought by the Great Depression, there had been something of a consensus. Government, directed by the will of the people as expressed through their votes, could be a powerful tool for good. Is there, for instance, a persistent problem with bad housing for low-income Americans? Under the New Deal consensus, publicly owned housing could be a big part of the answer. But by the 1980s, American were weary of fighting over government actions—ranging from the war in Vietnam to close-to-home issues such as school busing and public housing. What if we just shrank government's role in our lives?

The New Deal consensus had shaped policies throughout both Democratic and Republican presidencies, from FDR through Richard Nixon and Jimmy Carter. Likewise, the Reagan consensus would also carry great philosophical power, no matter which party held the White House, well into the 2020s.

In housing, as we have seen, the reality in 1980 was that government was deeply intertwined with multifamily construction—in ways that few people outside of the real estate industry understood. At the federal level, FHA mortgage insurance (introduced in 1935) and depreciation-based tax shelters (introduced in 1954) had ushered in the era of big suburban apartment complexes. Local governments' building codes, after decades of struggle, had finally become strong enough that both new and used housing were almost always fit to live in. On top of that bedrock, Washington had experimented with layering on additional subsidies to spark low-income housing construction. Section 236 and Section 8 Project-Based in the 1970s were the latest mechanisms to put extra dollars into businessmen's pockets.

Ironically, those dollars often were not regarded as government aid. Nationally syndicated financial columnist Sylvia Porter illustrated the mindset perfectly when Section 236 debuted: "Washington is eager to see you take advantage of these breaks in order to . . . pull private enterprise (as opposed to the federal government) into low-cost housing."[4]

That disconnect—the embrace of government help, as long as it went to "private enterprise"—set the stage for the housing policies of the 1980s. The programs we're about to discuss worked in ways that not only produced new low-income housing but also inspired powerful business leaders to advocate on their behalf.

North Carolina Housing Finance Agency

While Washington's Low-Income Housing Tax Credit would become the heartbeat of the system created in the 1980s, the first piece to be put in place was at the state level. Developers reinvented North Carolina's small and little-known Housing Finance Agency in an effort to partially make up for Washington's exit from affordable construction.

Our discussion so far in this book has been almost entirely about the federal government and local government—but next to nothing about state government. That changed as Reagan-era efforts to shrink the federal government had the unexpected effect of expanding North Carolina's state government into the urban low-income housing arena for the first time.

The North Carolina Housing Finance Agency had been created back in 1974, but for most of its initial decade it was a tiny operation focused on the countryside. Rural low-income people, many struggling to escape the old sharecropping system of agriculture, needed help securing low-interest, low-down-payment mortgages so they might buy a home. The NCHFA provided mortgage aid and did financial literacy education, making a small dent in the problem. Howard N.

Lee oversaw the agency.[5] He had grown up in a sharecropping family, risen to become one of the nation's first Black mayors of a white municipality, Chapel Hill, and now served as chief of North Carolina's Department of Natural and Economic Resources.

The agency's mortgage-aid dollars came from tax-free bonds issued by the state of North Carolina. What's a tax-free bond? A "bond" is a piece of paper saying that the government promises to repay a loan. Under a normal bond arrangement, the government borrows money from an investor, uses it for a public good, then pays it back with interest—giving the investor a profit.[6] Under the "tax-free" provision, the government charges the investor no income tax on that profit. The investor, nicely compensated by the tax saving, will be willing to take a smaller interest rate. So, if the state of North Carolina, for example, issued bonds to create a pool of mortgage money, it could charge homebuyers a below-market interest rate.

When John Crosland Jr. became chair of the NCHFA citizen advisory board in 1978, he brought a background sharply different from Howard Lee's.[7] Crosland not only headed his own John Crosland homebuilding firm, one of the largest in the state, but he was also the longtime president of the North Carolina Home Builders Association, a highly effective lobbying group. The building industry was North Carolina's "most persistent and muscled interest group," a newspaper profile noted, describing Crosland as "a man who parlays a dominant position in his industry into a dominant voice in public policy."[8] A state legislator put it simply: "People listen when John talks."[9]

Housing affordability was a frequent Crosland talking point. "For almost 50 years John Crosland has been building affordable quality homes—over 10,000 homes in more than 50 neighborhoods," ran a typical company ad in the mid-1980s.[10] "Affordable" was not synonymous with "low-income," a meaning that the term has taken in our own time. Instead, Crosland saw himself as a champion of a wide range of actions that could cut costs for developers and thus bring prices down for homebuyers and renters. Things that roused Crosland's ire included rules requiring curbs and gutters in new subdivisions or fire sprinklers in wood-frame apartments.[11] But his self-identification with affordability meant that Crosland was genuinely receptive when it came to issues of housing for the needy—much more receptive than any other homebuilder in the Charlotte market. Crosland had hired Paul Leonard back in 1973; the former preacher who had built homes for his low-income flock would become Crosland company president in the 1980s. And in those same years, John Crosland himself would become a trailblazing advocate for Habitat for Humanity (see the sidebar "Habitat for Humanity").

As new chair of the North Carolina Housing Finance Agency, Crosland looked for ways both to help needy North Carolinians and to aid his fellow homebuilders. Getting to know the agency's work, Crosland heard from advocates who wanted it to do more. "[The NCHFA] hasn't given any money to urban areas or for multifamily housing," pointed out Charlotte housing activist Don Carroll in 1980, calling for the agency to "issue bonds for long-term financing of multifamily housing."[12] Later that year, the NCHFA for the first time issued bonds for construction of low- and moderate-income apartments, creating a $24 million loan pool. All went to rural small towns, continuing Howard Lee's focus on the state's poorest areas.[13]

John Crosland chafed at what he regarded as Lee's narrow goal. Crosland and NCHFA attorney Travis Porter—who was also chief lobbyist for the North Carolina Home Builders Association—searched for a way to wrest control away from Lee and also from state treasurer Harlan Boyles, who did not like committing the state to big bond issues. The *Raleigh News and Observer* succinctly summarized what was at stake:

> Crosland and the [building] industry, which dominate the agency's board, have fought attempts by Howard N. Lee . . . to promote housing for the poor.
>
> Industry officials want to operate the agency as a financial institution that would not only provide housing for the poor but also boost the building industry.[14]

Crosland and Porter came up with an audacious strategy. They wrote a bill that took the NCHFA out of Lee's purview and put it in another wing of state government. The same bill stripped state treasurer Boyles of any authority to oversee NCHFA bond issues. "It's a special interests bill all the way," sputtered Boyles to the *News and Observer*. "It would put it (the agency) completely in the hands of one segment of our economy."[15]

And that is exactly what happened.

The aspect that ultimately won the legislature's approval, in addition to lobbying from builders, was Crosland's smart structuring of the agency's own finances so that—remarkably—it required no budget from state government. Every time the NCHFA sold bonds, it earmarked a few of those dollars to pay its staff expenses.

That didn't mean it cost the state nothing. The tax-free nature of the bonds still represented a substantial government subsidy. But to most observers, the arrangement made the NCHFA seem like a shining example of the idea that business, "freed" from government, can solve society's problems.

With its next bond issue, $52 million in 1983, the NCHFA agreed to lend in Charlotte and the state's other big cities. Wachovia Bank of Winston-Salem handled the sales and paperwork. As expected, the tax-free bonds worked their charm. Explained *Observer* business editor M. S. VanHecke: "The bonds permit developers to obtain 40-year financing at slightly more than 11 percent, unusually low in today's market," at a time when standard rates hovered near 16 percent.[16]

A great advantage of bonds was that they could be sold nationwide. This pulled new money into North Carolina housing. Said Gary Paul Kane, a tax and finance attorney who became staff director at the NCHFA in 1981, "All of a sudden we could appeal to all kinds of life insurance companies, pension funds and other investors."[17]

Two developers built projects in Charlotte under the 1983 bond issue. Westminster Corporation—the Weyerhaeuser affiliate we met in the Section 8 Project-Based discussion in chapter 6—constructed Grier Park Apartments in the Black neighborhood of Grier Heights. J. M. Dixon, another Greensboro firm, built Westside Apartments at Freedom Drive and Toddville Road. In keeping with recommendations of both HUD and also the City of Charlotte's scattered-site policy (see previous chapter), the two complexes each had fifty units.[18] Both were in African American areas but were not near any existing public housing.

During John Crosland Jr.'s tenure as chair, lasting to 1989, the NCHFA's tax-free bonds became a major force for multifamily affordable housing in North Carolina. "John gave the organization a sense of urgency," recalled Bob Kucab, the NCHFA's longtime paid executive. "Before John came, the financing activity for the organization totaled about $16 million a year. During the years John was chairman, the financing averaged about $160 million a year, so it increased ten-fold."[19]

Over time, the NCHFA would also be tapped to manage federal housing programs that required state-level decision-making. How do Section 8 rent vouchers get distributed? Which projects receive the scarce Low-Income Housing Tax Credit? As we learn about these programs in the next sections of this chapter, keep in mind that the NCHFA is part of what makes them go.

Section 8: From Project-Based to Vouchers

The housing voucher idea had been around for a while. President Johnson mentioned it in his 1965 speech launching HUD. President Nixon oversaw an early 1970s pilot called the Experimental Housing Allowance Program.[20] Low-income persons received vouchers that made up the gap between the rent they could afford (30 percent of their monthly income) and regular market-rate rent.

This differed from previous types of aid, which had all gone to developers of buildings.

With President Reagan in office, vouchers seemed like an idea whose time had come. They were "market-based," an attractive feature in the eyes of Reagan's followers. Renters could "shop" for the neighborhood and apartment of their choice—and the magic of "competition in the marketplace" would result in lower prices and better outcomes than under the heavy hand of government. HUD initiated the Section 8 voucher program in 1983, and it remains the United States' largest tool for affordable housing today (see chapter 9).[21]

Vouchers in place, Congress zeroed out the Section 8 Project-Based program in 1983, except for projects already in the pipeline.[22] Even the *Charlotte Observer* editorial board, long an advocate for public housing, liked Washington's fresh direction. Vouchers would sweep away "complicated and cumbersome" old policies that were "unnecessarily intrusive into the market," forecasted the *Observer*, "without reducing benefits to those who need help."[23]

Early optimism turned to criticism, however, as the effects of the 1983 cuts sank in. John Crosland Jr. offered a critique that must have surprised many observers. Crosland regularly contributed columns to the *Charlotte News* that railed against "excessive and costly government regulations that contribute to the rising cost of housing."[24] But when it came to constructing affordable multifamily apartments, Crosland knew from experience that government subsidies made the wheels turn.

"The government is really almost out of it," he complained to the *Observer* in 1985. "The only thing new they've introduced is the voucher.... The voucher goes with the individual.... And because it is not tied to a particular structure, it does not encourage the building [of new low-income housing]. It absolutely doesn't."[25]

Complaints like that were coming from every direction by 1985, locally and nationally. In Charlotte, people as different as high-powered businessman John Crosland and Caroline Myers at the homeless aid agency Crisis Assistance Ministry all agreed. "If [the federal] government is going to drop out," summed up Myers, "who is going to pick it up? So far nobody seems to have the answer."[26]

North Carolina Housing Trust Fund

One answer to Reagan's funding vacuum came in the form of a new state-level initiative, the North Carolina Housing Trust Fund. Betty Chafin Rash, an advocate for housing in her years on Charlotte City Council, played a major role in making it a reality by 1987.

The idea that a governmental entity might set aside a pool of dollars to be loaned or granted was on many lips in the early and mid-1980s. In Charlotte, urban geography professor James W. Clay of the University of North Carolina at Charlotte led a task force of local leaders, including Betty Chafin Rash and John Crosland Jr., on a 1981 trip to explore housing tools in Baltimore. They returned with a recommendation that Charlotte "create a self-sufficient loan program financed through a bond issue to make below-market home loans available to low- and moderate-income families."[27]

The idea didn't take hold immediately, but as Reagan's housing drought deepened, Betty Chafin Rash and others kept bringing up the trust fund possibility. Could it work at the state level? Rash, tapped to cochair a North Carolina Housing Commission in the mid-1980s, organized a series of public workshops across the state that hammered out details, built support, and generated news media coverage.

An initial workshop in March 1985 in Charlotte brought together elected officials, community activists, and business leaders to talk, at the request of the local Council for Children. Making that entity the convener helped position the trust fund as a broad community issue. "Of all the needs children in Charlotte face, the Council reports, more low-income housing is one of the most urgent," said an *Observer* editorial, noting that one-third of low-income single parents lived in subsidized housing.[28]

Rash's workshops caught the attention of a powerful ally, state senator Tony Rand of Fayetteville. A top dog at the capitol in Raleigh, Rand had a knack for finding issues that resonated statewide. He'd "launch a charm offensive and build consensus," Governor Mike Easley later recalled, "but if he felt you were hurting those in need, he could become a vicious foe."[29] Rand convened a study commission on the housing situation. Leaders from communities of every size agreed that housing aid, in the face of the Reagan drought, had become a North Carolina priority.

Senator Rand, now fully committed, cast about for a source of dollars to start the trust fund.[30] A recent court case had convicted oil companies of manipulating tax shelters to overcharge North Carolinians. The state could use the $19.6 million settlement to launch the trust fund. Black legislator Mel Watt (an ally—and Fourth Ward neighbor—of Harvey Gantt and Betty Chafin Rash), cosponsored Rand's bill.[31]

In August 1987, the North Carolina Housing Trust Fund became law.[32] The North Carolina Housing Finance Agency took on the task of managing it and making the decisions about which projects would receive loans or grants.[33] Over the years, the North Carolina Housing Trust Fund has tapped various income sources, including tax dollars appropriated annually by the state legislature starting in 2005. The trust fund aid, usually combined with other dollars, continues to be part of most affordable housing projects in North Carolina today.

Low-Income Housing Tax Credit: "The Last True Tax Shelter Left"

The North Carolina Housing Trust Fund provided part of the answer to the question of how the nation would handle Reagan's 1983 withdrawal of federal housing help. A much bigger piece of the puzzle arrived—quite unexpectedly—from Washington.

Three years of outcry from developers, housing advocates, and state and local elected officials—as we've seen in the North Carolina Housing Trust Fund discussion—chipped away at Congress's resistance to affordable housing. Legislators began looking to get back into the game, albeit in a new and small way. In 1986 President Reagan signed into law the Low-Income Housing Tax Credit program. LIHTC would become the linchpin of the housing system that continues today.[34]

LIHTC was something of an afterthought to massive Reagan-inspired fiddling with the US Tax Code in 1981 and 1986. As Reagan took office, Congress did yet another of its adjustments to depreciation rules—beloved by investors yet almost invisible to the general public. Something called the Accelerated Cost Recovery System kicked the deprecation tax shelter into overdrive, a massive gift to the US real estate industry. New rules set the "useful life" of a building at just fifteen years, half of what it had been previously. That meant that a developer could deduct an astounding 31 percent of a building's cost in the first three years. Developers danced with glee. New construction of income-producing buildings soared 56 percent by 1985, leading to an epidemic of overbuilding.[35] In Charlotte, multifamily permits went from about 1,500 units in 1982 to over 4,000 in 1985 as the wave neared its crest.[36] That exceeded even the frenzy of the early 1970s—similarly fueled by tax shelters. In both booms, you'll note, Washington's huge tax subsidy went almost entirely to market-rate projects, not to low-income.

Alarmed by the overbuilding, Congress backtracked. Its 1986 Tax Act reset the depreciation tax shelter to 1970s levels.[37] One new shelter appeared: the Low-Income Housing Tax Credit. It was a much smaller and tightly focused subsidy that gave investors an investment tax credit if they built low-income rental housing.[38]

What's an investment tax credit? Instead of mumbo jumbo about depreciation losses (which were arbitrary fictions, as we discussed in chapter 5), the investment tax credit gave an investor a straightforward tax reduction. That made it

Habitat for Humanity

As Charlotte and the nation coped with Washington's pullback from affordable housing in the early and mid-1980s, a nonprofit called Habitat for Humanity offered a ray of hope. The faith-based organization had begun as a self-help effort in rural Georgia in 1976. A minister named Millard Fuller organized neighbors, many of them African American, to cooperatively construct basic housing. Donors and volunteer builders worked together with each low-income family, which contributed its own "sweat equity" labor. At the end of the process, the family had a decent small house that it owned. By the early 1980s, Habitat was ready to expand its efforts across the South and beyond. One of the first places outside Georgia to try the Habitat approach was Charlotte.* A group of ministers, each joined by a lay leader in their congregation, visited Fuller in Georgia in 1981. John Crosland Jr., one of the lay leaders, offered the use of his company's Beechcraft jet for the trip.

They returned filled with inspiration. Crosland went congregation to congregation, gathering volunteers. In 1983 the group worked together to build a Habitat house in a depressed area called Optimist Park near downtown. The following year, Habitat's board with Crosland as chair hired a full-time staff director named Julia Maulden. She had served on the school board in the 1970s, one of the voices that convinced Charlotte to accept the Supreme Court's *Swann* busing decision, and then had worked in Africa as a Peace Corps volunteer.

Maulden and her allies invited former president Jimmy Carter to give a fundraising speech in 1985. He had just recently become involved with Habitat, pitching in on a work crew in New York City. Carter liked the energy he saw in Charlotte. In 1987 he and wife Rosalynn joined Charlotte volunteers for a weeklong building session that erected fourteen new Optimist Park houses in just five days—making national headlines. "This is the most exciting, challenging, unpredictable and gratifying thing I've ever done," the former president told the *Washington Post*.†

As exciting as Habitat was, constructing fourteen single-family houses at a time fell far short of meeting the huge need for affordable dwellings. Charlotte's waiting list for public housing had 2,000 names. An *Observer* editorial

(continued)

---

* Gaillard, *If I Were a Carpenter*, 53–88; Yockey, *Builder*, 224–29.
† "Carter Says Building Houses for the Poor One of 'Greatest Blessings,'" *Washington Post*, August 15, 1987.

applauded Habitat's accomplishments but cautioned, "Habitat represents a *limited* solution—a fledgling program overwhelmed by need."‡ Today, Habitat for Humanity remains one valuable component of Charlotte's approach to affordable housing. The organization is headquartered in the John Crosland Jr. Center for Housing, an old shopping plaza that holds a Habitat Re-Store furniture sales/recycling operation, as well as Julia's Cafe, a book-lined gathering spot that honors Julia Maulden.** There are now some 1,400 Habitat homes in the city.†† Owners of those dwellings, often in neighborhoods that are now gentrifying, are well-placed to reap some profits from the rising prices. When an owner wants to sell, the Habitat organization buys the property at the current market price, then rehabs it as needed and resells to a new low-income occupant.‡‡

By the way, perhaps the story of minister Millard Fuller's work with his poor neighbors reminds you of Paul Leonard? Leonard was the Charlotte preacher who helped low-income church members create Clawson Village (see chapter 5) before he joined the Crosland firm. Well, after Leonard retired from the business world, he became an active Habitat volunteer. When Millard Fuller stepped down from leadership of Habitat for Humanity International in 2004, its trustees chose Paul Leonard as the global organization's interim CEO.

---

‡ "An Epidemic: Housing Crisis for the Poor Getting Worse All the Time," *Charlotte Observer*, November 16, 1985.
** "Charlotte Habitat Gets $1 Million, Launches Drive," *Philanthropy Journal*, June 20, 2007, https://pj.news.chass.ncsu.edu/2007/06/20/133470/.
†† Tom Hanchett, "Inside Charlotte's Long Ride with Habitat for Humanity," *Charlotte Magazine*, August 25, 2021.
‡‡ Laura Belcher, Charlotte's Habitat CEO, interview by Tom Hanchett, July 18, 2019.

---

even more desirable than the previous depreciation-based tax shelter. "Note that these are federal credits, not ordinary tax deductions," explained the syndicated financial columnist Kenneth Harney. "Credits are better. They are dollar-for-dollar slices off the bottom line of your federal tax bill, after you've toted up what you think you owe Uncle Sam." In the wake of the 1986 Tax Act, Harney emphasized, "They're the last true tax shelter left."[39]

Here's how LIHTC works. If you put, say, $100 into a LIHTC construction project, you get to take $9 directly off your IRS tax bill.[40] That deduction happens every year for ten years—meaning a total of 90 percent of your investment comes back to you. Wow! And you still own your share of the building, which is almost certainly going up in value due to generally rising real estate values—so your initial $100 investment has turned into more than $190 in your hands. *And* you've been collecting rents all this time (though you've also had expenses for maintenance, tenant screening, filling out all the IRS paperwork, and the like).

So, the Low-Income Housing Tax Credit is a pretty valuable deal. Not everyone is willing to jump through all the hoops, but enough are so that demand for credits through the LIHTC program typically exceeds the supply. Washington allocates a tightly limited amount to each state each year. In North Carolina, the NCHFA drives the process to decide who gets the credits—with an independent panel appointed by the governor making the actual decision. It's quite competitive.[41]

If all of that sounds complicated, you'll understand why developers took a while to jump on the new opportunity, but jump they did. Only one Charlotte project got underway in 1988, the first year of eligibility. In 1989, four construction efforts launched—led by Fairmarket Square, developed by none other than John Crosland (see case study below). By 1997, a decade into the LIHTC era, Charlotte would boast eleven newly built apartment complexes subsidized by the tax break, a total of 733 living units.

The LIHTC rules also encouraged "acquisition and rehab." Charlotte would see eight such projects in the initial decade. Three abandoned cotton mills were renovated as low-income housing: the Hoskins Mill on the city's west side as well as the Johnston Mill and Mecklenburg Mill in a decaying former textile village north of downtown. The developer/owner of all three, with no previous rental experience, ran into financial troubles, and the buildings once again stood vacant after their fifteen-year LIHTC commitment ran out—but not before the Johnston and Mecklenburg rehabs helped stimulate revitalization of the surrounding area, today known as NoDa. Other investors acquired and updated three 1970s Section 221(d)(3) / Section 236 projects (see chapter 5), Orchard Park, Pressley Ridge (originally called Roseland, later Pressley South End), and Parker Heights, thereby extending their life. And a couple of existing apartment complexes in the low-income Black neighborhood of Grier Heights received thorough renovations by another LIHTC developer.

Although LIHTC projects were government-assisted "affordable housing," very much needed by low-income Charlotteans, they differed in an important way from the older "public housing" that continued to be owned and operated by the Charlotte Housing Authority. CHA housing projects served the city's neediest people, many having incomes below 30 percent of area median income. In contrast, federal rules said that tenants in LIHTC projects could make

60 percent of area median income. These were "working poor," people who were steadily employed in jobs that did not pay well, such as nursing or food service. A few LIHTC projects were structured to include some very-low-income renters, but that was rare.

By the 2010s, as we shall see in chapter 9, that LIHTC focus on 60 percent AMI would leave Charlotte far short of meeting needs for its poorest (30 percent AMI and below) citizens.

Charlotte's Innovative Housing Fund (Charlotte Housing Trust Fund)

Before we look at the case study of Fairmarket Square, there's one more piece of the affordable housing network to introduce. That is Charlotte's locally funded and administered Innovative Housing Fund (later reconfigured to create today's Charlotte Housing Trust Fund).

In 1987, with LIHTC deals about to happen, City Council asked itself whether it should reconsider its annual appropriations to build scattered-site public housing. Since the late 1970s, the city had regularly allocated a portion of its federal revenue sharing grant supplemented by local tax dollars—a total of about $2 million annually—to enable construction of about 100 units of affordable housing every year.[42]

Now with LIHTC a reality, council amended that policy, formally creating an Innovative Housing Fund in 1987. Public-private partnership with for-profit investors, a touchstone of the Reagan consensus, offered the hope of producing more housing without more public dollars. Projects already planned would go forward, "but for the first time in eight years the City has set aside no money for new ones this year or next," reported the *Observer* in 1987. "Money for low-income housing has been directed into an Innovative Housing Fund. The money will help pay for building low-income housing in partnership with private developers."[43]

In its eagerness to cultivate partnerships, City Council relaxed the policy against low-income concentrations that it had set in the 1973 *McKnight v. HUD* consent decree. Government-assisted apartment complexes had not been allowed within one-half mile of each other, nor in census tracts that were over 40 percent African American, nor in census tracts where more than half of residents made less than 80 percent of the city's median income.[44] Now council voted to drop those requirements in 1988. Summed up the *Observer*, "No rules require the public-private projects to be spread throughout the city."[45]

Some momentum from the scattered-site decade carried over into the new era. Among the first Innovative Housing Fund projects were two complexes in an upper-middle income and almost entirely white sector of suburban southeast Charlotte: McAlpine Terrace (112 units for elderly) and Glen Cove (50 two- and three-bedroom units for low-income) off Monroe Road.[46] Another complex, McMullen Wood, went up near Johnston Road and Highway 51 at the booming upscale southern rim of the city. Most projects, however, went into areas that already had a racial mixture or had existing low-income complexes.

While multifamily housing is the focus of this book, it is worth mentioning that the Innovative Housing Fund also aided single-family projects. Its very first activity in 1988 helped a number of public housing tenants step up to ownership. A row of new cottages along Summit Avenue in the Biddleville neighborhood adjacent to Johnson C. Smith University "turned twenty-four public housing tenants into homeowners and . . . last month won its second national award," reported the *Observer*.[47]

The Innovative Housing Fund would continue into the 2020s, assisting many types of short-term needs, such as emergency cash assistance for households facing eviction. The steady stream of dollars for construction of new apartments, however, would eventually be split off as a separate entity. At the request of City Council, Assistant City Manager Vi Alexander Lyles developed a proposal for a permanent Charlotte Housing Trust Fund.[48] It would be funded by a specific bond issue, to be approved by Charlotte voters every two years (see chapter 9).

Council launched the trust fund in 2001, and it remains a potent tool.[49] Lyles's detailed knowledge of housing issues would come in handy over the years. Elected as Charlotte's first female African American mayor in 2017, she would coax voters to approve over $100 million in bonds for the trust fund, making affordable housing a signature initiative for Charlotte in the 2020s (see chapter 9).

A LIHTC Case Study: Fairmarket Square by For-Profit Developer John Crosland

By the end of the 1980s, all the pieces were in place. From Washington: the Low-Income Housing Tax Credit. From Raleigh: the North Carolina Housing Finance Agency and its North Carolina Housing Trust Fund. From Charlotte: the Innovative Housing Fund.

John Crosland Jr. became one of the first developers in North Carolina to pull all components together. Back in 1979, he had built Fairmarket Plaza, 120 units for senior citizens on Plaza Road in east Charlotte, using Section 8 Project-Based support awarded by the NCHFA.[50] Now, with LIHTC available, Crosland proposed to expand the development, adding an adjacent pod of 60 apartments for families.[51]

Figure 7.1. Fairmarket Square on Plaza Road, 1991. Hanchett photo, 2023.

Crosland's architectural design for Fairmarket Square looked indistinguishable from nonsubsidized projects of the early 1990s. The three-story buildings featured wooden clapboard exteriors and homey gabled roofs—carefully calibrated to avoid any stereotypes of "public housing." The development's unremarkable appearance belied the complicated financing that made it work.

A Low-Income Housing Tax Credit worth just over $2 million formed the heart of the deal. Crosland had a sure shot at that. He chaired the North Carolina Housing Finance Agency, which managed the process that awarded the credits. He stepped down soon after receiving the credits "to avoid appearance of conflict," newspapers noted.[52]

In addition to the federal tax credits via the LIHTC program for Crosland and his co-owners in the LLC (limited liability corporation), a local bank put up $1.4 million, the City of Charlotte's Innovative Housing Fund provided a fifteen-year no-interest mortgage of $1.3 million, and the North Carolina Housing Trust Fund gave a fifteen-year no-interest second mortgage of $300,000.[53]

When City Council debated whether to make the Innovative Housing Fund loan, neighborhood groups pushed back. Adjacent Hampshire Hills, its streets of middle-income ranch houses developed by Crosland himself in the era of segregation, now held both Black and white homeowners. They complained that three other 1970s low-income projects already existed in a radius of less than a mile. And other nearby apartments from the early 1970s, including Crosland's Vista Villa directly across Plaza Road from Fairmarket, had seen rents slip as they aged. "We're already doing our part. We say enough's enough," said white resident Jerry McMurray. Agreed Anita Harvin from Bridlewood, a middle-class Black area, "We just don't need that in our neighborhood right now."[54] They worried that—as on West Boulevard two decades earlier—the concentration would foster perceptions that the area was undesirable. The big Harris Teeter supermarket in Hampshire Hills shopping plaza, they noted, closed its doors just as plans for Fairmarket Square were announced.[55]

As City Council voted on the Innovative Housing Fund loan, residents filled the council chamber. "Black and white, they wore checkerboard buttons to show that their middle-class area was integrated. 'We live the dream. We are an integrated community,'" testified McMurray. "But, he warned the Council, 'We are teetering on the edge.'"[56]

A few years previously, the neighborhood might have prevailed by pointing to city policies against concentrating low-income housing. Now those prohibitions were gone. Council's Republicans plus a few Democrats voted to make the loan.

"Poorly housed people never lobby us," said Republican council member Richard Vinroot. "They never write letters. They never come down to cheer or boo. But they are our responsibility, too."[57]

When Fairmarket Square opened, adjoining residents welcomed the tenants with a get-acquainted reception featuring "brownies, cakes, casseroles and good will."[58] Said Gary Howard, president of the Northeast Community Organization, "It was a mistake locating the apartments here, but we have no problem with the people. They are neighbors."

Howard's worries about perceptions of low-income concentration proved prescient, however. Hampshire Hills would continue to wrestle with empty stores and lack of a major supermarket into the 2020s.

Creating the Charlotte–Mecklenburg Housing Partnership

While most LIHTC developers were for-profit firms such as Crosland, a new nonprofit also joined the game.[59] Betty Chafin Rash provided the vision and coalition-building skill that brought into existence the Charlotte–Mecklenburg Housing Partnership in 1988 (renamed DreamKey Partners in 2021).

"We were looking at some of the major issues in Charlotte; where were opportunities for partnerships?" Rash later recalled.[60] Could new entities be structured to tackle housing and planning topics, bringing together city government, developers, neighborhood groups, and especially the city's fast-growing banks?

In the mid-1980s, Charlotte's two largest banks, North Carolina National Bank (NCNB, renamed NationsBank in 1991) and First Union, embarked on a remarkable growth spurt. Hugh McColl at NCNB discovered a legal loophole that allowed banks to merge across state lines, something that had been long prohibited. As NCNB and First Union led the United States into the era of interstate banking (NCNB/NationsBank would become Bank of America in 1998, the nation's first coast-to-coast bank), both banks felt a strong need to be community-minded.

An important anti-redlining law, the Community Reinvestment Act (CRA) passed by Congress in 1977, required financial institutions to invest especially in low-wealth neighborhoods. Charlotte bankers in charge of mergers and acquisitions knew that federal banking regulators would be watching for CRA compliance.[61] That made partnerships for affordable housing hugely attractive.

"The need for low-income housing was becoming a community crisis," Rash recalled years later. "Growth of the two big banks and the CRA created an environment ripe for public-private partnership to address the need."[62] She teamed up with Kathryn Heath, one of the early female executives at First Union bank, and the two dove into the task.[63]

"Kathryn Heath and I went to Boston to look at the housing partnership there," remembered Rash, "and came back and went to the banks, went to the city, [and] got, if I remember correctly, unanimous approval from the city to be a partner in this effort."[64] To shape the initiative, Rash continued her practice of convening public workshops. With the city's Community Development Office, she organized "The Housing Gap: A Charlotte Challenge," described by the *Observer* as a "marathon 12-hour conference at Charlotte's Radisson Plaza Hotel." More than 350 business and community leaders heard from speakers including urban development guru James Rouse from Maryland and Joseph Flatley, director of the Massachusetts Housing Partnership.[65] The public conference was "immediately followed by a retreat attended by 100 diverse stakeholders, organized by the Urban Institute at UNC Charlotte," Rash recalled. With that input, Heath and Rash drafted a formal proposal for the nonprofit Charlotte–Mecklenburg Housing Partnership (CMHP).

The CMHP would be "the vehicle for coordinating many of the public-private partnerships" on the horizon, the *Observer* reported.[66] Its twelve-member board and three-person staff would have time and expertise to "focus on securing financing and assembling land for low-income housing projects. Then it would seek proposals from ... developers, non-profit agencies and the Charlotte Housing Authority."[67] NCNB and First Union put up seed money, along with Duke Power, the Z. Smith Reynolds Foundation, and the city and county.[68] Board chairs would alternate between NCNB and First Union, with NCNB's John Boatwright holding the spot first.[69] Kathryn Heath and Betty Chafin Rash's proposal became reality in 1988.[70]

Patricia Garrett signed on as the CMHP's first executive director. She brought an unusual array of strengths. Raised in the physically demanding, no-nonsense world of dairy farming in poor rural North Carolina, she'd begun her work life teaching low-income kids in Head Start, then became a middle-school teacher, and then was tapped to run her hometown Community Action Agency. When President Nixon's 1973 moratorium on housing aid shut down a homebuilding program for farmers, Garrett wrote her county's first Community Development Block Grant. As Betty Chafin Rash got the North Carolina Housing Trust Fund going in 1987, Garrett served on its board and was elected chair. Rash and Ted Fillette recruited Garrett to take charge of the new CMHP the next year.[71]

Garrett's first project focused on former urban renewal land in Greenville, northwest of downtown along Statesville Avenue. In 1969 the city had booted out 600 families, knocked down every bit of the African American neighborhood, arranged for construction of the Interstate 77/NC 16 expressway interchange—and then done almost nothing with the remaining 283 acres for twenty years.[72] A for-profit company had constructed some houses in 1980 and then gone bankrupt, leaving unhappy residents and still-empty land.[73] The CMHP now took control. It went through a bidding process in which the Crosland company and the NCNB Community Development Corporation won contracts for the redevelopment, resulting in refinancing for existing homeowners and construction of over 100 new single-family houses for low-income buyers.[74]

Throughout the next three decades, the Charlotte–Mecklenburg Housing Partnership would keep coming back to the Statesville Avenue corridor, as we'll see in the next chapter—upgrading an area of duplex and single-family rental houses (rebranded "Genesis Park") in the 1990s, redeveloping the old Fairview Homes public housing with federal HOPE VI dollars in the 2000s, and replacing C. D. Spangler's FHA 608 Double Oaks apartments with a new mixed-income community called Brightwalk in the 2010s.

A LIHTC Case Study: Seversville Apartments by the Housing Partnership

The CMHP's initial foray into multifamily construction involved cleaning up another long-standing mess where previous efforts had failed. In Seversville, just west of downtown, the hulk of a former elementary school had stood vacant for almost twenty years. Charlotte–Mecklenburg Schools erected a modern replacement school on Bruns Avenue in 1968 but then did nothing with the

Figure 7.2. The Charlotte–Mecklenburg Housing Partnership built Seversville Apartments (*right rear*) and also renovated houses along Bruns and Katonah Avenues (*left*). Albert Dulin photo, 2021.

old structure on Sumter Avenue nearby. The fact that the racial makeup of the Seversville neighborhood was shifting surely had something to do with the neglect. Once all-white, Seversville became mostly Black in the early 1970s, one of several older neighborhoods that absorbed people displaced by the Brooklyn and Greenville urban renewal. In the mid-1980s, a coalition of Black and white churches proposed transforming the abandoned school into housing but could not make the numbers work. Now, with the new Low-Income Housing Tax Credit, might the project be doable?

Two provisions in the LIHTC law were the key.

One was a little-noticed rule that opened the door to nonprofits. Credits could be sold.[75] A nonprofit organization couldn't use a tax credit itself, since it paid no taxes. But it could sell the credit to a for-profit investor. Suddenly it made sense for nonprofits such as the CMHP to do tax credit housing.

A second subtle but important rule: the tax credits ran for ten years, but the property had to remain low-income for at least fifteen years. That long-term commitment caused some developers to shy away from LIHTC work. But the Charlotte–Mecklenburg Housing Partnership, a community-spirited nonprofit, was perfectly constituted to handle the long-term responsibilities.

The Seversville Apartments became the partnership's first multifamily rental project. The $2.5 million package utilized all the new financing tools of the 1980s.

- The CMHP won a Low-Income Housing Tax Credit. It sold the credit to Wachovia Bank, which gave the CMHP much of the cash needed for the project.
- For the rest, the North Carolina Housing Finance Agency arranged a low-interest loan from its new North Carolina Housing Trust Fund, and the City of Charlotte provided a loan from its Innovative Housing Fund.
- CMHP staff—supported by City grants plus aid from banks eager to meet Community Reinvestment Act guidelines—managed the complicated paperwork.[76]
- Even with all those subsidies, a CMHP spokesperson noted, "Most of the cost will be repaid . . . by income from rents."[77]

Pat Garrett got into the deal not simply to build forty-seven apartment units but also to help the surrounding neighborhood become stronger and more stable long past the initial fifteen years. That meant finding partners in the neighborhood, a daunting task in a place where most people were transient renters. Most people—but not all.

Wallace Pruitt, a Black homeowner who lived across the street from the school site, became the key facilitator. Neighbors regarded Pruitt as the "mayor" of Seversville, able to listen to community members, interact with city officials, and stay firm in advocating for neighborhood desires.[78] "Mr. Pruitt kind of took us on as a project. He's this great compromiser. I mean, he would persuade people that they really wanted to do it," Garrett recalled.[79] That persuading worked in both directions. "He'd call up and say, 'Now, this is what we want to do,' and we'd say, 'Okay.'" Pruitt insisted that the CMHP not just build new apartments but also rehab existing substandard dwellings.

"When we got the neighborhood to agree to the apartments, we committed to doing something with the houses, too," Garrett explained. Pruitt introduced Garrett to "people who had been there for a long time in that community and still needed a decent place to live. What we did is we ended up moving them to one of the other units while we renovated theirs and moved them back. . . . We were concerned that [if we did not keep them,] we were losing all the knowledge and the commitment to the community."

CMHP crews tackled the task of rehabbing some thirty existing houses on Bruns Avenue and nearby streets. "We acquired those and renovated them. In those days we were using HOME money [a federal housing-rehab subsidy program]. I remember having the HUD secretary come and visit. The rule was if you used HOME money you had to build on the same foundation, but you could take it down to the studs. And we took some of them all the way. They had a

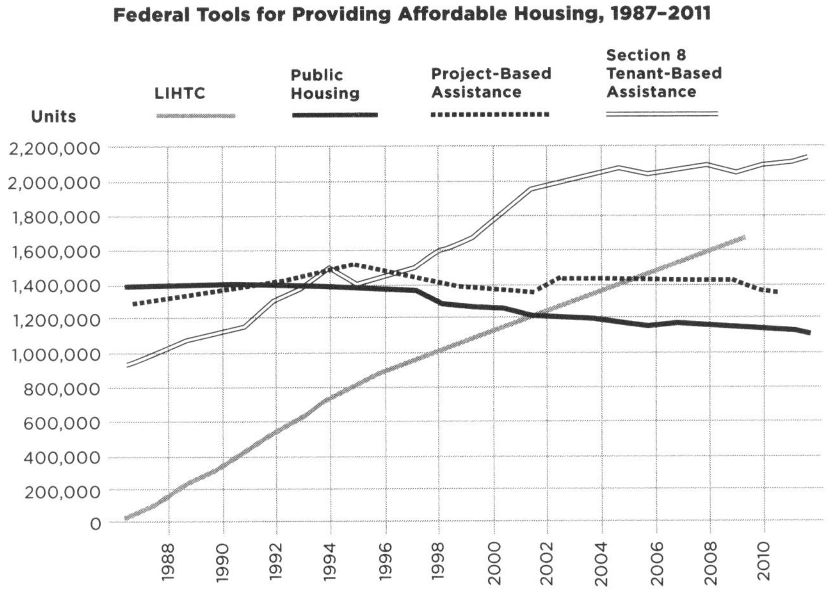

Federal Tools for Providing Affordable Housing, 1987–2011

Graph 7.1. Since the 1980s, traditional public housing declined while project-based aid remained roughly steady. Meanwhile, Low-Income Housing Tax Credit projects and Section 8 vouchers surged ahead in importance. Graph adapted from Vale and Freemark, "From Public Housing to Public-Private Housing."

partial wall or something, but that was 'renovation.' That wasn't 'new construction.' Hey, you do what you have to do."

Garrett also had an uncommonly strong sense of "what you have to do" when it came to ongoing maintenance of the Seversville Apartments. "We always wanted to manage the hell out of them. We wanted them to look better than anybody else. If it started looking bad—I used to do inspections. Every year I would go with our property manager and the company that we hired to do the property management on-site and walk every one of them. They knew I was coming, so that meant that the shades, the blinds that were broken got fixed. They knew the things I was going to be looking for."

All of the combined efforts helped Seversville stabilize. By 2002 the area was no longer considered a distressed neighborhood by city officials.[80] That didn't mean smooth sailing—in the 2010s, the Seversville area would be swept up in a wave of gentrification that buffeted every neighborhood near the center city (see chapter 9). But even then, the continued existence of Seversville Apartments, still affordable thanks to CMHP ownership, and the well-cared-for bungalows on Bruns Avenue meant that longtime residents retained some stake amid all the change.

Chapter Conclusion—Pluses and Minuses of LIHTC

With the dawn of the Low-Income Housing Tax Credit era, the federal government was largely out of the business of helping local governments add to their stock of new public housing. Washington continued to subsidize the buildings that already existed, and it would aid in constructing replacements for old, outmoded public housing units (as we shall see in chapter 8). But the total number of government-owned apartments froze at 1980s levels—and indeed has decreased steadily ever since.

We'll continue exploring the LIHTC era in the next chapters, beginning with a late 1990s federal initiative called HOPE VI. But three interim observations can be made here.

First, LIHTC and the network of programs that grew up around it basically worked pretty well. The combination of national, state, and local incentives forged during the 1980s has lasted almost forty years, far longer than any preceding system. LIHTC apartment complexes seem to have been well-designed and well-built and seldom have fallen into disrepair.

What has caused that success? The interplay of interests seems an important factor. Investors get tax credits over ten years but must ensure the project keeps serving its tenants for at least fifteen years. The North Carolina Housing Finance Agency board awards LIHTC competitively to projects that are best planned for long-term viability. The agency's North Carolina Housing Trust Fund, which has its own staff and board, also watches over projects until the loans are repaid. Ditto for the City of Charlotte's Innovative Housing Fund / Housing Trust Fund loans.

All of that was a great improvement over the housing programs described in earlier chapters. Creators of previous investor-developed projects held little long-term stake, which led to careless construction and lax upkeep. Likewise, projects owned by the Charlotte Housing Authority were at the mercy of elected officials, whose focus on savings for taxpayers often led to skimping on maintenance. In the LIHTC era, most of the worst physical problems with low-income housing disappeared—though stereotypes about such housing persisted in the minds of most Americans.

Second, for all that success, the LIHTC program has been sharply limited in its ability to make a big impact on America's shortage of affordable housing. Nationally, about $10 billion in credits would be given out each year by the 2010s.[81] That sounds large, but it works out to only about 63,000 apartments built annually nationwide.[82] By comparison, a recent study of needs in Charlotte pegs this one city's current shortfall at 28,000 units. As welcome as new LIHTC construction is, the pace falls further and further behind community need.

Third, LIHTC projects often fail to serve the people at the very bottom of the economic ladder. LIHTC regulations allowed tenants to make 60 percent or less of area median income.[83] At 60 percent AMI, that means most renters are "working poor," holding steady jobs that do not pay well, such as nurse assistant. That certainly meets an important need—but it leaves out the poorest Charlotteans.

There have been efforts to address this structural problem. The NCHFA requires that LIHTC developers accept housing choice vouchers and vouchers for veterans, which means that some households at 30 percent AMI can access the units.[84] Also, when it reviews applications for the scarce credits each year, the NCHFA lets applicants know that it likes to see 30 percent AMI units in the mix.[85] As well, nonprofit landlords such as the Charlotte–Mecklenburg Housing Partnership typically choose to include some 30 percent AMI units in their LIHTC projects.

But over time, a consequence of LIHTC rules would be that the nation's very poorest citizens would lose ground in the "post–public housing" era—introduced in the next chapter.

Table 7.1. Low-Income Housing Tax Credit Projects in Charlotte, 1987–1997

Development	Awarded	Annual allocation*	Opened	Units
†Orange & Sandalwood 115 Orange St 28205	1987	$14,488	1987	11
†Parker Heights 1505 Parker Dr 28208	1987	$28,771	1988	99
†Eastover Park Apartments 601 Alpha St 28205	1987	$3,804	1987	10
†Orchard Park Apartments 306 N Clarkson St 28202	1988	$45,119	1988	41
Winman Park 217 Bacon St 28288	1988	$52,618	1988	17
Saratoga Park Apartments 1234 Saratoga Dr 28208	1989	$62,732	1989	20
†Eastover Park Apartments 3126 Dunn St 28205	1989	$14,341	1989	13
‡Hoskins Mill phase 2 201 Hoskins Rd 28208	1989	$718,716	1989	189

Table 7.1. (*continued*)

Development	Awarded	Annual allocation*	Opened	Units
Fairmarket Square 5914 Fairmarket Pl 28215	1989	$217,218	1990	60
McAlpine Terrace/Glen Cove 6130 Pineburr Rd 28211	1989	$648,834	1990	162
Seneca Woods 1509 Seneca Pl 28209	1990	$182,144	1992	50
†Johnston Mill Apartments 401 E 36th St 28205	1991	$525,934	1993	99
Seversville Apartments 1707 Sumter Av 28208	1991	$177,537	1993	47
Summerfield Apartments 2352 Township Rd 28273	1992	$231,415	1992	53
McMullen Wood 6508 Walsh Blvd 28226	1992	$226,448	1993	55
Mill Creek Apartments 8498 Davis Lake Dr 28269	1993	$660,911	1995	180
Cheshire Chase Apartments 3724 Connery Ct 28269	1994	$325,364	1996	55
‡Mecklenburg Mill 3327 N Davidson St 28205	1994	$319,997	1996	60
St. Andrews Homes 3615 Central Av 28205	1995	$139,729	1996	34

* Multiply the annual allocation by ten years for total tax credit.

† Project included the acquisition and rehabilitation of existing structures.

‡ Project included both new construction and rehabilitation.

Note: LIHTC also aided a handful of smaller projects, under ten units, not included in this list.

Source: Table excerpted from Tom Hanchett, "Master List of Low-Income Multifamily Housing Constructed in Charlotte, 1940–2019," in the data collection of J. Murrey Atkins Library, University of North Carolina at Charlotte, https://doi.org/10.15139/S3/XQBOFW.

Income Limits
Who Is Eligible to Live in LIHTC Housing?

First, a Look Back

Early public housing had no Washington mandates about tenant incomes. Localities set their own policies. Tenants had to be able to pay at least some rent, since that was a big part of how housing authorities repaid construction loans. If tenants got a good job and their income rose too far, they could be evicted—which kept public housing out of competition with market-rate housing.

Policies started to change in the 1960s as, on one hand, President Johnson's Great Society attempted to uplift the poorest of the poor and, on the other hand, a wave of inflation upset previous calculations about housing costs. Initially, local authorities tried to cope with inflation by simply raising rents, which badly hurt tenants.

So Edward Brooke, the only African American in the US Senate, wrote the Brooke Amendment in 1969 that capped rents for subsidized housing at 25 percent (later 30 percent) of a tenant's income.* That had an unintended consequence. Local housing authorities now seriously lacked maintenance funds, so apartment complexes fell into disrepair. Congress began appropriating small annual maintenance subsidies, which continue today.

The Section 8 program in 1974 introduced the use of "percent of Area Median Income." Renters could make no more than 80 percent of their community's median income. That was not much of a limitation, since the poorest of the poor earned less than 30 percent AMI.

In 1981 under the Reagan administration, things tightened drastically. Congress required local housing authorities—which had previously had some flexibility in tenant mix, as long as all were under 80 percent AMI—to reduce the income cap to 50 percent AMI. And nearly half of units must be reserved for tenants under 30 percent AMI.

That sounded smart: serve those most in need. But again, there were unintended consequences. Public housing increasingly became the home of last resort for the poorest of the poor, almost entirely unemployed (rather than holding

(continued)

---

* Schwartz, *Housing Policy*, 154; Roessner, *Decent Place to Live*, 84–85, 152–53; Edson, "Affordable Housing," 196–97; Milgram, *Chronology of Housing Legislation*, 136.

a variety of low incomes, including the working poor). The *Charlotte Observer* reported that in Piedmont Courts in 1986, "81 percent of the residents are unemployed and 91 percent of the households are one-parent families headed by women."† A national scholar calculated that the median income of public housing residents slid from 41 percent of the US median in 1960 down to less than 20 percent in the 1990s.‡

Eligibility Limits under LIHTC, 1986–Present

As public housing became more focused on the very poor, the 1987 Low-Income Housing Tax Credit aimed at a different segment of low-income households.

LIHTC regulations defined "low-income" at 60 percent AMI. Households in that bracket, the working poor (see the sidebar "Some Definitions" in the introduction), certainly benefited from help. But they were not the lowest of low-income.

A few LIHTC projects included units aimed at 30 percent AMI. The nonprofit Charlotte–Mecklenburg Housing Partnership took pains to include 30 percent AMI households in its tenant mixes. Projects done under Washington's HOPE VI program, in which the Charlotte Housing Authority partnered with private investors (see next chapter), always included some 30 percent AMI households. But otherwise in the LIHTC program as a whole, units at 30 percent AMI were few or none.

From 1986 to the present, most low-income projects would be built by LIHTC-fueled partnerships. The 60 percent definition in the LIHTC program would lead to serious imbalances in Charlotte's affordable housing—described in chapters 8 and 9.

† "School Children Often Struggle to Succeed in Class," *Charlotte Observer*, November 9, 1986.
‡ Schwartz, *Housing Policy*, 147.

CHAPTER 8

Remix
Rediscovering Mixed-Income Housing, 1990s and Beyond

- Federal HOPE VI
- Local Nonprofit Charlotte–Mecklenburg Housing Partnership

The Low-Income Housing Tax Credit and the network of agencies that had sprung up around it during the 1980s rolled onward through the 2020s with few changes. Their mechanisms continued to funnel government aid to wealthy private investors in order to construct apartments for people in need. The kinds of projects produced, however, underwent considerable evolution.

Ideas about what constituted "good housing" shifted significantly during the 1990s and the following decade. At first, Charlotte-area LIHTC projects were just like those in the scattered-site era of the 1970s–1980s (see chapter 6). Most had about fifty units, arranged as a self-contained cluster of two- and three-story apartments—an island in an otherwise middle-class suburban area. During the 1990s, that started to change. Voices called for housing that would intermingle people of different incomes. Advocates for the poor, urban planning activists, and others from many backgrounds came to share a belief that reestablishing patterns of mixed land use—once the norm in America's cities—could bring a better future for everyone.

HOPE VI (pronounced "Hope Six," with HOPE standing for "Housing for People Everywhere"), a big new initiative from Washington, helped implement that vision starting in 1993.[1] The vast public housing projects of the 1940s–1960s had severe problems. So, HOPE VI offered to help redevelop them as mixed-income. Charlotte became a national leader, remaking five projects: Earle Village as First Ward Place, Dalton Village as Arbor Glen, Fairview Homes as Park at

Oaklawn, Piedmont Courts as Seigle Point, and Boulevard Homes as Renaissance West.

HOPE VI succeeded in important ways. People of every background indeed could live together, it proved. Such neighborhoods could be perceived as safe and desirable by all.

But HOPE VI fell short in replacing what it demolished. Charlotte's first redevelopment, Earle Village, built back less than half of the 409 public housing units it destroyed. Later projects did better; Park at Oaklawn, Seigle Point, and Renaissance West actually produced net *gains* in lowest-income units. Should the feds require one-for-one replacement? A conservative North Carolina senator named Lauch Faircloth argued against—and today his Faircloth Amendment still caps America's stock of public housing at 1990s levels.

This chapter tracks how HOPE VI began, nationally and in Charlotte. Then we'll see how other developers picked up HOPE VI ideas, notably the nonprofit Charlotte–Mecklenburg Housing Partnership (today known as DreamKey Partners). Two specific projects circa 2010 will illustrate the success: Brightwalk, where residents of different incomes intermingled, and Ashley Square in elite SouthPark, where retail shops mixed with upscale and subsidized apartments—and hardly anyone noticed or complained.

The Rediscovery of Mixed-Income Housing

The hottest new thing in urban development circa 1990 was actually an old place reimagined, a Boston public housing project radically rebuilt. The transformation of run-down low-income Columbia Point into a highly desirable mixed-income neighborhood renamed Harbor Point was spotlighted in no fewer than seven *New York Times* feature articles during 1987–92.[2] It would inspire Congress to create HOPE VI.

Several specifics of the Boston story are worth listing here. Built in 1953, Columbia Point was big, 1,500 units in high-rises, and it was in terrible shape by the 1980s with barely 350 units inhabited. Tenants led a revolt. HUD took Columbia Point away from the local housing authority and sold it to for-profit developer Corcoran Mullins Jennison.[3] Corcoran relocated tenants into two of the buildings. Then it demolished several towers, renovated others, and added 214 two-story townhouses. Corcoran also ripped out the old street system, where isolated courtyards were easily controlled by drug dealers, and laid in a new one with the buildings fronting on sidewalk-lined avenues. Finally, tenants moved into new or refurbished apartments—400 of them, compared with 350 before—intermingled among market-rate units.

"Harbor Point... aims to create a diversity of people, building function and shapes," marveled the *New York Times*.⁴ Today in the 2020s, it's hard to appreciate how radical that mixing sounded to most newspaper readers.

Harbor Point embodied cutting-edge ideas held by urban thinkers and antipoverty proponents. One influential writer was Jane Jacobs, whose *Death and Life of Great American Cities* called into question the lifeless "order" created by urban renewal. Density and variety, far from being bad, were actually the "source of immense vitality... a great and exuberant richness of differences and possibilities." Old existing neighborhoods fostered a "sidewalk ballet" in which storekeepers, shoppers, residents, and even the homeless interacted to create community. The variety of potential customers, plus the range of affordable business spaces, made such places hotspots of entrepreneurial innovation. "We need all kinds of diversity," she urged, "so the people of cities can sustain (and develop) their society and civilization."⁵

Jacobs's insights resonated with the era's rising environmental activism. The first Earth Day, in 1970, helped Americans begin to grasp the concept of "ecology." The natural world rested upon interactions of diverse living beings.

A city works like an ecology, observers realized. For it to function, different land uses and different people all interact together.⁶ Separating out components of a city was as misguided as the notion of separating aspects of nature. Isolate the bees from the flowers? Both die.

Sociologists came to the same realization. William Julius Wilson, one of the era's leading Black scholars, published his landmark study, *The Truly Disadvantaged*, in 1987.⁷ Economic and social isolation had created an "underclass" without role models or practical access to jobs and other opportunities. "Among the most important initiatives that government can undertake," summarized a proponent of Wilson's work, "are policies that reduce the concentration and isolation of very poor people in public housing."⁸

Calls grew to demolish big public housing projects.⁹ St. Louis had dynamited its notorious Pruitt-Igoe high-rises in 1972, and other cities dreamed of doing the same—especially as highly addictive crack cocaine sparked drug-dealer violence in the late 1980s.

With all of that in the air, Harbor Point seemed a beacon of hope. Longtime tenants liked the mixing. Previous public housing had "a stigma to it.... The school systems frowned on you," said one resident. "At least with mixed-income, the school systems don't know whether you're a doctor's child or an unwed mother's."¹⁰ Summed up another, "People said there would be too many cultures out here for it to work. But this place works."¹¹

Could it work in Charlotte? A growing cohort of young leaders were already thinking in that direction, beginning with efforts to create mixed-income housing in the center city's Fourth Ward and Third Ward.

In Fourth Ward, fewer than two dozen Victorian houses, most vacant, stood among weed-choked lots when activity began in the 1970s. A newcomer named Dennis Rash convinced North Carolina National Bank to fund low-interest home rehab loans. Soon middle-income townhouses sprang up on Hackberry Place—at the same time that Booth Gardens opened, a 130-unit low-income development by the Salvation Army.[12] NCNB financed both. Just down the block, architect Harvey Gantt and soon-to-be congressman Mel Watt, both leading Black advocates for affordable housing, built new homes for themselves.

Banker Hugh McColl liked Rash's energy and hired him to run a newly created NCNB Community Development Corporation (CDC).[13] Part of the job description required making connections with City Council. Rash responded with customary thoroughness: in 1981 he and City Council housing activist Betty Chafin were wed. They, too, chose to live in Fourth Ward.

The NCNB CDC became a game changer.[14] Congress had passed the Community Reinvestment Act in 1977, which required banks to actively lend in every part of the cities they served—a dramatic reversal of previous federally instigated redlining. The NCNB CDC functioned as a nonprofit developer, not merely lending but also initiating development projects. Nothing else like it existed in US banking. The CDC would inspire many imitators nationwide. In Charlotte it would become a major player in HOPE VI.

As Fourth Ward perked up, Rash and McColl looked to Third Ward, where they partnered with Black neighborhood leader Dr. Mildred Baxter Davis. The team built middle-income townhouses, attracting both Black and white professionals back to Third Ward, and they worked with MOTION to help existing renters, mostly Black, step up to home ownership.[15] "I wanted an integrated neighborhood—age, race, economic status," Davis told the *Observer*. "I've always been against putting 500 low-income people together. Then, you don't have anyone to inspire you, no good role models.... I feel as long as you have a mix of income, you always do better."[16]

With Fourth Ward and Third Ward on track, how about First Ward? The barracks-like Earle Village public housing seemed an insurmountable obstacle. Frequent shootings, including one that hit a passing city bus, frightened tenants and Charlotte leaders alike.[17] "When projects get as big as this, there's too many kids and too many people with no money hardly. What are the kids going to do?

They're going to get their energy off," said a tenant. "These large developments," a North Carolina housing official said bluntly in 1985, were "institutions" rather than homes. "What you wanted to do was encourage residents to be part of the community rather than to be in an enclave of their own."[18]

Fine words. But nothing changed.

Then came HOPE VI.

HOPE VI Begins:
Charlotte as a National Demonstration City

HOPE VI officially launched in 1993.[19] Washington aid would help remake old public housing projects. HUD offered direct onetime grants, and it also encouraged private investors to get involved using the Low-Income Housing Tax Credit program. Residents would be temporarily relocated, and existing buildings would be renovated or replaced. The final product would house all who had previously lived there (or other low-income people, if original inhabitants didn't wish to return). And it would also mix in higher-income households.

It was a bold vision. It would prove difficult to achieve.

Charlotte won a first-year HOPE VI grant. Nine cities nationwide—Atlanta and Charlotte were the only ones in the South—would hammer out the viability of the program on the ground.[20] What worked at Harbor Point might not work elsewhere. Earle Village would be Charlotte's test case. Could some of the existing buildings be upfitted? How long would construction take? Where would tenants go in the interim? Could rents from new middle-income residents cover some of the costs? Most basically: When all was completed, would middle- and upper-income people choose to live in an urban neighborhood with low-income neighbors?

NCNB CDC (renamed NationsBank CDC, then Bank of America CDC as its parent bank changed names over time) took the lead, arranging $10 million in LIHTC-subsidized private investment. The CDC and its investors would own the buildings; the Charlotte Housing Authority retained ownership of the land and would manage the rentals. Any profits would be split 50–50.[21] The CDC also brought in other allies, including the Charlotte–Mecklenburg Housing Partnership and Charlotte Center City Partners.[22] A large grant from HUD completed the package.

As the team remade Earle Village's eleven city blocks into a new neighborhood called First Ward Place, they discovered pros and cons of the Harbor Point model. On the upside, the architectural mixture pioneered in Boston worked well when translated to Charlotte, notwithstanding the fact that Earle Village had no high-rises. Local firm FMK Architects kept four of the old two-story Earle Village buildings, remodeling them to hold twenty-three townhouse apartments with inviting colonial-flavored porches.[23] Demolition crews cleared the rest of the site. Mid-rise apartment buildings, each three to four stories but differing in architectural finish, went up on several of the blocks. FMK arranged them to form mid-block courtyards that held playgrounds for children and parking for tenants, connected to the street by multiple driveways (unlike the single-entry arrangement that made older public housing a haven for crime). Each block also held some newly constructed townhouses. Single-family homes, as well, lined Eighth Street and a new avenue called Parkside Terrace. Davidson Street, a four-lane scar through the middle of the site, was narrowed and given a tree-shaded median.[24]

The project became an influential national model. It won multiple awards for architectural design and planning. The Urban Land Institute spotlighted it in a book of HOPE VI case studies.[25] HUD chose it as one of three examples of "the nation's best practices" in a 1996 pamphlet and specifically praised its single-family homeownership program in another how-to manual.[26] HUD secretary Henry Cisneros singled out the transformation as a prototype for other cities to emulate: "We can have Earle Villages all over the United States in a few years."[27]

Relationships with tenants—a hallmark of the Boston model—proved rocky in Charlotte, however. Ironically, part of the problem was that Earle Village was not in such terrible shape and all of its units were occupied. At Columbia Point, tenants had been relocated to empty buildings within the site during construction; at Earle Village, though, people were moved off-site to apartments scattered around Charlotte. That disrupted the "helping networks" that residents had forged, the informal webs of mutual aid that coped with childcare, transportation to jobs and health care, and so on. And that made for stressed, unhappy tenants. "We just want the apartments remodeled," said longtime resident Geraldine Jones. "We don't want 100-some people to be rooted up out of here."[28]

The scattering made it difficult to do "self-sufficiency training," a central feature of HOPE VI. The goal of HOPE VI was not to provide long-term housing but rather to be a temporary stepping stone to a life without government aid. Tenants would get classes in personal finance, budgeting, and saving, plus training for higher paying jobs. The Charlotte Housing Authority had begun such an effort in 1989 and boasted that 80 percent of people who chose to participate succeeded in getting off welfare.[29] CHA head Harrison Shannon, himself an African American who had grown up in public housing, believed fervently that HOPE VI projects must "require every able-bodied resident of public housing

Figures 8.1a–b. HOPE VI in First Ward. Townhouses, including some upfitted from former public housing (A), mingled with new mid-rise buildings (B), all oriented to the street. Hanchett photos, 2023.

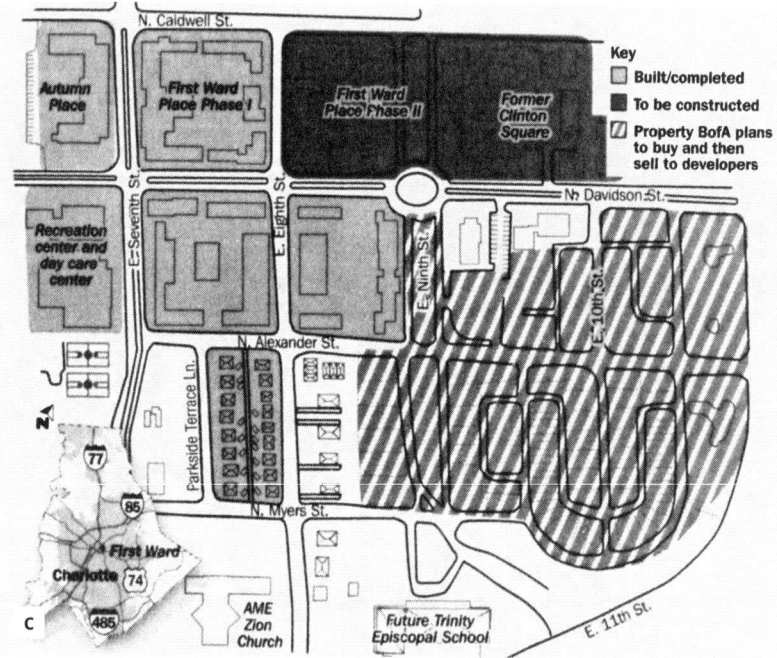

Figure 8.1c. Map from *Charlotte Observer*, June 14, 1999, showed Autumn Place senior apartments on Seventh Street, for-sale single-family homes along Eighth Street and Parkside Terrace, and two phases of apartment construction.

[except the elderly and the disabled] to participate in a family self-sufficiency program. They will have five years to come in and get it together."[30]

Five years and out—mandatory. That was frightening for many tenants, who already struggled to stay above water financially even with housing aid. Over the course of five years, a grandparent might need to drop out of the job market to become full-time caregiver for grandchildren; or a household member unexpectedly might struggle with addiction; or a missed rent payment might cause a poor credit history—all grounds for eviction.[31] And unexpectedly, a turning of the national economic tide made things worse. US household income, which had been rising for decades, turned downward around 2000. Market-rate rents, however, shot upward.[32] For many Americans in low-wage jobs, the possibility of climbing out of poverty evaporated—no matter how carefully one budgeted and saved. This is easier to see from today's vantage point than it was then. Policymakers and housing authority leaders—aware of past trends but insulated in their present middle-income lives—were much slower to recognize the mismatch than were poor people who lived it every day.

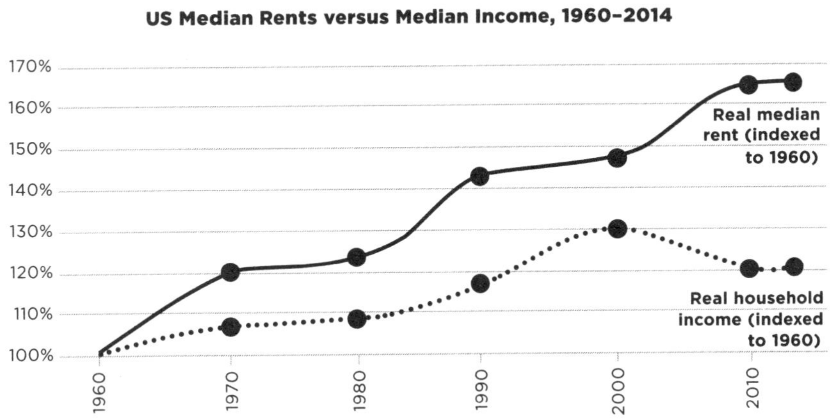

US Median Rents versus Median Income, 1960–2014

Graph 8.1. Inflection point circa 2000: incomes and rents in the United States began to diverge. US Census data; graph adapted from Woo, "How Have Rents Changed since 1960?"

Early discussions assumed that middle-income apartments and home sales would go far to balance reconstruction costs, allowing one-for-one replacement of low-income units. The numbers did not work out that way. "Of the 400 units torn down in Earle Village, 200 public housing units were built back in the new First Ward Place," noted a journalist.[33]

Very few Earle Village tenants returned when First Ward Place opened in 1998–2000. Initially 158 households indicated interest, but nearly all dropped out when faced with the requirement to agree to leave in five years. People who did not return found apartments at other CHA public housing or received Section 8 vouchers. "An additional 25 families bought homes at First Ward Place or elsewhere," noted a reporter.[34] The *Charlotte Observer* published a sharply critical weeklong series of articles in 1999, calling attention to the lack of returnees.[35] Responded CHA chief Charles Woodyard, "There's myth out there in the HOPE VI relocation efforts that people were thrown out in the streets. All families who left Earle Village are in much better housing situations, unless they violated their lease."[36]

Indeed, other public housing residents were willing to sign the agreement, and the new units filled immediately. Sandy Hoagland, whose family had lived in Earle Village, headed the First Ward Neighborhood Association in 2005. He told a reporter that tenants struggled with the five-year rule. But he also declared mixed-income First Ward Place a better place to live than Earle Village: "I embrace the mixture."[37]

Along with about 200 low-income units, First Ward Place eventually included 425 new market-rate apartments, townhouses, and single-family dwellings.[38]

Bank of America began construction on its own in 1999 on adjacent land that it marketed as the Garden District, developing a similar mixture of dwelling types (though no subsidized units).[39] Other developers also constructed small projects with condominiums or apartments; these included two low-rent initiatives by architect-entrepreneur David Furman and a complex for low-income elderly built by the United House of Prayer for All People, an African American religious denomination. Long-vacant nearby land filled out as well. A branch campus of the University of North Carolina at Charlotte and also a private academy named Trinity School joined the neighborhood, and the existing public school, First Ward Elementary, expanded in a new building.

Was First Ward Place a success? That depended on one's perspective. For tenants, the stigma of living in public housing decreased. Low-income households shared the same environment as wealthier neighbors. It was safer, too. "In 1995 the area that is now First Ward Place reported 331 criminal offenses. In 2002 there were 46," noted a visiting reporter.[40]

But the number of units for the very poor (under 30 percent of area median income) went down sharply. Earle Village had held 409 apartments; as in most US public housing, the majority of residents earned less than 30 percent AMI. In contrast, the new First Ward Place held barely 200 subsidized units—and just 132 of them went to that lowest-income group, the rest to 60 percent AMI tenants.[41] Displaced residents felt deep hurt. "Instead of talking about these pretty houses, you need to think about the people—the people who were cheated. And I'm one of them," exclaimed ex-tenant Jackie Abraham at a public meeting.[42]

From another perspective, as a test case for creating diverse neighborhoods, the transformation of Earle Village showed that HOPE VI could work. People would live together. Today in the 2020s, as the project nears a quarter-century in existence—the same point at which Earle Village seemed ripe for demolition—First Ward remains a pleasant place to live or visit. Few Charlotteans realize that the tree-lined streets hold a mix of low-income and market-rate housing.

Said banker Hugh McColl in 1999, "Our focus at First Ward Place was to produce a mixed-income community and revitalize a blighted area of the city. We wanted to create a neighborhood for families. We believe we were successful."[43]

HOPE VI Expands:
One-for-One Replacement versus the Faircloth Amendment

Earle Village's transformation generated enthusiasm for HOPE VI nationwide and in Charlotte. US congressman Mel Watt, an African American real estate attorney elected from Charlotte due in part to his housing and civil rights

Root Shock
Recognizing the Pain of Displacement

Charles Woodyard, African American CEO of the Charlotte Housing Authority during much of the HOPE VI era, looked back ruefully in 2021:

> I think I understand the human psychology behind it, but when I was going through it and immersed in it, I didn't understand it as well as I think I do now. And that is I always saw these communities—[big public housing projects] like Earle Village, Piedmont Courts, and Fairview Homes and Boulevard Homes—I saw those as artificial communities that the government had created to trap us. That's really the way I saw it.
>
> But the African Americans who lived there did not see it that way. They saw it as their community. It took me a while to understand that. I saw it as, "Man, we need to bust this up. Don't you get it? Don't you understand?" No, I didn't understand. That's who didn't understand. But I think both of us are right. I think they're right and I think I'm right. So there's got to be some understanding. I had to come halfway and understand their situation. I eventually did.*

Woodyard's growing empathy paralleled work by scholars and housing advocates. Mindy Thompson Fullilove, a medical doctor and professor of psychiatry at Columbia University, published an influential book in 2004 titled *Root Shock: How Tearing Up City Neighborhoods Hurts America, and What We Can Do about It*.† She carefully documented the "helping networks" in low-income neighborhoods that had been torn asunder by "urban renewal" in the 1960s and 1970s—and that were being disrupted again by HOPE VI.

Gardeners use the term "root shock" to describe how plants often struggle after transplanting. Destruction of a neighborhood, Fullilove showed, caused similar trauma for displaced residents.

---

*Charles Woodyard, interview by Tom Hanchett, June 28, 2021.
†Fullilove, *Root Shock*, 5–16, 178; Vale, *After the Projects*, 194–96.

advocacy, urged his colleagues on Capitol Hill to fund HOPE VI each year and helped get it extended from its initial 2003 conclusion to 2010.[44] Charlotte would eventually win five HOPE VI grants, making it one of the ten most active cities participating in the program.[45]

Loss of units at the lowest income level continued to generate controversy, both locally and nationally—which crystalized in countervailing efforts by Watt and his North Carolina counterpart in the US Senate, Lauch Faircloth.

- Watt wanted a strict policy of one-for-one replacement, he told an interviewer years later: "If you move a poor person out—wasn't race, couldn't do it based on race—but if you moved a low-income person out, you had to replace that unit with an affordable unit for a low-income person."[46]
- Senator Faircloth pushed Congress in the opposite direction. One of the nation's most conservative elected officials, Faircloth had long criticized public housing as a wasteful government gift to the undeserving poor. He proposed an amendment in 1998 to cap the net number of public housing units. Cities that redeveloped old complexes under HOPE VI or other HUD programs would be forbidden from any increase in apartments.[47]
- A third perspective on replacement came from urban leaders who loved HOPE VI as a tool for remaking neighborhoods. If one-for-one replacement slowed down a project, then do away with one-for-one replacement.

Which view would prevail? The three-way debate played out in the 1998 Quality Housing and Work Responsibility Act, an update to HOPE VI. When the dust settled and the bill became law, it formally expanded the HOPE VI philosophy of income-mixing to all HUD low-income initiatives, a win for Mel Watt and his allies.[48]

But on the issue of replacement and the Faircloth Amendment, urban leaders and business conservatives joined forces and won their goals. The Quality Housing and Work Responsibility Act officially waived any requirement that HOPE VI projects do full replacement.[49] And the Faircloth Amendment went into effect; the total number of public housing units in America would decline each year from the late 1990s to today.[50]

■ ■ ■ ■ ■

In Charlotte, however, the housing authority took to heart the criticisms made by Watt, the *Charlotte Observer*, and grassroots advocates. The next HOPE VI projects would build back nearly the same number of lowest-income (30 percent

AMI) units as were destroyed—while at the same time adding many units at 60 percent AMI. The key: construct some apartments off-site.

The innovation began with Dalton Village, remade as Arbor Glen, recalls Charles Woodyard. Raised in a family of Black educators in nearby Shelby, Woodyard earned a master's degree in public administration at the University of North Carolina at Chapel Hill and then joined the Charlotte budget office under future mayor Vi Alexander Lyles. His acumen in finance soon made him the vice president of real estate for the housing authority and then its CEO when Harrison Shannon departed in 2002. HOPE VI would become Woodyard's special realm of expertise: "Arbor Glen was my first."[51]

Dalton Village certainly needed expertise. Shoddily built as a Turnkey project, it had sparked massive protests from West Boulevard neighbors in 1970. Few mourned when HOPE VI was proposed. The Crosland firm would handle the project for the CHA, adept both at construction and also at luring LIHTC investors. Woodyard recalls that John Crosland Jr. himself expressed commitment, saying, "Dammit, we're going to do this. We're going to do affordable housing. [We're] not going to have to make a lot of money on it, but we're going to do it."[52]

Bulldozers took down all 300 units, then Crosland's crews built back 258 new apartments in three phases.[53] As in other HOPE VI projects, Crosland's for-profit investors owned the buildings (in order to reap LIHTC benefits) while the Charlotte Housing Authority retained ownership of the land. The CHA deeded part of the tract to the Charlotte–Mecklenburg Housing Partnership, which added fifty-four single-family dwellings (half at market rate, half for buyers with incomes at 80 percent AMI—including several who previously lived in public housing).[54] Unlike Earle Village, the Arbor Glen project included very little market-rate housing, but it did welcome a range of incomes on-site—some households at 30 percent AMI, some at 60 percent AMI, and a handful making the step up to homeownership.[55]

"We structured the deal so well," Woodyard later explained with pride, "we had enough money and cooperation from the city to finance stuff off-site."[56] Nia Point (the name honored a Kwanzaa value: financial strength for community goals) rose on Charlotte's west side along Booker Avenue near Johnson C. Smith University. Springfield Gardens went up in east Charlotte near Idlewild Road and Margaret Wallace Road.[57] Both held mixtures of tenants at 30 percent AMI and 60 percent AMI.

How did Arbor Glen score in terms of one-for-one replacement? If we lump together tenants at both 30 percent and 60 percent AMI, the project substantially *increased* the number of available units. Old Dalton Village held 300 households; Arbor Glen held 460.

If we look more narrowly at the poorest Charlotteans, making 30 percent or less of AMI, the number of available units fell slightly, from 300 to 255.

In Charles Woodyard's eyes, though, that number misses a key part of the deal.

"When we started tearing down these very large public housing communities, HUD would say, 'OK, you're not going to build back all the hard units.... [So] we're going to give you these Section 8 vouchers'.... Once they did that, they did not take away your statutory number of public housing units that you can have by law."[58]

In other words, HUD would continue its aid to existing public housing, plus increase its allocation of Section 8 vouchers—a net gain for affordable housing. At Arbor Glen, according to CHA records, Section 8 vouchers helped seventy-five households relocate to apartments in other neighborhoods off-site. If we assume that those folks were at 30 percent AMI, then the total units at lowest income actually rose.

Numbers aside, the new Arbor Glen was a much nicer place to live than Dalton Village. The North Carolina Housing Finance Agency gave Arbor Glen Phase I an award as the year's best affordable housing project in the state.[59] A reporter visiting three years later found "hope and stability." Said tenant James Byrd, seventy-four, who had lived in both iterations, "It's a heck of a lot better, nice and quiet. You just walk around and talk to your neighbors and be content."[60]

■ ■ ■ ■ ■

Charlotte's next HOPE VI effort, the transformation of Fairview Homes into Park at Oaklawn, did even better at helping people at all incomes, thanks to leadership by the nonprofit Charlotte–Mecklenburg Housing Partnership (CMHP).

Fairview Homes had been built in 1940 as Charlotte's first Black public housing, grim rows of flat-roofed two-story buildings (see chapter 2). Located in the struggling Statesville Avenue corridor a mile northwest of downtown, its 452 units made it Charlotte's biggest housing project.

Fairview stood next to two revitalization successes, Greenville and Genesis Park. The first was a mostly abandoned urban renewal tract until the CMHP began building homes for sale to low-income families.[61] Next, the CMHP bought up derelict rental houses on the other side of Oaklawn Avenue, kicked out drug dealers, and marketed what it now called Genesis Park to first-time

Figure 8.2. A: Arbor Glen, HOPE VI redevelopment of former Dalton Village by the Charlotte Housing Authority with Crosland. Hanchett photo, 2024. B: Park at Oaklawn, HOPE VI redevelopment of former Fairview Homes by the CMHP with Crosland. Multifamily in center foreground. Senior housing in right foreground. Single-family on curving street beyond. Albert Dulin photo, 2024.

homebuyers.[62] By the 1990s, a HOPE VI remake of Fairview Homes seemed a logical next step.

Initially, Bank of America CDC was the developer, but things fell apart when it couldn't guarantee one-for-one replacement.[63] So the Charlotte Housing Authority named the CMHP as master developer.[64] The CMHP's chief, Patricia "Pat" Garrett, brought in the Crosland firm to help arrange the LIHTC apartment component. She also wrote a HUD Section 202 grant for elderly housing; a block of apartments for senior citizens would help boost the number of lowest-income units in the package.[65]

As completed in 2005, Park at Oaklawn featured mixes of incomes on-site and also off-site. On-site, a dozen three-story apartment buildings, mixed-income, lined Oaklawn Avenue along with nine similar-looking apartment structures for seniors (called Anita Stroud Homes after a beloved Black community leader). Behind the apartments, new curving avenues held single-family houses.[66] Off-site, six apartment complexes sprang up around the city. They ranged from Montgomery Gardens, walkably located next to a Food Lion supermarket on Beatties Ford Road, to South Oak Crossing on the Lynx light rail line off South Boulevard, to Ashley Square at upscale SouthPark Mall (discussed later in this chapter).[67]

All intermingled residents at both 30 percent AMI and 60 percent AMI. Three of the off-site developments also added market-rate tenants to the mix.

In sum, the Park at Oaklawn HOPE VI initiative did increase the amount of affordable housing available in Charlotte, any way one chose to calculate it.

■ ■ ■ ■ ■

Charlotte's final HOPE VI redevelopments included off-site components from the start of their planning. On earlier projects, those efforts had begun after on-site construction surpluses became certain.[68] For the transformation of Piedmont Courts to Seigle Point and Boulevard Homes to Renaissance West, the outlying apartments were constructed first, as homes for relocated tenants.

By the beginning of the twenty-first century, Piedmont Courts just east of downtown had become a dangerous place, plagued by drug dealing and gunfire.[69] The CHA submitted a HOPE VI request in 2001, but HUD turned it down, citing insufficient replacement units. So, the CHA wrote a new plan in 2003 that fully utilized off-site as well as on-site components. Apartment buildings would be built at two locations about ten blocks away (one called McAden Court Apartments, the other named 940 Brevard), and many of the tenants would move there. All of Piedmont's 242 units would be demolished.[70] The new

Seigle Point would have on-site 120 units at 30 percent AMI, plus 104 units at 60 percent AMI and 30 at market-rate. The off-site buildings would ultimately hold 160 households at 30 percent AMI. To sum up, Piedmont Courts' existing 242 apartments for the very poor would be replaced by 280 new rental units at that 30 percent AMI level—*and* 60 percent AMI and market-rate residents would be added to the mix.[71] It was an impressive increase.

Across town on West Boulevard, the Renaissance West HOPE VI effort took aim at the much-maligned Boulevard Homes (see chapter 5). Again, the CHA brought forth a mix of incomes on-site, plus an increase in total units thanks to off-site components. That included purchasing the old Little Rock Homes (developed in 1971 by Reverend Leake, chapter 5) and building four new complexes elsewhere.

One notable aspect of Renaissance West was the CHA's codeveloper, Laurel Street Residential, led by Dionne Nelson—the first African American and first woman to play a top role in for-profit affordable housing development in the Charlotte region.[72] Nelson had learned her craft in the John Crosland organization, where she worked on HOPE VI projects helmed by Crosland's multifamily executive Jud Little. As Little contemplated retirement, he arranged for Crosland to spin off its affordable housing work to Nelson's Laurel Street.

The other noteworthy innovation at Renaissance West was an "educational campus" and an accompanying tenant-uplift organization, both the vision of the CHA's Charles Woodyard. At the time that Renaissance was being planned, an educator/activist named Geoffrey Canada was making headlines with his Harlem Children's Zone in New York City. A 2004 profile in the *New York Times Magazine* noted its success in providing educational services of all kinds—preschool, college, job training, coaching in parenting skills—for at-risk children and their families. Woodyard discovered that the ideas were being applied in a public housing setting, the East Lake HOPE VI neighborhood of Atlanta, by an organization called Purpose Built Communities. Woodyard set up a similar nonprofit, the Renaissance West Community Initiative.[73] Charlotte–Mecklenburg Schools built a public K–8 school on one side of the neighborhood's entrance. The Renaissance West Community Initiative raised philanthropic dollars to construct a pre-kindergarten "child development center" on the other side. And at the rear of the property, a new street connected directly with an existing branch of Central Piedmont Community College. A HOPE VI evaluator applauded Renaissance for "high-quality, mixed-income housing" and "a strong cradle-to-college education pipeline, and a suite of community services and facilities that lift up low-income families and attract middle-income ones."[74]

■ ■ ■ ■ ■

When Washington ended HOPE VI in 2010, Charlotte would have achieved one-for-one replacement of "lowest-income" housing units—if not for Belvedere Homes.[75] Constructed off Rozelles Ferry Road for white tenants back in 1953, Belvedere was beset by sinking foundations, asbestos and lead paint, and decades of deferred maintenance.[76] HUD awarded a HOPE VI demolition grant, and 170 families moved out and bulldozers rolled in 2004.[77] And then nothing happened.[78] Even with LIHTC and HOPE VI subsidies, developers found the site, ringed by industrial uses, to be undevelopable.[79] The twenty-three acres became a "business park," but as late as 2020 only a single new structure, headquarters of the Mecklenburg Bar Association, stood in the empty field.[80]

Non–HOPE VI Projects via LIHTC and/or the Charlotte Housing Trust Fund

While HOPE VI drama garnered hundreds of headlines during the 1990s and 2000s, two other types of affordable housing mostly flew under the radar in Charlotte. Together, Washington's ongoing Low-Income Housing Tax Credit program and the new Charlotte Housing Trust Fund helped create more units than HOPE VI.

The federal government underwrote thirty-eight LIHTC projects in Charlotte from 1998 to 2010. Exactly half of those were HOPE VI developments (discussed above)—and half were not. In other words, LIHTC aid was continuing to add to Charlotte's affordable housing at much the same rate as it had since the 1980s.

LIHTC projects did best in serving tenants at 60 percent AMI, since that was how Washington structured the program. A for-profit company named First Centrum, for example, built complexes called University Square and Honeycreek Seniors, both almost entirely at 60 percent AMI.[81] But a creative developer could do more mingling, as did Bank of America CDC when it mixed market-rate and subsidized units at Ten 05 West Trade, a big development at a prominent entry to the center city.[82]

■ ■ ■ ■ ■

In those same years, 1998–2010, the City of Charlotte formally created its own Charlotte Housing Trust Fund. City Manager Pam Syfert and her budget director, Vi Alexander Lyles, wanted to update the city budget line that had been

Figure 8.3. Sycamore Green (later renamed Ten 05 West Trade) mixed incomes and architectural forms. Developed by Bank of America CDC with LIHTC financing, 2003. Albert Dulin photo, 2021.

dedicated to assisting low-income housing since the 1970s, most recently called the Innovative Housing Fund. The new entity would be funded mainly by housing bonds—a tool that Charlotte had not previously used—which would be approved by voters every two years.[83] The bonds proved quite popular at the ballot box, raising a total of $47 million in the initial offerings in 2002 and 2004.[84] (When Lyles became mayor amid a 2010s housing crisis, expanding the trust fund would be her signature accomplishment—see chapter 9.)

The Charlotte Housing Trust Fund gave relatively small grants to assist projects where other finances came close but fell short. It made its first allocations in Fiscal Year 2002 and by the close of 2010 had assisted fourteen multifamily rental projects (new construction) and thirteen rehab projects (including dramatic improvements to the last large city-owned public housing project, Southside Homes) and also contributed to twenty "special needs housing" initiatives.

One innovative special needs project was McCreesh Place, a 2003 experiment in "supportive housing" whose success attracted national attention.[85] For men experiencing homelessness, it provided "housing first." A safe and secure apartment would be a first step to helping residents solve other problems in their lives—mental health, addiction, and so on. The facility won the admiration of neighbors; after initially opposing, they spoke enthusiastically in favor of a 2010 expansion.[86] It would inspire the Charlotte Housing Trust Fund to go on to aid Moore Place supportive housing, described in the book *The Hundred Story Home*, and also Dove's Nest, with temporary quarters for women recovering from addiction and domestic abuse.[87]

State-of-the-Art, 2010: Brightwalk and Ashley Square

Two projects summed up the state of the art in affordable housing in Charlotte as the 2010s began. Brightwalk, an ambitious initiative in the Statesville Avenue corridor, confirmed the ability of the Charlotte–Mecklenburg Housing Partnership to carry out mixed-income development at a large scale—without HOPE VI subsidies. Ashley Square, by the Charlotte Housing Authority, mingled not just different residential income levels but also added retail to the mix—and did it in the heart of SouthPark, Charlotte's most upscale shopping district.

■ ■ ■ ■ ■

Brightwalk represented another step in the Charlotte–Mecklenburg Housing Partnership's march of improvement along Statesville Avenue. With success achieved in the Greenville urban renewal lands, in Genesis Park, and in the Park at Oaklawn HOPE VI effort, could the CMHP tackle the vast, decaying complex known as Double Oaks? C. D. Spangler had built Double Oaks in 1949 with FHA 608 subsidies (see chapter 3) and then in 1981 sold it to a syndicate of Section 8 Project-Based investors who showed scant interest in maintenance once they reaped the tax advantages.[88] Double Oaks was privately owned, not public housing. It proved that market forces could do a much worse job than government when it came to low-income housing. By the time that the CMHP stepped in, barely 330 of the 576 units were habitable.[89]

CMHP chief Pat Garrett arranged to purchase Double Oaks in a foreclosure sale in 2007, aided by a loan from Wachovia bank. The Housing Partnership took great care to relocate the existing tenants, not simply offering immediate assistance but continuing rent supplements for as long as three years.

Crews cleared the eighty-six acres of its old one-story asbestos-shingled barracks. They laid a new street system that held a greenway park, tree-lined sidewalks, public art, and a daycare center—amenities shared by residents no matter what their wealth level. The low-income McNeel Apartments (named for Black westside neighborhood activist Luciel McNeel) and the Alexander Apartments (honoring Black political leader and housing advocate Fred Alexander) went up during 2008, followed by the low-income Stevenson Apartments and a pair of buildings for low-income senior citizens dubbed Gables I and II.[90] All were financed using LIHTC to lure private dollars, plus smaller grants from the Charlotte Housing Trust Fund. (The McNeel, for instance, had $4,925,230 in LIHTC plus $908,317 from the trust fund.) The buildings mixed tenants at various incomes, from as low as 25 percent AMI to 60 percent AMI, with the largest

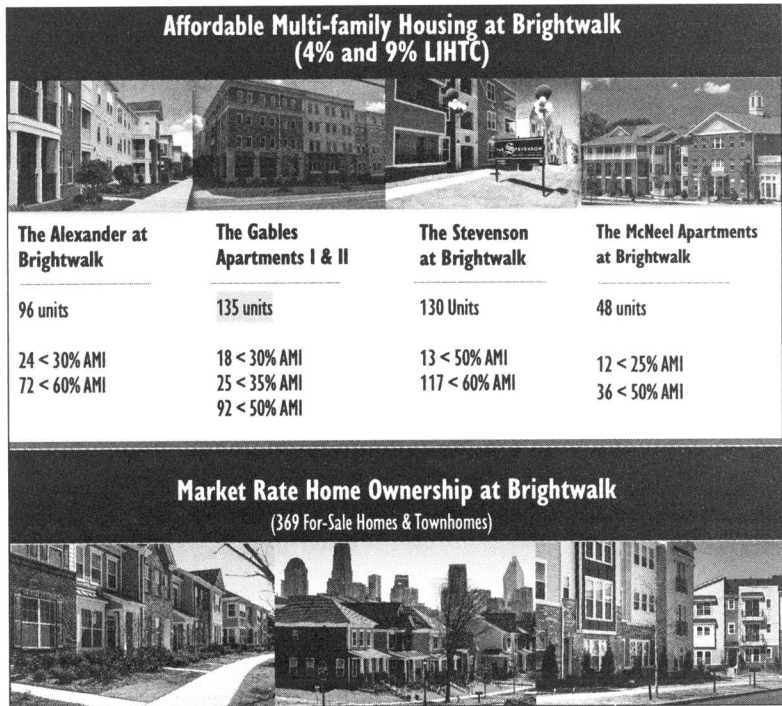

Figure 8.4. Brightwalk mixed low-income apartments and market-rate homeownership. 2018 graphic, DreamKey Partners.

number being at 50 percent AMI. Altogether, that totaled 409 units, more than Double Oaks had in its last days.[91]

Garrett made a point of starting with the low-income apartments—and then adding market-rate dwellings. She wanted to battle public perceptions head-on. Opponents often charged that low-income housing wrecked the desirability of adjacent market-rate homes. With big-time national suburban builder Standard Pacific as a partner, Brightwalk's townhouses and single-family homes began going up in 2012.[92] Initially, townhomes sold for $120,000. But almost immediately buyers began bidding up the prices. By 2021, the least expensive townhome listed for $315,000.[93]

"We discovered something that I think is absolutely remarkable," Garrett reflected in a 2020 interview: "People who have money are willing to pay high prices for a house and live next to low-income people if it's the right place; everything else has to be right. You got houses out there, $400,000 houses out there, and you're living next to—let's see, gosh, how many? Probably close to 400 if you consider Gables—poor people. Guess what? It works. You just have to make it right."[94]

CHAPTER 8

■ ■ ■ ■ ■

If you asked Pat Garrett about Brightwalk's shortcomings, she would point to the neighborhood's lack of retail. The CMHP tried hard to lure a supermarket, to no avail.

Ashley Square, in contrast, was able to build retail right into its construction plans.

To set the context for Ashley Square, let's drop back to the 1990s. Johnny Harris, a major south Charlotte investor, developed a chic mixed-use "village" close by SouthPark, the region's most upscale mall.[95] Called Phillips Place, it offered a main avenue lined with high-end shops that had office space on their second floors, plus a hotel and a cinema, all served by shared parking decks. Charlotte had never seen such an assemblage, and it required some massaging of the zoning code. But by the first decade of the twenty-first century, it was clear that Charlotteans embraced upscale mixed-use.

What if the mixture wasn't just upscale? Peter Pappas, a young developer who had worked with Johnny Harris and also with Crosland, began assembling land next to Phillips Place.[96] A key parcel held Live Oaks, a wood-frame complex of thirty-two apartments built by the Charlotte Housing Authority back in the scattered-site 1980s. Pappas approached CHA chief Charles Woodyard to try to work a deal.

Woodyard was already on the lookout. The CHA must partner with for-profit developers, he had come to believe, given the realities of aid from Washington. "HUD has been consistently cutting back on funding for the last 25 years, and they were our primary funding source," explained a Woodyard staff member. "This is the way for us to generate cash flow and build even more affordable housing."[97]

The Charlotte–Mecklenburg Housing Authority sold half of the nine acres to Pappas and kept the other half—a strategy that harvested dollars for the CHA while also ensuring that it would keep a large measure of control going forward.

- Pappas developed a series of four- to six-story apartment structures with restaurants and boutiques on the ground floors, all opening onto a new "stroll-able" Ashley Park Lane. At the entrance to the lane he built a two-story Whole Foods grocery.[98]
- The CHA partnered with Bank of America CDC to erect Ashley Square, utilizing LIHTC and the Charlotte Housing Trust Fund. It had retail space on Ashley Lane and 176 apartments on three upper floors: 140 at market-rate and 36 for residents at or below 30 percent AMI.[99]

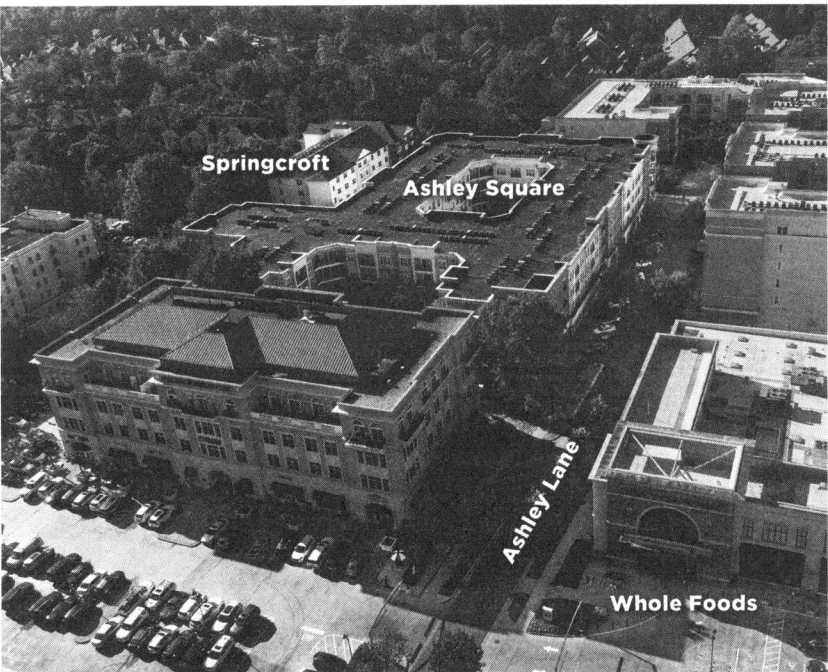

Figure 8.5. Ashley Square by Charlotte Housing Authority (Inlivian): mixed-income and mixed-use near elite SouthPark Mall. Albert Dulin photo, 2023.

- The CHA worked with the Charlotte–Mecklenburg Housing Partnership to create a four-story structure just off the lane, with 50 low-rent units for the elderly called Springcroft at Ashley Park.[100]

The result was a dense urban neighborhood, a seamless whole, lively and attractive. Noted the *Charlotte Observer*, "The project also underscores a shift in the Authority's philosophy about public housing. Instead of isolating poor people in their own developments, the theory goes, mix them among the gainfully employed." Roeshona Anderson, a longtime Live Oaks resident who walked to work at a nearby restaurant, looked forward to the project's completion. "People don't believe me when I tell them I live in SouthPark," she said. "This is one of the richest parts of North Carolina. Living here makes me want to be successful because I see success all around."[101]

Even though low-income units had nearly tripled, from thirty-two to eighty-six, complaints from neighbors were minimal. "The public housing tenants . . . live next to professionals paying $800 to $1200 a month in rent," reported the

Observer, "creating a true mixed-income community and a new revenue stream for the Authority."[102]

Affordable housing in a mixed-income, mixed-use setting could work—even in the priciest part of the city.

Chapter Conclusion

Brightwalk and Ashley Square showed that mixed-income—a far-fetched dream of a few forward-thinking urbanists two decades earlier—had become a bedrock feature of affordable housing by the start of the 2010s.

But the success of those two projects did not mean that neighborhood pushback evaporated, however. When the CHA proposed 60 percent AMI housing in elite Ballantyne, the *Observer* reported on a tense meeting of 300 neighbors:

> The residents' anger was simmering just below the surface when one neighbor stood and seized the microphone. . . . "My house is over a million, and I don't want that crap next to me."
>
> The crowd burst into loud and long applause. A minute later it was revealed that some of the prospective apartment residents would make 60 percent of area median income, or about $43,000 for a family of four.
>
> "$43,000?" the man said. "My jet costs that to go across the country."[103]

The *Observer* explained that about 35 percent of CHA tenants were elderly; another 40 percent were employed ("teachers, maids and others with low incomes but steady jobs"); and most of the remaining 25 percent were young unwed mothers—"hardly the portrait of a typical criminal." But the outpouring of emotion won the day. City Council canceled the project.

Indeed, time-consuming battles severely choked Charlotte's supply of affordable apartments. Ironically, however, when public housing did get built, as at Live Oak or McCreesh Place, neighbors who actually interacted with it year in and year out came to appreciate it and favor its expansion.

■ ■ ■ ■ ■

Before we move to the post-2010 decade, what can we say about the period covered in this chapter? The dozen years from 1998 to 2010 witnessed more dramatic changes in Charlotte's supply of low-income housing than any comparable period before or after.

- Mixed-income became the norm—combining the working poor (60 percent AMI) with lowest-income households (30 percent AMI), and sometimes also with market-rate residences and even retail.
- Big public housing complexes (over 150 units) owned by the Charlotte Housing Authority largely disappeared, with the exception of a handful of high-rises for senior citizens and Southside Homes for families.
- While HOPE VI decreased the number of CHA-owned units, LIHTC and the Charlotte Housing Trust Fund meant that Charlotte's supply of affordable housing continued to increase, albeit slowly.
- And at the same time, much of the previous housing stock continued to be in use—such as the Brookhill Village and Plaza Terrace complexes constructed under FHA 608, as well as the two dozen "scattered-site" developments from the 1970s and 1980s.

The way that Washington structured both HOPE VI and LIHTC meant that many "working poor" (60 percent AMI) now could find subsidized housing. That was good news.

But it carried the kernel of a problem that would become acute after 2010. Units for households earning below 30 percent AMI were becoming increasingly hard to find—as we will see in the next chapter.

Table 8.1. Low-Income Housing Tax Credit Projects in Charlotte, 1998–2015

Development	Awarded	Annual allocation++	Opened	Units
Charlotte Spring 4825 Spring Trace 28269	1997	$291,343	1999	76
Sparrow Run Apartments 1300 Pamlico St 28205	1997	$178,514	1999	32
Wallace Terrace Apartments 3720 Marvin Rd 28211	1997	$250,946	1999	32
†First Ward Place E 8th St 28202	1997	$875,865	1998	120
†Arrowood Villas 8825 Mount Carmel Ln 28217	1998	$224,692	2000	120
†First Ward Place II 550 E 8th St 28202	1998	$441,858	2000	72
Lincoln Heights Apts 2120 LaSalle St 28216	1998	$408,666	2000	60

Table 8.1. (*continued*)

Development	Awarded	Annual allocation++	Opened	Units
*Pressley Ridge 1210 Pressley Rd 28217	1998	$487,547	2000	505
Trinity Commons Apts 3015 Peach Bottom Ln 28205	1998	$127,856	2000	24
The Landings at Steele Creek 10701 Steele Creek Rd 28273	1999	$247,003	2001	48
Arbor Glen at Dalton Village 2305 Farmer St 28208	2000	$867,162	2002	144
Village of Rosedale at Sugar Creek 2925 Tiffany Rose 28206	2000	$452,224	2003	74
†The Gables at Druid Hills 2108 Statesville Av 28206	2001	$440,409	2003	63
Little Rock Apts 5712 Leake Av 28208	2001	$555,119	2003	242
†The Park at Oaklawn 1215 Rising Oak Dr 28206	2001	$885,307	2002	178
Pinecrest Manor 3713 Marvin Rd 28211	2001	$316,901	2003	44
*Stewart Stream 3410 Tennessee Av 28216	2001	$301,984	2003	57
†Ten 05 W Trade 1005 W Trade St 28202	2001	$279,325	2003	189
Arbor Glen II Clanton Rd 28208	2002	$867,062	2004	91
Honeycreek Seniors 4305 Sweet Honey Cir 28227	2002	$443,121	2004	78
Rosedale II 3829 Perennial Terrace 28206	2002	$208,807	2004	32
Rosedale II / Hope Haven 3925 Tiffany Rose Pl 28206	2002	not indicated	2004	32
Arbor Glen III 2305 Farmer St 28208	2003	$159,648	2005	24
†Rivermere Apts 3404 Dunn Commons 28216	2003	$244,338	2004	192
*Timber Ridge 7127 Barrington Dr 28215	2003	$189,381	2004	101

Table 8.1. (*continued*)

Development	Awarded	Annual allocation++	Opened	Units
Tyvola Crossing Apts 4425 W Tyvola Rd 28208	2003	$622,509	2005	80
Montgomery Gardens 5235 Garden Trace 28216	2004	$545,855	2006	76
Nia Point 1120 Mayfield Terrace 28216	2004	$619,526	2006	81
University Square Sr Apts 1715 Hedgelawn Dr 28262	2004	$284,460	2006	90
940 Brevard 940 Brevard St 28206	2005	$1,021,761	2008	100
Prosperity Creek Senior Apts 3705 Prosperity Church 28269	2005	$1,179,641	2007	168
†South Oak Crossing 7609 Kings Ridge 28217	2005	$307,106	2007	192
Springfield Gardens 9525 Springfield Garden 28227	2005	$634,917	2007	86
†Ashley Square 4845 Ashley Park Ln 28209	2006	not indicated	2010	174
†Seigle Point Apts 110 Winding Path Way 28204	2006	$1,000,000	2008	204
†The McNeel 1214 Kohler Av 28206	2007	$492,523	2010	48
†The Alexander 2425 Statesville Av 28206	2008	$1,000,000	2010	96
Cherry Gardens 506 Baxter St 28204	2008	$546,337	2010	42
†The Gables at Druid Hills II 1145 Kohler Av 28206	2008	$838,989	2010	72
*Randolph Hills 3449 Marvin Rd 28211	2009	$1,231,851	2011	168
Steele Creek Seniors 4314 Branch Bend 28273	2009	$1,021,612	2011	120
†Barringer Gardens 1842 West Blvd 28208	2011	not indicated	2015	85
†Boulevard Seniors (Renaissance) 1620 Brookvale St 28208	2011	not indicated	2013	110
Chambers Pt at Arsley 10124 Shaffer Valley 28273	2011	not indicated	2013	86

Table 8.1. (*continued*)

Development	Awarded	Annual allocation++	Opened	Units
The Retreat at Renaissance 3240 New Ren Way 28208	2011	$1,300,000	2013	110
*Strawn Tower II 1225 S Blvd 28203	2011	$766,234	2012	170
Westinghouse Senior Apts 10124 Shaffer Valley 28273	2011	$782,763	2013	86
†Boulevard Phase II (Renaissance) 1620 Brookvale St 28208	2012	not indicated	2014	74
Catawba Sr Housing 308 Mount Holly Rd 28214	2012	$565,201	2014	62
†The Residences at Renaissance 3610 Nobles Av 28208	2012	$865,439	2014	74
†Boulevard Phase III (Renaissance) 3610 Nobles Av 28208	2013	$482,622	2016	150
The Landing at Park Rd 3126 Park Rd 28209	2014	not indicated	2017	92
Allen Street Seniors 1321 Allen St 28205	2015	not indicated	201?	60
Rodden Square 6520 Mallard Creek Rd 28262	2015	not indicated	201?	98
Whitehall Crossing 2600 Arrowood Rd 28273	2015	not indicated	2017	96
Total complexes: 53				**Total units (including market-rate): 5,976**

*Project included acquisition and rehab of existing structures.

† Project included both market-rate and low-income units.

Note: Projects with ten or more units are included in this list. LIHTC also funded a handful of smaller projects.

Source: Table excerpted from Tom Hanchett, "Master List of Low-Income Multifamily Housing Constructed in Charlotte, 1940–2019," in the data collection of J. Murrey Atkins Library, University of North Carolina at Charlotte, https://doi.org/10.15139/S3/XQBOFW.

CHAPTER 9

The Tumultuous 2010s

- RAD, Inlivian, and Business-Driven Public Housing
- Cheap Money, K-Shaped Recovery, Gentrification, and Loss of NOAH
- Local Push for Affordable Projects—While Falling Further Behind

During the 2010s, affordable housing made headlines as never before, both nationwide and in Charlotte.

For public housing authorities, pressure intensified to pursue business-minded strategies. No longer was the focus on simply housing the poorest of the poor. Projects now often included market-rate rentals and lightly subsidized workforce housing, as well as units for lowest-income households. Authorities took on for-profit partners, both to develop projects and also to co-own them long-term. HUD created a program called RAD, which encouraged localities to sell their public housing to public-private investment consortiums.[1] In recognition of all the changes, the Charlotte Housing Authority renamed itself Inlivian in 2019.[2]

During the same decade, America slid into an affordable housing crisis. Ultra-low interest rates set by the Federal Reserve in 2008 launched an unprecedented era of cheap money, which continued into the early 2020s. Eager buyers bid up the prices of real estate.[3] In Charlotte, the median home price more than doubled from 2010 to 2022.[4] The hot market looked great—if you had enough wealth to get into the game. If you didn't, you watched in trepidation as once-affordable neighborhoods gentrified.[5] Observers called it a "K-shaped economy"—trending upward for some, downward for many others.[6]

Public unrest, provoked in part by the growing inequality, pushed housing to the top of the civic agenda in Charlotte. In 2016 a Black man named Keith Lamont Scott was shot by police. Months of protests, dubbed the Charlotte Uprising, raised calls for a wide range of systemic changes. Housing emerged as an important focus. Vi Alexander Lyles, elected in 2016 as Charlotte's first female

African American mayor, made affordable housing her prime issue. She got voters to approve two $50 million housing bonds. Local businesses and philanthropists added another $50 million. An impressive wave of new affordable housing projects opened during the late 2010s and early 2020s.

But all that construction, when measured against the naturally occurring affordable housing decrease, would leave Charlotte even further behind in meeting the needs of its lowest-income residents.

"We Are a Business": Charlotte Housing Authority in the Twenty-First Century

"[The CHA] is committed to helping people, but at the same time we are not a social service agency. We are a business," declared CHA chief Harrison Shannon as the housing authority entered the twenty-first century. The sea change in Washington's governmental priorities that had begun in the 1980s with Ronald Reagan was now undeniable. "The federal government will not provide us the necessary dollars that we need to get the job done," Shannon explained. "Consequently, we are looking to partner with people in the private sector."[7]

Shannon asked his vice president of real estate, Charles Woodyard, to launch a subsidiary called Horizon Development in 2001. "The Charlotte Housing Authority is creating for-profit and non-profit spinoff corporations to build low-income housing it now can't afford. 'We're going to operate more like a business,'" said the CHA's board chair.[8] Horizon Development Properties, the new nonprofit, would "own and operate developments, enter into partnerships with private developers and issue bonds on which the interest is tax-exempt."[9]

After Shannon retired in 2002, Woodyard stepped up to head the CHA. Federal dollars plus tenants' rents no longer covered local operating costs, as they had in public housing's early years. Washington "gives the Authority $220 for each of its approximately 3000 apartments and homes. But it costs just under $300 . . . to maintain each of those units." That left a $2.4 million annual shortfall, reported the *Charlotte Observer*.[10] Woodyard had to find ways to stem the losses. The CHA must, he declared, "act like a real estate company, not like a government agency."[11]

He looked around for old CHA properties that could be redeveloped. Tall Oaks in the fast-gentrifying Cherry neighborhood, the Barringer Hotel in the heart of downtown, and the Strawn Apartments for the elderly at the edge of the center city topped the list. "These communities are aging out," Woodyard said, and mere remodeling was not the answer. They should be totally rebuilt. The

Cheap Money and the K-Shaped Recovery

Among the factors that pushed up real estate prices during the 2010s were the cheap money policies of the Federal Reserve. In the depth of the 2008 Great Recession, the Fed cut interest rates to stimulate a recovery. That was standard US economic practice—but the Fed failed to bring the rates back up. Instead, it kept cutting. Mortgage rates dropped under 5 percent, then under 4 percent, and finally under 3 percent in 2020 and 2021. That was the lowest ever in American history.

We have seen throughout this book that low-interest loans were among the most powerful ways to stimulate construction of low-income housing. What the Fed did in the 2010s, though, was not targeted to affordable housing. It transformed the US real estate market.

The rates triggered a feeding frenzy. Borrowers bid up the prices of real estate. Median home values spiraled upward during the 2010s, doubling in many places. Rents went up as fast or faster.

Experts began talking about a "K-shaped recovery."* Cheap interest and seemingly ever-rising prices created exciting opportunities—for people who had enough income/assets to qualify for loans. If you already had some wealth, the go-go market could be very good. That was the up-sloping top leg of the K.

But many Americans were renters, not able to qualify for a big loan. For them the 2010s was a fearful time. Speculators, fueled by cheap money, bought up affordable properties and "upscaled" them. Rapid gentrification ate away at neighborhoods, slashing the supply of naturally occurring affordable housing. That was the bottom leg of the K.

---

*Lance Roberts, "Fed Study: How We Made the Top 10 Percent Richer Than Ever," Real Investment Advice, October 3, 2020, https://realinvestmentadvice.com/fed-study-how-we-made-the-top-10-richer-than-ever/; "Record Low Mortgage Rates Widen Historic U.S. Economic Divides," *Bloomberg Businessweek*, November 10, 2020, https://www.bloomberg.com/news/articles/2020-11-10/cheap-credit-is-widening-wealth-inequality-across-america-s-racial-lines. "In the record-setting housing market of 2021, homeownership has become the dividing line for a fractured economy that's racing toward extremes." "The New Real Estate Normal: In the Fracturing Economy, Any House Can Inspire a Bidding War," *Washington Post*, July 20, 2021. See also notes 3, 4, 5, and 6 earlier in this chapter.

CHA through its Horizon arm would seek to add other income levels and also add nonhousing uses.[12]

That approach carried risks. The more different strands woven into a project, the more chances for problems, both during development and later during operation. "Mixed-use projects require more time, more expense and create a number of obstacles from an operational and financial standpoint that other projects don't face," cautioned an executive at Charlotte's Grubb Properties, a leading for-profit mixed-use developer.[13] Variables could be mind-boggling—from finding retail tenants that would attract a fickle public, to meeting building codes that set different requirements for different land uses. Courting capital partners carried its own headaches, warned Jud Little at Crosland Properties: "Investors in such projects can also pose problems. Some are in for the long haul, while others see the project to completion, then sell."[14] No wonder that large for-profit real estate deals often take decades to come to fruition—assembling land, finding investors, lining up anchor-tenants, arranging bank loans for construction, and much, much more. Said the Grubb executive dryly: "Those kinds of projects can go awry."[15]

Indeed, the timetables for the ambitious Tall Oaks, Barringer, and Strawn redevelopments would extend past Woodyard's departure in 2011 and long into the tenure of the CHA's next chief, Fulton Meachem.

■ ■ ■ ■ ■

Tall Oaks in the Cherry neighborhood had come into existence as scattered-site public housing back in the early 1980s, a stabilizing presence in what was then a blue-collar Black neighborhood. Three decades later, the neighborhood found itself unexpectedly buffeted by intense changes.

The Cherry Community Organization (CCO), a Black citizens group active since the 1970s, owned numerous properties—dilapidated rental houses that had been seized by the city from absentee landlords and transferred to the CCO (see chapter 6).[16] In 2004 a Black developer named Stony Sellars made what sounded like a great proposal. If the CCO would sell him eight acres of old houses in the midst of the neighborhood, he promised to demolish the decaying dwellings, build at least thirty-eight new units for seniors and other low-income households, and develop the rest of the acreage as townhouses and single-family residences. To the CCO, which had been fighting neglect and disinvestment for decades, Sellars appeared to be a savior.

Hope soon gave way to angry disappointment. Sellars did build Cherry Gardens, a tax credit project via the LIHTC program serving forty-two low-income

Figure 9.1. Two Tall Oaks buildings (*left and center*) blend with a street of single-family houses in Cherry. Hanchett photo, 2023.

seniors.[17] But it quickly became clear that his new market-rate housing would not be aimed at blue-collar buyers, as the CCO had assumed, but instead would be priced at the top of the market, $600,000 and up.[18] Sellars recognized a burgeoning desire among high-income professionals (many of them white) for in-city homes—even if located in low-income environs. By 2016, Cherry's population, historically Black and blue-collar, had become 79 percent white and mostly well-to-do.

At that point, the CHA/Horizon stepped in. Could the CHA use its Tall Oaks land to help low-income people retain a foothold in Cherry?

The fifty existing public housing units, in two-story look-alike wood-frame buildings, fell to Horizon's bulldozers in 2016. In their place rose eighty-one units in two- and three-story buildings, each with different brick-and-clapboard exteriors. The architecture, by Black-led design firm Neighboring Concepts, blended deftly into the streetscape.[19]

Tall Oaks pointed up pluses and minuses of the business-minded approach.[20] The handsome and homey buildings, scattered on four different blocks, held many more residents, all below median income. Instead of fifty households at lowest-income, there were now eighteen at 30 percent AMI and sixty-three at 60 percent AMI.[21]

But if you looked closely at those numbers, you realized that the most-needy Charlotteans (people at 30 percent AMI) had once again lost ground.

■ ■ ■ ■ ■

While the Cherry effort mingled income levels, the Barringer and Strawn projects aimed to mix in retail as well. That proved to be a much more time-consuming challenge.

The twelve-story Barringer, built in 1940, had languished as downtown hotels lost favor with American travelers, and in 1979 the CHA had converted it to public housing.[22] It was often used as "swing space," where tenants lived while other complexes were being rebuilt. By 2014 it stood vacant, mothballed by the CHA as Fulton Meachem pursued redevelopment.

The Barringer site, the rest of the block (owned by Bank of America), and the adjoining block of Tryon Street (government-owned public library and Spirit Square arts facility) were hot properties in a now-booming downtown. Meachem and the other owners enlisted an out-of-town master developer to devise a plan. Early drafts had the CHA/Horizon retaining an ownership stake. But by 2020 the developer was calling for Meachem to sell the Barringer land.

Meachem refused. He'd learned a big lesson at Live Oak/Ashley Square in SouthPark and at Tall Oaks in Cherry. Putting new low-income housing on an existing site stirred little opposition. But acquiring fresh land almost always triggered neighborhood resistance, time-consuming at best, project-killing at worst. If the CHA ever wanted to build affordable housing downtown, it must keep a tight hold on its land.

Meachem pulled out of the Seventh and Tryon consortium. With Maryland-based developer Urban Atlantic, he put together a seven-story project with retail on the ground level and 353 apartments above. It would be "luxury, mixed-income housing," said Meachem, while at the same time including 106 low-income households at 80 percent, 50 percent, and 30 percent AMI.[23] For the CHA, it would be a profit center, generating income for affordable housing work elsewhere. Construction started in 2023. Planning and deal-making had taken almost a decade.

Strawn, a much larger project, would take even longer. The sixteen-acre site on South Boulevard was at a gateway to downtown, an area newly popular as "South End." The CHA had built a tower and several one-story structures, a total of 316 units in all, for low-income seniors back in 1971. Now, in boom times, could the land be redeveloped more densely?

In 2004 the CHA identified the site as one it would like to redo if finances allowed.[24] It rezoned the land for mixed-use in 2010 and then hired the national Urban Land Institute to draft a plan for what might fit.[25] In 2016, the

Boston-based Fallon Company signed on to lead creation of Centre South: "725 mixed-income apartments (145 to be affordable for between 65 to 85 percent of Area Median Income), 20 for-sale townhouses, 57,000 square feet of retail, a 330,000-square-foot office building and a 180-room hotel," reported the *Charlotte Business Journal*.[26] At the same time, the CHA moved occupants out of the Strawn Tower, renovated it and moved them back in, and demolished the one-story units.[27] But at that point, visible progress ceased. Critics began asking what was taking so long—and also called attention to the small number of affordable units in the package.

"Patience Is a Virtue in Developing Affordable Housing," Meachem fired back in an op-ed.[28] Centre South might not be creating new lowest-income units, he admitted, but it would preserve 170 existing units in the Strawn high-rise. If Charlotteans supported the CHA's "mission to develop, operate and provide quality housing in sustainable communities of choice for residents of diverse incomes," they needed to recognize that "ambitious, complex and transformative projects" took time.

Indeed, the Centre South delays closely paralleled the types of setbacks that dragged out other big mixed-use efforts. "Four Huge Developments Have Stalled," noted *Observer* reporter Ely Portillo in 2018.[29]

Centre South ceremonially broke ground in 2020.[30] But as this book moved to publication in 2025—twenty-five years after the initial announcement—actual construction had not yet begun.

RAD Fosters Public-Private Ownership: The End of "Public Housing"?

A little-heralded change from Washington played into the business-driven approach that Fulton Meachem—and other public housing CEOs across the nation—pursued during the 2010s and 2020s. In 2011 under President Barack Obama, HUD launched a new program called RAD (Rental Assistance Demonstration).[31] The innocuous name gave no hint of the audacious impact. RAD would open fresh funding sources—and drastically change public housing's ownership.

As we begin to look into RAD, you'll recall that Congress sends dollars each year to local housing authorities to help them operate their projects.[32] Over time, due to a multitude of pressures including inflation and also conservative resistance to "coddling" the poor, that HUD budget line has gotten trimmed tighter and tighter. Periodically, Congress has searched for other ways to assist low-income housing. (Such was the reasoning behind the Low-Income Housing Tax Credit begun in 1986. Its tax breaks came via the Internal Revenue Service—a separate pot of money from HUD.)

RAD operated on the same principle: tap federal money outside of HUD's public housing budget and use those government dollars to attract private dollars.[33] It added a fresh twist: utilize the ongoing stream of federal operating money as a creative leveraging tool. To make it happen, HUD resurrected the old Section 8 Project-Based program, largely dormant since the 1980s. Here's how it all worked:

1. The local housing authority would set up LLCs (limited liability companies) to own each of its public housing projects.
2. HUD would shift its regular aid allocation from its "public housing" budget to its "Section 8" budget. (As we have seen previously, Congress is much more comfortable making appropriations for Section 8, regarded as a boon to the real estate industry, than it is funding "public housing," seen as a giveaway to the poor.)
3. The aid would be "Section 8 Project-Based." In regular Section 8, tenants got portable housing choice vouchers that they could use with any landlord who would accept them. Under Project-Based rules, in contrast, the vouchers stayed with a particular building. That meant a guaranteed income stream for the LLC.
4. The guaranteed income stream was almost like gold. Investors loved it. They would gladly loan money to an LLC (or buy any bonds it might issue) because they knew that dollars would be streaming in predictably over the years to pay back the borrowing.
5. The LLC could use those dollars *today* to remedy delayed maintenance issues—no waiting for local or national government appropriations.
6. Under RAD the housing authority could even sell part of its ownership stake to private investors. (Private investors could take tax benefits under LIHTC; see chapter 7.) With that immediate cash in hand, the authority could build new stuff, such as adding retail or rental housing for higher income tenants. In fact, the authority could set up entirely new LLCs to construct new housing projects. (In all cases, HUD required that the housing authority retain at least a 51 percent stake so that it controlled the LLC.)

In short, explained HUD, the RAD strategy offered a "reliable income stream for operations and maintenance and better attracts private investment for capital needs of the property."[34]

RAD incorporated lessons that HUD had learned from mistakes during the earlier HOPE VI program. RAD guaranteed that renters had the "right to remain" or, if temporarily moved off-site, were guaranteed the right to return. RAD required one-for-one replacement: "Public Housing Authority must retain or replace units on a one-for-one basis." And RAD offered a way to get around the notorious Faircloth Amendment, which had blocked any increase to total public housing units. Because the LLCs no longer received money from HUD's "public housing" budget, they were exempt from Faircloth.[35]

The Charlotte Housing Authority went all-in on RAD. By 2020, according to the agency's annual report, it had "converted a total of 3,179 Public Housing units to Project Based Voucher (PBV) units and is on schedule to convert 100 percent of the agency's Public Housing inventory by end of FY 2022."[36] New capital investments blossomed. At First Ward Place, for example, the buildings constructed under HOPE VI, now showing a quarter-century of wear, were recapitalized and spruced up; the RAD-inspired LLC applied for a fresh round of tax credits via the LIHTC program to sweeten the pot.[37] Elsewhere around the city, the Charlotte Housing Authority contemplated—for the first time in many years—constructing totally new housing projects. The agency's Horizon Development Properties listed plans for seven mixed-income apartment complexes in 2021, each co-owned with private LIHTC developers. They would offer "clients a chance to move into a community not historically known as being federally subsidized."[38]

As the 2020s began, the long-term effects of RAD were less clear, however. It represented a huge change in the meaning of "public" housing. Since the 1940s, the term had meant that local government had full, direct ownership. Now, though, private entities controlled up to 49 percent of ownership. What would that mean over the coming years? What would happen as the private partners used up their tax credits from the LIHTC program? Would they lose interest in maintenance? Would they bring pressure to convert projects to market-rate?

Housing expert Alex F. Schwartz was among the national voices skeptical of RAD. "Public housing has proven to be the most durable of the nation's low-income housing programs," he wrote in 2021. "The secret to the longevity of public housing is its public ownership. Unlike virtually all other types of subsidized housing, public housing guarantees perpetual low-income occupancy."[39] Would that guarantee continue to exist for America's neediest residents?

The CHA Becomes Inlivian

With so many changes underway, Fulton Meachem decided that it was time to rename the Charlotte Housing Authority. His team talked with tenants, community members, and funding partners who agreed that "housing authority" carried strongly negative connotations. In 2019 they coined an entirely new word, Inlivian, rooted in "enliven."[40]

Inlivian's goals did not specifically mention housing the poorest of the poor. It now aimed to "play a vital role in expanding the supply of permanent mixed-income units in Charlotte by maximizing real estate assets through acquisition, rehabilitation, and development of permanent workforce, market rate, and affordable units in desirable neighborhoods."[41]

To be sure, Meachem promised, Inlivian would continue to maintain a large inventory of lowest-income housing and also provide "supportive services" that helped clients cope with life challenges and, hopefully, move away from government assistance. But that was just one "line of business" among many. Inlivian, said its goal statement, "will utilize vital expertise in development, technology, property management, social service provision, and other areas to generate various lines of business on a fee-for-service basis to other government, non-profit, and for-profit entities . . . [to] Create and Enhance Diverse Income Streams."[42]

Inlivian, in summary, no longer saw itself solely as a builder and maintainer of housing for Charlotte's lowest-income residents. It was a diversified corporation, said Meachem, pursuing an "innovative approach to housing, real estate development, property management and resident services."[43]

"We never thought about it as getting out of the affordable housing business. It was all about creating more opportunities for us and the families we serve," he emphasized. "Because the numbers, at the end of the day, all these math problems, they have to work financially."[44]

A Frenzy of Gentrification: Rapid and Huge Loss of NOAH

During the first decade of the 2000s, people in older Charlotte neighborhoods started talking about a surprising phenomenon: teardowns. You could detect it in the demolition permit statistics. In the early and mid-1990s, it had been rare to see an old house or duplex torn down. Mecklenburg County issued just fourteen single-family demolition permits in 1994. But that started to change, part of a national phenomenon in which people with money and choice began to question their ever-longer commutes to far-flung suburbs. By 2004, Mecklenburg demo permits were running 300–400 per year. Wealthy close-in neighborhoods felt the pressure first. Elite old-line Myers Park, which held some post–World War II ranch-style houses along with earlier mansions, saw the relatively modest dwellings snapped up, torn down, and replaced. "Livable Houses Razed for 'Monster Houses,'" headlined the *Charlotte Observer* in 2004, the first story on the trend.[45]

SOID
Source of Income Discrimination

Housing choice vouchers (often referred to as "Section 8") have been an important tool since the 1980s, as we have seen. HUD gives to each local housing authority a number of vouchers, which the authority assigns to people in need. With the voucher, people can rent in any market-rate apartment; they pay part of the rent (up to 30 percent of their income) and the voucher covers the rest. It's a market-based solution that enables people to choose to live wherever economic opportunities are strong.

At least that's the theory.

In reality, a sizable number of apartment owners refuse to take the vouchers. "Landlords just say ... 'We don't accept Section 8.' Period," Inlivian CEO Fulton Meachem says with frustration.* It's not a new problem, but Charlotte's intensified focus on housing affordability and economic opportunity in the late 2010s made it a priority for some city leaders.

In 2019, seventeen Charlotte organizations, ranging from Inlivian and Habitat for Humanity to veterans' groups, mobilized to convince the City Council to make "Source of Income Discrimination" (SOID) illegal under Charlotte's fair housing ordinance.†

One point they emphasized: HUD allocated nowhere near enough vouchers to serve every family that qualified, and that allocation was not going up, despite Charlotte's rapidly rising population. Some 6,000 households languished on the city's waiting list. The typical wait was five years.

With that in mind, another statistic was heartbreaking. Due in part to SOID, "one in five households that receives a voucher in Charlotte doesn't find housing in time to use it" before its expiration date, reported the *Observer*.

And it wasn't just Section 8. Vouchers from the Veterans Administration for homeless veterans, as well as disability checks provided by other agencies, were

(continued)

---

*Fulton Meachem, interview by Tom Hanchett, June 22, 2022; A. Fulton Meachem, "Issue Brief: Housing for Everyone—Addressing Barriers to Opportunity," undated report by Inlivian emailed to Tom Hanchett, June 27, 2022; Webb and Melvin, "Appendix C."

†"Housing Groups Want to Ban Rental Source of Income Discrimination," *Charlotte Observer*, December 17, 2019; "Housing Organizations Try to Stop 'Income Discrimination,'" Spectrum News, December 16, 2019, https://www.ny1.com/nyc/all-boroughs/news/2019/12/16/housing-organizations-try-to-stop—income-discrimination-; Webb and Melvin, "Appendix C."

being turned down, said Ryan Carter, Habitat for Humanity's point person on the issue.‡

To document the problems, Meachem says, "we interviewed about seventeen different apartment communities, all on the Blue Line"—the new commuter rail corridor intended to spur high-density residential construction. "And every one of them—except for the three that were [built partly with Charlotte's] Housing Trust Fund and the Low-Income Housing Tax Credit—from all of them, the answer to this simply was, 'We don't accept Section 8.'

"When you're not evaluating people based on your screening criteria [but instead] based solely on the fact that they have a housing choice voucher, that is discriminatory. It impacts mostly women, right? Mostly African American women with children. Which again pushes that group of individuals further and further down the economic ladder."**

Even as the SOID coalition lobbied for legislation, Inlivian also met directly with landlords to try to address concerns. Explained Meachem:

> We work very hard with the Greater Charlotte Apartment Association—as well as we created our own advisory board of housing providers and landlords throughout Charlotte to give us some of their issues with the housing choice voucher program.
>
> Then we started developing incentives to address those issues.
>
> Some people didn't like the inspection [mandated by HUD and carried out by Inlivian].... So instead of doing them every year, we started moving those to every two years.
>
> We started to say, OK, well maybe we need some incentives monetarily as well. And so we said, "We'll give [landlords] a $250 signing bonus if they sign for the housing choice voucher program."
>
> Another thing we do is say, "Hey, well, if you have a resident and they leave"—'cause people move—"we'll pay you in that time in between, fourteen days. We'll pay you fourteen days in between the time a person moves out, another person moves in. So you still have some level of continuous income going on." What that normally is, is make-ready time [in which landlords do cleaning and minor renovations]. And you're not making any income during that period of time. We say that we will pay you during

(continued)

---

‡ Webb and Melvin, "Appendix C."
** Meachem interview.

that downtime . . . if you lease to a person with the housing choice voucher program.

And then finally we said, "OK, we know that you get security deposits. But we'll also pay a thousand dollars more than your security deposit for any damages that a resident will cost."

All these things we put in place to incentivize housing providers. Because again, they are not the bad guy. I understand that they are here to make money. And trust me, I'm not against anybody making money. I just think that . . . when it comes to housing, everybody should have that opportunity to . . . actually live where they want to.[††]

In 2022, after three years of lobbying, the City Council voted to outlaw Source of Income Discrimination—but only in apartment projects that had used government land or Charlotte Housing Trust Fund aid.[‡‡] For most landlords, SOID rules still don't apply.

[††] Meachem interview.
[‡‡] "Charlotte Landlords May Reject Tenants with Rent Vouchers," *Charlotte Observer*, April 4, 2022; "Charlotte Wants More Landlords to Accept Vouchers," Axios Charlotte, July 5, 2022, https://charlotte.axios.com/301600/charlotte-wants-more-landlords-to-accept-vouchers/. "Charlotte became the first city in North Carolina to implement protections against source-of-income discrimination." "City Makes Renting Easier for Section Eight Voucher Holders," *Charlotte Observer*, August 24, 2022.

The demolition wave declined slightly with the 2008 recession but then began rising even more sharply as Washington's rock-bottom interest rates propelled the K-shaped recovery. Demolitions spread beyond the already-desirable neighborhoods in southeast Charlotte. Suddenly prospective homeowners and speculators were buying up old rental houses in blue-collar Black neighborhoods such as Seversville and Biddleville on the city's west side near Johnson C. Smith University.

Demolition stats shot upward. Nearly 800 single-family homes in Mecklenburg bit the dust in 2016 alone, along with an untold number of duplexes and other apartments. They were usually among the most affordable housing in their neighborhoods. The replacement dwellings "reset" the housing price-point in the vicinity, not only for the new houses but also for existing ones. On State Street in Seversville, for instance, you could buy a home for about $60,000 in the early years of the 2000s. Fifteen years later that figure had jumped tenfold to about $600,000.[46] Rents went up proportionately.

If you were lucky enough to own your house, that could produce a windfall, though it was tough finding anything that you could buy with the money. Most Black people on State Street were not owners, however. They rented from landlords who now saw big profit in selling. Many of the families had memories of being displaced back in the era of urban renewal or in the HOPE VI years. Even though this time the causes of displacement were different, the effect was the same. By the end of the 2010s, most of Seversville's lifelong Black residents were gone.

All across the city, rents rose relentlessly. Median rent for a one-bedroom apartment hovered around $900 a month in Charlotte at the start of the 2010s. By the end of the decade, it was up about 60 percent to nearly $1,500 a month.[47]

To put it another way, NOAH was disappearing. As said many times in this book, most people who need low-income housing have found it not in subsidized units but in older market-rate places. Those were now vanishing. "Approximately 51 percent of rental units were low-cost in 2010. By 2018 only 25 percent were low-cost," reported the University of North Carolina at Charlotte's Urban Institute.[48]

Charlotteans often assumed that the hot market was a local thing. Indeed, Charlotte did rank among the fastest growing metro areas in the United States, appearing in the top dozen year after year.[49] As people streamed in, they put heavy demand on the existing housing stock.

But in actuality, similar price jumps were happening in many parts of the United States. "Rising rents won't let up in 2016 and will continue to set new records. The next year will bring the least affordable median rents ever," forecast the real estate research firm Zillow at mid-decade. "Highest Ever" US median rent became a recurring headline year after year.[50]

At the same time, incomes stagnated. The gap that had begun to open around 2000 between America's average workers and those in the upper reaches of the economic pyramid now widened. If you were wealthy, the national economy had a rosy glow. If you weren't, the future held less and less hope. Minimum wage stopped rising: $7.25 an hour in 2009 and exactly the same a dozen years later.[51]

I'll say that again. Minimum wage stopped rising. It stood at $7.25 an hour in 2009 and $7.25 a dozen years later.

Even as median rent shot up 60 percent.[52]

In Charlotte, the *Observer* compared incomes in the city's neighborhoods and found inequality on the upswing: "The difference between the highest and lowest median incomes in 2016 was about $103,000. That's up more than $3,000

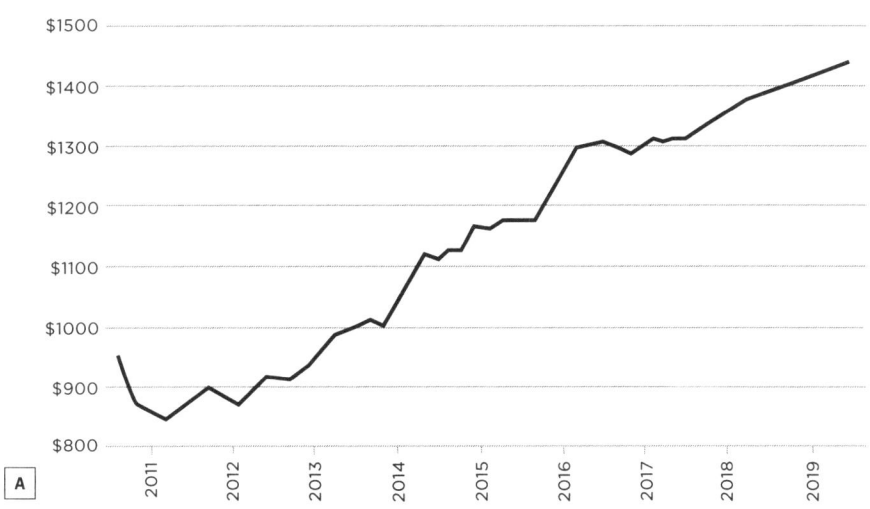

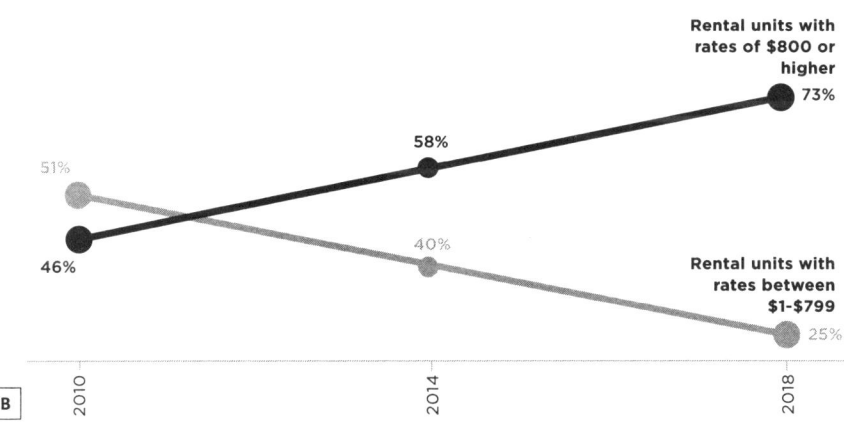

Graph 9.1. A: Apartment rents took off as America came out of the 2008 recession. Zillow data; graph adapted from Griffin, "Single-Family Construction." B: NOAH (naturally occurring affordable housing) apartments became scarce during the 2010s. Graph adapted from Anderson, Charlotte–Mecklenburg: 2020 State of Housing Instability and Homelessness Report.

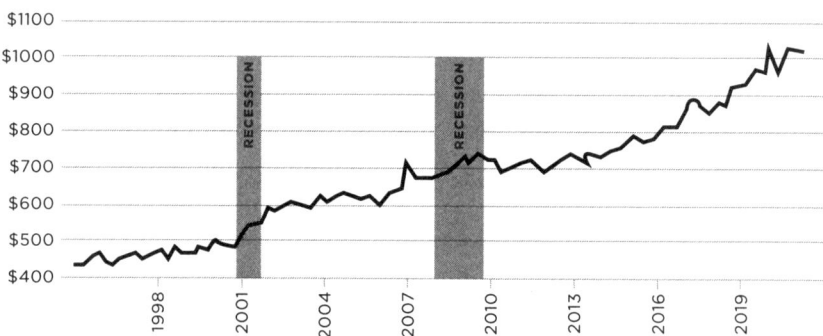

Graph 9.2. Rapidly rising rents were a national problem, not unique to Charlotte. Graph adapted from US Census Bureau, "Quarterly Residential Vacancies and Homeownership, Third Quarter 2019."

from five years prior."[53] Nationally, a *Wall Street Journal* analysis of 2007–19 data showed that "households in the bottom 20 percent of incomes had seen their financial assets, such as money in the bank, stock and bond investments or retirement funds fall by 34 percent since the end of the 2007–2009 recession. Those in the middle of the income distribution have seen just four percent growth"—at the same time that upper-income wealth soared, year upon year.[54]

While the K-shaped real estate market played a big role in pushing up housing prices during the 2010s, additional factors exacerbated the situation. One that observers frequently mentioned: young adults, squeezed by an economy that made it tough to save enough to put a down payment on a house, continued to rent longer. That bigger demand drove rents upward.[55] Charlotte experienced a boom in construction of new apartments aimed at the most affluent part of the young cohort, while less wealthy friends crowded into existing units.[56]

Older apartment complexes became a hot commodity. Investors snapped them up, did minimal renovations, and then jacked up the rent.[57] "The share of rental units priced for very low-income households in Charlotte has decreased since 2000, while the number of these households significantly increased over that same period," said the 2018 study *Housing Charlotte*, with alarm. In just the past four years, "the city lost more than half its supply (nearly 28,000 units) of large-scale NOAH for households earning 50 percent of area median income or below."[58]

New transit construction also played a part in the rising housing prices—but only in limited areas. The north-south Lynx light rail line that opened in 2007 and was extended in 2018 sparked neighborhood transformations around some of its stops near uptown, particularly in South End and also the Optimist Park vicinity where new mid-rise apartment buildings sprouted by the dozens. It was tempting to blame the Lynx for housing woes, but if you looked carefully, tear-downs were now everywhere. Heavy machinery showed up at a house one day, and rubble-filled dump trucks departed the next, leaving the land scoured clean and ready to build upon. It happened most often within four or five miles of uptown but otherwise seemed to pay little attention to social geography or public investment.[59]

Yet another upward force on real estate prices came from wealthy out-of-town investors. Wall Street financial firms began buying up single-family homes to lease out.[60] The business model called for regularly raising rents, decreasing maintenance, and being merciless on any tenants who fell behind. The trend appeared nationally during the mid-2010s and gathered momentum as the 2020s began. Charlotte's strong population growth made the city very attractive to these national players. A 2021 report by Realtor.com "put Charlotte at No. 2 on the list of housing markets most negatively impacted by investors. That means investors are buying more homes than they sell in the Charlotte area, taking away local inventory. In the Charlotte market, investors were shown to have a significant impact, taking away 287 homes from the local inventory" in a single month in 2021—and thus pushing up the prices for the remaining homes on the market.[61]

Whatever the exact mix of forces, people who depended on NOAH increasingly found themselves screwed. Lamented a Charlotte social worker, "They're tearing down affordable neighborhoods. I mean, places where you'd have private owners that would maybe work with somebody [who had trouble making the rent], they're gone, you know?"[62]

In a city where the wealthy and the less well-to-do usually lived miles apart, would Charlotte leaders ever recognize what was happening?

Big Push for Affordable Housing after 2016

The first wake-up call came from Berkeley, California, in 2014. A scholar named Raj Chetty published a study of economic opportunity in fifty major US metro areas. Where did a person at the bottom of the ladder have the best shot at climbing to the top? Charlotte ranked dead last, fiftieth out of fifty.[63] The abysmal showing grabbed the attention of city leaders. What could be done to improve the situation?

Chetty's team did not nail down the exact factors involved, but one was a "spatial mismatch" in which well-to-do neighborhoods with good jobs had few

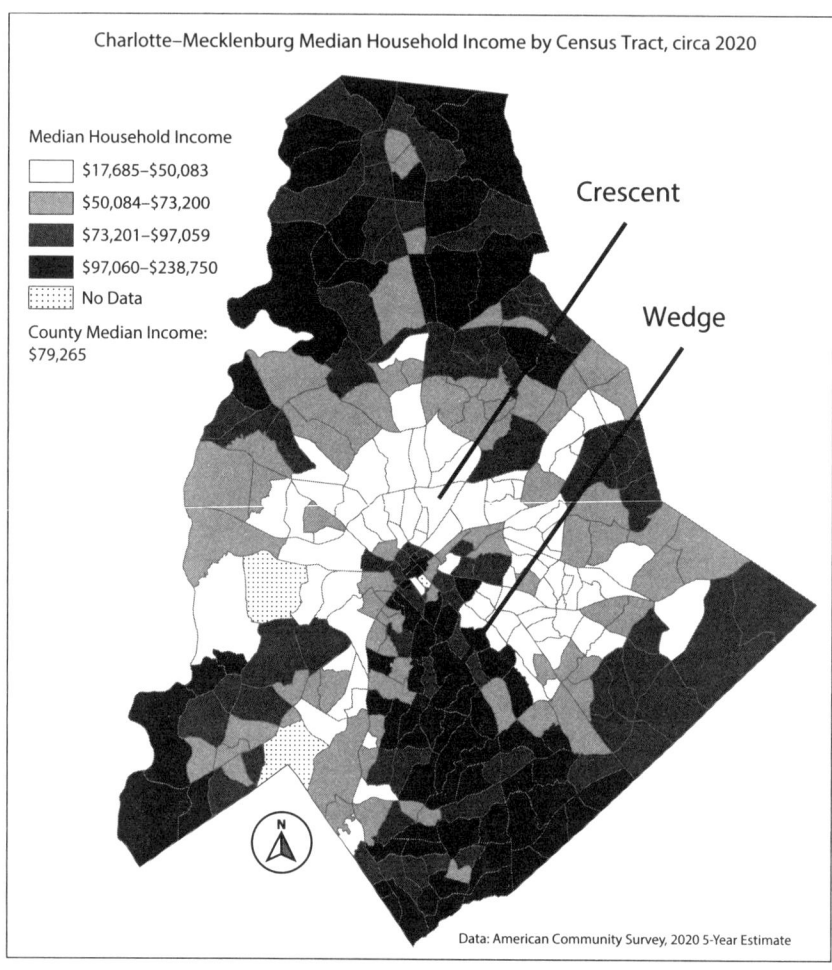

Map 9.1. Income levels clustered in an upscale wedge to the south and a less-prosperous crescent across the center of Mecklenburg County. Courtesy of UNC Charlotte Urban Institute.

affordable living units for folks who needed those jobs. Local Charlotte leaders began to acknowledge and discuss what came to be called the "wedge and crescent": upscale residents concentrated in the south, counterpointed by a crescent of much less prosperous neighborhoods across the center of Mecklenburg County. Charlotte's scattered-site public housing and later efforts such as Ashley Square had placed some projects in the southward wedge of wealth. But not nearly enough.[64]

The second wake-up call arrived after the Keith Lamont Scott shooting on September 20, 2016.[65] Two days of chaos rocked the city, wrenching it into the national spotlight. For established leaders, dealing with inequality became a topline concern. A coalition of young activists who called themselves the Charlotte Uprising worked hard to keep the issues hot during the weeks and months that followed. Well-planned marches and other nonviolent protests continued for more than a year.[66] The Uprising coalition included a fresh generation of African American leaders, among them Bree Newsome, who had first made national headlines when she climbed a flagpole at the South Carolina capitol to take down the Confederate flag in 2015.[67] Other key organizers in the Uprising came from immigrant-rights work: Latino leaders Oliver Merino and Stefania Arteaga, Southeast Asian Coalition organizers Tin Nguyen and Cat Bao Le.[68]

Within days of the shooting, housing issues bubbled to the top. *Charlotte Observer* journalist Ely Portillo reported on a Black speaker at an October 2 City Council meeting who linked the protests to the rapid displacement in gentrifying neighborhoods: "What we're looking at now, that's the effect."[69] Bree Newsome launched the Housing Justice Coalition, saying, "It's important to realize that the amount of anger and hurt that is felt is not totally about the killing that happened Tuesday."[70] A writer for the national online CityLab of Bloomberg News urged Charlotte leaders to "form a long-term vision" to "protect against resident displacement."[71] Headlined the *Charlotte Observer*: "Keith Lamont Scott Shooting Sparks Calls to Fix Charlotte Affordable Housing Shortage."[72]

But would Charlotte's politicians and business leaders actually do anything? As the Uprising kept the pressure on via marches and protests, a sequence of national and local events sparked real action in Charlotte. For the first time in decades, public debate focused intensely on *how* to *sharply increase* the supply of affordable housing and also on *whom* that housing should be for.

- **October 2016: 5,000 units pledged.** All eleven members of City Council signed a letter, drafted by councilmember Vi Lyles, pledging to create 5,000 affordable housing units in the next three years.[73]
- **April 2017: National study puts focus on ELI (under 30 percent AMI).** The Urban Institute in Washington, DC, released a study of what they termed ELI—or extremely low-income—housing. Since the 1980s, most "affordable housing" construction had been funded by the Low-Income Housing Tax Credit—which mainly reached households who earned 60 percent of area median income. But what about the poorest of the poor: under 30 percent AMI? The analysis dramatically reset the terms of housing discussions. "Every U.S. County Has an Affordable Housing Crisis," headlined Bloomberg.[74] In Mecklenburg County, only 27 ELI units existed for every 100 ELI households, an abysmal figure.

- **May 2017: *The Color of Law* proves government culpability in housing inequality.** The highly readable best-selling book relentlessly documented decades of practices by national and local governments that systematically blocked Black citizens from housing opportunities. Author Richard Rothstein reached the ears of many decision-makers via appearances on NPR's *Fresh Air* and *All Things Considered*.[75] Also that spring, Matthew Desmond's book *Evicted*, an emotionally powerful exposé of forces that kept millions of Americans teetering on the edge of homelessness, won the Pulitzer Prize.[76]
- **November 2017: Voters elect Vi Lyles as mayor.** While her background in housing was not much mentioned during the campaign, Lyles's election as Charlotte's first Black female mayor signaled the voters' embrace of change. That echoed in the City Council election, where all seats went to young people of the "millennial" generation—including Black, dreadlocked Braxton Winston, who'd been on the front lines of the 2016 protests.[77]
- **Early 2018: Voices demand change.** During 2018, more and more calls came from every direction. "What we're looking for is action. Concrete sustainable change," demanded local NAACP president Corrine Mack.[78] Real estate developer Clay Grubb, in an *Observer* op-ed, criticized Mayor Lyles as "not bold enough."[79]
- **August 2018: *Housing Charlotte: A Framework* sets 20 percent ELI requirement.** The detailed policy document approved by City Council laid out over forty pages of actions that local government would undertake. A key requirement: any housing developed with land or subsidies acquired from the city or county must set aside at least 20 percent of units for extremely low-income households. This was a big milestone. In a city where real estate interests wielded great power, no such requirement had ever been made.[80]
- **September 2018: Artist spotlights displacement at Brookhill.** Locally based, nationally active Black photographer Alvin C. Jacobs opened a photo exhibition at the Gantt Center in uptown Charlotte. It put a human face on the struggle of residents in Brookhill Village (an early FHA 608 project; see chapter 3) to stay in their apartments as gentrification rolled in from South End. Jacobs's art built upon ongoing efforts by Rev. Ray McKinnon, Lisa Stockton Howell, and others affiliated with the adjacent South Tryon Methodist Church, which had strong crosstown connections in wealthy Myers Park. Altogether, the activists' mix of incomes, ages, races, and energies helped make Brookhill a powerful symbol of displacement.[81]

- **October 2018: "Millions Go to Housing, but Poor Can't Afford It."** A hard-hitting *Observer* article by reporters Fred Clasen-Kelly and Juliana Rennie made sure that Charlotteans grasped the long-standing shortfall in ELI. There was now enough affordable housing to serve Charlotte's 60 percent AMI households—hooray!—but people below that level were hurting.[82] "From 2002 through March 2018, [the Charlotte Housing Trust Fund] provided developers money to build about 4,500 apartments and houses, but records show only about 1,300 were affordable to households making less than 30 percent of area median income. That's $25,100 a year for a family of four."[83] The story profiled specific struggling renters, including a school custodian and a nurse assistant. For many Charlotteans, even those who had actively supported LIHTC-aided affordable housing efforts, it was a startling wake-up call.
- **November 2018: Voters approve $50 million housing bond.** Mayor Lyles asked voters in 2018 to OK $50 million in new bonds for the Charlotte Housing Trust Fund, up from the $15 million typically sought every two years.[84] They not only did that but also added another $50 million in the next bond election.[85] Corporations and nonprofits pledged over $50 million more.[86]

By 2018, barely two years after housing surfaced as a major concern in the wake of the Keith Lamont Scott shooting, Charlotte had big dollars ready to spend on affordable housing. It also had that intangible essential: political will. Not only Mayor Lyles and City Council but also a broad collection of community members now pushed passionately and vocally for action.

A group called OneMECK was one example. New activists—Justin Perry and Rosalyn Allison Jacobs (Black) and Pete and Mary Kelly (white)—joined with longtime advocates Ted Fillette (white) and westside minster Rev. Ricky Woods (Black). They arranged a "community read" of *The Color of Law*. The public library gave away hundreds of free books, publicized community discussions, and helped bring author Richard Rothstein to town for an evening at Reverend Woods's First Baptist Church West.[87] A diverse crowd overflowed the large sanctuary and filled the gymnasium.

Journalists kept housing on the front burner. In June 2019 reporter Pam Kelley published a deeply researched overview of Charlotte's recent housing efforts: "From Brooklyn to Ballantyne: The Story behind Charlotte's Affordable Housing Crisis."[88] It documented how governmental and private actions had stymied housing efforts, from the "urban renewal" of Brooklyn through the efforts that

Vi Alexander Lyles
Persistent Voice for Affordable Housing

A key reason that housing moved to the forefront of public discussion and action in Charlotte after 2016 was the leadership of Vi Lyles. Decades of personal engagement gave her a high level of understanding of the issue, as well as expertise with the tools to address it.

"It has always been something that has had a lot of meaning for me," she reflected in a 2022 interview. She grew up "in a southern community—I went to George Washington Carver Elementary School. I remember ... that there were families that lived in shotgun houses right across the street from my school in Columbia, South Carolina, [where] you could see the dirt [floors inside them] still."*

Her family was part of a southern tradition of African American builders; Black masons and carpenters were often leaders in the construction field in the decades after slavery. "My grandfather, I have pictures of him with a wagon and a mule, building the first basement [on the] main street of Columbia. My father and his brother continued that business. Now, my brothers run that business [Taylor Brothers Construction]. We are a third-generation family in construction and still in Columbia."

She came to Charlotte as one of the first Black students at Queens College, earned a master's in public administration at the University of North Carolina at Chapel Hill, and then joined the city's budget office in 1975.† Among her initial tasks: developing the five-year Capital Improvement Plan that included the first allocations for the fledgling scattered-site housing initiative.

During the 1980s she rose to be Charlotte's budget director, the highest-ranking Black woman in local government. Her ally and mentor was Pam Syfert, a white woman just a few years older, who followed a similar trajectory from researcher to budget director.‡ When Syfert broke the glass ceiling into top management as city manager in 1996, she appointed Vi Lyles as assistant city manager.

As Lyles moved up the ladder, housing issues were always part of her respon-

(continued)

---

* Vi Alexander Lyles, interview by Tom Hanchett, August 10, 2022. See also Lyles's bio at "2018 BE Entrepreneurs Summit," on the website Black Enterprise Entrepreneurs Summit, June 6–9, 2018, https://events.bizzabo.com/206192/agenda/speakers/262848.
† "Hall of Famer Chooses City Hall, Knowing It Can Be a Force for Good," *Charlotte Observer*, August 8, 1998.
‡ "Pamela Syfert, City Manager," profile posted in 1999 on the website Governing, https://www.governing.com/poy/pamela-syfert.html.

sibility. One example: when Betty Chafin Rash and Kathryn Heath launched the Charlotte–Mecklenburg Housing Partnership, Lyles was the city's liaison.** Another example: when Bank of America sought to buy city land to be part of the mixed-income apartments now known as Ten 05 West Trade, Lyles handled the transaction, demanding that the bank guarantee that the housing would stay affordable.†† A third example: when the Charlotte Housing Authority created Horizon Development Properties to buy and develop real estate, it named Assistant City Manager Vi Lyles to the entity's board.‡‡

Lyles seldom called attention to herself, projecting the persona of a friendly, unflamboyant civil servant. But her quiet competence caused elected leaders to look to her. In 2000, Syfert and City Council asked her to draft recommendations in advance of the council's annual planning retreat.*** Lyles responded with a proposal that the city begin issuing bonds to create a pool of dollars to aid low-income housing. That became the Charlotte Housing Trust Fund—the city's chief affordable housing tool.

All of that positioned Lyles to lead in shaping Charlotte responses to the protests sparked by the Keith Lamont Scott shooting. Now a member of City Council (elected after her retirement as assistant city manager in 2004), she took the initiative to draft the letter signed by council members that promised construction of 5,000 units of affordable housing. "We've got to give this community something that they can rely upon that will actually show that we care about people," she recalls thinking.††† Housing became that top action item.

A year later, voters elected her mayor. From that office, she pushed for two unprecedented $50 million housing bond issues—approved by a whopping 75+ percent of voters in 2018 and 2020—and helped arrange similar commitments from foundations and corporations.‡‡‡

** "They Often Agree, So What Makes Democrat Vi Lyles Different from Mayor Jennifer Roberts?," *Charlotte Observer*, October 15, 2017.
†† "City and B of A Still Far Apart on Lot Price: Affordable Housing at Stake," *Charlotte Observer*, January 18, 2001.
‡‡ "Low-Income Units to Come from Spin-Offs," *Charlotte Observer*, July 18, 2001.
*** "Council Retreat," minutes of the Charlotte City Council, February 8, 2001, minutes book 115, pp. 842–44, American Legal Publishing's Code Library, https://codelibrary.amlegal.com/codes/CharlotteNC/latest/m/2001/2/8. Former city manager Pam Syfert confirmed that Lyles suggested the use of bond funding to set up the Charlotte Housing Trust Fund. Pam Syfert, interview by Tom Hanchett, March 28, 2022.
††† Lyles interview.
‡‡‡ "Charlotte Approves Bonds for Streets, Housing," *Charlotte Observer*, November 5, 2020.

blocked low-income housing in upscale Ballantyne during the 2010s. Even if you'd been following newspaper coverage over the years, seeing it all together was a shock. Soon after Kelley's article, Ballantyne's chief developer announced plans to include 175 apartments at 80 percent AMI in its next construction phase—not extremely low-income, for sure, but Ballantyne's first-ever housing for below-median households.[89]

The civic leadership of ministers such as Rev. Ricky Woods and Rev. Ray McKinnon fired up other religious congregations across the city. A few Black churches had constructed affordable apartments over the years. The United House of Prayer for All People had built Grace Emmanuel Village Apartments in First Ward back in the 1980s. St. Paul Baptist began working in 2015 with Dionne Nelson's Laurel Street Residential to erect low-income Allen Street Apartments in the blocks near its historic sanctuary in the fast-gentrifying Belmont neighborhood.[90] Now other Black churches—and white churches as well—began to ponder: Could their land or other resources be used to follow the Bible's call to shelter the poor?

Wealthy and historically white Covenant Presbyterian Church in Dilworth joined with the Charlotte–Mecklenburg Housing Partnership to develop a big mixed-income LIHTC apartment complex next to a supermarket on Freedom Drive. Marsh Properties donated 7.8 acres, congregation members raised $2 million, and the Charlotte Housing Trust Fund chipped in $4.5 million. The 185 apartments would include 129 below-market-rate units at various levels of AMI. It broke ground at the end of 2018, with the name Mezzanine.[91]

Charlotte Housing Trust Fund payouts ramped up dramatically as proposals moved through the application pipeline. The fund OK'd eight projects with 950 units in July 2019 and nine developments with 1,400 units in April 2020.[92] That represented a sharp increase from the early 2010s, when the pace was often two or three deals each year.

The city hired a national nonprofit firm with a long track record, the Local Initiatives Support Corporation (LISC), to help administer the various funds and also connect Charlotte with national investors.[93] The nonprofit's portfolio included the Charlotte Housing Opportunity Investment Fund, the $50 million in corporate and private commitments raised by Foundation for the Carolinas. Ralphine Caldwell, LISC's local executive, had previously worked for the Charlotte–Mecklenburg Housing Partnership.

Most of the projects were new construction, but some added beds at Charlotte's homeless shelters while others renovated existing NOAH apartment complexes. Critics complained that beds were temporary accommodations and should not be counted as "affordable housing." In contrast, everyone applauded the NOAH

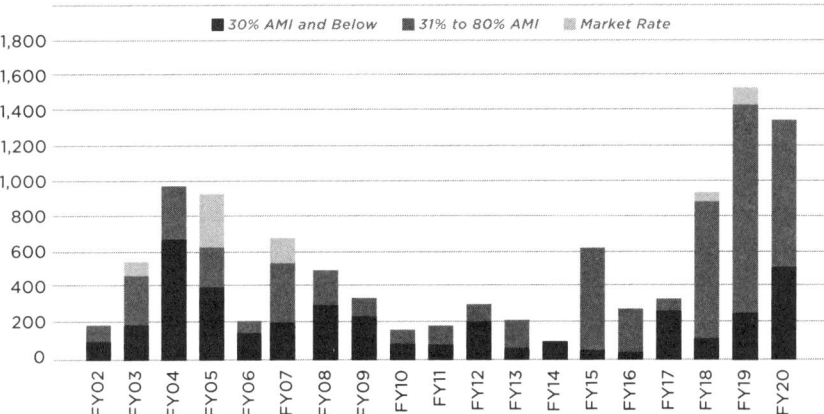

Graph 9.3. After years of assisting one to three projects annually, the Charlotte Housing Trust Fund ramped up sharply in 2018. At the urging of housing activists, it also started reporting how many units were at 30 percent AMI (extremely low-income). Graph adapted from Anderson, *Charlotte–Mecklenburg: 2020 State of Housing Instability and Homelessness Report.*

projects. A provision of the 2018 *Housing Framework* had set NOAH preservation as a goal. Renovating existing apartments while keeping rents low required less cash than building from scratch. It was faster, too. "New construction can take up to two years for approval and competition, but housing advocates say that many more affordable units disappear during that time when investors buy older properties, flip them and raise rents," explained the *Charlotte Observer*.[94]

One of the NOAH allocations in 2021 went to help Ascent Housing—a private investment group—purchase The Pines on Wendover, an existing forty-four-unit complex located just off upscale Randolph Road.[95] Aware of growing enthusiasm for affordable housing, Ascent's chief Mark Etheridge structured a Housing Impact Fund. Public-spirited investors would put money into the fund with the expectation that they would see a modest but steady return. Ascent would buy older apartments where rents were already relatively low. It would improve maintenance but keep rents under the city median, with 30 percent of units set aside for very-low-income households (30 percent AMI or less).[96] It was a new thing—but with historical roots reaching back to the earliest days of low-income housing. It paralleled the work of Julius Rosenwald (see chapter 2) and other civic-minded capitalists whose limited-dividend companies had built affordable apartments before the advent of public housing nearly a century earlier.

Figure 9.2. Waiting to sign up for a Mezzanine apartment. Alvin C. Jacobs photo for Axios Charlotte, January 27, 2020.

■ ■ ■ ■ ■

For all of the efforts of the 2010s, however, Charlotte closed out the decade with many fewer apartments for low-income households than it had at the start. The "upscaling" of 28,000 NOAH units in old multifamily complexes, noted in the 2018 *Housing Charlotte* study, far exceeded the total number of units built by the Charlotte Housing Authority, Low-Income Housing Tax Credit developers, and all others since the beginning of time. According to one careful estimate, Charlotte now needed 23,060 additional affordable dwelling units.[97]

On a wet January day in 2020, Mezzanine, the church-sponsored development rising on Freedom Drive, began accepting sign-ups from prospective tenants.[98] Alvin C. Jacobs snapped a photo of the crowd. Over 1,000 people stood in the rain for a chance at just 129 apartments. It was a heart-wrenching reminder that Charlotte's affordable housing shortage remained devastatingly deep.

A Problem Called Brookhill

Brookhill Village became a problem that defied solution in the 2010s. The twists and turns that led to that situation offer a useful look back at the history of affordable housing in Charlotte.

Developer C. D. Spangler had used FHA 608 subsidies to create Brookhill in 1951—privately owned "low-rent" housing (see chapter 3). Under FHA 608 regulations, it was advantageous to have two separate entities, one to own the buildings, the other to own the land. So Spangler set up Brookhill Village, Inc., which got the FHA 608 aid to construct and own the buildings. Spangler kept the land, leasing it under a ninety-nine-year lease to Brookhill Village, Inc.

Over the years, Spangler (wearing his Brookhill Village, Inc. hat) sold the buildings to businesspeople who used fresh subsidies (such as accelerated depreciation, which applies only to buildings, not land—see chapter 5) to fix them up.

(*continued*)

Figure 9.3. Brookhill Village, 2021, with Charlotte skyline in the distance. Clayton Hanson photo, courtesy of UNC Charlotte Urban Institute.

But those investors lost enthusiasm when tax breaks ran out, and they allowed maintenance to lapse. Meanwhile, Spangler had kept the land, which he put into a trust for his heirs.

Through it all, Brookhill remained in private hands. Yes, it held low-income residents. But it was never "public housing" owned by the Charlotte Housing Authority (now Inlivian). Nor was it controlled by a community-minded nonprofit such as DreamKey Partners. Brookhill remains a private, for-profit venture—just as it had been created by FHA 608 so long ago.

In the late 2010s, with many units boarded up, Brookhill became a highly visible "poster child" for Charlotte's housing problems. Booming upscale apartment construction in South End rolled nearer and nearer. Evocative images of Brookhill's tenant community by photographer Alvin C. Jacobs, along with civic activism led in part by Rev. Ray McKinnon, whose church adjoined the property, struck a chord with many Charlotteans who were already angry in the wake of protests that followed the 2016 Keith Lamont Scott shooting.

Could a deal be worked out whereby some redeveloper would acquire the decaying buildings and rebuild with a mix of low-income and market-rate? During the 2010s and early 2020s, a succession of housing advocates attempted to use tools such as the Low-Income Housing Tax Credit in combination with the Charlotte Housing Trust Fund (see chapter 7) to "make the numbers work."

But there was a fundamental problem. Under US law, buildings on leased land become property of the landowner when the lease ends. In other words, any developer of affordable housing would lose it when the ninety-nine-year lease ran out in 2049.

The Housing Trust Fund's board very much wanted to help. But it knew that big bucks would be needed, since the project had to pay off before the land lease ended.* How much should the fund invest, considering that the same dollar amount elsewhere would likely provide more apartments?

(continued)

---

*David Boraks, "Charlotte City Council Supports $3M for Brookhill—with Strings Attached," WFAE, October 27, 2020, https://www.wfae.org/local-news/2020-10-27/charlotte-city-council-supports-3m-for-brookhill-with-strings-attached; "A Developer Had Big Plans for Brookhill. Now He's Backing Out," Axios Charlotte, March 15, 2022, https://charlotte.axios.com/291277/brookhill-developer-sells-interest-in-the-project-after-funding-issues/; "Affordable Housing Still Planned for Charlotte's Brookhill," *Charlotte Observer*, March 17, 2022; DreamKey Partners CEO Julie Porter, written communication to Tom Hanchett, August 29, 2022.

A potential developer made a proposal that requested $13 million in aid. The trust fund countered with an offer of $3 million, part of a loan and tax credit package to be underwritten by the Local Initiatives Support Corporation (LISC), the national housing nonprofit that the city had contracted with to assist with Charlotte's affordable housing.

LISC took a careful look at the proposal and concluded that the lease situation made it too risky, not viable to underwrite. The deal collapsed.

At this writing in 2022, Brookhill still languishes.

Figure 9.4. A: Demetrice Locket (*right*) raised daughter Ki-ra (*center*) at Brookhill while working as a hospital technician. With a family friend (*left*), they ready Ki-ra to begin college at UNC Greensboro. Lisa Stockton Howell photo.
B: Brookhill youngster. Alvin C. Jacobs photo, 2018.

EPILOGUE

After a Whole Book about Affordable Housing, Where Are We?

- Affordable Housing in the COVID Years
- Lessons of History
- A Way Forward

COVID arrived in March 2020. And things got worse. The pandemic virus, which swept the United States well into 2022, helped push earlier inequities into hyperdrive. The K-shaped economy became unmistakable.

Though COVID got all the blame, one big driver of inequality was cheap money—now made even cheaper. The Federal Reserve cut interest rates yet again at the start of 2020, just before COVID appeared.[1] That put mortgages under 3 percent for the first time in history, where they stayed into 2022.[2] Eager buyers, both individuals with low-rate mortgages and also corporate investors wielding well-leveraged hedge funds, competed for properties, often bidding above the asking amount. Real estate prices rose even more sharply than before.[3] It became almost impossible to find an apartment under $1,000 a month in Charlotte.

Then add the dislocations of the COVID pandemic. Businesses shut down; employees were abruptly laid off. And still rents rose.[4]

Tent camps of nearly a thousand homeless people appeared along Interstate 277 in the shadow of uptown's glittering skyscrapers.[5] No longer was it easy for prosperous Charlotteans to be oblivious to the city's housing crisis.

In the short term, governments instituted rent assistance programs and eviction moratoriums—beyond the scope of this book. Looking toward the longer term, the search for systemic solutions continued with added urgency. The City of Charlotte announced a pilot program to give owners of low-rent apartments a property tax break, which they would use to reduce rents for tenants earning

228 ■ EPILOGUE

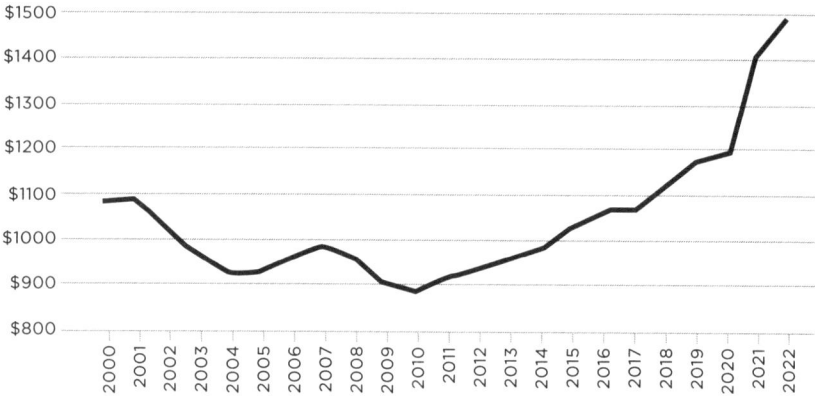

Figure 10.1 (*top*). Tent city along Interstate 277, February 2021. Travis Dove photo, 2021.
Graph 10.1 (*bottom*). Apartment rents in Charlotte began rising as low interest rates kicked in after the 2008 recession. The trend accelerated when the Fed cut rates to an all-time low in early 2020. Graph adapted from Chu, "State of Housing and Jobs."

under 30 percent AMI.[6] A grassroots group called Restorative Justice CLT pushed hard for the county to mandate more affordable housing in the planned redevelopment of former Brooklyn urban renewal lands.[7]

In mid-2022, the Federal Reserve finally began inching up interest rates. That brought hardship for anyone seeking to buy a home, but it also offered wider hope. Might the upward spiral of real estate prices slow or even halt?[8]

Lessons from History

After tracking eight decades of affordable housing in Charlotte, what themes stand out?

"You're writing a history of affordable housing in Charlotte? That'll be a real short book!" I heard that often while working on this project. Maybe you thought it, too.

But as we've seen in this volume, there's been a great deal of hard work and accomplishment over many years. A wide variety of approaches—by government, by business, by many types of partnerships—have been put into practice. Over 180 apartment complexes have been constructed, 150 of them in use today.

Yet severe shortages persist.

If we are going to really address the situation, it helps to know what's been tried in the past and what's being done in the present.

What's Been Tried, Phase 1

The four decades from the start of public housing in 1940 through Ronald Reagan's presidency were a period of experimentation. America tried a lot of affordable housing strategies that didn't work very well.

Big government-owned projects, Fairview Homes and the like, held as many as 500 households in bare-bones accommodations isolated from the rest of the city. The isolation, the concentrated poverty, and the reluctance of government officials to spend tax dollars on adequate maintenance caused deep problems. That gave public housing a bad image from which it has yet to recover.

Putting subsidy dollars directly into private developers' hands worked no better. By the way, that was not some "neoliberal" innovation of the 1970s or 1980s, as some scholars erroneously claim, but instead has been ongoing from FHA 608 and accelerated depreciation in the 1950s up to the present day.[9] In Charlotte the worst abuses happened under HUD's Section 221(d)(3), Section 236, and Turnkey programs around 1970. Charlotteans still recall with anger the construction of five big low-income developments along West Boulevard.

A bright spot in those early decades was Charlotte's energetic scattered-site initiative—one of the best such programs in the United States. An interracial coalition, inside and outside of government, used federal revenue-sharing dollars and local tax money to construct nearly a dozen complexes starting in the mid-1970s. Architecturally similar to for-profit apartments and capped at fifty households, they were built in upscale as well as less-wealthy sectors of the city. Developments such as Gladedale on elite Providence Road blend in so well that neighbors today are often unaware they exist. Charlotte proved that it could mobilize "political will"—that important intangible—to make progressive policy a reality.

What's Been Tried, Phase 2

The modern era of affordable housing finance began circa 1986 after President Reagan ended previous programs. Washington's Low-Income Housing Tax Credit provides tax breaks that give wealthy people a profit if they invest in affordable housing. That subsidy is augmented by state and local dollars (via the North Carolina Housing Finance Agency, the North Carolina Housing Trust Fund, the Charlotte Housing Trust Fund). This is our current system—the basis for all new affordable housing construction today.

Ideas about what constituted "good housing" changed during the 1990s, in the United States as a whole and in Charlotte. Advocates of every background worked to create affordable housing that mixed incomes and that blended with the surrounding city. The HOPE VI program (aided by LIHTC subsidies) remade many big old projects as more livable mixed-income places—though in the process it disrupted "helping networks" that existing residents had created. First Ward, Arbor Glen, Seigle Point, and Renaissance West have fared well over the years; unlike the old public housing, they remain desirable places two decades or more after construction. And they've inspired subsequent mixed-income success stories, notably Brightwalk by nonprofit DreamKey Partners.

But at the same time, America's stock of traditional public housing (that is, owned by local government) has shrunk year after year from the 1990s to the present. The HOPE VI program had the side effect of decreasing the number of units for the most-needy households (earning under 30 percent of area median income). That tendency became intentional US policy in 1998 when the Faircloth Amendment decreed that cities could never increase their net amount of public housing.

There are additional federal constraints. The tax credits provided by the LIHTC program and related funds are extremely limited. Washington gives out far less than enough to meet the nation's affordable housing shortfall.

And the LIHTC regulations define "low-income" as households making 60 percent AMI. That means that many projects have no units for the poorest of the poor, at 30 percent AMI.

Even in the best of times, subsidies have reached only a small slice of Charlotte's poor. "Among households in Mecklenburg County that earn less than 30 percent of area median income, only about one quarter receive a housing subsidy," writes Ken Szymanski of Charlotte's Apartment Association. "That means about three-quarters are left to fend for themselves."[10]

No Affordable Housing at the Scaleybark Lynx Stop?!?

The tight limits on LIHTC available from Washington doomed one of Charlotte's most highly sought affordable housing projects.

In 2008 the city set aside land near the Scaleybark Station of its new Lynx light rail line for mixed-income apartments. It agreed to sell the land to developer Peter Pappas, based on his detailed plans for a mixed-income, mixed-use development.

Pappas submitted applications, year after year (at his own expense), to the LIHTC gatekeepers at the North Carolina Housing Finance Agency, to no avail. The NCHFA actually liked the project; it just didn't have credits to allocate to it. "The state said there is a cap of two projects for the Charlotte area in each award cycle," explained the *Observer*. "There wasn't enough money," confirmed NCHFA spokesperson Margaret Matrone. "It doesn't mean it wasn't a good project."

In other words, the problem lay not in anything that Charlotte government did or did not do. Nor was it due to lack of effort by the developer. Instead, as with hundreds of solid proposals nationwide every year, lack of credits available from Washington crippled a project that many people had worked hard for.

After a decade of attempts, the city pulled the plug on the deal. The absence of affordable housing along the mass transit corridor became a widely discussed issue. Headlined a 2018 *Observer* article, "We Missed a Major Opportunity."[*]

[*] "Downturn Stalls Scaleybark Project," *Charlotte Observer*, August 3, 2011; "'We Missed a Major Opportunity': Housing Lags near New Charlotte Light Rail," *Charlotte Observer*, April 1, 2018; "Developer Cut after Inaction on Affordable Housing," *Charlotte Observer*, June 1, 2018.

What Now? What Next?

We now know, after all that trial and error, how to build affordable housing that is desirable for both tenants and neighbors and that remains attractive and well maintained over time.

Mixing is the key. Mixing people who have different incomes. Mixing low-rent units into market-rate communities. And doing it in every part of the city.

History proves that mixed housing works well. Developments built during the scattered-site era and thereafter are thriving. No public outcry calls for their closure. When surrounding residents have an opportunity to object to a project such as Ashley Square, which replaced existing public housing with a larger number of low-rent units in higher density buildings, there is little or no push-back. Low-income residents generally turn out to be good neighbors.

But that doesn't mean that adding new low-income housing is easy. Not at all. The current system with its array of public and private entities requires a big investment of money, time, and bureaucracy on every proposed project. Only specialists can navigate the complexity.

And people still cling to the old stereotype of bad public housing. They continue to fight new projects "tooth and nail," as Harvey Gantt put it. Government officials, nonprofit organizations, and for-profit developers who attempt a new project usually spend years upon years working to overcome opposition—with only a small chance that a proposal will get built.

■ ■ ■ ■ ■

In the late 2010s, a series of local events and national trends—the 2016 Keith Lamont Scott protests, the rapid upswing in housing prices driven in part by artificially low US interest rates, the K-shaped economy that brought prosperity for upper-income people even as lower-income households fell ever further behind—made affordable housing a glaring issue in Charlotte.

Since 2016, local leaders have impressively marshaled the political will to get affordable housing constructed. Two bond issues totaling $100 million pumped up the Charlotte Housing Trust Fund. Nongovernmental sources committed over $50 million more. Churches and other public-spirited entities gave not only cash but also land. Even the family who runs Brooks Sandwich Shop, a long-beloved cinder-block hotdog joint, donated a two-acre tract where Habitat for Humanity will build townhouses.[11]

During the last years of the 2010s and first years of the 2020s, crews completed well over a thousand affordable units annually in Charlotte, both new construction and NOAH renovations. That's a big advance from the 200–400 units previously added in a typical year.

But that achievement was tempered by the continuing bias toward 60 percent–80 percent AMI tenants. Barely a third of the total was available to people at 30 percent AMI.

More sobering, all those hard-won apartments made only a tiny impact on the shortage. We are falling further and further behind. Estimates put Charlotte's shortfall for 30 percent AMI households at 23,000 units. At today's pace, it would take more than seventy years to house people *currently* in need—not even

Mixed-Housing and Economic Advancement

Harvard scholar Raj Chetty, whose 2014 study had shockingly placed Charlotte last among fifty US metro areas in terms of opportunity for people to climb the economic ladder, revisited the city in 2023.

Charlotte's progress was being studied closely by his Opportunity Insights research team, he said, which found much to commend. For example: the Charlotte Housing Trust Fund's many projects showed an impressive level of commitment by city leaders and voters. The education-rich environment at Renaissance West, where schools from pre-K to college now surrounded Inlivian's new housing, was improving outcomes for residents.

Chetty's research, nationwide, was now tracking specific actions that sparked upward mobility. What worked best were interpersonal interactions that could lead to friendships. Proximity, by itself, did not bring advancement. But without being proximate, it was unlikely that encounters across lines of income and race would take place.

Chetty summed up his decade of data-gathering: "Mixed income areas have higher economic mobility."*

---

*Raj Chetty, "2023 Chancellor's Speakers Series: Dr. Raj Chetty," UNC Charlotte, November 14, 2023. Similarly: "Where We Build Homes Helps Explain America's Political Divide," *Washington Post*, November 24, 2023. Chetty's research is ongoing in the 2020s. *Charlotte Opportunity Initiative: 2020 Report*, Opportunity Insights, https://opportunity insights.org/wp-content/uploads/2020/11/OI-CharlotteReport.pdf; Steve Harrison and Lisa Worf, "Updated Chetty Study Data Paints Surprising Picture of Economic Mobility in Charlotte," WFAE, March 1, 2022, https://www.wfae.org/race-equity/2022-03-01/updated-chetty-study-data-paints-a-surprising-picture-of-economic-mobility-in-mecklenburg-county. Charlotte was part of a Chetty experiment to improve housing vouchers: Kriston Capps, "How a Section 8 Experiment Could Reveal a Better Way to Escape Poverty," Bloomberg CityLab, August 4, 2019, https://www.bloomberg.com/news/articles/2019-08-04/a-cheap-powerful-tool-to-beat-housing-segregation. A roundup of results: Heycke, "New Approach," 10–12.

---

considering those losing out as naturally occurring affordable housing continues to vanish.

HUD chief Henry Cisneros, interviewed for an article on affordable housing shortages in the 1990s, described the situation that persists today: "It's like bailing water out of the boat while at the other end someone's got a hose and they're filling it from the ocean."[12]

■ ■ ■ ■ ■

In early 2022, reporters Lauren Lindstrom from the *Charlotte Observer* and Danielle Chemtob with Axios Charlotte independently interviewed local leaders about progress on low-income housing. "Charlotte's Been Funding Affordable Housing This Way for 20 Years. Is It Working?" headlined Lindstrom's essay.[13] The answers that both journalists heard were surprisingly unanimous.

Malcolm Graham, a Black liberal City Council member with extensive experience in real estate development, said flatly, "Fifty [million in bonds] isn't enough." Council colleague Ed Driggs, a white conservative from the city's most affluent district, wavered on whether the city should prioritize housing or infrastructure investments, but he agreed that the recent $50 million housing bond represented "really a drop in the bucket."[14]

Julie Porter of the nonprofit DreamKey Partners hoped that bond goals could at least double, to $100 million. That would put Charlotte in line with other growth hotspots such as Atlanta and Austin, Lindstrom noted. City Manager Marcus Jones, though traditionally wary of increasing bonded indebtedness, agreed that $50 million "may not be enough." Financier Mark Etheridge urged more dollars for NOAH preservation; otherwise, "we're never going to make progress in our housing crisis."[15]

Brian Collier at the Foundation for the Carolinas, the philanthropic fund known for its close ties to Charlotte business leaders, had been deeply involved in promoting the bond issues and the private fundraising. The experience gave him serious reservations. "Now, we've already proven that at the current levels, that is inadequate," he told Chemtob. She summed up, "Collier and others want to see the housing bond substantially increased. To match the scale of the problem, Collier says, would require billions of dollars."[16]

"Billions" popped up often as I talked with local experts. What's really needed for the Charlotte Housing Trust Fund? "$1 billion." And how much in LIHTC from Washington annually? "$8 billion would be a good start." That's almost as much as the feds are willing to allocate annually to the *entire United States* under America's current affordable housing policy.[17]

A Way Forward

If we aim to have housing for everyone, our current system can't achieve that goal. That is the lesson of this book.

Our shortfall, decade after decade, is not the result of uncaring local politicians or incompetent administrators. From the scattered-site era to today, Charlotte has been quite active in construction of subsidized affordable housing. And those apartments are quite good places to live. But there aren't nearly enough.

For eighty years, America's approach has been to subsidize individual projects. That's what all the tools described in this book have in common, from Charlotte's initial public housing projects aided by federal grants to the current system in which private investors get tax breaks for constructing affordable apartments.

Currently, each project is a one-off custom effort. A public-spirited initiator (whether a government agency, a nonprofit advocate, or a private developer) negotiates with Low-Income Housing Tax Credit gatekeepers and with the state and local trust fund gatekeepers for a slice of extremely limited subsidy dollars. Along the way, there are myriad ways for neighbors and elected officials to delay, any of which can quash the effort. If all parts of the subsidy package don't snap into place, the project dies.

Are there other, more sweeping approaches that might actually conquer Charlotte's affordable housing problems?

One audacious proposal that's been floated nationally: create a federally funded "universal basic income" set at a level that enables every household to afford housing. Presidential candidate Andrew Yang ran on that platform in 2020, dropping out of the race but not before stimulating serious discussion.[18]

A related possibility would be to greatly increase the US minimum wage. Labor shortages during the COVID pandemic pushed many employers to set their own minimums at double the prevailing $7.25. Some corporations, such as giant retailer Target, went to $24.[19] That is the number whereby an employee could afford to rent a $1,000 per month apartment (the rock-bottom price in Charlotte in the early 2020s), spending no more than 30 percent of his or her income. A truly livable minimum wage would need to be well above $24 per hour.

A more conservative, focused strategy would be to require developers to include affordable units in every multifamily project.

Each new apartment complex would have a set percentage—20 percent, say—of units for households at 30 percent AMI and 60 percent AMI.

By making that a requirement of *every* development project, it might overcome some of the stigma that now exists. More importantly, it would ensure that low-income households can live near good jobs and schools—the tools needed to overcome poverty. Neighbors who now reflexively cry "increased traffic" as they fight new projects might discover that adding housing near workplaces could actually shorten workers' commutes and *decrease* traffic.

Could such a requirement ever happen? It *is* happening—just not in Charlotte and North Carolina. Nearly 900 municipalities in twenty-five states have what is sometimes called "inclusionary zoning."[20] Instead of using zoning to exclude low-income renters from certain areas (as Charlotte did when it introduced zoning in 1947; see chapter 4), how about using the zoning tool to *include*?

Under North Carolina law, a policy known as the Dillon Rule says that localities cannot take any actions that are not specifically allowed by the state legislature. So far, North Carolina's legislators have turned a cold shoulder to inclusionary zoning. But that could change. As the affordable housing shortage becomes undeniably worse in city after city, will urban officials and real estate leaders band together to win authorization?

The notion of making affordable units a requirement in all rental developments actually has a strong historic precedent.

We've seen it in Charlotte's own housing history. Recall the adoption of the building code of 1948. It mandated that developers must provide a toilet and indoor plumbing in each apartment.

City Council briefly considered setting up a subsidy program, in which developers would apply for public dollars every time they put in a bathroom. Can you imagine how cumbersome that would have been—and how few bathrooms we would now have?

For years, the plumbing requirement seemed an impossible dream. Critics called it "socialism," said it would push up rents, said it would make it impossible for developers to operate, said it would destroy housing affordability. They said it would never happen.

But after much wrangling, it did happen. Real estate leaders branded it the Realtors' Standard House Ordinance and lobbied political officials to vote in favor. Once the new law took hold, property investors discovered it was no deep hardship: because everyone had to do the same thing, no particular building owner was put at a competitive disadvantage. Developers absorbed the cost of bathrooms into their overall cost of doing business. We came to regard bathrooms as a basic right, not just for low-income tenants but for the health of our entire community.

We can do the same for affordable housing.

A Few Words about Methods and Sources

Some Benefits of the Case Study Approach

Looking at one city over the entire time span of subsidized housing, from circa 1940 to the 2020s, brings insights that are often missed by scholars using other methods. In midsize Charlotte, it is possible to become knowledgeable about the full range of housing—not just federal programs but also state, local, and private initiatives—and to follow those stories over the long term.

That knowledge sparks fresh questions. Some examples:

- How did NOAH (naturally occurring affordable housing—the largest source of low-rent dwellings) work? And how has that changed over time?
- How did federal aid for market-rate apartments—FHA subsidies starting in the 1930s, accelerated depreciation tax shelters starting in the 1950s—pave the way for subsequent low-income programs?
- Perhaps the biggest government intrusion into the affordable housing market was the adoption of building codes; how did that come to pass?
- How have federal initiatives interacted with each other, with existing housing, and with state and local forces?
- How have we come to the point, currently, where most "affordable housing" is built for people earning 60 percent of area median income rather than for the poorest of the poor earning less than 30 percent AMI?

Charlotte's story won't be exactly your town's story. But what happened here will raise useful questions as you probe your own community's experience. Understanding that history can help all of us—policymakers and ordinary citizens as well—advocate for better programs that will improve housing opportunities for all Americans.

What Books Are Good Starting Points for a Newcomer to the History of Housing?

- Recent highly acclaimed works have alerted many Americans to housing issues: Matthew Desmond, *Evicted: Poverty and Profit in the American City* (2017), winner of the Pulitzer Prize; Richard Rothstein, *The Color of Law: A Forgotten History of How Our Government Segregated America* (2018), four weeks on the *New York Times* bestseller list; Keeanga-Yamahtta Taylor, *Race for Profit: How Banks and the Real Estate Industry Undermined Black Homeownership* (2019), short-listed for the Pulitzer.
- The best technical overview of the US government's housing programs, past and present: Alex F. Schwartz, *Housing Policy in the United States*, 4th ed. (2021).
- An empathetic look at the evolution of one housing complex, seen through the eyes of tenants, planners, and reformers (its redevelopment circa 1990 helped inspire HOPE VI and other mixed-income affordable housing nationally): Jane Roessner, *A Decent Place to Live: From Columbia Point to Harbor Point—A Community History*, 2nd ed. (2000).
- A pioneering study of housing over time in America's biggest city: Richard Plunz, *A History of Housing in New York*, rev. ed. (2016).
- Two introductions to academic discussions: Elizabeth J. Mueller and J. Rosie Tighe, eds., *The Affordable Housing Reader*, 2nd ed. (2022); John F. Bauman, Roger Biles, and Kristin M. Szylvian, eds., *From Tenements to the Taylor Homes: In Search of an Urban Housing Policy in Twentieth-Century America* (2000).

Is There a "Master List" Showing Federal Programs That Have Produced Low-Income Housing?

Nope. Nor is there a source that tells when particular programs shut down—in part because even when a program stops funding new projects, the existing apartments usually continue to receive aid.

That's frustrating, but here are places to start:

- Grace Milgram, *A Chronology of Housing Legislation and Selected Executive Actions, 1892–2003: A Report by the Congressional Research Service*, printed for the Committee on Financial Services, US House of Representatives,

March 2004 [SuDoc Y 4.F 49/20:108-D], https://www.govinfo.gov/content/pkg/CPRT-108HPRT92629/html/CPRT-108HPRT92629.htm.
- Charles L. Edson, "Affordable Housing—An Intimate History," *Journal of Affordable Housing and Community Development Law* 20, no. 2 (Winter 2011): 192–213, https://pdf4pro.com/view/affordable-housing-1-an-intimate-history-3c8526.html.
- Maggie McCarty, *Introduction to Public Housing*, Congressional Research Service, January 3, 2014, [SuDoc LC 14.23:R 41654/], https://fas.org/sgp/crs/misc/R41654.pdf.

ACKNOWLEDGMENTS

Brookhill Village pushed me into this project. During 2018–19, Charlotte's news media was filled with stories about that old low-income project located two miles south of downtown. As gentrification rolled through the area, would its longtime tenants lose their homes? Would city leaders mobilize aid so it could be redeveloped for mixed-income, including its current residents?

Brookhill redevelopment was running into two stumbling points, it turned out.

- One: Brookhill Village was privately owned. It *looked* like public housing, rows of identical bare-bones barracks. But it had been privately developed (with federal assistance) back in 1951, and it remained in the hands of one of North Carolina's richest families. Huh?! What was the history behind all of that?
- Two: the government aid that was now available for redevelopment rested on something called the Low-Income Housing Tax Credit—which was targeted to help tenants with incomes at 60 percent of Charlotte's area median income, not the 30 percent AMI that most Brookhill tenants made. Again, how had that come to be?

As I followed stories by reporters Pam Kelley, Fred Clasen-Kelly, Ely Portillo, Danielle Chemtob, Lauren Lindstrom, and others, I was embarrassed to realize how little I knew about all of this. I'd helped write a book documenting the early decades of US public housing (*From Tenements to the Taylor Homes: In Search of an Urban Housing Policy in Twentieth-Century America*, John F. Bauman, Roger Biles, and Kristin M. Szylvian, eds.). And I'd written a whole volume exploring how Charlotte's "built environment" had developed (*Sorting Out the New South City: Race, Class, and Urban Development in Charlotte, 1875–1975*). Maybe I should find time to do some additional research into this affordable housing situation?

I knew three knowledgeable folks to start with. Attorney Ted Fillette, longtime housing advocate with Legal Aid; Laura Belcher, current head of Charlotte's Habitat for Humanity; and Pat Garrett, retired CEO of the highly effective nonprofit Charlotte–Mecklenburg Housing Partnership (now DreamKey

Partners), each graciously sat down for interviews. Their conversations began my journey but left me with many more questions than answers.

Then came COVID. As society went quiet during 2020–22, I had time on my hands to pursue the research.

I am grateful for encouragement from Ken Schorr of the Charlotte Center for Legal Advocacy, Jeff Michael and Lori Thomas of the Urban Institute at the University of North Carolina at Charlotte, Mindy Thompson Fullilove at the New School for Social Research, Frye Gaillard at the University of South Alabama, Alexander von Hoffman of the Kennedy School at Harvard, and Rolf Pendall, chair of the Department of Urban and Regional Planning at the University of Illinois at Champaign-Urbana.

For comments and suggestions, I thank thoughtful readers Maddy Baer, Ted Fillette, Annetta Watkins Foard, Pamela Grundy, Colleen Hammelman, Lisa Stockton Howell, Rosalyn Allison Jacobs, Greg Jarrell, Pam Kelley, Vi Alexander Lyles, Fulton Meachem, Julie Porter, Betty Chafin Rash, Jim Rothstein, and Ken Szymanski and critical audiences at Charlotte's Aldersgate, Carriage Club, and Senior Scholars.

I am indebted to history makers who sat for interviews or communicated with me informally, including Laura Belcher, Zelleka Biermann, Don Carroll, Betty Chafin Rash, Ted Fillette, Pat Garrett, Pete Kelly, Paul Leonard, Jud Little, Vi Alexander Lyles, Fulton Meachem, Julie Porter, Maggie Ray, Pam Syfert, Mel Watt, Debbie Williams, Ricky Woods, and Charles Woodyard.

For research assistance, I thank Ted Fillette, J. Michael Moore, Lydia Sawyer Hanchett, Julie Porter and Fred Dodson, Laura Belcher, Zelleka Biermann, Fulton Meachem and Kenya Lewis, and David Carlson. And for graphics assistance, thanks are due Katie Zager, Albert Dulin, and Irene Morris.

I am especially grateful to energetic archivists: at UNC Charlotte's J. Murrey Atkins Library, Dawn Schmitz and her Special Collections team, as well as data librarian Reese Manceaux; and at the Charlotte Mecklenburg Library, the staff of the Robinson-Spangler Carolina Room including John O'Connor, Tom Cole, Shelia Bumgarner, Meghan Bowden, and Sydney Carroll.

Thanks to UNC Press, particularly the painstaking copyediting by Julie Bush and Erin Granville.

This book is for Carol Sawyer. Her help, in so many ways, propelled this project from start to completion. Her passion for social justice inspired every page.

NOTES

Abbreviations

CDBG Community Development Block Grant
CN   *Charlotte News*
CO   *Charlotte Observer*
JMAL J. Murrey Atkins Library, University of North Carolina at Charlotte
RNO   *Raleigh News and Observer*

Introduction

1. Desmond, *Poverty*, 91–93; Jackson, *Crabgrass Frontier*, 294–95; Howard, *Hidden Welfare State*, chapter 5; Hanchett, "Other 'Subsidized Housing.'"
2. "Charlotte May Use Property Taxes to Fund More Rent Vouchers," *CO*, November 3, 2021.
3. Zelleka Biermann, "HTF Activity Summary: Public Records Request Final," Charlotte Housing Trust Fund spreadsheet emailed to Tom Hanchett on November 16, 2021, in the data collection of JMAL, https://doi.org/10.15139/S3/XQBOFW. Julie Porter, CEO at the nonprofit housing developer DreamKey Partners, adds a caveat: "Just because HTF approved seventeen apartments, that doesn't mean they are going to be funded." The North Carolina Housing Finance Agency uses the Charlotte list as a starting point, weighed against lists from other cities, as it allocates the scarce LIHTC. Julie Porter, written communication to Tom Hanchett, August 29, 2022.

Chapter 1

1. "Treloar, William House," Charlotte–Mecklenburg Historic Landmarks Commission, July 3, 1984, http://landmarkscommission.org/2016/10/28/treloar-william-house/.
2. "For Rent or Sale," *Charlotte Chronicle*, January 7, 1887.
3. The *Charlotte Future 2040 Comprehensive Plan* (www.cltfuture2040plan.com) and its Unified Development Ordinance ended single-family-only zoning and allowed small apartment structures (duplexes, triplexes) on corner lots in all areas. "In a Major Vote, Charlotte Officials Approve New Development Rules," Axios Charlotte, August 23, 2022, https://charlotte.axios.com/306173/in-a-major-vote-charlotte-leaders-approve-new-development-rules/; Andy Thomason, "Can Charlotte Re-sort Itself?," *The Assembly*, November 13, 2023, www.theassemblync.com/place/charlotte-zoning-reform/.
4. Hanchett, *Sorting Out*, 146–52.
5. "Excellent Investment," *CO*, February 15, 1920.
6. Love, *Plum Thickets*, 116.
7. Florida, "How Poor Americans Get Exploited by Their Landlords."

Chapter 2

1. On FDR's persistent pattern of aiding the middle class and then extending programs to low-income Americans, see Leuchtenburg, *Roosevelt and the New Deal*.
2. Franklin D. Roosevelt, "Remarks re NIRA—'To Put People Back to Work,'" speech, June 16, 1933, file no. 637, box 15, Master Speech File, 1898–1945, Franklin D. Roosevelt Presidential Library and Museum, Hyde Park, NY, www.fdrlibrary.marist.edu/_resources/images/msf/msf00656.
3. Fairbanks, "From Better Dwellings."
4. Howard's *Garden Cities of Tomorrow* inspired investors to create a pair of experimental communities in England, Letchworth (1903) and Welwyn (1920). "The Fight to Preserve a Pioneering Planned Town," *The Economist*, April 15, 2021. The phrase "dark satanic mills" came from beloved British writer William Blake's poem "Jerusalem." On the phrase's widespread application to the Industrial Revolution, see "Pastures Green and Dark Satanic Mills: The British Passion for Landscape," Princeton University Art Museum, 2016, https://artmuseum.princeton.edu/art/exhibitions/1758.
5. Plunz, *History of Housing*, 94–96.
6. Plunz, *History of Housing*, 117–20.
7. Buder, *Visionaries and Planners*, 168–69; Wright, *Building the Dream*, 205–6. "The *Oxford English Dictionary* lists the first published usage of 'superblock' as occurring in 1928, in reference to Clarence Stein and Henry Wright's project for Radburn, New Jersey." Whiting, "Super!," 22. On superblocks in Charlotte, see Morrill, *Reconnaissance Survey of Superblock Apartment Projects*. On the national scene in this era, another influential project that featured courtyard greenspaces between buildings was Stein and Wright's Sunnyside Gardens, a 1924 apartment community in Queens, New York, funded by Metropolitan Life Insurance under a limited-dividend arrangement. Sunnyside Gardens Preservation Alliance website, accessed November 4, 2024, https://sunnysidegardens.us/preservation/; Kroessler, *Sunnyside Gardens*. Financing described in Winnick, *Rental Housing Opportunities*, 122–24.
8. "Rehabilitation Brings Massive Chicago Development Back to Its Heyday," *Affordable Housing Finance*, July 7, 2017, www.housingfinance.com/developments/rehabilitation-brings-massive-chicago-development-back-to-its-heyday_o.
9. Chase, Horak and Keylon, *Garden Apartments of Los Angeles*; von Hoffman, "Why They Built Pruitt-Igoe," esp. 186.
10. Crawford, *Building the Workingman's Paradise*, 168–73; Stephenson, *John Nolen*, 139–48.
11. Milgram, *Chronology of Housing Legislation*, section viii.
12. Radford, "Federal Government and Housing." To read the act itself: "National Housing Act (1934)," Living New Deal, accessed November 4, 2024, https://livingnewdeal.org/glossary/national-housing-act-1934/.
13. The text of the 1934 National Housing Act is available on the FRASER website, accessed November 4, 2024, https://fraser.stlouisfed.org/files/docs/historical/martin/54_01_19340627.pdf.
14. Vandell, "FHA Restructuring Proposals," 307. The FHA evidently issued some Section 207 mortgages for middle-income projects as early as May 1937—an experiment intended to pave the way for "certain proposed amendments in the law [that] would permit

a large expansion of limited-dividend operations . . . financing rental accommodations for families in the middle-income groups." "Developments Making Gains," *CO*, May 2, 1937. The expansion of Section 207 was part of the National Housing Act Amendments of 1938 (Public Law 75–424) officially signed on February 3, 1938. Milgram, *Chronology of Housing Legislation*, 13. Only twenty-two projects, located in eleven states, had been initiated under the original low-income version of Section 207. "Unit Program Proves Helpful," *CN*, March 20, 1938.

15. Milgram, *Chronology of Housing Legislation*, 13; "Unit Program Proves Helpful," *CN*, March 20, 1938.
16. "FHA Rental Housing Is Safe Investment," *CO*, August 7, 1938.
17. Quoted in Radford, "Federal Government and Housing," 108.
18. The term "exclusive neighborhood" meant one protected by deed restrictions. The FHA actively promoted the "protection provided by zoning and suitable deed restrictions." The Dilworth and Eastover neighborhoods both had restrictions that barred African Americans, among other provisions. "FHA to Hold Meeting Here: Charles Hayes Diggs of Land Planning Division Will Assist Builders," *CN*, May 22, 1938.
19. Charlotte–Mecklenburg Historic Landmarks Commission, *Myrtle Square Apartments*; "Myrtle Avenue Apartments to Cost $400,000," *CO*, December 3, 1937; "Begin Building Job Next Week: FHA Inspector Asked to Be on Hand for Erection of Myrtle Apartments," *CO*, December 29, 1937; "Impressive Myrtle Apartments Ready to Open" (special section), *CO*, August 7, 1938. Two other men partnered with Blythe in the Myrtle project, fellow Charlotte contractor F. N. Thompson and Raleigh real estate man Alan O'Neal, who developed a similar FHA project in his home city called the Raleigh Apartments. "Two Property Deals Involve $500,000," *CO*, August 2, 1949.
20. "F. J. Blythe's Funeral Today," *CO*, March 9, 1957. Joe L. Blythe also cofounded First Federal Savings and Loan in Charlotte, which by 1950 had used the FHA aid to finance more than 1,400 homes around the city. "Bankers Honor Joseph Holt," *CO*, January 14, 1950.
21. Hanchett, "Financing Suburbia."
22. "Begin Building Job Next Week," *CO*, December 29, 1937.
23. "Myrtle Apartments Now Ready for Occupancy," *CN*, August 7, 1938; "Myrtle Apartments Have Ideal Conveniences and Attractions," *CO*, August 7, 1938.
24. E. C. Goode handled the project for A. Lloyd Goode Construction. "New Company Gets Charter," *CO*, February 12, 1939; "Project Will Cost $200,000," *CO*, February 21, 1939; "Alson (Allison) Lloyd Goode," on the Find a Grave website, accessed November 4, 2024, www.findagrave.com/memorial/192852358/alson_allison_-lloyd-goode. Architect for Alson Court was Washington, DC, firm Raymond C. Snow, who made a specialty of drawing designs that would readily meet FHA approval. Projects included Summerville Apartments in Birmingham, Octavia Gardens in Mobile, Forest Apartments in Montgomery, and Redmont Gardens in Tuscaloosa. Raymond C. Snow, advertisement in *CO*, August 20, 1939. Nephews of Alson Goode converted Alson Court to condominiums: "Eastover Landmark's New Owners Plan for Condos," *CO*, March 13, 1996.
25. Sources indicate that 9.2 percent of multifamily deals are financed with FHA-insured loans in the 2020s; that figure seems to cover *all* projects, not just new construction. "FHA Multifamily and the Apartment Industry Fact Sheet," National Multifamily

Housing Council, accessed November 4, 2024, www.nmhc.org/advocacy/issue-fact-sheet/fha-multifamily-and-the-apartment-industry-fact-sheet/.

26. FDR repeated that language in his "Remarks re NIRA—'To Put People Back to Work'" speech (see note 2 above).

27. The Wagner–Steagall Act was technically an amendment to the 1934 legislation that had authorized the FHA. Low-income housing had been permitted under Section 207 of the initial 1934 legislation, as noted above, but few developers felt motivated to go after the slim profits available. On the first low-income project financed via the FHA, located in suburban Washington, DC: "Apartment Plan Wins Help of FHA," *New York Times*, February 24, 1935.

28. "United States Housing Act of 1937 (Public Law 7–412), September 1, 1937," as summarized in Milgram, *Chronology of Housing Legislation*, 11; McDonald, "Public Housing Construction." For a detailed description of financing under the act: "75th Anniversary of the Wagner–Steagall Housing Act of 1937," FDR and Housing Legislation on Franklin D. Roosevelt Presidential Library and Museum website, accessed November 4, 2024, www.fdrlibrary.org/housing.

29. "City-Wide Group to Push for Slum Clearance: Drive against Squalor Gains Momentum," *CO*, February 12, 1937; "Councilmen Seek Anti-Slum Move," *CN*, February 10, 1937. Cora Harris was fascinating activist who deserves more study. Daughter of *Charlotte News* founder Wade Harris, she became one of Charlotte's first female reporters, wrote for national publications, and was regarded as an expert on gardening and landscape architecture (she was a fellow of the Royal Horticultural Society). "Gives Report of FHA Work," *CO*, October 8, 1936. "Cora Harris Dies: Was News Columnist," *CO*, January 19, 1983; "Deaths and Funerals: Cora A Harris," *CN*, January 19, 1983. "Cora Harris Dies," *CN*, January 19, 1983. First Lady Eleanor Roosevelt invited her to a meeting of female New Deal allies at the presidential residence. "Mrs. Roosevelt Aids Destitute," *CO*, November 27, 1932.

30. "Housing Authority Makes First Report: Summary Contained in Illustrated Booklet 'Building a Better Charlotte,'" *CO*, March 3, 1940. "FHA Lists Charlotte as Housing Possibility," *CO*, July 14, 1938; "Praise Heaped on B & P Club: Women Are Lauded for Their Efforts in Getting Housing Project Underway," *CO*, February 19, 1939.

31. "Teddy Burwell to Head Housing Survey," *CO*, February 7, 1939. Among the employees on the WPA survey was Fred Alexander, who became a major Black advocate for better housing, as discussed in chapters 3 and 4.

32. "FHA Lists Charlotte as Housing Possibility."

33. "J. A. Jones Bids on Federal Job," *CO*, October 10, 1935; "Jones Is Low Bidder on Big Federal Job," *CO*, January 5, 1937; "Jones Works on Nashville Job," *CO*, February 20, 1936; "Interesting Carolina People," *CO*, October 20, 1940.

34. "Charlotte Company Gets $850,000 Job," *CO*, March 4, 1938.

35. "Housing Work Is Described," *CO*, February 24, 1939.

36. "Housing Plans Sent to USHA Officials," *CO*, August 20, 1939. USHA staffer Charles Wagner, an associate project planner, worked closely with the designers and visited Charlotte during the planning process. "Housing Expert Visits City Thursday," *CO*, February 21, 1939.

37. "How Fairview Homes Will Look," *CO*, February 11, 1940.

38. "How Fairview Homes Will Look." These facilities were expanded soon after the projects opened: "Extra Housing Units Planned," *CO*, November 23, 1941. Alson Lloyd Goode—developer of the Alson Court FHA apartments in Eastover—got the contract to erect Fairview Homes, while an out-of-town company from Greensboro won the Piedmont Courts job. "Fairview Homes Opening Marks Climax of Housing Movement," *CN*, July 28, 1940; "Piedmont Courts Almost Ready for Tenants," *CN*, November 10, 1940.
39. "Contracts Awarded for Piedmont Courts," *CO*, November 28, 1939. On enlargement of Piedmont Courts: "USHA Earmarks $309,000 for Local Projects: Adds $340,000 to Resources for Work Here," *CO*, October 29, 1939; "Housing Authority Makes First Report," *CO*, March 3, 1940.
40. "Refrigerator Order Biggest: Units for City's Two Low-Cost Housing Projects Occupy 11 Freight Cars," *CO*, July 28, 1940.
41. "Negro Project to Be Opened," *CO*, June 19, 1940; "Public to See Housing Units," *CO*, June 23, 1940; "Negro Housing Project to Open July 15," *CO*, July 6, 1940.
42. "Three Units of Piedmont Courts in City Are Opened," *CO*, December 11, 1940.
43. "Housing Project Renting Opens Monday: Tenants Now Must Be Living in Poor Homes," *CO*, September 8, 1940. On Frye's background: "Relief Set-Up Is Announced," *CO*, November 4, 1932.
44. "Housing Project Renting Opens Monday." The "no boarder" rule marked a sharp break from tradition (see chapter 1).
45. "Interesting Carolina People," *CO*, October 20, 1940. The income limit of "five times the rent" meant that families might pay 20 percent of their income for housing—a better ratio than the 30 percent that later became standard in US low-income housing. For more on Charlotte's public housing policies during the 1940s: "Incomes Not Too High: Housing Board Sees No Reasons for Evictions," *CO*, January 25, 1947.
46. "Negro Housing Project to Open July 15," *CO*, July 6, 1940.
47. "Housing Plan in Good Shape," *CO*, July 24, 1971.
48. "City Facing Difficulties in Keeping Housing Terms," *CO*, September 13, 1942.
49. Fullilove, *Root Shock*; Stack, *All Our Kin*. A firsthand account of such networks in Charlotte's Brooklyn: Love, *Plum Thickets*.
50. "48 Vets Move into New Units," *CO*, November 19, 1946; "Full Title to Morris Field Homes to Be Asked by City: New U.S. Law Now Provides for Transfer," *CO*, October 12, 1949; "Morris Field Homes Are Dead: An Obituary," *CO*, September 30, 1955.
51. "Plan 43 Duplexes in Army Housing Project," *CO*, July 4, 1941. Stonewall Jackson Homes were funded via the Lanham Act, a wartime housing authorization. Hanchett, "Roots of the 'Renaissance.'"
52. "Housing Authority Gives Two-Year Report," *CO*, October 23, 1947. "Body Approves Housing Move: County Board Agrees to Ask Transfer of Homes to Charlotte Housing Authority," *CO*, May 14, 1946; "Base Housing Unit Action Awaits Bill," *CO*, June 5, 1947; "Housing Title Is Transferred: Federal Authority Turns Over Ownership of Stonewall Jackson Homes to Association," *CO*, April 2, 1949.
53. "Negro Housing Unit Planned," *CO*, May 20, 1950. Southside was extensively renovated by the CHA in 2006: "Reservations Make a Difference to Low-Income Residents," *CO*, June 10, 2006. Southside held 400 apartments, while Belvedere had 200. "98 Additional Housing Units Are Released," *CO*, February 26, 1952. For early photographs of Southside

Homes, see papers of contractor Beaumert Whitton, MS 0117, box 6, folder 2, Manuscript Collections, JMAL.
54. "200-Unit Housing Project: Belvedere Homes Work Slated to Begin Jan. 2," *CO*, December 28, 1951; "Architect's Sketch of Belvedere Homes," *CO*, March 16, 1952.
55. In the Housing Act of 1949, signed into law July 15, 1949, Truman won the appropriation of "up to $308 million a year for 40 years to enable construction, through local housing authorities, of 810,000 publicly-owned dwelling units in six years." "Truman Housing Bill Is Passed by House," *CO*, June 30, 1949; "Local Housing Board to Seek New Projects," *CO*, July 1, 1949.

Chapter 3

1. FHA 608 is noted in the history of housing policies compiled by Washington's Congressional Research Service: Milgram, *Chronology of Housing Legislation*, section viii. But academic scholars have largely ignored the FHA 608 story. See, for instance, Mueller and Tighe, *Affordable Housing Reader*; and Plunz, *History of Housing*. Alex F. Schwartz titles chapter 7 of his voluminous *Housing Policy in the United States* "Privately Owned Rental Housing Built with Federal Subsidy"—but starts his narrative with FHA 221(d)(3) in 1961. The case study approach of *Affordable Housing in Charlotte*—examining what actually got built over time in a particular city—puts FHA 608 on historians' research agendas for the first time.
2. "FHA Head Here: Great Post-War Housing Program Seems Assured," *CN*, January 31, 1945.
3. "FHA Approves Builders' Plans for 235 New Houses," *CO*, May 10, 1945; "225 New Housing Units for City Are Approved," *CO*, March 17, 1945; "Crosland to Build Skyland Road Homes at Cost of $95,000," *CO*, August 5, 1945.
4. "Housing Needs Are Discussed," *CO*, January 11, 1946.
5. "Hundreds Live in Makeshift Homes in City," *CO*, November 13, 1946; "Housing for Charlotte Vets Lags after Whirlwind Start," *CO*, August 9, 1946.
6. "FHA Allots Billion for Rental Homes," *New York Times*, April 15, 1947. A billion in 1948 would equal about $12.18 billion in 2021.
7. The "various 'liberalizing' developments in the Federal program . . . allow a net return of 6½ per cent on the total cost of the project." "FHA Allots Billion for Rental Homes." Life insurance companies became large lenders to FHA 608 apartments. Hanchett, "Financing Suburbia."
8. "Meeting Held in Charlotte: FHA Financing Program Explained at Conference," *CO*, February 7, 1947.
9. "Liberal Terms May Break Crisis in Year: FHA Mortgages Bring Boom in Rental Field," *CO*, November 30, 1947; National Park Service, "Modern Apartment Complexes in Georgia."
10. "Liberal Terms May Break Crisis in Year."
11. FHA 608 loans were long-term and amortized (i.e., paid off both the interest and principal over time), running twenty-eight, thirty-three, or forty years. "Liberal Terms May Break Crisis in Year." For a close look at initial financing and at operating expenses over time for FHA 608 projects: "Appendix B: Operating Experience in FHA 608 Rental Projects, 1951 to 1956," in Winnick, *Rental Housing Opportunities*, 271–86, also 16–17.

12. FHA, *Planning Rental Housing Projects*; "FHA Impact on the Financing and Design of Apartments," *Architectural Forum*, January 1950.
13. "Apartment Skyscrapers Banned in N.C. but OK in Other States," *CN*, January 23, 1950. The FHA's South Carolina regional office issued no such prohibition. FHA 608 underwrote the eighteen-story Cornell Arms tower—said to be the tallest building between Richmond and Miami—which remains a landmark adjacent to the University of South Carolina in Columbia. "Eighteen Story Apartment Hotel to Arise at Sumter-Pendleton," *The State* (Columbia, SC), February 8, 1948.
14. "Liberal Terms May Break Crisis in Year," *CO*, November 30, 1947.
15. On Moore's FHA-aided single-family work: "FHA Approves Builders' Plans for 235 New Houses," *CO*, May 10, 1945.
16. "$800,000 Apartment Planned for Charlotte," *CO*, December 10, 1947. In contrast, Moore and other developers built "low-cost" houses under the FHA's postwar program that sold for $5,000 each. "Crosland to Build Skyland Road Homes at Cost of $95,000," *CO*, August 5, 1945.
17. "$800,000 Apartment Planned for Charlotte."
18. Connelly did design a shopping cluster on Selwyn at Colony Avenue, but it was nearly a mile away. "Three Concerns Given Charters," *CO*, August 26, 1948; "Contract Is Awarded for Shopping Center," *CO*, December 26, 1948; "Colony Center Is Now Open," *CO*, September 3, 1949.
19. Selwyn-Queens Apartments in Myers Park still stood at this writing in the early 2020s. Younts Apartments had been replaced with a newer development. "Beautiful Selwyn-Queens Apartments Completed," *CO*, October 24, 1948; "Younts to Build Two Apartments: $250,000 Sum Will Be Spent on Selwyn Ave.," *CO*, January 8, 1948; "Younts Realty Perfects Plans for Big Three-Place Opening," plus related articles and advertisements, *CO*, February 6, 1949; "Paul Younts Active in Civic Life," plus related articles about his two Selwyn Avenue projects as well as Plaza Terrace, *CO*, November 12, 1949. Another active FHA 608 developer was V. P. Loftis, who launched both the Forest Apartments (still extant in the 2020s) on Vail Avenue in Elizabeth and the Berkmore (now the Berkeley office condos) on Morehead Street in Dilworth. "Work Will Begin Soon on Forest Apartments," *CO*, February 8, 1948; "Issue Permits for Projects," *CO*, August 1, 1948; "Berkmore Set to Begin Work," *CO*, February 8, 1948; "Berkmore Apartments to Be Ready in August," *CO*, June 12, 1948; "Developments Rise in State," *Robesonian* (Lumberton, NC), February 10, 1956. Marsh, still a leading firm in Charlotte multifamily housing in the 2020s, created Oakcrest in Sedgefield: "Marsh to Build 76 Apartments," *CN*, July 12, 1948; "Construction to Begin on Apartment Project," *CO*, July 13, 1948; "Builds Modern Housing Units," *CO*, September 12, 1948; "Families Move into Oakcrest," *CO*, December 5, 1948.
20. "Housing Work Begins Today," *CO*, May 4, 1948.
21. "Charlotte Developer C. D. Spangler, Sr., Dies of Heart Attack," *CO*, October 12, 1987. C. D. Spangler Jr., interview by Amy Blitz, July 2001, HBS Entrepreneurs Oral History Collection, Baker Library, Harvard University; "Sales Reported by C. D. Spangler," *CO*, April 27, 1941; "C. D. Spangler Jr., Tough, Efficient and Very, Very Private," *CO*, December 19, 1982; "C. D. Spangler Jr., Former UNC President and Charlotte Businessman, Dies," *RNO*, July 23, 2018; "Harvard Business School Alumnus and Great Benefactor

Dies at 86," Harvard Business School, Newsroom, July 30, 2018, www.hbs.edu/news/releases/Pages/dick-spangler-obituary.aspx; "In Memoriam: C. D. Spangler," *Carolina Alumni Review*, July 23, 2018, https://alumni.unc.edu/news/former-unc-system-president-c-d-spangler-54-dies-at-86/.

22. "Shrewd Businessman: UNC President's Other Side," *Greensboro News and Record*, May 21, 1995; Covington and Ellis, *Story of NationsBank*. At Camp Lejeune, Spangler constructed federally subsidized Tarawa Terrace in the early 1950s, with over 1,000 apartments, a shopping center, a fire station, and a sewer plant—all owned and operated by the Spangler company. "Spangler Gets Big Job at Camp Lejeune," *CO*, March 8, 1951; "Fore Named to Executive Post with Spangler Firm," *CO*, May 19, 1951. Spangler also built post–World War II military family housing at Fort Lee in Virginia and Fort Hood in Georgia. Peeler et al., *Housing an Air Force and a Navy*.

23. "Million Dollar Apartment Planned—Work Will Start Soon on 250-Unit Project Here—Tryon Hills, Inc., Is Chartered," *CN*, March 8, 1948; "Building Bits," *CO*, December 26, 1948.

24. "Spangler Plans Negro Housing Project," *CO*, September 28, 1948; "Committee of Realtors Makes Estimate: Proposed Housing Site Valued at $45,000," *CN*, December 4, 1948, mentions the landfill.

25. "Relief Is Forecast in Rental Housing," *CO*, August 22, 1948; "We Are Proud of Our Part in Developing These Great Projects," *CO*, February 28, 1950; "These Apartment Buildings Typical of Many That Have Been Erected Here in the Post War Years," *CN*, January 31, 1951.

26. "Apartment Work Begins," *CN*, May 3, 1948.

27. Early publicity suggested that Tryon Hills would have 87 one-bedroom units and 154 two-bedroom units. The actual total was 250 units. "Housing Work Begins Today," *CO*, May 4, 1948; "Huge Housing Project Is Announced," *CO*, March 9, 1948.

28. "With Assembly-Line Housing, Charlotte Builder Is Making History," *CO*, June 27, 1948. Spangler would use the same assembly-line process at Double Oaks: "Eighty-Five Negro Rentals Ready Next Month," *CO*, July 31, 1949.

29. "With Assembly-Line Housing, Charlotte Builder Is Making History."

30. The first three names shown for Tryon Hills in the 1952 city directory, the earliest to list the development, were William H. Tucker, Robert R. Harwell, and Louis A. Wintzer.

31. "Miss Wall, Mr. Long Are United in Marriage," *CO*, April 30, 1949.

32. "'Get Involved' Was Always His Mantra: Fred Alexander Was Charlotte's First Black City Council Member of the Twentieth Century," *CO*, February 19, 2012; "Fred Alexander's Contributions," *CO*, February 15, 1980; "Charlotte Legislator Dies at 70," *CO*, February 14, 1980; Fred D. Alexander Papers, MS 0091, Manuscript Collections, JMAL, https://findingaids.uncc.edu/repositories/4/resources/427. Biographical note in finding guide confirms he was named for abolitionist Frederick Douglass.

33. Gaillard, *Dream Long Deferred*, 15–17; "Who We Are," on the Alexander Funeral Home website, accessed April 14, 2024, www.alexanderfunerals.com/history; Bishir and Hanchett, "Houser, William H."

34. Vann and Jones, *Durham's Haiti*, 127.

35. "Masons Purchase Lot," *CO*, February 3, 1949.

36. "Teddy Burwell to Head Housing Survey," *CO*, February 7, 1939.

37. Boger, *Charlotte 23*, 6.
38. "Study Proposal for 500 Negro Rental Houses," *CO*, September 22, 1948. Spangler's bid got him sixty-two acres, with twenty-three of those reserved for a park. "Only One Bidder Seeks City Land Lease: C. D. Spangler Submits Offer for Property," *CO*, January 15, 1949; "Negro Housing Project Gets Go-Ahead Signal," *CO*, February 17, 1949; "$1,800,000 and $2,535,000 Housing Projects Planning in City: Will Provide 740 Units," *CO*, June 15, 1949.
39. "Eighty-Five Negro Rentals Ready Next Month," *CO*, July 31, 1949.
40. "Eighty-Five Negro Rentals Ready Next Month."
41. "Big Housing Project for Negroes Opened," *CO*, September 28, 1949. City directories for 1951 and 1952 listed James C. Clemmons, a carrier for the post office, along with spouse, Willie M. Clemmons, at 916 D. Druid Circle.
42. "Teachers Elect Jefferson," *CO*, September 21, 1949; "Pan-Hellenic Council to Hold Meet Today," *CO*, November 21, 1954.
43. "Colored Cage Game Tonight," *CO*, February 1, 1945.
44. "John H. Moore Heads Phalanx Fraternity," *CO*, January 14, 1944; "Dedication Service Is Held by Church," *CO*, July 10, 1950.
45. "Negro Housing Project Gets Go-Ahead Signal," *CO*, February 17, 1949.
46. "Big Housing Project Is Planned for City," *CO*, June 3, 1950.
47. "Eighty-Five Negro Rentals Ready Next Month," *CO*, July 31, 1949.
48. "Work Begins Soon on Negro Housing," *CO*, March 1, 1950. The Newland project was often referred to as "an addition to" Double Oaks. "Project Permit Granted," *CO*, April 4, 1950. The Newland Road application slid into the FHA office in Greensboro just hours before FHA 608 funding expired on March 1, 1950. "Two Housing Projects OKed," *Asheville Citizen*, March 1, 1950; "Seek Statesville Ave. Development: City to Take Bids on Tract November 21," *CO*, October 9, 1949.
49. "City to Buy 11-Acre Tract as Site for Negro School," *CO*, March 9, 1950.
50. "Building Development to Cost $5,750,000: C. D. Spangler to Begin Work Soon on 978 Rental Units," *CO*, December 18, 1949. The article reported on Brookhill and several other projects, including forty-five single-family houses built adjacent to Double Oaks and sold to Black buyers.
51. "York Road Favored for Negro Housing Project," *CO*, October 9, 1949; "September Work Date Set for 418-Unit Negro Housing," *CO*, August 5, 1950; "$2 Million Negro Housing Job Begins Thursday," *CO*, October 31, 1950.
52. In reality, Spangler also controlled Brookhill Village, Inc., though the project's contractor, F. L. Taylor, was listed as president on the ninety-nine-year lease document. Ground lease: C. D. Spangler, landlord, and Brookhill Village, Inc., tenant, November 1, 1950, deed book 1474, pp. 386–405 ("under agreement dated January 1, 1950"), Mecklenburg County Register of Deeds, Charlotte, NC. On Spangler's ownership of Brookhill Village, Inc.: "Secretary of State Thad Eure today chartered a $400,000 housing project in Charlotte. The Brookhill Villlage, Inc., was sponsored by John D. Shaw and C. D. Spangler." "Charters Project," *Statesville (NC) Daily Record*, September 8, 1950. See also "New Corporations," *RNO*, September 9, 1950; "Brookhill Village, Inc., Is Given State Charter," *CO*, September 9, 1950.
53. The 1954 investigation into the FHA 608 program produced hundreds of pages of

testimony, including several discussions of land-lease arrangements. This exchange about a New York City project was typical:

> *Chairman [Sen. Homer Capehart]*: Let me ask you this question: In this particular case, they did not sell or include the land as part of the project. They took a 99-year lease at $76,960 a year. Is that the general pattern of what happened in New York City?
>
> *Mr. McKenna [Housing and Home Finance Agency]*: That is true of New York, and also of some other areas. . . . It is a very lucrative means of getting another windfall, so far as the sponsor of the project is concerned.
>
> *Chairman*: The law, of course, says that whoever has the land lease in case of default on a mortgage owns the property. In other words, [the FHA] cannot repossess without purchasing his land or making a deal.

FHA Investigation: Hearings before the Committee on Banking and Currency, Part 2, 30. See also Part 1, 374.

54. "Schul Forum Series," UNC Charlotte Urban Institute website, October 26, 2021, https://ui.charlotte.edu/our-work/schul-forum-series.
55. "Boom in Construction of Luxury Apartments Meets Big City Needs," *Asheville Citizen*, November 14, 1949.
56. "Boom in Construction of Luxury Apartments Meets Big City Needs"; "Low-Priced Housing Program Is Lauded," *CO*, April 27, 1950.
57. "FHA Approves Loans for Rent Units Here," *CO*, March 25, 1949.
58. "Marsh to Build 76 Apartments," *CN*, July 12, 1948.
59. On Westwood: "Plans 300 Unit Housing Job," *CO*, December 17, 1949. This was revised to 270 units when the building permit was obtained. "Spangler Files for $1,274,000 Building Permit," *CO*, June 10, 1950. Charlotte developer John Crosland Jr. would buy Double Oaks, Tryon Hills, and Westwood and renovate them in the early 1980s. Yockey, *Builder*, 197–200; "Revenue Bonds to Help Revamp Privately Owned Housing Project," *CO*, March 13, 1983. Westwood would be demolished in the early years of the 2000s.
60. "FHA Approves Loans for Rent Units Here," *CO*, March 25, 1949.
61. "W. A. Thompson to Head Firm," *CO*, September 12, 1947. Thompson also developed FHA 608 apartments in Asheville. "Charlotte Man in Big Project," September 29, 1949. C. D. Spangler was a small stockholder in Thompson's firm during the construction of Selwyn Village, and his property management staff handled rentals initially.
62. "Apartment Would Cost over $3 Million," *CO*, February 20, 1949; "Construction of Apartment Slated in August," *CO*, June 15, 1949; "Selwyn Village Seeks Permit for 234 Units," *CO*, October 12, 1949; "Loan Approved for Apartment," *CO*, November 11, 1949. Selwyn Village sold as condominiums in 1979. "Selwyn Village Spawned City's Leaders," *CO*, November 21, 1981.
63. "FHA to Issue Commitments for Projects," *Asheville Citizen*, June 30, 1949.
64. "Asks Revision of '608': Wherry Urges Change to Protect Pending Applications," *New York Times*, February 25, 1950. Congress appropriated $500 million to cover the final big rush, agreeing to accept applications in-process by February 15, 1950. "Low Priced Housing Program Is Lauded," *CO*, April 27, 1950. It helped that Harry Truman personally lobbied Congress on behalf of Section 608. For example, Harry Truman, "Special

Message to Congress on Housing," February 23, 1948, American Presidency Project, www.presidency.ucsb.edu/documents/special-message-the-congress-housing.
65. "Two Housing Projects OKed," *Asheville Citizen*, March 1, 1950. Spangler's expansion of Double Oaks northward along Newland Road was one of the last two to make it under the deadline.
66. "FHA Takes Over Eight Modern Florida Apartments: *Tampa Tribune* Blasts Agency," *CO*, June 17, 1951.
67. "FHA Foreclosures Rise on Developments in State," *Robesonian*, February 10, 1956; "Apartment Headache Given $200,000 Pill," *CO*, September 2, 1956.
68. "FHA Foreclosures Rise on Developments in State"; "Turnback Figures Are Low on FHA-Insured Projects," *CO*, September 2, 1956.
69. "FHA Takes Over Eight Modern Florida Apartments: Tampa Tribune Blasts Agency," *CO*, June 17, 1951.
70. "Local Housing Wages Rapped: AFL Asks Investigation of Pay Scales at FHA-Guaranteed Projects," *CO*, April 27, 1950; "Section 608 Projects—Prevailing Wage Violations," 92–93.
71. "Sins and Section 608," *Harvard Crimson*, April 27, 1954; "Housing: Subsidized Fraud," *Time*, January 18, 1971.
72. Quotations from *FHA Investigation: Report of the Senate Committee on Banking and Currency, Pursuant to S. Resolution 229*, 123. The elder Trump testified at length, calling the FHA's accusations "completely untrue and very unfair." *FHA Investigation: Report*, 52, 393–418; Brockenbrough, *Unpresidented*, 35–36.
73. "How Uncle Sam Helped a Charlottean Strike It Rich," *CO*, July 26, 1959.
74. "How Uncle Sam Helped a Charlottean Strike It Rich."
75. FHA, *Sixteenth Annual Report*, 5; Harry Truman, "Annual Budget Message to the Congress: Fiscal Year 1948," January 10, 1947, American Presidency Project, www.presidency.ucsb.edu/documents/annual-budget-message-the-congress-fiscal-year-1948.
76. "FHA Mortgages, Loans in N.C. Total $419 million," *CN*, June 11, 1954.
77. "History of the Glen Lennox Apartments and Shopping Center," Town of Chapel Hill website, accessed April 14, 2024, www.townofchapelhill.org/Home/ShowDocument?id=7328.
78. "Ardmore Historic District," Living Places website, accessed November 4, 2024, www.livingplaces.com/NC/Forsyth_County/Winston-Salem_City/Ardmore_Historic_District.html.
79. "List of Original Sponsors of Tar Heel Housing Developments through FHA Announced," *RNO*, April 21, 1954; "Charles Bennett Deane," NCpedia, accessed April 14, 2024, www.ncpedia.org/biography/deane-charles-bennett; York with Sharpe, *Growing Up with Raleigh*; Hutchins with York and York, *Cameron Village*. The York family used part of the FHA 608 proceeds to launch what became Cameron Brown Mortgage, a major financial force in North Carolina on its own and later as part of First Union National Bank (predecessor to today's Wells Fargo).
80. "Huge $8–$10 Million Suburban Charlotte Project Is Planned," *CO*, December 18, 1952. Mott did the land planning at Cotswold, while Charlotte's dependable Charles Connelly provided the architectural designs. "Apartment Project Gets Underway," *CO*, June 25, 1953; "Rising Suburban Area Links Shopping, Home," *CO*, June 1, 1954. In

North Carolina, Mott had previously drawn the plans for Cameron Village in Raleigh, which clustered single-family homes and FHA 608 apartments around a shopping plaza. Hutchins with York and York, *Cameron Village*.

81. Anderson with assistance from Butts, *Charlotte–Mecklenburg*, 28.
82. "600 New Dwelling Units Voted by City Council," *CO*, December 22, 1949. An FHA deputy commissioner made similar points in a 1951 interview: "Section 608 was not the low-cost housing program. It was intended to relieve the shortage of rental accommodations for middle-income families. The law provided that the projects be of standard quality and provided through normal building and real estate channels. The rents were dictated mainly . . . by the construction costs which FHA felt it had to approve to get builders into the field." The stimulus worked: "When the builders came in, they came with a rush. They made money." "FHA Takes Over Eight Modern Florida Apartments: Tampa Tribune Blasts Agency," *CO*, June 17, 1951.

Chapter 4

1. The term "urban renewal" was introduced in Congress's 1954 Housing Act, a revision of the 1949 Housing Act. On slum clearance/urban renewal, the classic history is Hirsch, *Making the Second Ghetto*. Most recently, see Fairbanks, *War on Slums*.
2. Scholars often assume that the 1949 Housing Act and 1954 Housing Act required that new public housing be constructed on the cleared lands. Richard Plunz, for instance, stated categorically that the "Housing Act, as it was finally passed in 1949, stipulated that public housing be built in areas where slums were to be razed." Plunz, *History of Housing*, 272. Plunz's assumption was not correct.
3. Scholars have paid scant attention to the process whereby building codes became local law. They note when codes were first instituted in America's biggest cities or point to actions such as Herbert Hoover's creation of a model building code in 1921 that localities could adopt. Hayden, *Building Suburbia*, 121; Schiesl, *Politics of Efficiency*. But code adoption did not follow automatically. It required long battles on the ground—as described in this chapter and also in Hanchett, "Roots of the 'Renaissance.'"
4. V. S. Woodward, "Housing and Its Relation to Health in Our City," typescript in folder 5, box 98, John Nolen Papers, Rare and Manuscript Collections, Cornell University Library, Ithaca, NY.
5. Women's clubs took the lead in municipal health efforts both in Charlotte and nationwide. The Charlotte Women's Club held meetings with the mayor on the issue as early as 1910. "Civics Department Asks for Better Enforcement of Sanitary Laws," *CN*, February 10, 1910. On the growth of women's clubs during the Progressive Era and their focus on "municipal housekeeping," see Beard, *Women's Work*; Blain, *Clubwoman as Feminist*, 73–119; Birch, "From Civic Worker to City Planner"; and Flanigan, "Gender and Urban Political Reform." On such activities in the South: Scott, *Southern Lady*, 159–63; Gilmore, *Gender and Jim Crow*.
6. Ogle, *All the Modern Conveniences*.
7. "Dr. C. C. Hudson, Health Officer," *CN*, September 23, 1917; "Health Officer Elected by the Commissioners," *CO*, September 23, 1917; "Public Mass Meeting on Next Tuesday Night," *CO*, September 27, 1917.
8. "15,000 in City Use Well Water," *CO*, July 28, 1918.

9. "Health Meeting Brings Out Many," *CO*, October 3, 1917; "Health Campaign to Be Waged in the City: New Superintendent of Health, Aided by U.S. Experts, to Clean Up Charlotte," *CO*, October 20, 1917.
10. "Here to Install Better System: Surface Closets Will Be Made Much More Sanitary," *CO*, December 18, 1917; "Campaign On for Health: Over 2400 Sanitary Closets to Be Constructed; Notices Being Served," *CN*, April 18, 1918. Perhaps due to his lack of impact in Charlotte, Hudson resigned in 1920 to become public health chief for Richmond. "Warren's Election Pleases Rankin," *CN*, February 9, 1920.
11. "For several years in his annual reports Dr. McPhaul [W. A. McPhaul, city health officer] recommended a new health code, but not until this year has the plan been authorized." "Code of Health Is Authorized for This City," *CN*, September 25, 1929. "Most important of the new measures was the plumbing, sewer and sanitation ordinance." "Council Votes on Three City Codes," *CO*, January 7, 1930. "City Ordinance: An Ordinance with Reference to Public Health," published verbatim in the *CN*, February 22, 1930. McPhaul, hired in 1920, came from a similar post in Montgomery, Alabama. "Health Officer Takes Up Work," *CN*, October 15, 1920. Soon after getting Charlotte's new ordinance passed, he was lured away to head a larger and better-funded health department in Florida. "Dr. M'Phaul Will Be City Health Officer in Pensacola," *CN*, February 21, 1932.
12. "Will Ask Council to Finance Housing Survey," *CN*, February 13, 1935.
13. For more on the large impact of the women's clubs on civic issues in the early twentieth century, see note 5 above.
14. "White People Exist in Areas of Misery," "Councilmen Seek Anti-slum Move," "Council Asked to Investigate Slum Sections," "Anti-slum Campaign of the News Given High Commendation," all in the *CN*, February 10, 1937.
15. "White People Exist in Areas of Misery."
16. "Council Asked to Investigate Slum Sections," *CN*, February 10, 1937.
17. "Praise Heaped on B. & P. Club," *CO*, February 19, 1939. On the WPA survey, see "Teddy Burwell to Head Housing Survey," *CO*, February 7, 1939. The last mention of that survey in the newspapers: "Results of a WPA housing survey recently completed have not been compiled." "$309,000 for New Buildings," *CN*, October 29, 1939.
18. "City to Launch Drive on Slum Dwellings: Homes Must Have Running Water," *CN*, May 5, 1940.
19. Hanchett, "Roots of the 'Renaissance,'" 296–99.
20. "Planning Body Shaping Law to End Slums," *CO*, November 15, 1945.
21. "Real Estate Board Advances Slum Clearance Program: Plan Designed to Eliminate Blighted Areas," *CO*, February 5, 1945; "Housing Act Would Better Conditions: 'Standard House' Ordinance Studied," *CN*, November 16, 1945; "Plan to Tighten Law to Require Hot Water Also," *CO*, November 28, 1945; "Housing Authority Opposes Any 'Period of Grace': Takes Issue with Request for Five Years," *CN*, December 1, 1945.
22. "Real Estate Board Advances Slum Clearance Program: Plan Designed to Eliminate Blighted Areas," *CO*, February 5, 1945.
23. "Councilmen Adopt City Slum Clearance Ordinance," *CO*, December 12, 1945.
24. "Enforcement Not Near for Slum Clearance Law," *CO*, August 19, 1947; "Council Urged to Enforce Slum Clearance Law," *CO*, October 23, 1947.
25. C. C. Dauer, "Prevalence of Poliomyelitis in 1948," *Public Health Reports*, June 10, 1949,

733–40; "Two New Polio Cases are Reported in City," *CN*, July 24, 1948. And on the same page of the newspaper: "Bethel Asks Housing Ordinance Be Enforced."
26. "Fearful 1948 Polio Epidemic Crippled Children, United City," *Greensboro News and Record*, August 29, 1999.
27. "Don't Panic over Polio," *Maclean's*, August 1, 1948.
28. "City Gets Housing Drive Underway," *CN*, August 3, 1948. Real estate leaders frequently stated the quid pro quo: they would consider complying if the city would "guarantee that the Charlotte Housing Authority will not step in and build a great many new units which would compete with the 2,000 to 3,000 houses in the $3 to $5 weekly rent class envisioned by the realtors." "Real Estate Board Advances Slum Clearance Program," *CN*, February 5, 1945.
29. "Council Streamlines Slum Clearance Program," *CO*, August 19, 1948; "More Time to Install Baths in Slums Expected," *CO*, August 15, 1948.
30. "More Time to Install Baths in Slums Expected."
31. "Machinery Started to Enforce Housing Law: Move to Step Up Sanitary Program," *CN*, July 29, 1948.
32. "Slum Program Result Should Be Seen Soon," *CN*, July 29, 1948.
33. "Real Estate Board Advances Slum Clearance Program," *CO*, February 5, 1945.
34. "Council Streamlines Slum Clearance Program," *CO*, August 19, 1948; "More Time to Install Baths in Slums Expected," *CO*, August 15, 1948.
35. Federal urban renewal officials pushed the new housing code in many cities, an attempt to stop the ongoing creation of slums. Ted Fillette, written communication to Tom Hanchett, March 25, 2022.
36. As recently as 2021, 73 of North Carolina's 100 counties had no minimum housing standards. Korie Dean and Taylor Buck, "Thousands without Adequate Plumbing Could Be Helped by Minimum Codes," Carolina Public Press, February 23, 2021, https://carolinapublicpress.org/42729/thousands-without-adequate-plumbing-could-be-helped-by-minimum-codes/.
37. "As 2020 Begins, Many Lake Arbor Residents Still Looking for New Homes," *CO*, January 21, 2020.
38. On the importance of informal "helping networks" among low-income Americans, the pathbreaking study was Fullilove, *Root Shock*.
39. "Slum Clearance Big Property Value Aid," *CN*, July 14, 1953; "For Redevelopment: No Federal Funds Needed, Says Allen," *CO*, June 29, 1952.
40. "Slum Prevention, Not Slum Clearance, Is Housing Code's Biggest Accomplishment," *Architectural Forum*, October 1950, 176; "In *Post* Article: Charlotte's Slum Clearance Cited," *CO*, January 28, 1953; "These Slumlords Got Smart," *Saturday Evening Post*, January 31, 1953, www.saturdayeveningpost.com/issues/1953–01–31/. A similar, larger effort by Baltimore, headed by soon-to-be-famous developer James Rouse, took the main spotlight in both the *Forum* and *Post* articles. See also *The Baltimore Plan*, a twenty-minute film produced by Encyclopedia Britannica, 1953, on YouTube, www.youtube.com/watch?v=-52MmEdIqOU.
41. "These Slumlords Got Smart."
42. "Loan System Set Up for Slum Clearance," *CO*, December 24, 1949. On the shift nationally, see von Hoffman, "Lost History of Urban Renewal."

43. "Council's Slum Program Decision Looming Wednesday," *CO*, March 19, 1950.
44. Emphasis added. Wheaton, "Housing Act of 1949," 18.
45. Minutes of the Charlotte City Council, March 22, 1950, Meeting Minutes 1936–1978, City of Charlotte, www.charlottenc.gov/files/sharedassets/city/v/1/city-government/departments/documents/clerks-office/minutes/1948-1951/minutes-1950/march-22-1950.pdf.
46. "Suburb for Negroes," *CO*, September 22, 1912; "Model Suburb for Colored People to Be Developed," *Charlotte Chronicle*, September 23, 1912.
47. "Council Slates Study of Slum Clearance," *CO*, August 2, 1951.
48. "For Redevelopment: No Federal Funds Needed, Says Allen," *CO*, June 29, 1952; "Planners Eye Redevelopment of Slum Areas," *CO*, February 24, 1956.
49. "Low Investment: Negligible Taxes: Brooklyn Homes Give Owners High Returns," *CO*, January 11, 1960.
50. Hanchett, *Sorting Out*, 229–32.
51. Hanchett, *Sorting Out*, 245–47.
52. "Offer Names for Boulevard," *CO*, November 2, 1948; "Boulevard Is Nearing Completion," *CO*, October 25, 1949; "City Requests Survey for Link of Boulevard," *CO*, November 22, 1949. The final section opened in 1955. "Saves Three Minutes: Independence Link Opened to Traffic," *CO*, November 24, 1955; Hanchett, *Sorting Out*, 239–40.
53. "Charlotte's Brooklyn Doomed by Progress?," *CO*, February 23, 1956.
54. "Must Designate Area: Next Slum Step Up to Planners," *CO*, January 15, 1958.
55. "Better Living Conditions Sought: NAACP to Push Improvement Program," *CN*, January 23, 1950. Kelly Alexander had won national notice for revitalizing Charlotte's lapsed NAACP chapter in the early 1940s. By 1950 he also headed North Carolina's statewide NAACP and served on the national board. "Alexander Is Elected to National Board of NAACP," *CN*, January 4, 1950.
56. Letter from Charlotte NAACP to Charlotte Redevelopment Commission, January 1960, box C112, group III, NAACP Papers, quoted in Newkirk, "Development of the National Association for the Advancement of Colored People," 103. A *CO* report made the same point: "Low Investment: Negligible Taxes: Brooklyn Homes Give Owners High Returns," *CO*, January 11, 1960.
57. "NAACP Asks Stronger Voice in Slum Plan," *CO*, January 5, 1960; "Redevelopers Dispute NAACP's Claim," *CN*, June 23, 1960.
58. "Redevelopers Dispute NAACP's Claim." Sawyer's comments appeared in a transcript of the subsequent City Council meeting in which the Redevelopment Commission presented the hearing results to elected officials. "Hearing on the Brooklyn Area General Neighborhood Renewal Plan," minutes of the Charlotte City Council, August 22, 1960, pp. 38–42, Meeting Minutes 1936–1978, City of Charlotte, www.charlottenc.gov/files/sharedassets/city/v/1/city-government/departments/documents/clerks-office/minutes/1960-1963/minutes-1960/august-22-1960.pdf.
59. "Redevelopers Dispute NAACP's Claim"; "Hearing on the Brooklyn Area General Neighborhood Renewal Plan," 38–42.
60. Public hearing in February 1961 on clearing an initial eight blocks: "The hearing is one of two that must be held before the Charlotte Redevelopment Commission can begin buying land. . . . Following today's hearing the commission is expected to formally adopt

the plans and send them to the Council for action." "Slum Clearance Hearing Is Today," *CO*, February 22, 1961.
61. "Plea Made to Council: Public Housing Sought for Negroes," *CO*, December 5, 1961.
62. "Plea Made to Council."
63. "Empty Building: Four Firemen Hurt in Brooklyn Blaze," *CO*, August 17, 1963.
64. "What to Do 'til the Bulldozer Comes? Slum Clearance, Expressway Plans Create Hazardous, Empty Homes," *CO*, August 26, 1963; "Not Just Urban Renewal: Many Forces Adding to Housing Squeeze," *CO*, October 14, 1962.
65. "Slum Aid Snagged on Alternate Housing," *CO*, October 9, 1962.
66. "Pre-Fab Slum: Artist Critical of Earle Village," *CN*, April 12, 1967; "A Visit to Earle Village," *CN*, October 13, 1967; "Earle Village Gets a Needed Hand," *CO*, May 11, 1967; "Low Income Housing Needs Remain as Major Challenge," *CO*, May 27, 1967.
67. "Low Income Housing Needs Remain a Major Challenge."
68. "Pre-Fab Slum: Artist Critical of Earle Village," *CN*, April 12, 1967; "A Visit to Earle Village," *CN*, October 13, 1967.
69. "Earle Village Gets a Needed Hand," *CO*, May 11, 1967.
70. "Statistical Summary of Urban Renewal Program, October 1972," Charlotte Redevelopment Commission Records, digitized image in the Evolution of Housing Policy Documents, Manuscript Collections, JMAL, accessed April 14, 2024, https://repository.charlotte.edu//islandora/object/mss:73085#page/1/mode/1up.
71. "Urban Renewal High Bidder Proposes Convention Site," *CO*, February 17, 1971.
72. "Warehouse Provision Cut Out of Brooklyn Land-Use Plan," *CO*, July 27, 1970. Alexander had previously made a motion to consider putting low-income housing on a pair of persistently vacant Brooklyn urban renewal parcels. That motion, too, received no second. "Council Vetoes 'Island' Housing," *CO*, February 26, 1969.

Chapter 5

1. Historians who have discussed the public-private housing programs launched in the 1960s seldom mentioned accelerated depreciation. For instance: Schwartz, *Housing Policy*, chapter 7 ("Privately Owned Rental Housing Built with Federal Subsidy"); Edson, "Affordable Housing"; Orlebeke, "Evolution of Low-Income Housing Policy." The best in-depth history of the era noted the importance of tax considerations but treated accelerated depreciation as a given rather than as something that Congress created and revised over time. Von Hoffman, "Calling Upon the Genius of Private Enterprise." Washington's misplaced trust during these years in what President Johnson termed "the genius of private industry" was devastatingly documented in a recent study of FHA 235: Taylor, *Race for Profit*. Except for von Hoffman, few scholars have taken a similarly skeptical approach to FHA 236 and its companions. Nor have they documented abuses on the ground, as Taylor did.
2. "Almost as an afterthought, accelerated depreciation was allowed for buildings as well as machinery and equipment in 1954." Verdier, *Real Estate Tax Shelter Subsidies*, 23. Real estate guru Louis Winnick helped investors discover the tax shelter: "The newer depreciation schemes . . . encourage new rental investment by substantially increasing the potential cash take-out during the first few years and by providing a tax offset to the investor." Winnick, *Rental Housing Opportunities*, 151. It is no coincidence that the United States

also saw an upsurge in construction of shopping malls and office parks starting in the late 1950s, hot on the heels of the tax change. Hanchett, "U.S. Tax Policy and the Shopping Center Boom." Charlotte experienced an unprecedented wave of office construction—far beyond actual demand—at exactly the same time as the apartment boom. "Offices Outnumber Tenants: Half a Million Square Feet of Space May Be Vacant by Next Year," *CO*, August 15, 1971.

3. On the 1960 IRS regulation that made the depreciation tax shelter especially lucrative for doctors and other professionals, encouraging limited partnerships: Brown, "Taxability of Unincorporated Medical Associations"; Verdier, *Real Estate Tax Shelter Subsidies*, especially 26–27. According to a study of one office building in Charlotte: "Even if the building were struggling financially, the partners could write off a certain amount each year for depreciation . . . [which] worked to move individuals into a lower tax bracket. . . . For every dollar invested, partners could write off three dollars on their tax forms, which added up to an attractive bonus." Watt, "East Independence Plaza Building," 5.

4. Verdier, *Real Estate Tax Shelter Subsidies*, especially 26–27; Brown, "Taxability of Unincorporated Medical Associations."

5. Verdier, *Real Estate Tax Shelter Subsidies*, especially xiv.

6. "LBJ Proposes Legislation to Curb Inflationary Trend," *CO*, September 9, 1966; "Building Up in February but Still Below a Year Ago," *CO*, March 29, 1967; Romer and Romer, "Narrative Analysis of Postwar Tax Changes," 43–45.

7. Increasing the early depreciation write-off "drastically altered current tax consequences associated with housing and real estate development." "Chapter EE. Effect of Tax Reform Act on Housing," 117 Cong. Rec. 10610 (daily ed. April 15, 1971). "In the Tax Reform Act of 1969, Congress reduced substantially the accelerated depreciation allowed for [most types of] buildings. Accelerated depreciation was continued at its pre-1969 level for newly constructed rental housing, however, giving this form of construction a comparative tax advantage over office buildings, shopping centers, and other commercial buildings. [The 1969 act] also added a new provision permitting certain amounts spent to rehabilitate low-income rental housing to be written off or amortized on a straight-line basis over a period of only five years . . . in effect a form of super-accelerated depreciation." Verdier, *Real Estate Tax Shelter Subsidies*, 23.

8. Charles Ervin, the city's biggest builder, for example, "has sold virtually all of its projects in the area to syndicates," i.e., limited partnerships. "Apartment Permits Zip Ahead of Houses at Two-to-One Rate," *CO*, January 30, 1972; "Builders Fight for Renters: Charlotte's Apartment Boom Roars On," *CO*, May 6, 1973; "Charlotte's First Apartment Boom Struck in Early 1970s," *CO*, May 20, 2018.

9. "Woodlake-Foxfire Tax Anomaly Is Explained," *CO*, March 25, 1972. Similarly, "Making 25 Percent on Apartments," *San Francisco Examiner*, September 7, 1969.

10. "132-Unit Complex: Crosland Making Jump into Apartment Field," *CO*, November 21, 1970.

11. Sperbeck, "Suburban Multifamily Vacancy Rates." "At the beginning of the [1960s] decade there was for all practical purposes no apartment construction" in Minneapolis's suburb of New Hope, for instance. By late 1969, "about 45 percent of all residential units in New Hope are apartments." "Two Running for Mayor, Four for New Hope Council," *Minneapolis Star*, October 28, 1969; "Apartments for Rent: Sign of New Suburban

Boom," *Minneapolis Tribune*, September 29, 1968; "'Bigness' Hitting Apartment Boom," *Minneapolis Star-Tribune*, June 11, 1972.
12. "Builders Fight for Renters: Charlotte's Apartment Boom Roars On," *CO*, May 6, 1973.
13. See "Mecklenburg County, North Carolina" on Wikipedia, accessed April 14, 2024, https://en.wikipedia.org/wiki/Mecklenburg_County,_North_Carolina.
14. "This $58 Million Fund Will Buy, Save Affordable Housing from Vanishing in Charlotte," *CO*, November 3, 2020.
15. "New Tax Loophole: Big Profits Possible in Low-Cost Housing," *CO*, January 24, 1970.
16. "N.C. Fund Aims to Untie Housing Red Tape," *CO*, July 15, 1966. Section 221 had been introduced in the Housing Act of 1954, initially targeted very narrowly at providing low-interest mortgages to nonprofits that would build or renovate single-family homes and multifamily projects to serve people displaced by other federal actions (such as highway construction). The Housing Act of 1959 expanded eligibility, allowing for-profit developers to receive those mortgages. In the Housing Act of 1961, Section (d)(3) removed the "displaced persons" requirement—but only for nonprofit developers. The Housing Act of 1964 opened Section (d)(3) to for-profit developers. Milgram, *Chronology of Housing Legislation*, section viii; Schwartz, *Housing Policy*, chapter 7; von Hoffman, "Calling Upon the Genius of Private Enterprise."
17. "N.C. Fund Aims to Untie Housing Red Tape."
18. Milgram, *Chronology of Housing Legislation*.
19. United States, *Tax Incentives to Encourage Housing in Urban Poverty Areas*, 173.
20. In an interesting throwback to early twentieth-century low-rent apartment financing, all four were "set up as limited dividend companies. Under the limited dividend arrangement, a sponsor may not take more than six percent of the total proceeds from the project per year. The remainder of the funds is held in escrow for maintenance and upkeep until the government decides it may be released." "Four Low-Rent Housing Projects Clear Hurdle: FHA Gives Tentative Approval," *CO*, July 27, 1967. If money remained in the escrow at the end of the forty-year mortgage, the owner received it as profit. "The Almost-Poor Getting Housing," *CO*, August 22, 1968.
21. "Four Low-Rent Housing Projects Clear Hurdle"; "Work Starts Soon on Low-Rent Units," *CO*, January 16, 1968. As the project came to fruition, the FHA underwrote a second phase, doubling it to 504 apartments. "Roseland to Be Doubled in Federal Project," *CN*, April 23, 1969; "Two New Housing Projects Lift 387 Families Out of Slums," *CO*, December 2, 1968.
22. "Developer Plans Low-Rent Housing Project," *CN*, March 24, 1967; "133 Housing Units for Lower Income Persons Planned," *CO*, March 5, 1968; "Private-Owner, Low-Income Housing Planned for City," *CO*, March 24, 1967; "Four Low-Rent Housing Projects Clear Hurdle."
23. "Four Low-Rent Housing Projects Clear Hurdle"; "Housing Agency Faces Debate over Contract," *CO*, February 5, 1978. Parker Heights Ltd. owned the apartments: forty-four shareholders including Harvey Gantt—who said he held less than a 1 percent interest and took no tax loss. "Two Candidates Talk about Their Holdings," *CO*, September 21, 1979. Hawkins subsequently attempted a similar project in white east Charlotte, blocked by neighbors. "Rent-Subsidy Apartments: Eastside Project Planned for Low-Income Families," *CN*, March 3, 1970.

24. "City, Church, U.S. to Build Neighborhood: 540 Low-Moderate Income Units Set," *CO*, October 11, 1968; "Two New Housing Projects Lift 387 Families Out of Slums," *CO*, December 2, 1968. The project was built in two phases and opened in 1971, holding 240 units. "Little Rock Apartments Win Final U.S. Approval," *CO*, March 6, 1970; "More Low-Income Housing OKed," *CO*, March 11, 1970; "Low Rent Projects: Housing Trouble Brings Probers," *CN*, March 16, 1970; "Rowe Motley: Midas Touch Gone Sour," *CO*, August 28, 1977.

25. "Housing Groups to Join Hands," *CO*, November 6, 1969. Urban Systems Development Corp. would eventually participate in at least four Charlotte projects circa 1970, all discussed below: Little Rock Homes phases 1 and 2 under FHA 221(d)(3) and FHA 236; Village Town Houses under FHA 236; and Dillehay Courts under HUD Turnkey I. Thanks go to community historian J. Michael Moore for alerting me to Urban Systems Development Corp.'s involvement. On the corporation elsewhere: "Firm to Direct Urban Renewal," *RNO*, May 12, 1968; "Plans Announced for $651,800 Housing Project Here," *Nashville (NC) Graphic*, July 24, 1971.

26. "City, Church, U.S. to Build Neighborhood: 540 Low-Moderate Income Units Set," *CO*, October 11, 1968.

27. I am grateful to J. Michael Moore for this deed research.

28. The rent structure at Little Rock was interesting. Rather than bringing down rents across the whole project, the subsidies were calculated based on income of each tenant, lifting them up to pay market-rate rent. This foreshadowed the Section 8 Housing Choice Voucher Program initiated in the 1980s (see chapter 7). "Two New Housing Projects Lift 387 Families Out of Slums," *CO*, December 2, 1968. The family-adjusted rent supplement was different from the more usual arrangement in which all apartments rented for a fixed below-market amount. "The Almost-Poor Getting Housing," *CO*, August 22, 1968.

29. "No One Takes the Blame for Crumbling Complex," *CN*, April 19, 1979. The for-profit buyer was National Investment Development Corporation of Los Angeles. "Little Rock Apartments to Be Rebuilt with Grant," *CN*, July 29, 1980; "Notice of Public Hearing on Proposed Multi-family Housing Revenue Bonds," *CO*, September 9, 2002; deed book 4092, p. 379, Mecklenburg County Register of Deeds, Charlotte, NC.

30. The UPI wire service story ran in many newspapers, for instance: "Break in Taxes Saved," *San Francisco Examiner*, September 7, 1969; "Romney Wins Round in Housing Tax Fight," *Decatur (IN) Daily Democrat*, September 2, 1969.

31. Staats, *Section 236 Rental Housing*, 21–22; von Hoffman, "Calling upon the Genius of Private Enterprise."

32. Staats, *Section 236 Rental Housing*, 65–66. Ginnie Mae was created as a spin-off from Fannie Mae, the Federal National Mortgage Association, which had routinely purchased and serviced FHA mortgages since 1938. Stuart, *Discriminating Risk*.

33. Staats, *Section 236 Rental Housing*, 72; von Hoffman, "Calling upon the Genius of Private Enterprise."

34. Staats, *Section 236 Rental Housing*, 69.

35. Fribourg Navigation Co. v. Commissioner of Internal Revenue, 86 S.Ct. 862 (1969), https://supreme.justia.com/cases/federal/us/383/272/. "Cites Court Ruling Aiding Taxpayers," *St. Louis Post-Dispatch*, May 8, 1966. "The Federal income tax shelter through accelerated depreciation which is available to Section 236 mortgagors is real

and substantial. However, the tax benefits are substantially exhausted within a ten-year period. Consequently, the tax shelter benefits offer little, if any, incentive to long-term ownership and sound management. To the contrary, the tax shelter benefits tend to promote construction and short-term ownership, as opposed to long-term investment and ownership." Muhonen, *Report on Audit*, 52–53.

36. P. Smith, "Federal Tax Aspects." In one Boston project, a developer invested $82,000 in putting a project together, then sold shares to investors "seeking paper depreciation losses," earning himself "a gross profit... of $334,260." "US Gives Money to Rich to Get Housing for Poor," *Boston Globe*, October 28, 1971.

37. "Cost-of-Living Catching Up with Low-Cost Housing," *CO*, August 19, 1971.

38. Schwartz, *Housing Policy*, 179–80. One of the most aggressive FHA 236 developers nationally was Fred Trump. In the 2010s his son, US president Donald Trump, remained partial owner of properties such as Brooklyn's Starrett City, "today the biggest subsidized housing project in America." "Will Donald Trump Slash the Kind of Federal Housing Programs that Made His Family Rich?," *CO*, January 13, 2017; "Brooklyn's Starrett City, with Trump as Investor, Finds a Buyer," Bloomberg, September 6, 2017, www.bloomberg.com/news/articles/2017-09-06/brooklyn-s-starrett-city-with-trump-as-investor-finds-a-buyer; "Landlord-in-Chief's Public Housing Investment Gets a Sweet Tax Break," *St. Louis Post-Dispatch*, June 22, 2017.

39. Staats, *Section 236 Rental Housing*.

40. "Will Need Outweigh Council's Ban on Further Westside Public Housing?," *CO*, February 5, 1971; "Milton Road Not Public Housing," *CO*, August 26, 1971; "Barrington Oaks Grand Opening," *CO*, February 24, 1973. Rehabbed with LIHTC in 2003 as Timber Ridge Apartments: Novogradac and Company, "LIHTC Properties in North Carolina's 12th District (Alma Adams–D) through 2015."

41. "Grand Opening... Village Town Houses" ad in *CO*, February 15, 1974. Today the complex is called Norcross Townhomes, 1801 Griers Grove Road.

42. "Will Need Outweigh Council's Ban on Further Westside Public Housing?," *CO*, February 5, 1971. On Foundation for Cooperative Housing: "Non-Profit Housing, N.Y. Style," *CO*, July 23, 1954; "Cheap Homes for Builders to Launch Managua's Rebirth," *CO*, February 11, 1973; "Global Communities 101," Borgen Project website, accessed November 4, 2024, https://borgenproject.org/global-communities-101/.

43. "Cost-of-Living Catching Up with Low-Cost Housing," *CO*, August 19, 1971; "Home Builders Told Government Low-Income Housing on Upswing," *CO*, July 18, 1970. A study of Black involvement in Section 236 construction in Miami: Connolly, *World More Concrete*.

44. "They're Prepared to Help Build, Clear Out Slums," *CO*, April 22, 1971; "Model Cities Units to Ask Council for Lending Agency," *CO*, November 23, 1970; "Poor May Get 'Sweat-of-Brow' Houses," *CO*, March 19, 1975. On Model Cities nationally: von Hoffman, "Into the Wild Blue Yonder."

45. Nelo Alford, interview by Tom Hanchett, November 27, 2020.

46. "Poverty Focal Issue of Urban Homes," *CO*, August 14, 1971; "Charlotte's Clawson Village Stands as a Little Landmark on the Road to Integration," *CO*, June 21, 1981; Paul Leonard, interview by Tom Hanchett, March 2, 2020; Leonard, *Music of a Thousand Hammers*; Leonard, *Where Is Church?*

47. Leonard recalls that planning was underway before Nixon's 1973 moratorium. Leonard, *Where Is Church?*, 75–78; Yockey, *Builder*, 153–54. On Orchard Park: "Low-Income Housing to Be Built in Third Ward," *CN*, December 22, 1975; "Housing to Beat Bulldozers to Renewal Area," *CO*, July 7, 1976; Leonard interview. Leonard has a photocopy of the Orchard Park mortgage in his files. On Greenhaven: "In Greenville Urban Renewal Area: North Side to Get Apartments," *CN*, February 25, 1977; "Greenville Is Opening Its Doors to Returning Former Residents," *CO*, November 3, 1977. MOTION created one more low-income apartment project: ten-unit Victoria Townhouses, W. Fourth Street and Victoria Avenue, a partnership with for-profit developer Westminster, 1983. "Third Ward Low-Income Units Full," *CN*, March 30, 1983. It would be demolished circa 2010, replaced by a luxury mid-rise apartment building. City Council ended funding for MOTION in 1984. "Phil Berry Resigns from MOTION, Inc.," *CO*, June 26, 1984; "U.S. Sues to Recover $200,000 Loan," *CN*, January 25, 1985.
48. Burnstein, "New Techniques in Public Housing"; von Hoffman, "Calling upon the Genius of Private Enterprise."
49. "Turnkey Leasing Benefits Explained: 350 Attend Seminar," *Oakland Tribune*, November 3, 1968.
50. Weaver began experimenting in 1966 with Turnkey pilot projects. He fully implemented the initiative as part of the 1968 Housing and Urban Development Act. Von Hoffman, "Calling upon the Genius of Private Enterprise"; Catz, "Historical and Political Background"; "Turnkey Plan Noted," *New York Times*, December 10, 1967.
51. "Turnkey III: Over Hurdle to Home Ownership," *CO*, July 21, 1970.
52. At least two other Charlotte projects were built as Turnkey Leased Housing. I have not been able to track down construction specifics about Coronet Way Apartments off Rozelles Ferry Road nor Keyway Apartments off Dr. Carver Drive near West Boulevard, but they had similarly shoddy construction and angry tenants. "Some Public Housing Fees Cut," *CN*, November 17, 1976; "Mrs. Fields Goes to Bat for Her Keyway Neighbors," *CN*, March 13, 1980.
53. The brothers' ventures included a firm called Wright Homes that manufactured prefab houses. "Housing Industry Now in Operation by Durham Group," *RNO*, December 16, 1956; "Richard H. Wright Dies at Durham," *Chatham Record* (Siler City, NC), March 7, 1929. The younger Wright married a Charlotte debutante soon after Pitts Drive opened. "Anne Gibson Sullivan Marries Richard Harvey Wright III," *CO*, October 31, 1970. On legal troubles at other points in Wright's career: "Housing Project at Issue: Two Plead Innocent in Fraud Case," *CN*, February 19, 1980; "Company Head Faces Embezzlement Charge," *RNO*, June 2, 2001.
54. The 1965 leasing policy was known as FHA Section 23. "Turnkey Leasing Benefits Explained," *Oakland Tribune*, November 3, 1968. On Section 23 leasing generally: Friedman and Krier, "New Lease on Life"; Edson, "Affordable Housing," 197. An update on May 17, 1982, to HUD's *Low-Rent Leased Housing Handbook* 7430.1 included a notation to remove a circular dated April 9, 1968, and titled "'Turnkey' Leased Housing Proposals." I have not located a copy of that 1968 document. See www.hud.gov/sites/documents/74301TRNPIHH.PDF.
55. "Turnkey Leasing Benefits Explained."

56. "'Each Project Must Be Judged on Its Own,'" *Oakland Tribune*, November 3, 1968.
57. "Housing Unit's Flaws Still Not Repaired by Builder, Authority Says," *CO*, November 10, 1970; "Housing Plan Gets Conditional OK," *CO*, July 14, 1970.
58. "Housing Plan Gets Conditional OK."
59. "Public Housing Repairs Warm Tenants," *CO*, January 11, 1976.
60. "Grant to Charlotte Housing Authority for the Acquisition and Renovation of the Pitts Drive Apartment Project, Approved," minutes of the Charlotte City Council, June 21, 1976, Meeting Minutes 1936–1978, City of Charlotte, www.charlottenc.gov/files/sharedassets/city/v/1/city-government/departments/documents/clerks-office/minutes/1976-1978/minutes-1976/june-21-1976.pdf; "CHA Criticized on Budget: Top Officials Say Many of Report's Suggestions Had Already Been Started," *CO*, September 16, 2001.
61. "Problem Unanticipated: Authority to Correct Soil," *CN*, December 15, 1970.
62. "Public Housing Projects Crawling with Complaints," *CO*, August 10, 1971; "Officials Soured: Turnkey Housing Problems May Halt Future Projects," *CO*, May 13, 1972; "Suit Filed in Dillehay Dispute," *CN*, July 19, 1972.
63. The initial developer, Vector Corporation of Greensboro, sold to Tennessee-based Whittaker Corporation, which subsequently also backed away, selling the project at discount to the CHA. "Officials Soured"; "Suit Filed in Dillehay Dispute"; "Housing Board Won't Buy Townhouses," *CN*, June 5, 1973; "Developer Offers City a Deal on Once-Rejected Housing," *CO*, May 24, 1973.
64. On Vinson's involvement, see for Little Rock Apartments: "Housing Project Gets Fast OK," *CO*, November 19, 1968. For Boulevard Homes: "Big Project Threatened by Freeze," *CN*, March 8, 1969.
65. "U.S. Gives Money to Rich to Get Housing for Poor," *Boston Globe*, October 28, 1971.
66. "Dan C. Summers, Sr.," obituary notice, *CN*, November 3, 1978; "Builder Will Ask Turnkey Housing OK," *CO*, February 20, 1968; "Firm Offers Turnkey Job on Public Housing Unit," *CN*, February 19, 1968. The project followed a tradition of naming public housing after CHA officials, in this case R. I. Dalton, an eighteen-year member of the CHA board. "Final Approval Near on Housing Project: Authority Would Buy West Blvd. Complex," *CN*, September 28, 1968; "HUD OKs 300 Units for City," *CO*, April 18, 1969; "Housing Future Bright for Crowded Poor," *CO*, January 25, 1970. Like Richard H. Wright III, Cam Summers Jr. also had a financial interest in a manufacturer of prefabricated building components. "Company Is Shooting for $3 Million Mark," *CO*, April 13, 1969. On HUD's enthusiasm for prefab housing: "Builders Consider Systems," *Bensenville (IL) Register*, November 21, 1969.
67. Excellent Turnkey explanation: "Builder Will Ask Turnkey Housing," *CO*, February 20, 1968. See also "HUD OKs 300 Units for City," *CO*, April 18, 1969; "Apartment Destroyed by Fire," *CO*, October 18, 1969; "Public Housing Will Open in March," *CO*, January 15, 1970; "Architects Lend Talents to Housing," *CO*, June 14, 1970; "Summer Firm Didn't Build Boulevard Homes," *CO*, June 16, 1970; "Housing Future Bright for Crowded Poor," *CO*, January 25, 1970; "Information on Low-Income Housing Prepared by City Manager's Office," minutes of the Charlotte City Council, March 31, 1969, 444, Meeting Minutes 1936–1978, City of Charlotte, www.charlottenc.gov/files/sharedassets/city/v/1/city-government/departments/documents/clerks-office/minutes/1968-1971/minutes-1969/march-31-1969.pdf.

68. "Public Housing Trouble: Economics and Attitudes," *CN*, March 4, 1969. For a look back at the 1964 integration of Piedmont Courts, Charlotte's first public housing for whites, see "Project's Early Hope Fades to Despair," *CO*, March 30, 1986.
69. "West Boulevard: Zoning Battle Blocks Low-Income Housing," *CO*, March 23, 1967; "Council Halts Public Housing Work after 7000 Sign Petition: Crowd of 200 Jam Chamber," *CO*, March 4, 1969; "City Seeks Temporary Housing Project Delay," *CO*, March 25, 1969; "Council Takes Charge of Public Housing: Two Westside Units OK'd over Protest," *CO*, April 1, 1969; "Westside Group to Fight at Polls," *CN*, April 1, 1969; "Suit Filed to Block Little Rock Project," *CN*, April 21, 1970.
70. "Negroes Oppose Apartments," *CO*, May 24, 1969; "'It Looks Like a Long Fight': Westside Housing Feud Pits Negroes against Negroes," *CO*, March 31, 1970. On African American pushback against subsidized housing in greater Miami: Connolly, *World More Concrete*.
71. "Information on Low-Income Housing Prepared by City Manager's Office," minutes of the Charlotte City Council, March 31, 1969, 444, Meeting Minutes 1936–1978, City of Charlotte, www.charlottenc.gov/files/sharedassets/city/v/1/city-government/departments/documents/clerks-office/minutes/1968-1971/minutes-1969/march-31-1969.pdf. Similarly on the Little Rock apartments, built under Section 221(d)(3): "Council's Edict Can't Block Project—Officials," *CO*, January 28, 1970.
72. "Nine Negroes File Housing Suit: 'Effective' Integration Plan Asked," *CO*, July 25, 1970; "Hoax Wires to Builders Fail to Delay Bid Opening," *CN*, September 17, 1970. The first person on the list of plaintiffs happened to be a chef named America McKnight, a homeowner on James Street off West Boulevard. "Mr. America 'Mac' McKnight," obituary, *CO*, August 23, 1993.
73. "Officials Soured: Turnkey Housing Problems May Halt Future Projects," *CO*, May 13, 1972; "Housing: Poor Results but Rich Subsidies for Some," *CO*, October 21, 1972. On Pine Valley, see, for instance, "Or Face Lawsuit: Developers Told to Finish Project," *CN*, April 4, 1972.
74. Taylor, *Race for Profit*.
75. "For City's 43,000 Poor, This Year Will Be Different," *CN*, February 26, 1973.

Chapter 6

1. On scattered-site housing in the United States: Rubinowitz and Rosenbaum, *Crossing the Class and Color Lines*; Hogan, *Scattered-Site Housing*. On Section 8 Project-Based: *Overview of the Section 8 Housing Programs*, "Summary" section. To explore debates among Washington policymakers on public housing funding and siting in this era, see von Hoffman, "Into the Wild Blue Yonder"; and Freemark, "Myth #5."
2. Johnson, "Special Message to Congress on the Nation's Cities."
3. "New Housing Program: Congress to Get LBJ's Urban Affairs Message," *Daily Independent* (Kannapolis, NC), March 2, 1965; "LBJ's Plan to Mix the Rich and the Poor," *San Francisco Examiner*, May 2, 1965.
4. "Program of the Chicago Freedom Movement," July 1966, CRMvet.org, www.crmvet.org/docs/66_cfm_program-july.pdf. I am grateful to Lydia Hanchett for locating this material. For a recent analysis by a Chicago-based Black journalist: Michael Romain, "Fifty Years after King's Chicago Campaign, Racism Still Burdening Black Suburbs, Say

Housing Experts," *Village Free Press* (Proviso Township, IL), August 19, 2016, www.vfpress.news/articles/housing/50-years-after-kings-chicago-campaign-racism-still-burdening-black-suburbs-say-housing-experts/. On the national context of what was sometimes termed the "open housing" movement: Ritter, "Discriminating Priority of Integration."

5. Polikoff, *Waiting for Gautreaux*; Bostic and Acolin, "Affirmatively Furthering Fair Housing." A study tracked low-income families who moved to Chicago suburbia under *Gautreaux*. The moves "significantly increase[d] children's future lifetime earnings, employment, and wealth." Eric Chyn, Robert Collinson, and Danielle Sadler, "The Long-Run Effects of Residential Racial Desegregation Programs: Evidence from *Gautreaux*," March 29, 2023, *Quarterly Journal of Economics* (forthcoming), https://robcollinson.github.io/RobWebsite/CCS_Gautreaux.pdf.

6. Oliveri, "Legislative Battle." The Fair Housing Act was formally Title VIII of the Civil Rights Act of 1968. LBJ's attorney general Ramsey Clark drafted the legislation: "Ramsey Clark, Attorney General and Rebel with a Cause, Dies at 83," *New York Times*, April 10, 2021.

7. "Longtime Judge Had Civil Rights Background: Family, Colleagues Said Jim Lanning Was Fair and Helpful to All," *CO*, July 11, 2015. Kevin Davis (Lanning's widow), interview by Tom Hanchett, December 1, 2020. During his year at Legal Aid, Lanning got the Charlotte Housing Authority to institute formal eviction appeal procedures for the first time. "By Housing Attorney: Eviction Appeal Procedures Outlined," *CN*, September 16, 1968.

8. Before filing the *McKnight* suit itself, Lanning began by lodging a complaint with HUD secretary George Romney charging that HUD's loan for a new low-income project off North Tryon Street adjacent to existing low-income Tryon Hills would perpetuate segregation. "Housing to Be Cancelled in Tryon Hills—Lawyer," *CO*, November 9, 1969.

9. "Nine Negroes File Housing Suit: 'Effective' Integration Plan Asked," *CO*, July 25, 1970. The first name on the list of plaintiffs was America "Mac" McKnight, a homeowner off West Boulevard. "Mr. America 'Mac' McKnight," obituary, *CO*, August 23, 1993. Other plaintiffs included longtime civil rights activists Dr. Reginald Hawkins and Rev. Coleman Kerry. "Hoax Wires to Builders Fail to Delay Bid Opening," *CN*, September 17, 1970.

10. "Public Housing Program Hits Temporary Lull," *CO*, October 19, 1987.

11. Rev. Richard A. Macon and the Barringer Woods Improvement Committee worked energetically to oppose the low-income apartment expansion prior to filing the lawsuit: "Negroes Oppose Apartments," *CO*, May 29, 1969; "Residents Promise 'Fight to the Hilt,'" *CN*, January 28, 1970; "The Poor? WE ARE the Poor, Says Housing Foe," *CO*, January 30, 1970; "Westside Unit Seeks Injunction," *CN*, February 7, 1970; "Get Barricade," *CN*, February 10, 1970; "Oppose Leake Project: Westsiders Fear Housing Switch," *CN*, March 31, 1970; "Housing Project Fight Taken to Washington," *CO*, March 28, 1970; "Testimony Heard in Housing Suit," *CN*, May 5, 1970; "Invisible No More: Prosperous Blacks Say Goodbye to the Ghetto," *CO*, October 12, 1970.

12. "Suit Attacks Leake Project," *CO*, April 21, 1970; "Judge Studies Plea for Ban on Housing," *CO*, May 6, 1970; "Barringer Woods: Charlotte Getting Protests, Lawsuit," *CO*, February 16, 1971.

13. "800 Blacks Cheer on School Fight Leaders," *CO*, August 11, 1969.
14. *Margaret Green Harris, et al., v. United States Department of Housing and Urban Development, et al.*
15. Daly would combine the *Harris* suit with a second lawsuit in 1974 on behalf of a laundry owner in First Ward who asserted that the city's assistance for businesses displaced by urban renewal was deficient under the Federal Uniform Relocation Act: *Mitchell Kannon, et al., v. HUD and the City of Charlotte*. Ted Fillette, interview by Tom Hanchett, April 9, 2021. On *Harris* and *Kannon*, see, for instance, "Lawsuit Threatens Hotel Plan," *CN*, July 19, 1980.
16. "Public Housing Still Undispersed," *CN*, March 19, 1971; "Court Rulings May Help Public Housing Effort," *RNO*, March 7, 1971; "Suits Blamed for Model Cities Stall," *CN*, June 9, 1971; "City Promises a Housing Plan," *CN*, June 9, 1971.
17. "Public Housing Still Undispersed."
18. "Power in Charlotte: Tom Ray," *CN*, April 20, 1982; W. Thomas Ray Papers, MS 0104, Manuscript Collections, JMAL, https://findingaids.uncc.edu/repositories/4/resources/454. Tom Ray's spouse, Maggie Ray, would become deeply involved in forging the community coalition that made *Swann* busing work. Gaillard, *Dream Long Deferred*. Upon appointment to the Charlotte Housing Authority, Ray removed himself from the westside lawsuit and turned it over to another attorney. "McDuffie Hits Gluck Selection," *CO*, January 11, 1972; "Leaders Showed Foresight in Housing," *CO*, August 17, 1988.
19. W. Thomas Ray and Robert G. Anderson, "Charlotte Housing Authority, Long Range Planning Committee, Report—Phase I, September 1972," photocopied, spiral-bound report given by Maggie Ray to Tom Hanchett, quotations from pages 8 and 51.
20. "Public Housing: A New Policy Is Shaped," *CO*, July 4, 1975. See also "Blacks' Housing Suit Settlement Seems Likely," *CO*, April 27, 1973; "City Agrees to Provide Scattered Housing: Settlement Will Cancel Two Housing Lawsuits," *CN*, April 30, 1973.
21. Robert C. Sink, "Memorandum to Commissioners of the Housing Authority—Subject: Site Selection for Conventional Public Housing," June 28, 1979, 16; "Plan to Encourage the Production of Low and Moderate Income Housing in Charlotte (FY 1975–1978)," City of Charlotte, May 1974, both in the collection of former Charlotte Housing Authority attorney Robert C. Sink, shared via email with Tom Hanchett, October 2023. The 1973 consent decree guided city actions as late as 1988. "Public Housing: A New Policy Is Shaped," *CO*, July 4, 1975; "Assurance of Equity Is the Essential Ingredient of Scattered Site Housing Policy," *CN*, June 6, 1979; "Three-Year Plan Will Affect Very Fabric of Neighborhoods: Public Housing, a Collision of Needs, Emotions," *CO*, May 9, 1983; "City May Stay with Its Own Public Housing," *CO*, July 29, 1988.
22. "City Agrees to Provide Scattered Housing," *CN*, April 30, 1973.
23. "CDBG: A 25-Year History"; von Hoffman, "Past, Present, and Future of Community Development"; von Hoffman, *House by House*.
24. Both major party candidates, Democrat Hubert Humphrey and Republican Richard Nixon, promoted revenue sharing during the 1968 presidential campaign. "Federal-City Revenue Sharing Advised: Urban Centers' Plight 'Aggravated by Financial Distress,'" *CO*, September 19, 1968. Nixon signed revenue sharing into law in 1972, and dollars first became available at the start of 1973. "Will Revenue Sharing Hurt Poor? Nobody Seems Sure," *CO*, June 27, 1973; Freemark, "Myth #5."

25. "Nixon Wants Tax-Sharing for States," *CO*, August 9, 1969.
26. "Major Housing Bill Is OKed," *CO*, August 16, 1974. CDBG funding became available January 1, 1975. Milgram, *A Chronology of Housing Legislation*, section viii. CDBG dollars could not be used directly to build local public housing, but they could pay for related costs such as planning and administration, park construction, and rehab of existing dwellings. Orlebeke, "Evolution of Low-Income Housing Policy," 33; Schwartz, *Housing Policy*, 240–43.
27. "HUD Objects to City Plans for Housing," *CO*, June 11, 1979. George Selden, a resident of upscale Myers Park in his sixties, remained on City Council and staunchly opposed scattered-site plans. He believed that "government ought not to interfere with 'personal values' on which housing patterns are based," reported the *Observer*. "'[F]or government to place low-income families in upper income neighborhoods would create disruption,'" Selden said. "'I want to specifically point out that I have made no reference at all to race in that.'" "Mixing Low-Income Homes with High Hit," *CN*, March 19, 1971. Similar rhetoric in 1979: "Expense of Five Housing Sites Is Examined," *CN*, July 21, 1979. At Community Development, Sawyer finally retired in 1981 and City Council hired an African American replacement, Harry Jones, who worked to rehabilitate houses rather than bulldoze neighborhoods. "City Agency Gains Director, Direction," *CO*, June 13, 1981. Jones left for a job in Dallas, replaced by another African American with a similar outlook: "Jay Walton to Take Over City Agency," *CO*, August 17, 1984. Jones would return to be Charlotte's first Black city manager, 2000–2013. "Harry Jones, 'Model of . . . a Professional Public Servant' Remembered," *CO*, February 21, 2017.
28. "$500k would be used for scattered-site public housing; still another $50,000 will purchase and distribute park equipment to 23 neighborhood park sites to be located at schools. These are part of the city's response to an out-of-court settlement of the scattered-site housing suit." "Revenue Sharing: An Afterword," *CN*, July 17, 1974; "The Local Way: Work on Housing Pays Off," *CO*, June 9, 1974.
29. "Public Housing, a Bold Step: Scattered Site Plan Off to a Good Start," *CN*, February 11, 1975.
30. "Scattered Site Concept Can Work," *CO*, April 7, 1971. The *CN* echoed Claiborne's call for scattered-site development: "Charlotte Should Consider Smaller Housing Projects," *CN*, August 16, 1971.
31. "The Public Views Housing Better Than Its Leaders," *CO*, February 21, 1972.
32. "Public Housing: A New Policy Is Shaped," *CO*, July 4, 1975.
33. "Construction May Start Soon on Scattered Housing Projects," *CN*, October 9, 1976; "Housing Projects Lag, Authority Board Told," *CO*, March 21, 1979; "Leafcrest, Two Years Later," *CN*, August 1, 1981. Ted Fillette recalled funding details: (a) The initial four complexes were built with revenue sharing dollars. CHA operated them; city retained ownership. (b) The subsequent seven complexes were built with CDBG dollars. CHA owned and operated them. (c) Revenue sharing was related to CDBG but not exactly the same. Revenue sharing dollars had almost no strings attached. In contrast, CDBG could be used only in targeted neighborhoods only for specified types of projects. Fillette interview, April 9, 2021. The city made an embarrassing error in its scattered-site program. It set aside no money for major maintenance. "With HUD public housing, when it got to be dilapidated, you'd just go to HUD and say 'I need five million dollars to fix this up.'"

But with locally built scattered-site projects, there was no such backstop, CMHP's Pat Garrett later explained. By 1993, several of the projects needed rehab; wooden exterior finishes had not handled weather well. So the city arranged to sell four of the complexes to CMHP, which had a sufficient income stream to do the rehabs. Pat Garrett, interview by Tom Hanchett, July 20, 2022; "Who'll Pay for Upkeep?," *CO*, March 31, 1993; "Charlotte Mecklenburg Housing Partnership, New Owners of Pence Road Units, Say Renovations on Tap," *CO*, February 27, 1995.

34. "Public Housing Fanning Out," *CN*, July 14, 1979. Leafcrest, Cedar Knoll, Sunridge, and Meadow Oaks all were open by the following summer: "No One to Pay More Than $250: Rents Limited in Public Housing," *CO*, July 16, 1980.
35. "Money for Subsidized Housing Sought," *CO*, December 12, 1977.
36. The at-large system had been instituted in 1917 to solidify white elite control. Hanchett, *Sorting Out*, 211–13, 226–27, 254–56.
37. "Districting Ends Era of Clout for Affluent Southeast Charlotte," *CO*, April 20, 1971; "A 'Yes' Day: Voters Approve All Bonds, Council Districts," *CO*, April 20, 1971; "Blacks Held Balance of Power," *CO*, April 21, 1977; Gaillard, *Dream Long Deferred*, chapter 10.
38. Gantt had been appointed to City Council in 1974, filling the "Black seat" of retired trailblazer Fred Alexander. Chafin had first won election in 1975. The visibility gave them momentum to run at-large in 1977. Chafin, with the highest vote total, became mayor pro tem in 1977, presiding over council meetings.
39. "City Council Gets New Look," *CO*, November 9, 1977.
40. The allocation for scattered-site housing fluctuated over the years, supplemented by local tax revenues at times. The $2 million was the amount in annual budgets from 1983 to 1987. "No Sweet Home: 19,000 Housing Units Needed for Poor in Charlotte—Council Looks at Policy," *CO*, July 28, 1988.
41. "With Gantt Off Council, Votes Go Conservative," *CN*, February 23, 1980.
42. Ted Fillette, interview by Tom Hanchett, May 12, 2019.
43. Fillette interview, May 12, 2019. The requirement to provide housing came under the Uniform Relocation Act, which became US law in 1970.
44. Phyllis Lynch was still in her twenties when she began making headlines as a Black political and neighborhood organizer. "Phyllis Lynch . . . 'There Are No Instant Adults,'" *CO*, November 24, 1976; "Cherry Forms Corporation to Revive Area," *CO*, December 22, 1977. On Lynch's Cherry Community Organization and its real estate efforts, see also Ted Fillette, interview by Sarah Thuesen, March 2, 2006, interview U-0185, Southern Oral History Program Collection (#4007), Southern Historical Collection, Wilson Library, University of North Carolina at Chapel Hill, https://docsouth.unc.edu/sohp/U-0185/excerpts/excerpt_9452.html.
45. Fillette interview, May 12, 2019.
46. "City to Build Apartments for Poor, Displaced Persons," *CN*, March 23, 1982; Fillette oral history with Thuesen; Johnson, "Charlotte Housing Tour."
47. Fillette interview, May 12, 2019.
48. Fillette interview, May 12, 2019.
49. "Judge Indicates City Violating Housing Pact," *CO*, October 18, 1980; "Hicks Named to Monitor Relocations," *CO*, June 3, 1981; "City Faulted in Relocating People," *CO*, November 19, 1981; "City Might Take 'Last Resort' to House People," *CO*, March 5, 1982;

"U.S. Judge Reviews City's Progress in Relocating Displaced Families," *CO*, June 9, 1982. Indeed, right from the start in 1978, the city had been in violation of Judge McMillan's orders to build public housing in response to *Harris*. "Housing Projects behind Schedule," *CO*, February 22, 1978.

50. Ted Fillette, interview by Mary Newsom, January 17, 2005, in Newsom's possession; Don Carroll, interview by Tom Hanchett, July 13, 2021.
51. "Five to Supervise New Housing in Third Ward, Five Points," *CN*, May 3, 1982. Interviews with Louise Sellers and Mildred Dwiggins Swift who helped get West Downs built: "Biddleville Was a Good Place to Grow Up," *CO*, January 2, 1986.
52. The YWCA ran after-school programs at Live Oaks and six other suburban public housing complexes. "Can Their Afternoons Be Saved: Live Oaks Faces End of Its Budget," *CO*, January 12, 1992.
53. Also spelled "Savannah." "Council Agrees to Buy Two Housing Sites," *CN*, March 4, 1980; "Finding New Uses for Three Old Houses," *CO*, December 16, 1984.
54. "City Buying Two Tracts for Public Housing," *CO*, October 4, 1984. What became Mallard Ridge Apartments was initially referred to as "Muddy Pond Lane." "Housing: Bite the Bullet," *CN*, January 11, 1980.
55. "I'll Speak Out: For Decades Luciel McNeel Has Been a Mentor to Politicians and Force for Change in Charlotte," *CO*, June 5, 1994.
56. All quotations from Fillette in this section on Gladedale are from Fillette, interview by Hanchett, May 12, 2019.
57. "Providence Housing Neighbors Want Someone to Listen," *CN*, October 22, 1980. "If HUD's comments are favorable, the Authority will ask City Council . . . to allocate about $101,000 in local funds to add to the $196,000 that HUD has agreed to pay for the project." "For Family Moving In, Opposition to Public Housing Was No Issue," *CO*, March 6, 1983; "Gladedale Joins to Help Youth Attend Day Camp," *CO*, May 27, 1984.
58. A historical overview of federal aid to low-income housing, including Section 8 vouchers: McCarty, *Introduction to Public Housing*, especially 5–6. Also Milgram, *Chronology of Housing Legislation*.
59. From 1974 to 1983, Section 8 was almost entirely project-based. The term "Section 8," by the way, came from Section 8 of the 1937 Housing Act, under which it was authorized. *Overview of the Section 8 Housing Programs*.
60. "In the new construction program, HUD contracts with builder/developers to make rent subsidy payments to them on behalf of eligible renters for up to 30 years (40 years if the project is financed by state or local housing agencies)." Verdier, *Real Estate Tax Shelter Subsidies*, especially xix.
61. McCarty, *Introduction to Public Housing*, 6.
62. "Low-Income Housing," *CO*, October 30, 1975; "HUD Extension of Invitation for Preliminary Proposals," *CO*, February 23, 1976.
63. "Council Makes Housing a Top Priority: High Rise for Elderly a Step Closer," *CO*, April 6, 1977.
64. "Elderly Gain More Housing," *CO*, October 8, 1978. Charlottetown Terrace, recently renovated, stands today at 1000 Baxter Street. Park Towne Terrace remains desirable today amid upscale surroundings on Fairview Road at Park South Drive.
65. "Elderly Gain More Housing," *CO*, October 8, 1978; "Red Carpet Treatment: Former

Inn Becomes Home to Handicapped, Elderly," *CO*, February 29, 1980. Both have been demolished.
66. "Protests Prompt Call for Housing-Projects Review," *CO*, June 28, 1977.
67. "Money for Subsidized Housing Sought," *CO*, December 12, 1977. Evidently several types of multifamily construction were eligible for the $5 billion; according to another news report, "about one-third of the money was used for the Section Eight program." Compare these two reports: "Protests Prompt Call for Housing-Projects Review," *CO*, June 28, 1977, and "Money for Subsidized Housing Sought," *CO*, December 12, 1977.
68. "Protests Prompt Call for Housing-Projects Review." "For the first time, ... Section Eight will be eligible for the GNMA program. In the past they have been specifically excluded." "HUD Releases Condo Funds," *Naples (FL) Daily News*, January 25, 1976.
69. Westminster's link to Weyerhaeuser: "Southport, State Feud over Waste Treatment Plant," *RNO*, January 31, 1982. Westminster also developed market-rate single-family homes in the Stonehaven section of east Charlotte: "Daybreak ... Homes by Westminster," ad in *CO*, January 15, 1984.
70. "Elderly Gain More Housing," *CO*, October 8, 1978; "Rent-Subsidized Complex Likely on Arnold Drive," *CN*, November 10, 1980.
71. Very early in his career, while still a minister, Leonard cofounded the Charlotte Fair Housing Association. See statement by the association on interconnections between neighborhood segregation and the *Swann* decision: "Housing Group Speaks to Schools," *CN*, May 21, 1969.
72. "Crosland to Build More Apartments," *CO*, March 26, 1978.
73. "Crosland to Build More Apartments."
74. "Money for Subsidized Housing Sought," *CO*, December 12, 1977; "In Apartment Department," *CN*, May 23, 1978; "Hollis House: New Facility for Elderly and Handicapped Persons," ad in *CO*, December 31, 1978.
75. "Money for Subsidized Housing Sought"; "Elderly Gain More Housing," *CO*, October 8, 1978; "Elderly Finding Home at Fairmarket Plaza," *CN*, December 31, 1979; "Fairmarket Plaza Apartments Now Leasing: Housing for the Elderly and Handicaps," ad in *CO*, January 17, 1980.
76. "Future of Housing Aid for Poor Faces Closed Doors," *CO*, September 13, 1981; Yockey, *Builder*, 198–200, 231; Paul Leonard, interview by Tom Hanchett, March 2, 2020.
77. "Leaders Showed Foresight in Housing," *CO*, August 17, 1988. And much earlier: "Charlotte May Be Ahead on Schools, Housing," *CO*, May 6, 1973. On the Yonkers situation, see article carried in many US newspapers: "A City Divided: U.S. Court's Order on Housing Tears Yonkers Apart," *Atlanta Constitution*, August 10, 1988.
78. "Yonkers: Learn from Charlotte," *CO*, August 31, 1988. Similarly, a deeply researched essay in 1996, which used Charlotte as a case study of a US city doing relatively well in affordable housing, marveled at Charlotte's suburban scattered-site apartments. Jason DeParle, "Slamming the Door," *New York Times Magazine*, October 20, 1996, especially 95, 105.
79. "Scattered-Site Rehabs Have Luxury Price Tags," *Chicago Tribune*, May 15, 1987. Eventually the Chicago Housing Authority built 900 scattered-site units. Polikoff, *Housing the Poor*, 212.
80. Pastor et al., *Regions That Work*, 15, 129, 142, and chapter 6. "Charlotte's scattered-site

program was generally considered one of the nation's most successful." S. Smith, *Boom for Whom?*, 217. Also Douglas, *Reading, Writing, and Race*, 248.
81. Six towns did exist near the edges of Mecklenburg County: Matthews, Mint Hill, Pineville, Huntersville, Cornelius, and Davidson. All were well beyond Charlotte's rim at that time, and, except for the college town of Davidson, none were wealthy suburbs.
82. Lord and Rent, "Residential Satisfaction"; Hogan, *Scattered-Site Housing*, 30–32.
83. Vivian Puryear and John G. Hayes, "Impact of Scattered Site Public Housing on Residential Property Values," Hayes-PA.com, January 1990, www.hayes-pa.com/Documents/Impact%20of%20Scattered%20Site%20Public%20Housing%20on%20Property%20Values.pdf. The quotation is from a summary of the Puryear and Hayes study in Hogan, *Scattered-Site Housing*, 163. Puryear and Hayes's essay drew upon research by Vivian Puryear, "The Effects of Scattered-Site Public Housing on Residential Property Values" (master's thesis, University of North Carolina at Charlotte, 1989). See also Galster et al., *Assessing Property Value Impacts*.
84. Hogan, *Scattered-Site Housing*, xv, xvi. Similar findings about both tenant satisfaction and adjoining property values: "Leafcrest, Two Years Later," *CN*, August 1, 1981.
85. Harvey Gantt, interview by Pamela Grundy, July 6, 2021, in Grundy's possession.
86. Gantt interview.

Chapter 7

1. For an overview of LIHTC: Schwartz, *Housing Policy*, chapter 5; McClure, "Future of the Low-Income Housing Tax Credit Program?"
2. "Transcript of President Reagan's News Conference," *Washington Post*, August 13, 1986. The joke predated Reagan. A Newspapers.com search indicates it first appeared in newsprint in a speech by Democratic senator Edmund Muskie to the US Conference of Mayors. "Yankee Joke," *Wilmington (DE) Morning News*, February 1, 1976.
3. "Government is not the solution to our problem; government is the problem." "First Inaugural Address of Ronald Reagan," January 20, 1981, Avalon Project, Yale Law School, https://avalon.law.yale.edu/20th_century/reagan1.asp.
4. "New Tax Loophole: Big Profits Possible in Low-Cost Housing," *CO*, January 24, 1970.
5. "Howard Lee, Founder, Howard N. Lee Institute," Keenan Institute of Private Enterprise, accessed November 4, 2024, https://kenaninstitute.unc.edu/people/howard-lee/.
6. Jenkins, *Bonds of Inequality*.
7. "Housing Agency OK'd," *CO*, April 12, 1974; "Named Chairman," *CO*, September 14, 1978; "Charlotte Tries to Make Homeowners of Renters," *CO*, April 12, 1979; "Low Income Buyers Can Get Mortgage Aid," *CO*, April 26, 1980. An early 1980s description of the agency: Bill Finger, "From Wall Street to Four Oaks, NC: The North Carolina Housing Finance Agency," *NC Insight*, August 1982, 2–15. (This entire issue of *NC Insight*, published by the School of Government at the University of North Carolina at Chapel Hill, explored affordable housing: https://nccppr.org/1982/08/01/.) A 2010s description: Farmer, "Testimony of Scott Farmer."
8. "Crosland, Tate at Home in Building Industry," *CO*, April 27, 1987; "Kingmakers: Panel Names 13 People Who Wield Influence without Raising a Finger," *CN*, April 19, 1982.
9. "Crosland, Tate at Home in Building Industry."
10. "WTVI Premiere House," *CO*, January 25, 1986.

11. "Crosland, Tate at Home in Building Industry," *CO*, April 27, 1987.
12. "Five Big Cities Hoping to Pool Their Clout in Raleigh," *CO*, May 30, 1980.
13. "Legislative Committees Appropriate $7 Million," *CO*, June 24, 1980; "Charlotte Gets Low-Income Apartments," *CO*, June 13, 1982.
14. "Builders Seek New Home for State Agency," *RNO*, June 2, 1981; Yockey, *Builder*, 211; "Howard Nathaniel Lee," Wikipedia, accessed April 14, 2024, https://en.wikipedia.org/wiki/Howard_Nathaniel_Lee.
15. "Builders Seek New Home for State Agency."
16. "Charlotte Gets Low-Income Apartments," *CO*, June 13, 1982. Wachovia added whipped cream and a cherry on top; because the state was guaranteeing the bonds, the bank told investors they could cash in the bonds in just five years—which made the investors happy to accept an even lower rate of return.
17. Yockey, *Builder*, 212; Bill Finger, "An Interview with Gary Paul Kane," *NC Insight*, August 1982, 47–52, https://nccppr.org/wp-content/uploads/2017/02/Interview_Grimsley_and_Kane.pdf. Also Finger, "From Wall Street to Four Oaks, NC," in the same issue.
18. "Charlotte Gets Low-Income Apartments," *CO*, June 13, 1982.
19. "Under the Dome: Builders Seek New State Home for Agency," *RNO*, June 2, 1981; Yockey, *Builder*, chapter 13.
20. Hogan, *Scattered-Site Housing*, 7; Schill, "Distressed Public Housing."
21. Hogan, *Scattered-Site Housing*, 8; Rosen, *Voucher Promise*. "Today [in 2014], vouchers—numbering more than 2 million—are the primary form of assistance provided under Section 8, although over 1 million units still receive project-based assistance under their original contracts or renewals of those contracts." Quoted from *Overview of the Section 8 Housing Programs*, "Summary" section.
22. *Overview of the Section 8 Housing Programs*. For a history of federal aid to low-income housing, including Section 8 vouchers: McCarty, *Introduction to Public Housing*, especially 5–6; Milgram, *Chronology of Housing Legislation*, section viii.
23. "A Simpler Form of Housing Aid," *CO*, October 15, 1981.
24. "Will Regulations Push Home Costs Out of Reach?," *CN*, August 2, 1978; Yockey, *Builder*, 194–96, 202–3. Said NCHFA ally C. D. Spangler Jr., "If the government just told John Crosland, 'You build a house the best you can, and we will relieve you of the code requirements and inspections,' my guess is that John could build the same house he's building now for twenty-five percent less." Yockey, *Builder*, 217.
25. "An Epidemic: Housing Crisis for the Poor Getting Worse All the Time," *CO*, November 16, 1985.
26. "An Epidemic: Housing Crisis for the Poor Getting Worse All the Time."
27. "Task Force Suggests City Use Bond Issue for Home Loan Fund," *CO*, July 16, 1981. For a roundup of trust fund initiatives in 1985: urbanist Neil Pierce's syndicated column, "Innovators Search for Affordable Housing Ideas," *CO*, November 9, 1985.
28. "New Idea for Low-Cost Housing," *CO*, March 12, 1985. News media stories sparked by Betty Chafin Rash's workshops made housing a top-of-mind issue. For instance, "Housing Burden Shifting to State, Local Government," *RNO*, May 18, 1986; "N.C. Facing Severe Shortage of Low-Income Housing," *Rocky Mount (NC) Telegram*, June 22, 1986; "Housing Funds Urged as Issue for State Legislature," *RNO*, June 27, 1986.

29. "Housing Burden Shifting to State, Local Government," *RNO*, May 18, 1986; "'One of the Last Democratic Power Brokers': Former NC Sen. Tony Rand Dies," *RNO*, May 1, 2020.
30. "'One of the Last Democratic Power Brokers.'"
31. "Legislator to Propose Fundraising Limits," *CO*, May 1, 1987; "Low Income Housing, Tax Bills Advance," *RNO*, August 9, 1987.
32. "Budget Bill Passes as Storm Clears," *CO*, August 14, 1987; "Senate OKs Creation of Housing Trust Fund," *RNO*, August 14, 1987; "North Carolina Housing Trust Fund," on the North Carolina Housing Coalition website, accessed November 4, 2024, https://nchousing.org/policy-advocacy/north-carolina-housing-trust-fund/. Also "Our Financing," on the NCHFA website, accessed November 5, 2024, www.nchfa.com/about-us/our-financing. Funded by excise tax on real estate transfers: "North Carolina Introduces Legislation to Dedicate Funding for State Housing Trust Fund," Spring 2011, on the Housing Trust Fund Project website, accessed November 4, 2024, https://housingtrustfundproject.org/north-carolina-introduces-legislation-to-dedicate-funding-for-state-housing-trust-fund/; Robert Kucab, interview by Michael Cai, March 24, 2020, American Predatory Lending and Global Financial Crisis, Duke University, https://predatorylending.duke.edu/histories/robert-kucab/. "Don Saunders, Bob Kucab and I designed the state Housing Trust Fund on a napkin in a bar. Nobody kept the napkin! [laughs] I've talked about that to Bob Kucab; we just don't know where the napkin went." Pat Garrett, interview by Tom Hanchett, July 20, 2022.
33. Initially, the North Carolina Housing Trust Fund money went to energy conservation repairs in existing low-income homes. "$2 Million Available in Energy Rehab Grants," *RNO*, July 14, 1988; "$1.4 Million Available for Low-Income Houses," *RNO*, December 28, 1989; "House OKs Funds for NC Housing Trust," *RNO*, September 29, 1992.
34. Two recent discussions of LIHTC history and effectiveness: McClure, "Future of the Low-Income Housing Tax Credit Program?"; Vale and Freemark, "From Public Housing to Public-Private Housing."
35. Gordon, Hines, and Summers, "Notes on the Tax Treatment of Structures"; Malcom R. Riley, "The Reality behind Retail Overbuilding," *Shopping Center World*, May 1991, especially 288.
36. "Apartment Boom in '85 Sets Record," *CO*, January 17, 1986; "Apartment Boom Sounds," *CO*, August 7, 1985; "Apartments Adding 'Extras': Development Surge Gives Renters Options," *CO*, August 7, 1985. Nationally, apartment construction starts jumped 76 percent from January 1984 to January 1985, according to an Associated Press story. "Housing Starts Boosted by Surge in Apartments," *San Francisco Examiner*, February 19, 1985. In Los Angeles: "Suddenly the Renter Is King: Apartment Building Boom Creates Competitive Market," *Los Angeles Times*, September 7, 1986. In small-town Hickory, North Carolina: "Apartment, Condo Building Booms in Hickory," *CO*, October 18, 1984. The 1986 Tax Act ended the building spree. "The limited-partnership tax shelter, a major source of capital to finance new apartments in recent years," had triggered the boom but was now rescinded: "This Tax Shelter Loses Some Luster," *CO*, October 20, 1986; "Apartment Boom Now Only a Flicker," *CO*, October 20, 1986; "Metro Housing Starts Drop 35.4 Percent in June," *Atlanta Constitution*, July 25, 1987.
37. The 1986 Tax Act set "useful life" (today called "depreciable life") of rental residential

buildings at 27.5 years. Income-producing real estate—including multifamily housing—remained a tax shelter. That continues today. A good nontechnical summary of the system in the first decade of the twenty-first century: "Tax Breaks Abound for Realty Investors," *CO*, March 9, 2002. Also Gravelle, *Depreciation and the Taxation of Real Estate*. I am grateful to tax advisor David Carlson, CPA, for assistance with depreciation tax shelter research.

38. As with other programs we've discussed in this book, the LIHTC's proponents were not limited to a single political party. An influential study by the Congressional Budget Office in 1977, commissioned by Democratic budget hawk Senator William Proxmire, put forth a proposal that closely foreshadowed the LIHTC. His Refundable Investment Tax Credit would have worked "almost exactly like a direct construction grant from HUD, except that it would be provided by the IRS through the tax system. Under this option, the builder/developer would be entitled to a tax credit equal to a percentage of the initial cost of the building." Verdier, *Real Estate Tax Shelter Subsidies*, especially xvi.

39. "Real Estate Tax Shelter Moves Ahead in Congress," *RNO*, May 29, 1988. By the way, accelerated depreciation write-offs remained in place for *all* new income-producing buildings. What changed was the way that extra sweetening was provided for low-income projects.

40. "Low-Income Housing Tax Credits" section of the NCHFA website, accessed November 4, 2024, www.nchfa.com/about-us/our-financing. Using accountants' calculations, the yield is considered to be slightly less than 90 percent. Because one has to wait for that return (rather than have the cash in hand right now to reinvest), accountants say that the "present value of money" works out to a 70 percent yield rather than 90 percent. Thanks to CPA David Carlson for his assistance with this explanation.

41. The three-person North Carolina Federal Tax Reform Allocation Committee, created in 1987, looks at rankings compiled by the NCHFA and makes the actual decision. "New Housing Program Designed to Spur Low-Income Investment," *Rocky Mount (NC) Telegram*, August 4, 1987. More recently: Madison Fisler Lewis, "State to Gain $403.6 Million in Affordable Apartments," NCHFA website, August 14, 2017, www.nchfa.com/es/node/15589.

42. In 1986, as Washington cut back its CDBG program, Charlotte voted to levy a five-cent property tax hike to replace the missing federal funds. It boosted its annual housing allocation to $2.5 million in 1988. "Recipe for Roofs: 19,000 Housing Units Needed for Charlotte Poor, Elderly," *CO*, July 28, 1988.

43. "Public Housing Program Hits Temporary Lull," *CO*, October 19, 1987; "City Must Decide Its Involvement in Low-Income Housing Business," *CO*, October 19, 1987. Bucking a Reagan-era trend, City Council did not slash its own housing appropriation and expect the private sector to pick up the slack. Instead, it upped its commitment. "The City, which already planned to set aside $2.5 million a year over the next five years into the Innovative Housing Fund, has added another $9 million": "Housing Plan Hits Financial Bump," *CO*, July 10, 1988.

44. "Committee Back Giving Housing Projects Leeway," *CO*, August 17, 1988.

45. "Public Housing Program Hits Temporary Lull," *CO*, October 19, 1987; "City Must Decide Its Involvement in Low-Income Housing Business," *CO*, October 19, 1987; "Recipe for Roofs: 19,000 Housing Units Needed for Charlotte Poor, Elderly," *CO*, July 28, 1988.

On earlier debates over Charlotte's location policy for low-income housing: "Council Torn on Public Housing," *CO*, July 18, 1982 (specifically mentions Hampshire Hills); "City Council Revamping Public Housing Policy," *CN*, May 6, 1983; "Public Housing: A Collision of Needs, Emotions," *CO*, May 9, 1983.

46. Trinity Group, a for-profit entity led by housing advocate and former Presbyterian minister Neil Leach, partnered with builder McDevitt & Street to develop the project, which was immediately sold to First Union Bank. The Charlotte Housing Authority selected the tenants and handled ongoing management. The Innovative Housing Fund loaned the developers $500,000 to buy the land and agreed to give the CHA a yearly stipend for fifteen years to reduce tenants' rent. "Location Is Question of Political Clout," *CO*, July 31, 1990; "Low-Income Housing before City Council," *CO*, January 17, 1989; "Council OKs 162 Units in Stonehaven," *CO*, January 18, 1989; "Housing Project Proposed: 198 Units Near Stonehaven," *CO*, September 2, 1988.

47. "City Must Decide Its Involvement in Low-Income Housing Business," *CO*, October 19, 1987; "Housing Plan Hits Financial Bump," *CO*, July 10, 1988; "City Plans Two Dozen New Homes: For-Profit Firms Join Charlotte in Project," *CO*, June 18, 1986. Mel Watt, a pioneering Black attorney in Charlotte who specialized in real estate law, wrote what he recalled as "soft second" mortgages for the Summit Avenue project: once the owner succeeded in paying off the main mortgage, the city would forgive the second mortgage, converting it into a grant. Watt would go on to become a major national leader in real estate finance, heading the Federal Housing Finance Agency under President Barack Obama. Mel Watt, interview by Tom Hanchett, January 21, 2020.

48. "Council Retreat," minutes of the Charlotte City Council, February 8, 2001, minutes book 115, pp. 842–44, American Legal Publishing's Code Library, https://codelibrary.amlegal.com/codes/CharlotteNC/latest/m/2001/2/8. Vi Lyles was the point person in drafting housing recommendations in her role as assistant city manager, 1996–2004. Pam Syfert, city manager in those years, confirmed that Lyles suggested the use of bond funding to set up the Charlotte Housing Trust Fund. Pam Syfert, interview by Tom Hanchett, March 28, 2022. For more on housing bond debates: "Housing Strategies: Report Has Much Good, but a Few Troubling Parts," *CO*, October 10, 2000; "Council Approves Budget for 2002: Timing of Housing Bonds in Question," *CO*, June 5, 2001; "Vote on Affordable Housing Bonds Set," *CO*, June 26, 2001. Initially proposed at $40 million, that first bond issue was trimmed to $20 million and passed by voters in November 2002. "Affordable Housing Lands on the Ballot," *CO*, November 3, 2002. The trust fund was formally created in late 2001, part of city officials' preparations in advance of the vote on the bonds. "Three Housing Reforms Up for Review," *CO*, November 11, 2001; "Volunteers Needed for Housing Advisory Board," *CO*, February 17, 2002. For an official overview of the Charlotte Housing Trust Fund, consult the Affordable Housing section of the City of Charlotte website, accessed November 5, 2024, www.charlottenc.gov/Streets-and-Neighborhoods/Housing/Affordable-Housing.

49. "Millions Go to Housing, but Poor Can't Afford It," *CO*, October 21, 2018; "The Housing Trust Fund's Role: More Affordable Housing Is Needed, but Don't Overlook Accomplishments," *CO*, April 9, 2008.

50. "Money for Subsidized Housing Sought," *CO*, December 12, 1977; "Elderly Gain More

Housing," *CO*, October 8, 1978; "Fairmarket Plaza Apartments Now Leasing: Housing for the Elderly and Handicaps," ad in *CO*, January 17, 1980.
51. "Charlotte Developer Resigns from NC Housing Agency," *CO*, August 10, 1989; Jud Little, email to Tom Hanchett, April 7, 2020 (Little headed Crosland's apartment division 1988–2007); "Northeast Neighbors Finding Fairmarket's Folks Fit in Fine," *CO*, July 17, 1991; Novogradac and Company, "LIHTC Properties in North Carolina's 12th District (Alma Adams–D) through 2015."
52. "Housing Agency Head Will Resign to Avoid Appearance of Conflict," *RNO*, August 19, 1989. On developers' initial lack of interest in the LIHTC both nationally and in North Carolina: "Real Estate Tax Shelter Moves Ahead in Congress," *RNO*, May 29, 1988; "Mortgage Lenders Decreasing," *CO*, January 22, 1989.
53. "Partnership Puts Rents within Reach: Public-Private Venture Finances Apartments," *CO*, November 16, 1990; "Northeast Neighbors Finding Fairmarket's Folks Fit in Fine," *CO*, July 17, 1991.
54. "Neighbors Come Out Fighting: Crosland Project Is Not Welcomed," *CO*, July 11, 1989.
55. "Hampshire Hills: A Shopping Center Struggling for Business," *CO*, February 7, 1990. A Giant Genie supermarket that opened in 1990 while Fairmarket Square was under construction closed after barely a year. "Giant Genie to Close: Profits Never Materialized at Store on the Plaza," *CO*, February 2, 1992.
56. "City OKs Loan for Housing: 7–4 Vote Boosts E. Charlotte Project," *CO*, September 12, 1989.
57. "City OKs Loan for Housing: 7–4 Vote Boosts E. Charlotte Project."
58. "Residents Get Sweet Welcome," *CO*, October 14, 1990; "Northeast Neighbors Finding Fairmarket's Folks Fit in Fine," *CO*, July 17, 1991.
59. On nonprofit developers of affordable housing nationally, see, for instance, Bratt, "Quadruple Bottom Line."
60. Betty Chafin Rash, interview by Tom Hanchett, January 23, 2018.
61. Pat Garrett, interview by Tom Hanchett, August 24, 2019. While banks' worries about the CRA made them receptive to aiding the startup of the Charlotte–Mecklenburg Housing Partnership, ultimately the CRA focused more on single-family home ownership than on multifamily rentals. Schwartz, *Housing Policy*, 221–25. On CRA actions by Charlotte banks, see, for instance, "'CR1' Loan Allows Three Percent Down Payment," *CO*, July 18, 1992; "Profits Lower, But Banks' CRA Loans Bring Rewards," *CO*, January 10, 1997. In Charlotte, "I cannot think of a single project caused by a CRA protest": housing attorney Ted Fillette, email to Tom Hanchett, October 11, 2023.
62. Betty Chafin Rash, written communication to Tom Hanchett, March 20, 2022.
63. "Bank's Tenth Legion Award Goes to Kathryn Heath," *CO*, September 25, 1999; "Hard Work for Housing Supported," *CO*, February 20, 1991. Future mayor Vi Alexander was the city's liaison during creation of the Charlotte–Mecklenburg Housing Partnership. "Charlotte Mayoral Election," *CO*, October 15, 2017.
64. Rash interview; "Group Proposes Nonprofit Effort to Stem Charlotte Housing Problem," *CO*, November 20, 1987. On the Boston Housing Partnership, chartered in 1983, see "Our History" on the Metro Housing Boston website, accessed November 4, 2024, www.metrohousingboston.org/about/. On the Massachusetts Housing Partnership,

launched in 1985, see "About Us" on the Massachusetts Housing Partnership website, accessed November 4, 2024, www.mhp.net/about-us.
65. "Housing for Poor Addressed," *CO*, November 21, 1986.
66. "Recipe for Roofs: 19,000 Housing Units Needed for Charlotte Poor, Elderly," *CO*, July 28, 1988.
67. "Group Proposes Nonprofit Effort to Stem Charlotte Housing Problem," *CO*, November 20, 1987; "Forum Supports Low-Income Housing Idea," *CO*, November 22, 1987.
68. "Group Examines Housing Options," *CO*, January 1, 1989. Government support continued:

> Councilmember Cannon said over the past four years the Council has funded the Partnership for about $500,000 from the innovative housing fund and another $1.5 million from the Community Development Block Grants. They have a request this year for $1 million from the innovative housing funds, which is taxpayer dollars and $1 million from the Community Development Block Grant. He asked why that is being requested or recommended.
>
> [*City Manager Pam Syfert*]: The City Council set up the Housing Partnership Board in 1989 and identified which agencies would be represented on that. They agreed to put $2 million of innovative funds in[,] which lasted for about three years[,] and then staff approached the Partnership and suggested that they begin using Block Grant money in order to free up some of the innovative money for things the City wanted to do with those funds.

Minutes of the Charlotte City Council, June 10, 1997, minutes book 111, p. 108, American Legal Publishing's Code Library, https://codelibrary.amlegal.com/codes/CharlotteNC/latest/m/1997/6/10.
69. Rash, written communication to Tom Hanchett, March 20, 2022.
70. "City Proposes Money, Staff for Housing Partnership," *CO*, March 2, 1988; "Group Examines Housing Options," *CO*, January 1, 1989.
71. Garrett interview, August 24, 2019.
72. "Renewal OKed for Greenville Neighborhood," *CO*, September 26, 1989. The partnership initially took control of twenty-six acres and planned to build 105 new houses on suburban-style quarter-acre lots. "NCNB Proposes Rebuilding of Neighborhood near Uptown," *CO*, September 6, 1989; "Fulfilling a Twenty-Year Pledge: Charlotte Attempts to Make Good on Neighborhood's Revival," *CO*, October 11, 1989; "Charlotte Attempts to Make Good," *CO*, October 16, 1989; "Program Turns Renter into Homeowner," *CO*, February 22, 1990.
73. "Greenville Area Gets New Start," *CN*, September 13, 1982. The 1980 effort used some of HUD's last Section 235 money: "Resettling Greenville: First of 100 New Houses Occupied in Redeveloped Neighborhood," *CO*, August 28, 1980. Background on HUD Section 235: Taylor, *Race for Profit*; Gotham, "Separate and Unequal"; McClaughry and Percy, "Troubled Dream"; "FHA Refinance Loans for Section 235 Mortgages," FHA.com, September 12, 2018, www.fha.com/fha_article?id=1800.
74. "Rebuilding a Neighborhood: Greenville Homes Get Underway," *CO*, December 9, 1990.
75. Eventually a few savvy banks created a national market that bought credits from entities

such as the CMHP at a discount and sold them to wealthy individuals and corporations who desired a tax break. But it took a while for that system to come into being. Sale of credits was not noted in newspaper articles on LIHTC when it moved through Congress in 1986. As late as 1988, widely published financial columnist Kenneth Harney made no mention of the provision: "Use of Last Real Tax Shelter Better in '88," *Atlanta Constitution*, May 29, 1988. A project that spring described it as an innovation: "A corporation will have to be formed to sell low-income housing tax credits" to outside investors. "New Rochelle Fund Helps Keep MacLeay Project Alive," *Marmoneck (NY) Daily Times*, April 17, 1988.

76. "Seversville Is on Its Way with Low-Cost Apartments," *CO*, August 23, 1992; "Affordable Housing Envisioned at Former School Site," *CO*, September 23, 1991; "Housing Fund Money Grows Scarcer: Panel Meets Today to Discuss Budget," *CO*, May 3, 1993.
77. "Seversville Is on Its Way with Low-Cost Apartments."
78. "Housing Work Gives Neighbors Hope," *CO*, March 30, 1995. Pruitt headed the Seversville Community Organization from the 1980s to the 2010s. "Summit to Honor Ten Leaders," *CO*, June 2, 2013; "Recreation Center Named to Honor Pruitt," *CO*, August 2, 2009.
79. All quotations from Garrett in this section on Seversville are from Garrett interview by Tom Hanchett, August 24, 2019.
80. "Revived Seversville Has Reason to Celebrate," *CO*, June 28, 2002.
81. Sources vary on the amount of LIHTC offered annually. For instance, $10.9 billion: "An Introduction to the Low-Income Housing Tax Credit," Congressional Research Service, 2021, https://fas.org/sgp/crs/misc/RS22389.pdf. Or $8 billion: "Low Income Housing Tax Credit (LIHTC)," HUD User, Office of Planning, Development and Research, 2020, www.huduser.gov/portal/datasets/lihtc.html. For a critical view: Everett Stamm, "An Overview of the Low-Income Housing Tax Credit (LIHTC)," Tax Foundation website, August 11, 2020, https://taxfoundation.org/low-income-housing-tax-credit-lihtc/.
82. "LIHTC Funding Recovers: Will It Last?," *Multi-Housing News*, April 3, 2020, www.multihousingnews.com/post/lihtc-funding-recovers-will-it-last/.
83. In 2018, the income limit was raised to 80 percent AMI. "Introduction to the Low-Income Housing Tax Credit."
84. Ted Fillette, email to Tom Hanchett, April 4, 2021.
85. Garrett interview, July 20, 2022.

Chapter 8

1. Vale, *After the Projects*; Schwartz, *Housing Policy*, 160–73. Advocates for the poor often criticized HOPE VI: Williams, "From HOPE VI to HOPE Sick?" See also the thoughtful analysis in Popkin et al., *Decade of HOPE VI*, 44–45.
2. From the *New York Times*: "Architecture View: Out of a Failed Project Comes a Design for Living," September 13, 1987; "Community Rises from Boston Slum," November 15, 1987; "Focus Boston: Rundown Reborn," March 13, 1988; "Experiment in Housing: Boston Tries Gentrifying around the Projects," July 10, 1988; "Focus Boston: An Experiment in Urban Transformation," January 14, 1990; "Boston War Zone Becomes Public Housing Dream," November 23, 1991; "Boston: A Redevelopment Project Thrives," December 27, 1992. An Associated Press article carried in many newspapers: "A Utopian

Housing Experiment," *Asheville Citizen*, October 2, 1988. A United Press International story: "Reborn Project Swaps Squalor for New Pride," *Miami Herald*, February 19, 1989. A *Christian Science Monitor* syndicated article: "Cities Transform Housing Projects into Mixed-Income Apartments," *Atlanta Constitution*, April 23, 1988.

3. The government retained ownership of the land, giving Corcoran Mullins Jennison a ninety-nine-year lease at one dollar a year. "Community Rises from Boston Slum." Corcoran pulled in investors by offering the rapid depreciation tax break instituted by Reagan in 1981—though the preparations dragged on so long that tax law changed again in 1986. So local officials successfully beseeched the US Congress to grant Corcoran an extension to continue using the pre-1986 "depreciation provisions that now make housing an attractive investment." "Hope amid Decay in Boston Project," *New York Times*, July 13, 1986. The project subsequently also took advantage of the new tax credits via the Low-Income Housing Tax Credit program when they became available in 1987. "State Offers Tax Credits for Rentals," *Boston Globe*, June 26, 1987. Chevron refinanced the complex in 1991, putting up $34 million in exchange for tax credits. "Boston War Zone Becomes Public Housing Dream."

4. "Out of a Failed Project Comes a Design for Living," *New York Times*, September 13, 1987.

5. Both quotes from Nathaniel Rich, "The Prophesies of Jane Jacobs," *The Atlantic,* November 2016.

6. Charlotte attorney and housing activist Tom Ray: "During the last decade we as a society have begun to realize that problems are related," pointing to air pollution as an ecological parallel. W. Thomas Ray and Robert G. Anderson, "Charlotte Housing Authority, Long Range Planning Committee, Report—Phase I, September 1972," photocopied, spiral-bound report given by Maggie Ray to Tom Hanchett.

7. Wilson, *Truly Disadvantaged*. An important follow-up documented how segregation had been historically constructed: Massey and Denton, *America Apartheid*. For an overview of such research, read Charlotte native Fulwood, "Costs of Segregation." See also Polikoff, *Waiting for Gautreaux*, 253 and onward.

8. Schill, "Distressed Public Housing," 499. On the trend toward income mixing in public housing: Schwartz, *Housing Policy*, 350.

9. On this trend over time: Goetz, *New Deal Ruins*, especially chapter 2, "Dismantling Public Housing."

10. Quoted in Roessner, *Decent Place to Live*, 174.

11. "Project Is What Public Housing Ought to Be," *Atlanta Constitution*, July 17, 1993.

12. "It's Townhouses for Fourth Ward," *CN*, February 27, 1977. Rash: "Our objective from Day One was to build a multi-racial, multi-income-level neighborhood base," quoted in "Fourth Ward Took a Kinder Approach," *CO*, January 29, 1978; "Elderly and Disabled Find New Downtown Home," *CO*, January 15, 1978; "$3.5 Million Townhouses to Be Built in Fourth Ward," *CN*, August 30, 1978.

13. Smith and Graves, "Corporate (Re)Construction of a New South City"; "Unofficial Mayor of Fourth Ward Uses Tenancy, Energy and a Gift for Gab to Get Things Done," *CO*, September 19, 1982; "A Miracle Right Here: In Four Years, Back from the Dead," *CO*, October 28, 1979.

14. On CDCs nationally: von Hoffman, "Past, Present, and Future of Community De-

velopment." Locally: Blevins and Hanchett, *Bank That Built*, 43–46. The Community Reinvestment Act particularly tracked banks' home loans in low-income and minority neighborhoods but also required "federal agencies to consider how well a bank has served those neighborhoods when considering its request for merger or acquisition." Underwriting a CDC helped meet that requirement. "First Union to Hear Pleas on Loan Policy," *CO*, March 31, 1989.

15. "Third Ward Plan Turns into Reality," *CO*, June 21, 1982; "Third Ward Home, Condo Build-Up Gets New Life," *CN*, April 4, 1984; "Renaissance Slow to Move into Former Scrapyard Site," *CO*, September 4, 1986; "Hail of Interest Greets Newborn Third Ward Project," *CO*, August 22, 1981. MOTION was an offshoot of Model Cities. Nationally, see Weber and Wallace, "Revealing the Empowerment Revolution."

16. "'A Friendly Atmosphere,' Says Third Ward Matriarch," *CO*, September 2, 1984.

17. "Public Housing's Legacy of Problems," *CO*, December 8, 1985. The violence reached a high point in 1993, the year that Charlotte won its first HOPE VI grant. Chuck McShane, "1993, Charlotte's Deadliest Year," *Charlotte Magazine*, November 21, 2013, www.charlottemagazine.com/1993-charlottes-deadliest-year/.

18. "Public Housing's Legacy of Problems." As early as 1983, Charlotte Housing Authority board member Sam Smith Jr. expressed deep misgivings about Charlotte's sprawling pre-1980s public housing complexes: "So many of the early public housing developments were much too large. We know that now. They were put on the west side because the people don't have the clout to fight them." "A Jungle? Many Areas Don't Live Up to Crime-Ridden Image," *CN*, April 21, 1983.

19. On specific links between Harbor Point and HOPE VI: Roessner, *Decent Place to Live*, 293–94; "Project Is What Public Housing Ought to Be," *Atlanta Constitution*, July 17, 1993. HOPE legislation had begun in the early 1990s with titles I through V, promoting homeownership and nonprofit rehab of single-family homes, among other goals. Abt Associates Inc. et al., *Historical and Baseline Assessment of HOPE VI*; Hostetter, "Emotions of Public Housing Policy," 164–66. Hostetter's dissertation focused on HOPE VI in Charlotte.

20. "Earle Village Getting a $34 Million Federal Facelift: Housing Authority Plans a 'Complete Metamorphosis' for First Ward Development," *CO*, August 28, 1993. Earle Village/First Ward as a model to be emulated: Porter, *Engaging the Private Sector in HOPE VI*. Centennial Park in Atlanta is sometimes credited as the South's first HOPE VI project, but Charlotte shared that honor. The redevelopment of Atlanta's Techwood Homes (America's very first Washington-funded "public housing" project back in the 1930s) began planning in 1990 with local dollars—part of Atlanta's preparations for the 1996 Olympics. HOPE VI funding was added in August 1993, the same day the Earle Village grant was announced. "HUD Takes 'Public' Out of St. Martin St.," *Atlanta Constitution*, August 28, 1993; Naparstek et al., *HOPE VI*, esp. 17–30; Tracy, "HOPE VI Mixed-Income Housing Projects Displace Poor People."

21. HUD pledged $34 million to the project. Hostetter, "Emotions of Public Housing Policy," 8.

22. The CMHP got involved to help "provide home ownership opportunities for people that were in their self-sufficiency program." Some bought homes in the CMHP's Park at Oaklawn project; CMHP counselors helped others purchase elsewhere in the city.

Retired CMHP chief Pat Garrett, interview by Tom Hanchett, July 20, 2022. Garrett's successor Julie Porter recalled that the CMHP also gave a $1.2 million loan to the HOPE VI project. Julie Porter, written communication with Tom Hanchett, August 29, 2022.

23. "First Ward Place," Carocon, accessed November 4, 2024, https://carocon.com/projects/first-ward-place/. Also "First Ward Place," FMK Architects, accessed November 5, 2024, www.fmkarchitects.com/work/affordable-housing/first-ward; "First Ward Starts Over with Middle Class Living beside Public Housing Residents," *CO*, January 18, 1998.
24. "Earle Village Plan Targets Crime, Traffic," *CO*, October 20, 1993.
25. Porter, *Engaging the Private Sector in HOPE VI*.
26. *Moving Up to the American Dream: From Public Housing to Private Ownership* (Washington, DC: HUD, July 1996); *Issue Brief: Neighborhood Development / Renewal* (Washington, DC: HUD, May 30, 1996).
27. Cisneros, "Legacy for a Reinvented HUD."
28. "Earle Village Getting a $34 Million Federal Facelift: Housing Authority Plans a 'Complete Metamorphosis' for First Ward Development," *CO*, August 28, 1993. On helping networks: Fullilove, *Root Shock*.
29. "Self-Sufficiency Best for Charlotte's Poor," *CO*, July 10, 1999.
30. "Bottom Line for Future of Public Housing: Move In, Move Up—Move Out," *CO*, April 19, 1998. The stepping-stone metaphor was part of the initial 1993 pitch for HOPE VI in Charlotte. "Earle Village Getting a $34 Million Federal Facelift: Housing Authority Plans a 'Complete Metamorphosis' for First Ward Development," *CO*, August 28, 1993.
31. Housing officials, both national and local, gradually realized that some public housing residents would never become upwardly mobile. These included "'hard-to-house' public housing residents, including families with special needs (multigenerational households, large families, disabled residents), 'lease violators' (with back rent payments, criminal histories, illegal residents on the lease), and residents with substance abuse or mental illness who are at risk of becoming homeless." Popkin et al., *Decade of HOPE VI*, 44–45. Another large group in that category: grandparents raising their grandchildren. Baker et al., "Grandparents Raising Grandchildren."
32. Woo, "How Have Rents Changed since 1960?" "The share of cost-burdened renters increased by a stunning twelve percentage points between 2000 and 2010, the largest jump of any decade dating back at least to 1960. The cumulative increase in the incidence of housing cost burdens is astounding. In 1960, about one in four renters paid more than 30 percent of income for housing. Today [in 2012], one in two are cost burdened." Joint Center for Housing Studies of Harvard University, "Rental Housing Affordability." For a pop-culture look at the same phenomenon: Ryskamp, "Life in 'The Simpsons' Is No Longer Attainable."
33. "Housing Crisis Squeezing Out the Poor: Success with Bricks, but Not with Earle Village's People," *CO*, June 14, 1999; "Charlotte Eyes New Future for Old Apartments: City, Developers Seek to Revamp Public Housing Sitting on Pricey Land," *CO*, September 5, 2004.
34. "Charlotte Eyes New Future for Old Apartments." For interviews with some of the earliest new tenants, see "A New Way of Living: Uptown Homes Blend Communities," *CO*, March 23, 1998.

35. "Housing Crisis Squeezing Out the Poor: Success with Bricks, but Not with Earle Village's People," *CO*, June 14, 1999.
36. "Public Housing to Get Makeover: Charlotte to Redevelop with a Private Partner," *CO*, September 5, 2004.
37. "Renewing an Area and Some Attitudes," *Tampa Bay Times*, October 2, 2005.
38. "Renewing an Area and Some Attitudes." By 2005, the Bank of America CDC was developing projects in fifteen cities, including Tampa.
39. "Renewing an Area and Some Attitudes."
40. "Renewing an Area and Some Attitudes"; "First Ward's Revival Is Second to None: Once Crime-Ridden, Hot Uptown Destination Gets a National Award," *CO*, November 21, 2004. On crime trends and HOPE VI in Charlotte more generally: Chuck McShane, "1993: Charlotte's Deadliest Year," *Charlotte Magazine*, November 21, 2013. Crime reduction in Earle Village earned mentions in national studies including Popkin et al., *Decade of HOPE VI*, 44–45. Nationwide, violent crime decreased markedly following HOPE VI redevelopments: "Neighborhoods and Violent Crime."
41. "Bottom Line for Future of Public Housing: Move In, Move Up—Move Out," *CO*, April 19, 1998.
42. "Advocates Take City to Task on Affordable Housing," *CO*, June 29, 1999. On difficulties encountered by voucher holders: "Bank Won't Keep Promise: 'Productive' Talks Reported in Fairview Homes Renewal," *CO*, December 2, 1999.
43. "Housing Crisis Squeezing Out the Poor: Success with Bricks, but Not with Earle Village's People," *CO*, June 14, 1999; "Keep Vows to Tenants, Group Tells City," *CO*, June 17, 1999.
44. "Watt Urges Funding of HUD Grant, Criticizes Bush Plan to End Program That Improves Communities," *CO*, October 10, 2006; US Congress, House, *Reauthorization of the HOPE VI Program*, 33–34.
45. Gress, Cho, and Joseph, *HOPE VI Data Compilation and Analysis*, 15. Thanks to Ken Szymanski for bringing this to my attention.
46. Mel Watt, interview by Tom Hanchett, January 21, 2020. Watt and CHA chief Charles Woodyard testified at a HOPE VI reauthorization hearing in Washington in 2007. "Watt said he wanted to ensure that one-for-one replacement of housing units was carried out," quoted in "Congressional Hearing: Public Housing Screening Debated," *CO*, June 22, 2007. On Watt's ongoing efforts for one-for-one replacement: "Old Project to Be Rebuilt at Loss of Low-Rent Units," *CO*, October 7, 2000. Transcript of the 2007 hearing can be found in US Congress, House, *Reauthorization of the HOPE VI Program*, especially 23–24, 33–34, and also appendix titled "Written Testimony of Charles Woodyard, President/CEO of the Charlotte Housing Authority," 116–33.
47. Jared Brey, "What Is the Faircloth Amendment?," Next City, February 9, 2021, https://nextcity.org/daily/entry/what-is-the-faircloth-amendment. Also "Alexandria Ocasio-Cortez Knows How to Fix Housing: The First Step to Addressing the Country's Housing Affordability Problem Is to Repeal the Faircloth Amendment," *New York Times*, January 4, 2021. Constraints posed by the Faircloth Amendment were still on Woodyard's mind years later: Charles Woodyard, interview by Tom Hanchett, July 28, 2021.
48. Schwartz, *Housing Policy*, 167–68; Vale, "Future of Planned Poverty."
49. "The Quality Housing and Work Responsibility Act of 1998 . . . rewrote Section 24 and

fully excused the HOPE VI program from the requirement of one-for-one unit replacement." Williams, "From HOPE VI to HOPE Sick?" A Congressional Research Service summary of the Quality Housing and Work Responsibility Act of 1998 said, "Eliminates the one-for-one replacement requirement." Milgram, *Chronology of Housing Legislation*, 310. A recent HUD publication referring to the Faircloth Amendment: US Department of Housing and Urban Development, *Guide to Public Housing Repositioning*, 20. One-for-one replacement was temporarily waived for HOPE VI projects in 1995. Vale, "Future of Planned Poverty," 22; Vale, *After the Projects*, 100, 402–3; Schwartz, *Housing Policy*, 167.

50. Brey, "What Is the Faircloth Amendment?" Also "Alexandria Ocasio-Cortez Knows How to Fix Housing: The First Step to Addressing the Country's Housing Affordability Problem Is to Repeal the Faircloth Amendment," *New York Times*, January 4, 2021. "From 1995 when the one-for-one replacement rule was initially suspended, through 2019, PHAs [local Public Housing Authorities] had demolished or otherwise removed about 570,781 units from the public housing stock. Partially offsetting this loss was the concurrent construction of 148,459 units of public housing, resulting in a net loss of 422,322 units during this period." Schwartz, *Housing Policy*, 167. On the continued applicability of the Faircloth Amendment in the 2020s, see US Department of Housing and Urban Development, *Guide to Public Housing Repositioning*, 20; "Faircloth-to-RAD: New Pathway to Create Deeply Affordable Housing," Department of Housing and Urban Development, accessed November 6, 2024, www.hud.gov/sites/dfiles/Housing/documents/Faircloth-to-RAD_Fact_Sheet.pdf; "On One-Year Anniversary of Innovative 'Faircloth-to-RAD' Initiative, HUD on Track to Create Nearly 1850 New Affordable Housing Units," HUD press release 22-085, May 3, 2022, HUD Archives, US Department of Housing and Urban Development, https://archives.hud.gov/news/2022/pr22-085.cfm.

51. Woodyard interview, June 28, 2021.

52. Woodyard interview, June 28, 2021.

53. First phase: 92 garden apartments + 52 apartments for elderly = 144 low-income units. Arbor Glen II: 91 low-income units. Arbor Glen III: 23 low-income units (including 8 at 30 percent AMI). Novogradac and Company, "LIHTC Properties in North Carolina's 12th District (Alma Adams–D) through 2015"; the Charlotte Housing Trust Fund was utilized for Arbor Glen III only: Zelleka Biermann, "HTF Activity Summary: Public Records Request Final," Charlotte Housing Trust Fund spreadsheet emailed to Tom Hanchett on November 16, 2021, in the data collection of JMAL, https://doi.org/10.15139/S3/XQBOFW.

54. "Arbor Glen," DreamKey Partners (formerly CMHP) website, 2021, www.dreamkeypartners.org/arbor-glen/.

55. "Written Testimony of Charles Woodyard," in US Congress, House, *Reauthorization of the HOPE VI Program*, 128. Data on the CMHP's single-family homes comes from organization's current CEO, Julie Porter, written communication to Tom Hanchett, September 7, 2022.

56. Woodyard interview, June 28, 2021.

57. Building permit to "Charlotte Housing Authority, Crosland Contractors," *CO*, June 21, 2006. Previously the newspaper noted creation of a "Crosland Springfield Gardens LLC," *CO*, September 24, 2004.

Notes to Pages 182–184 ■ 285

58. Woodyard interview, June 28, 2021.
59. "On the Move," *CO*, December 15, 2003. The award was specifically for the ninety-two-unit phase I of the affordable apartments. The project also had fifty renovated units plus elderly housing. "Housing North Carolina Awards Recognize Affordable Developments in Six Cities," North Carolina Housing Finance Agency website, October 21, 2003, www.nchfa.com/news/housing-north-carolina-awards-recognize-affordable-developments-six-cities.
60. "Makeover Brings Hope, Stability to Arbor Glen," *CO*, September 6, 2006.
61. "Rebuilding a Neighborhood: Greenville Homes Get Underway," *CO*, December 9, 1990.
62. As a symbol of the transformation, the CMHP convinced the city to rename Kinney, Gibbs, and Wyat Streets as Genesis Park Place, Rush Wind Drive, and Brewton Drive. "Names from Bad Days Pulled from Neighborhood's Streets," *CO*, June 11, 1994; "Marlene Jackson, 2000 Genesis Park Place," testimony in minutes of the Charlotte City Council, June 9, 1997, minutes book 111, p. 51, American Legal Publishing's Code Library, https://codelibrary.amlegal.com/codes/CharlotteNC/latest/m/1997/6/9; Feins, *Solving Crime Problems*, 6, 45, 61, 65; Gaillard, *If I Were a Carpenter*, 83–87.
63. "Bank Won't Keep Promise on Housing," *CO*, December 13, 1999; "Renewal at a Price: Rebuilt Project to Bring Loss of Homes for the Poor," *CO*, October 7, 2000; "Housing for the Poor: Mistakes Mount in Transforming Public Housing," *CO*, August 19, 2001; "B of A Leaves Fairview Project: Housing Authority Must Find New Developer to Rebuild Public Housing," *CO*, August 16, 2001; "217 Low-Rent Units to Be Lost at Fairview Homes," *CO*, October 7, 2000; "Broken Vow Can't Be Taken to the Bank," *CO*, August 17, 2001.
64. Pat Garrett, interview by Tom Hanchett, August 24, 2019; "Affordable Housing: Non-Profit Will Develop Site," *CO*, August 29, 2001.
65. Garrett interview, August 24, 2019; "Affordable Housing: Non-Profit Will Develop Site."
66. Jud Little, email to Tom Hanchett, April 7, 2020 (Little headed Crosland's apartment division 1988–2007); "A New Day for Public Housing: Complex Mixes Assisted Renters, People of Higher Incomes," *CO*, May 13, 2003; "A House Wasn't All That She Won," *CO*, August 25, 2005.
67. Montgomery Gardens contained seventy-six two- and three-bedroom apartments. It used about $8 million in HOPE VI dollars, plus tax credits and other subsidies. "Apartments Open amid Debate over HOPE VI: Federal Program That Helped Pay for Housing Facing Cutbacks," *CO*, October 24, 2006; "Watt Urges Funding of HUD Grant, Criticizes Bush Plan to End Program That Improves Communities," *CO*, October 10, 2006. Other off-site pieces of the Park at Oaklawn HOPE VI project: Rivermere, northwest Charlotte; Prosperity Creek, northeast Charlotte; purchase of existing Stonehaven East NOAH apartments in east Charlotte.
68. "Nia Point, Springfield Gardens, Montgomery Gardens, all of those were great successes. . . . Off-site housing program became a fixture in HOPE VI for us. . . . I don't know [how] it's done [elsewhere] around the country." Woodyard interview, June 28, 2021.
69. In Piedmont Courts in 1986, "81 percent of the residents are unemployed and 91 percent of the households are one-parent families headed by women." "School Children Often Struggle to Succeed in Class," *CO*, November 9, 1986; Kelley, *Money Rock*.

70. "Tenacity Wins at Piedmont Courts," *CO*, June 4, 2004; "HUD OKs Key Housing Revamp: Charlotte's Notorious Piedmont Courts to Be Fully Replaced," *CO*, June 3, 2004; "Replacing Piedmont Courts: City Gives Project Best Shot," *CO*, August 4, 2003; "Mix of Subsidized, Market-Rate Housing Shows Shift in Strategy," *CO*, November 3, 2008. Piedmont Courts had 368 units when initially constructed. In 1985–86, the CHA reduced the number to 242 in order to give more space to parking and playgrounds. "Rescuing Piedmont Courts," *CN*, October 2, 1985.
71. "Written Testimony of Charles Woodyard," in US Congress, House, *Reauthorization of the HOPE VI Program*, 132.
72. Laurel Street described the project thus: "Renaissance provides 334 new housing units targeted to all income levels. The community includes tax credit and market-rate units, serving working families, seniors, and the disabled.... Phase one, The Retreat at Renaissance, a 110-unit seniors building, was completed in September 2013.... Phases two and three, The Residences at Renaissance, are a total of 224 mixed-income family units completed in May 2014 and July 2016, respectively. [The complex also included] a 14,000 square foot LEED for New Construction certified clubhouse" with a swimming pool, meeting space, and administrative offices for the complex. From the Laurel Street website, accessed November 15, 2024, https://laurelstreetres.com/development/renaissance/.
73. "Affordable 'Village' to Rise in Place of Crime-Plagued Project: Renaissance to Replace Boulevard Homes with Housing, Education Sites," *CO*, September 24, 2012.
74. Rohe et al., *Boulevard Homes HOPE VI*, 22–24. "Renaissance West serves as the community quarterback for this innovative neighborhood redevelopment initiative to improve economic mobility and end intergenerational poverty. We believe in the extraordinary impact of a holistic, place-based approach that includes mixed-income housing, a cradle-to-career education continuum, and wraparound services including health, after school, academic support, recreation, and job training programs." From the Renaissance West Community Initiative website, accessed November 5, 2024, www.rwci.org/. See also "Who We Are" on the Purpose Built Communities website, accessed November 4, 2024, https://purposebuiltcommunities.org/who-we-are/; and "Affordable 'Village' to Rise in Place of Crime-Plagued Project: Renaissance to Replace Boulevard Homes with Housing, Education Sites."
75. Given the various difficulties of counting HOPE VI replacement units, I am not confident in this number—but by my calculations, Charlotte actually produced 84 more replacement units for renters at 30 percent AMI than it demolished under HOPE VI—until the Belvedere non-replacement is included. Those 170 demolished units pushed the balance sheet into negative territory: in total in Charlotte, 86 more units were torn down than were added under HOPE VI.
76. "City-Owned Housing Costly to Fix, Replace: Residents at Belvedere Homes Say the Buildings Should Just Be Torn Down," *CO*, June 14, 2001.
77. "HUD OK's Key Housing Revamp: Charlotte's Notorious Piedmont Courts to Be Fully Replaced," *CO*, June 3, 2004; "HOPE VI Demolition Grants: FY 1996–2003," HUD.gov, October 2004, www.hud.gov/sites/documents/DOC_9890.PDF; "And the Walls Came Tumbling Down," Creative Loafing Charlotte, December 19, 2001, https://clclt.com/charlotte/and-the-walls-came-tumbling-down/Content?oid=2347473.
78. "Housing Authority Looks at Bold Plan," *CO*, February 9, 2003; "City-Owned Housing

Costly to Fix, Replace: Residents at Belvedere Homes Say the Buildings Should Just Be Torn Down," *CO*, June 14, 2001.
79. "Ex Site of Decrepit Homes May Get Biz Park," *CO*, January 23, 2007.
80. "On the Road to Revitalization? Business Park May Arise at Former Site of Dilapidated Housing Complex: Officials Back Idea for Rozelles Ferry Corridor," *CO*, February 21, 2007; "Proposal for 27-Acre Business Park Advances," *CO*, July 22, 2007; "Housing Authority Looks at Bold Plan," *CO*, February 9, 2003; "City-Owned Housing Costly to Fix, Replace: Residents at Belvedere Homes Say the Buildings Should Just Be Torn Down," *CO*, June 14, 2001.
81. Novogradac and Company, "LIHTC Properties in North Carolina's 12th District (Alma Adams–D) through 2015"; Biermann, "HTF Activity Summary." I am grateful to Ms. Biermann, the Charlotte Housing Trust Fund's sole administrator throughout its first two decades, for gracious assistance in this research.
82. Novogradac and Company, "LIHTC Properties in North Carolina's 12th District (Alma Adams–D) through 2015"; Biermann, "HTF Activity Summary."
83. Lyles recommended the creation of the trust fund at a staff retreat in early 2001 and council made it law late that year. "Council Retreat," minutes of the Charlotte City Council, February 8, 2001, minutes book 115, pp. 843–45, American Legal Publishing's Code Library, https://codelibrary.amlegal.com/codes/CharlotteNC/latest/m/2001/2/8; "Rules Aim for More Subsidized Housing—Developments Can Include More Units but Spacing Changes," *CO*, November 27, 2001. Lyles and Syfert shared a passion for housing policy. They had earlier been the city's point persons for creation of the Charlotte–Mecklenburg Housing Partnership in 1988. On Lyles: "They Often Agree, So What Makes Democrat Vi Lyles Different from Mayor Jennifer Roberts?," *CO*, October 15, 2017. On Syfert: Betty Chafin Rash, written communication to Tom Hanchett, March 20, 2022; Pam Syfert, interview by Tom Hanchett, March 28, 2022.
84. City Council decided in 2001 to place affordable housing bonds on the November 2002 ballot. Housing advocates urged $40 million; council trimmed that to $20 million, which the voters approved. "Vote on Affordable Bonds Set: Affordable Housing Strategy Aims to Help Fulfill Demand for 30,000 Rental Units," *CO*, June 26, 2001; "Housing Bonds: Affordable Housing Lands on the Ballot," *CO*, November 3, 2002. On Charlotte's previous reluctance to issue housing bonds: "Cities Can Use Bonds in Housing Initiatives," *CO*, June 16, 1999; "Housing Strategies," *CO*, October 10, 2000. The $47 million in bond money raised in 2002 and 2004, while impressive, fell far short of estimates that $76 million would be needed to solve low-income housing shortages. "Money Hits Home: Can Charlotte Afford $76 Million a Year to Build on Housing Trust Fund's Success?," *CO*, January 28, 2006.
85. The three-story apartment building on North Davidson Street housed sixty-three men initially, later expanded to ninety-three. "Neighbors Now Favor Expansion," *CO*, May 25, 2010; "Haven for the Homeless: Grateful Residents Find Safety, Comfort at McCreesh Place," *CO*, December 14, 2007. To trace the growing interest in the "supportive housing" approach in Charlotte: "Make Room for the Poor, Housing Group Says," *CO*, February 22, 1998; "She's the Heart of This Home: Social Worker Wears Many Hats in Quest to Create Affordable Housing," *CO*, December 14, 2003.
86. "Neighbors Now Favor Expansion," *CO*, May 25, 2010; Lori Thomas, "Housing First

Works: Report Sheds Light on Program to End Homelessness," UNC Charlotte Urban Institute blog, November 12, 2020, https://ui.charlotte.edu/story/housing-first-works-report-sheds-light-program-end-homelessness/.
87. Izard, *Hundred Story Home*. Dove's Nest, operated by the Charlotte Rescue Mission, provided short-term beds during recovery from abuse or addiction. "Residential Treatment for Addiction: Where Broken Lives Are Mended—Dove's Nest Provides a Safe Place for Women as They Begin Recovery," *CO*, February 24, 2007; "Partnering to Provide More Lifeboats," *CO*, October 17, 2010; "Dove's Nest and Its Women Beat the Odds," *CO*, September 23, 2012.
88. "Future of Housing Aid for Poor Faces Closed Doors," *CO*, September 13, 1981; Yockey, *Builder*, 198–200, 231; Paul Leonard, interview by Tom Hanchett, March 2, 2020.
89. The total of 576 units does not match exactly the numbers noted earlier in this book. That may reflect renovations done over the years. "Council OKs $25 Million for Renewal Endeavor," *CO*, June 24, 2007.
90. "Mature Renters Get Dibs on Apartments: The Gables at Druid Hills Were Developed for Folks 55 and Older," *CO*, September 24, 2003; "The Housing Partnership Celebrates Grand Opening of New Housing Development Named for Political Trailblazer," Dreamkey Partners, November 9, 2017, https://dreamkeypartners.org/housing-partnership-celebrates-grand-opening-new-housing-development-named-political-trailblazer/.
91. Net loss/gain of units at Brightwalk: 576 low-income units were demolished (many uninhabitable, about 330 actual residents); 409 low-income units were built. "Affordable Housing Summit," Dix Edge Area Study, City of Raleigh, March 18, 2021 (DreamKey Partners' case study starts about halfway through the slide deck), https://cityofraleighodrupal.blob.core.usgovcloudapi.net/drupal-prod/COR22/DixEdgeAffordableHousingSummitDaytimePresentation.pdf; Biermann, "HTF Activity Summary."
92. "Brightwalk: A Town Center in the City's Midst," *CO*, June 30, 2012; Jarvis Holiday, "The $25 Million Hood," *Charlotte Magazine*, December 2008, www.charlottemagazine.com/the-25-million-hood/.
93. "Affordable Housing Summit," Dix Edge Area Study, City of Raleigh, March 18, 2021 (DreamKey Partners' case study starts about halfway through the slide deck).
94. Garrett interview, August 23, 2019.
95. The theater opened in 1996, shops in 1997, hotel in 1998. "Phillips Place: Birth of a Notion," *CO*, October 28, 2008. Johnny Harris's grandfather, North Carolina governor Cameron Morrison, had owned Morrocroft farm in the 1930s. The family developed part of those holdings as SouthPark Mall in the 1970s.
96. "Phillips Place: Birth of a Notion." On Pappas's previous work with Crosland: "Birkdale Village Caters to Yuppie Market," *CO*, April 11, 2002.
97. "From Public Housing, a Public Place," *CO*, December 26, 2005. The CHA needed "to act like a real estate company, not like a government agency," Woodyard urged. "He Aims to Alter Rules of Public Housing," *CO*, December 29, 2006.
98. "Big Buildings, Nightlife in SouthPark's Future," *CO*, June 12, 2013; "Whole Foods Plans Store Near SouthPark in 2012," *CO*, November 4, 2010.
99. Novogradac and Company, "LIHTC Properties in North Carolina's 12th District (Alma Adams–D) through 2015"; Biermann, "HTF Activity Summary"; "Will

Ballantyne Get Public Housing?," *CO*, February 21, 2010; "Putting a New Face on 'Projects' of Old," *CO*, June 5, 2010; "Legal Notices... Ashley Square at SouthPark," *CO*, September 1, 2009; "Crosland Affordable Apts. Leasing Fair for Charlotte Communities," *CO*, January 20, 2010.
100. "Putting a New Face on 'Projects' of Old"; "Some Don't Want Affordable Housing Near them," WSOC TV, May 30, 2018, www.wsoctv.com/news/some-don-t-want-affordable-housing-near-them/759688359/.
101. "From Public Housing, a Public Place," *CO*, December 26, 2005.
102. "SouthPark Public Housing in Balance," *CO*, February 20, 2006.
103. "Fears, Facts and Low-Income Housing," *CO*, February 28, 2010; "From Brooklyn to Ballantyne: Charlotte's Affordable Housing Crisis," *CO*, June 17, 2019.

Chapter 9

1. On the business-minded transformation of public housing, including RAD: Vale and Freemark, "From Public Housing to Public-Private Housing"; Schwartz, *Housing Policy*, 157–59, 169–73.
2. "Charlotte Housing Authority Is Now Inlivian," *CO*, November 19, 2019; "Inlivian? It's No Laughing Matter," *CO*, November 24, 2019.
3. Real estate prices rose even in areas that were adding little or no population. "Home Prices Rise, Building Surges: Costs Push Starter Homes Out of Reach of Many Memphis Residents," *Commercial Appeal* (Memphis), February 2, 2020. Nationally: Schwartz and McClure, "Why Building More Homes Won't Solve the Affordable Housing Problem"; Elizabeth Renter, "First-Time Homebuyers Priced Out in Major Metros, Even before Pandemic," NerdWallet, May 20, 2020, NASDAQ.com, www.nasdaq.com/articles/first-time-home-buyers-priced-out-in-major-metros-even-before-pandemic-2020-05-20.
4. "Home Prices in Charlotte Reach Record Highs, Leaving Many Behind," *Queen City Nerve* (Charlotte), July 9, 2021, https://qcnerve.com/home-prices-in-charlotte/. The Charlotte region median home price was $140,024 in 2010, $313,000 in 2021. Childress Klein Center for Real Estate, *State of Housing in Charlotte Report*; Szymanski, "In Charlotte Housing Debate, Let's Look at Underlying Factors." Nationally: Desmond, "Unaffordable America."
5. Feldman, "Gentrification, Urban Displacement and Affordable Housing." "In the record-setting housing market of 2021, homeownership has become the dividing line for a fractured economy that's racing toward extremes." "The New Real Estate Normal: In the Fracturing Economy, Any House Can Inspire a Bidding War," *Washington Post*, July 20, 2021. For instance, in small-town New York State: "As Home Prices Soar in Unlikely Places, the Most Vulnerable Residents Pay the Price," *Washington Post*, June 9, 2021. Similarly in Washington, DC: "Opinion: Goodbye, Chocolate City," *Washington Post*, August 14, 2021.
6. The metaphor "K-shaped recovery" first appeared during the COVID pandemic of 2020–21 and then became more widely applied. Financial advisor Jake Ablin seems to have coined the term: "Today's Economy and Markets Brought to You by the Letter 'K,'" CressetCapital.com, August 26, 2020, https://cressetcapital.com/post/todays-economy-and-markets-brought-to-you-by-the-letter-k/. Bloomberg news service

picked it up from Ablin: "Christmas Shopping Poised to Show Inequity in 'K-Shaped Recovery,'" *CO*, September 29, 2020. On "K-shaped" economic trends beyond the pandemic: Lance Roberts, "Fed Study: How We Made the Top 10 Percent Richer Than Ever," RealInvestmentAdvice.com, October 3, 2020, https://realinvestmentadvice.com/fed-study-how-we-made-the-top-10-richer-than-ever/; Lance Roberts, "The K-Shaped Recovery. A 'V' for Some, Not for Most," RealInvestmentAdvice.com, October 12, 2020; "Lack of Savings Worsens the Pain of Coronavirus Downturn," *Wall Street Journal*, April 15, 2020; "Record Low Mortgage Rates Widen Historic U.S. Economic Divides," *Bloomberg Businessweek*, November 10, 2020, www.bloomberg.com/news/articles/2020-11-10/cheap-credit-is-widening-wealth-inequality-across-america-s-racial-lines?embedded-checkout=true; Neal Rockwell, "A New Book Tells Us What Is Really behind the 'K-Shaped Recovery,'" Uneven Earth, February 23, 2021, https://unevenearth.org/2021/02/a-new-book-tells-us-what-is-really-behind-the-k-shaped-recovery/; Kevin Wack et al., "Who the K-Shaped Recovery Is Leaving Behind," American Banker, August 23, 2021, www.americanbanker.com/list/who-the-k-shaped-recovery-is-leaving-behind. Journalist Christopher Leonard (using the term "asset inflation" rather than "K-shaped economy") traced the genesis to the Federal Reserve's low interest rates, which "stoked demand for assets like stocks, corporate debt and commercial real estate." The stock market doubled in value during the 2010s with little connection to actual economic indicators. Leonard criticized the Fed for "taking a risky path that would deepen income inequality [and] stoke dangerous asset bubbles . . . , driving up prices across markets . . . which primarily benefited the very rich." Christopher Leonard, "The Fed's Doomsday Prophet Has a Dire Warning about Where We Are Headed," Politico, December 28, 2021, www.politico.com/news/magazine/2021/12/28/inflation-interest-rates-thomas-hoenig-federal-reserve-526177. See also Leonard's book *Lords of Easy Money*.

7. "Bottom Line for Future of Public Housing: Move In, Move Up—Move Out," *CO*, April 19, 1998; "Housing Agency to Build Its Own," *CO*, November 1, 2000.
8. The Horizon Development Properties' five-member board, led by Woodyard, included three CHA board members: Lucy Bush, Tom Hunter, and Ray Jones. The same four people also served on the seven-member Horizon Acquisition board, joined by Assistant City Manager Vi Alexander Lyles. "Low Income Units to Come from Spin-Offs," *CO*, July 18, 2001; "Horizon Development Properties," incorporation announcement, *CO*, March 26, 2001.
9. The CHA's "Horizon group" also included a for-profit real estate purchasing arm called Horizon Acquisition and a property management/tenant-relations entity called Blue Horizon Management. "Blue Horizon Management Company," Cause IQ, updated January 5, 2024, www.causeiq.com/organizations/horizon-development-properties,562246833/. Horizon Acquisition would buy and sell property on the open market, assembling tracts for Horizon Development Properties to develop. "Low Income Units to Come from Spin-Offs."
10. "Housing Agency to Build Its Own," *CO*, November 1, 2000.
11. "He Aims to Alter Rules of Public Housing," *CO*, December 29, 2006. Woodyard put in place a "cost-center" system of accounting, like that used by commercial real estate companies. It treated each property as its own profit-and-loss equation, matching income from rents against maintenance expenses of that particular site. Previously, all

maintenance had been in one budget line, with dollars doled out by executive decision—which made it easy for particular sites to be neglected. Under the new system, each site was expected to generate revenue for its own upkeep. Charles Woodyard, interview by Tom Hanchett, June 28, 2021.

12. The CHA's board chair elaborated: "If you can create an income stream, you can use it to help carry the low-income housing." "CHA Makes Shift to Mixed Use," *Charlotte Business Journal*, March 15, 2004, www.bizjournals.com/charlotte/stories/2004/03/15/story2.html. Similarly, "Charlotte Eyes New Future for Old Apartments: City, Developers Seek to Revamp Public Housing Sitting on Pricey Land," *CO*, September 5, 2004; "Public Housing to Get Makeover: Charlotte to Redevelop with a Private Partner," *CO*, September 5, 2004; "Low-Income Housing Plan a Test for Council: Neighbors Say Roads Can't Support Density at Weddington Road," *CO*, January 19, 2014.
13. "CHA Makes Shift to Mixed Use."
14. "CHA Makes Shift to Mixed Use."
15. "CHA Makes Shift to Mixed Use."
16. "Cherry Forms Corporation to Revive Area," *CO*, December 22, 1977; Ted Fillette, interview by Sarah Thuesen, March 2, 2006, interview U-0185, Southern Oral History Program Collection (#4007), Southern Historical Collection, Wilson Library, University of North Carolina at Chapel Hill, https://docsouth.unc.edu/sohp/U-0185/excerpts/excerpt_9452.html.
17. The Charlotte Housing Trust Fund required that eleven of those units be for seniors under 30 percent AMI. Zelleka Biermann, "HTF Activity Summary: Public Records Request Final," Charlotte Housing Trust Fund spreadsheet emailed to Tom Hanchett on November 16, 2021, in the data collection of JMAL, https://doi.org/10.15139/S3/XQBOFW.
18. "Cherry Residents Resist Developer: Both Sides Agree That New Housing Would Displace Many," *CO*, November 21, 2006; "Cherry Ripe for a Fix-Up," *CO*, November 8, 2006; "Shaping Cherry's Future: Development Could Change Area—for Better or Worse," *CO*, January 14, 2007. The Cherry Community Organization successfully sued Sellars for breach of contract. The North Carolina Supreme Court ruled that Sellars must compensate the CCO—but Sellars had declared bankruptcy and sold the land to another corporation. The situation remained in limbo in 2022. "Jury Finds Developer Broke His Affordable Housing Pledge," *CO*, September 7, 2018; "Cherry Residents Win Ruling from NC Supreme Court after Failed Affordable Housing Deal," *CO*, May 8, 2022.
19. "New Housing Moving Ahead in Cherry," *CO*, August 25, 2015; "Affordable Housing Units for Cherry Win Council Approval," *CO*, March 17, 2015; "Charlotte Housing Authority Plans Major Cherry Redevelopment," *CO*, February 25, 2015; "Eviction History Brings Challenges as Low-Income Sites Redeveloped," *CO*, December 27, 2016; "For Immediate Release: Wait List Opening," public notice, *CO*, September 3, 2017.
20. The project utilized $1.2 million from the Charlotte Housing Trust Fund, plus $8.2 million in Low-Income Housing Tax Credits. "New Housing Moving Ahead in Cherry"; "LIHTC Properties in North Carolina's 9th District," Novogradac and Company. Dionne Nelson's Laurel Street group (the new incarnation of longtime LIHTC developer Crosland; see previous chapter) put together the financing. "A PHA Success Story in

Developing Tax Credits/RAD Housing," Banks Law Firm, accessed November 4, 2024, https://bankslawfirm.com/pha-success-story-developing-tax-creditsrad-housing-video-available/; "City OKs Sale of Cherry Land for Affordable Apartments," Laurel Street, November 25, 2014, https://laurelstreetres.com/city-oks-sale-cherry-land-affordable-apartments/. See also Novogradac and Company, "LIHTC Properties in North Carolina's 12th District (Alma Adams–D) through 2018" and "LIHTC Properties in North Carolina's 9th District (Dan Bishop–R) through 2018."

21. Biermann, "HTF Activity Summary"; "Affordable Housing Units for Cherry Win Council Approval," *CO*, March 17, 2015. Tall Oaks' first phase was to be followed by a five-story mid-rise development with "workforce housing for families making $38,500 to 77,040" (50 percent to 100 percent of AMI), including "law enforcement professionals and people in the education, health care and services industries." "CHA Plans Changes to Historic Cherry," *CO*, February 19, 2015. But disagreements over zoning and density stalled the second phase into the 2020s. See "Inlivian 2021 Moving to Work Annual Plan," appendix F, www.inlivian.com/wp-content/uploads/2020/10/FY2021MTW Plan_PublicCommentDraft-1.pdf.

22. Morrill, *Survey and Research Report on the Barringer Hotel*. The Barringer, also known as the Cavalier Inn, was renamed Hall House under the CHA. "Elderly Gain More Housing," *CO*, October 8, 1978.

23. "Construction Starts on Mixed-Income Trella Apartments Uptown," *CO*, January 23, 2023; "Preservation Group Seeks to Save Uptown Hotel from Demolition," *CO*, August 2, 2020; "Seventh and Tryon Plan Revives Affordable Housing Uptown Debate," *CO*, May 23, 2020; "Uptown Plan Faces Critics over Affordable Housing," *CO*, March 8, 2020.

24. "Charlotte Eyes New Future for Old Apartments: City, Developers Seek to Revamp Public Housing Sitting on Pricey Land," *CO*, September 5, 2004.

25. "Site for Dilworth Project Rezoned: Housing Authority's Plan Includes Condos and Businesses amid Low-Income Housing," *CO*, September 21, 2010.

26. "Substantial Mixed-Use, Mixed Income Development Coming to Dilworth," *Charlotte Business Journal*, October 19, 2016, www.bizjournals.com/charlotte/news/2016/10/19/substantial-mixed-use-mixed-income-development.html; "Mixed-Income Development Announced for Dilworth," *CO*, October 19, 2016.

27. "Housing Authority Wants to Redevelop Prominent Property," *CO*, December 10, 2015; "Strawn Tower," Miles McClellan Construction website, accessed November 4, 2024, https://mmbuildings.com/construction-projects/senior-living/strawn-tower/.

28. "Patience Is a Virtue in Developing Affordable Housing," *CO*, August 12, 2018.

29. "Four Huge Developments Have Stalled in Charlotte," *CO*, July 29, 2018.

30. "$400 Million Development to Break Ground in Dilworth after Years of Planning," Axios Charlotte, October 16, 2020, https://charlotte.axios.com/235889/400-million-development-to-break-ground-in-dilworth-after-years-of-planning/; "What's Happening Now—and Later—with Queen City's Skyline," *CO*, May 16, 2021. The project's website, Centre South, made no mention of the affordable component: https://centresouth.com/, accessed November 4, 2024.

31. Schwartz, *Housing Policy*, 157–59, 169–73. Newspapers did not give RAD much coverage, likely because it sounded like a complicated and technical bureaucratic adjustment without obvious real-world impact. Among the earliest stories nationally: "$1.5M Later, New Gamble for a Housing Program," *Atlanta Constitution*, April 10, 2013. It quoted the

leader of the Housing Authority of Marietta: "We see this as an excellent opportunity to get out of the public housing business." The newspaper explained that by getting out of public housing ownership "and into the project-based voucher contracts, under the Section 8 program, housing authorities also get out of a lot of legal requirements." On the launch of Savannah's first RAD project: "The Week in Review," *Atlanta Constitution*, January 13, 2013. In North Carolina, fewer than a dozen newspaper stories mentioned RAD during its first decade—a sharp contrast with the hundreds of articles devoted to HUD's earlier HOPE VI program. See the online newspaper archive Newspapers.com.

32. A refresher on Washington's history of assisting with the operating costs for local public housing, from US Department of Housing and Urban Development, *Guide to Public Housing Repositioning*:

> Initially, Congress authorized the Federal Government to issue bonds to finance the development of new Public Housing and PHAs were required to set rents at levels necessary to meet basic operating costs, i.e., no Federal subsidies were provided for operations or capital improvements. By the 1950s and 1960s, as properties were aging and as the predominant incomes of new residents were lower, PHAs were no longer able to meet operating needs solely based on the rents that residents could afford. To protect these families from high rent burdens, the Brooke Amendment to The Housing and Urban Development Act of 1968 capped tenant rents at 25 percent of a family's adjusted income. The cap has subsequently gone up to 30 percent of the family's adjusted income. Although essential to reducing tenant rent burdens, the Brooke Amendment accelerated the financial strain on Public Housing by reducing revenues. To offset the impact of these reduced rental incomes, Congress, over the next several decades, incrementally introduced a series of programs to provide operating and capital subsidies.

33. US Department of Housing and Urban Development, *Guide to Public Housing Repositioning*. On a successful RAD project in New York City: "A Rebirth in the Bronx: Is This How to Save Public Housing?," *New York Times*, August 5, updated August 8, 2021. Criticism of New York City's RAD initiative, dubbed PACT: "When New York City Public Housing Goes Private It Can Get Worse," Bloomberg Equality + CityLab, January 27. 2022, www.bloomberg.com/news/articles/2022-01-27/nyc-public-housing-privatization-worse-for-tenants-says-human-rights-watch. An explanation of PACT and RAD in New York: "Executive Summary: NYCHA's Final Amendment to the Annual PHA Plan for FY 2017," undated and unsourced document online at NYC.gov, accessed November 4, 2024, https://www1.nyc.gov/assets/nycha/downloads/pdf/FY2017-Annual-Plan-Amendment-Exec-Summary-en-101817.pdf.

34. US Department of Housing and Urban Development, *Guide to Public Housing Repositioning*, 3.

35. US Department of Housing and Urban Development, *Guide to Public Housing Repositioning*, 20–21. HUD specifically recommended using RAD as a tool to overcome limitations set by the Faircloth Amendment. "Faircloth-to-RAD: New Pathway to Create Deeply Affordable Housing," Department of Housing and Urban Development, accessed November 6, 2024, www.hud.gov/sites/dfiles/Housing/documents/Faircloth-to-RAD_Fact_Sheet.pdf.

36. "Inlivian 2021 Moving to Work Annual Plan," appendix F. For a list of the agency's early

RAD conversions: US Department of Housing and Urban Development, *Charlotte Housing Authority FY 2018 Moving Forward*, appendix K. A national study of thirty-six metro areas in 2019 showed Charlotte to be one of the most enthusiastic adopters of the RAD approach. Schwartz, *Housing Policy*, 171–72.
37. "Inlivian 2021 Moving to Work Annual Plan."
38. "Notice of Public Hearing on Proposed Multifamily Revenue Bonds, Financing by Inlivian," *CO*, January 11, 2021. "Completion and lease-up" were "anticipated in 2021" for "Archdale Flats—Family (202), Archdale Flats—Seniors (131), Abbington on Mt. Holly (102), Freedom Flats (220), Ashley Flats (150), Evoke Living at Westerly Hills (156), and Evoke Living at Arrowwood (168)." "Inlivian 2021 Moving to Work Annual Plan," 8–11 and appendix F. By the way, HUD has a RAD mapping tool, not for use by the public: "RAD (Rental Assistance Demonstration) Minority Concentration Analysis Tool," in the Office of Policy Development and Research section of the HUD User website, accessed November 4, 2024, www.huduser.gov/portal/maps/rad/home.html.
39. Schwartz, *Housing Policy*, 170.
40. "'A Great Deal of Stigma': Charlotte Housing Authority to Change Its Name to 'Inlivian,'" *CO*, November 18, 2019; "Charlotte Housing Authority Is Now Inlivian," *CO*, November 19, 2019; "Inlivian? It's No Laughing Matter," *CO*, November 24, 2019.
41. "Inlivian 2021 Moving to Work Annual Plan," 5.
42. "Inlivian 2021 Moving to Work Annual Plan," 6. On Inlivian's social services work, see 28–29.
43. "'A Great Deal of Stigma': Charlotte Housing Authority to Change Its Name to 'Inlivian,'" *CO*, November 18, 2019.
44. Fulton Meachem, interview by Tom Hanchett, June 22, 2022.
45. "Livable Houses Razed for 'Monster Houses,'" *CO*, April 11, 2004; "Residents Fight 'McMansion' Wave—Tear-Downs Draw Ire of Some," *CO*, June 5, 2008; "Down with the Old, Up with New and Big: Demand for Close-In Neighborhood Space Gives Rise to Tear-Downs," *CO*, July 6, 2014; "What Used to Be There? The Rapid Pace of Demolitions Is Reshaping Charlotte," *CO*, September 7, 2017. As late as 2004, the teardowns seemed a very limited phenomenon. A city study that year concluded that "gentrification is not a threat to Charlotte neighborhoods." "Council Members Want Protections for Poor Neighborhoods," *CO*, December 9, 2004. Awareness slowly grew: "Life on Upswing in Neighborhoods near Center City," *CO*, August 4, 2008; "Protection from Gentrification: Charlotte Should Consider Capping Property Tax Hikes," *CO*, April 8, 2014; "Gentrifying Areas Targets of Aggressive Investors," *CO*, 2019.
46. Annetta Watkins Foard, a longtime Black homeowner on State Street, interview by Tom Hanchett, February 10, 2022. I am grateful to Rev. Ricky Woods of First Baptist Church West for introducing me to the housing price reset phenomenon.
47. Nathan Griffin, "Single-Family Construction Once Dominated Mecklenburg."
48. "Median rent [in the Charlotte area] remained constant between 2010 and 2013; however, it has increased steadily between 2013 and 2018." Anderson with assistance from Butts, *Charlotte–Mecklenburg*, 15–17.
49. The United Nations ranked Charlotte number one in a study predicting the expansion of major US cities during 2010 to 2030. "Charlotte and Raleigh Top U.N. List of

Fastest-Growing Large U.S. Cities," UNC Charlotte Urban Institute website, August 27, 2014, https://ui.charlotte.edu/story/charlotte-and-raleigh-top-un-list-fastest-growing-large-us-cities.
50. "Median Rent Reaches All-Time High," Housing Wire, April 26, 2019, www.housingwire.com/articles/48891-median-rent-reaches-all-time-high/. Similarly: "Rising Rents for Millennials Give Rise to New Bread of Lender," *Wall Street Journal*, May 13, 2019.
51. "History of Changes to the Minimum Wage Law."
52. Griffin, "Single-Family Construction Once Dominated Mecklenburg." On rising rents nationally: "Median Rent Reaches All-Time High," Housing Wire, April 26, 2019; "Rising Rents for Millennials Give Rise to New Breed of Lender," *Wall Street Journal*, May 13, 2019. Rising rents continued into the 2020s—"Rent increases of 20 percent or more ... in many cities": "What's Driving the Huge U.S. Rent Spike?," Bloomberg CityLab, October 5, 2021.
53. The study calculated the median income in each city zip code. "Charlotte's Household Income Gap Widens," *CO*, June 17, 2018.
54. "Lack of Savings Worsens the Pain of Coronavirus Downturn," *Wall Street Journal*, April 15, 2020; Lance Roberts, "Fed Study: How We Made the Top 10 Percent Richer Than Ever," RIA Advice, October 6, 2020, https://realinvestmentadvice.com/fed-study-how-we-made-the-top-10-richer-than-ever/.
55. Patrick Sisson, Jeff Andrews, and Alex Bazeley, "The Affordable Housing Crisis, Explained," Curbed.com, May 15, 2019, https://archive.curbed.com/2019/5/15/18617763/affordable-housing-policy-rent-real-estate-apartment; Jeff Andrews and Patrick Sisson, "U.S. Housing Marker Continues Rebound, despite Inequality, Says Harvard Report," Curbed.com, June 19, 2018, https://archive.curbed.com/2018/6/19/17476360/housing-market-rebound-inequality-harvard-state-of-nations-housing.
56. Griffin, "Single-Family Construction Once Dominated Mecklenburg." "The Charlotte region has seen about 40,000 new apartments deliver since 2015, with rents jumping about 20 percent in that same period." "Where the Next Wave of Apartments around Charlotte May Rise," *Charlotte Business Journal*, December 3, 2019, www.bizjournals.com/charlotte/news/2019/12/03/where-the-next-wave-of-apartment-developments.html?ana=wsoc; "Charlotte Faces Questions over Future Growth Plans," *CO*, August 12, 2018.
57. Childress Klein Center for Real Estate, *State of Housing in Charlotte Report*.
58. "Housing Costs Outpacing Wage Gains in Charlotte, according to New Report," *CO*, June 6, 2018; City of Charlotte Office of Housing and Neighborhood Services, *Housing Charlotte*, 17. The trend continued into the 2020s: "Finding an affordable apartment in the Charlotte area is a challenge. Finding one for less than $1,000? Nearly impossible, new data show. Only one percent of apartments in Mecklenburg County rent for less than $1,000." "Charlotte, Mecklenburg Rent: One Percent of Apartments under $1000," *CO*, January 31, 2022.
59. Delmelle, Nilsson, and Schuch, "Rail Transit."
60. The financial news media began to remark on big investors moving into the single-family rental market in the mid-2010s. "Charlotte's Single-Family Home Market Ranked

Number Three for Investing and Renting," *Charlotte Business Journal*, December 24, 2013, www.bizjournals.com/charlotte/blog/going_green/2013/12/charlotte-single-family-home-no-3-investing-rent.html. By the 2020s the trend was unmistakable: "Home Prices in Charlotte Reach Record Highs, Leaving Many Behind," *Queen City Nerve*, July 9, 2021; Ely Portillo and Justin Lane, "Wall Street–Backed Landlords Now Own More Than 11,000 Single Family Homes in Charlotte," UNC Charlotte Urban Institute, June 9, 2021, https://ui.uncc.edu/story/wall-street-backed-landlords-now-own-more-11000-single-family-homes-charlotte. A related trend: "Built-to-Rent Suburbs Are Poised to Spread across the U.S.," *Wall Street Journal*, June 7, 2021.

61. "Investors Making It Tough for Local Home Buyers," *Charlotte Business Journal*, July 29, 2021; "With Investors Knocking, Charlotte HOAs Are Starting to Change Their Rules," *CO*, October 2, 2021. Investors bought nearly one-third of all houses sold in Charlotte during 2021. "Investors Are Buying One in Four Homes in Raleigh, One in Five in Durham," WRAL TechWire, February 24, 2022, https://wraltechwire.com/2022/02/24/investors-are-buying-1-in-4-homes-in-raleigh-1-in-5-in-durham/.

62. Thomas, *Housing First Charlotte-Mecklenburg Research and Evaluation Project*.

63. Chetty et al., "Where Is the Land of Opportunity?" Chetty's study stimulated lively national discussion, including high-profile magazine articles that spotlighted Charlotte. Alana Semuels, "Why It's So Hard to Get Ahead in the South," *The Atlantic*, April 4, 2017, www.theatlantic.com/business/archive/2017/04/south-mobility-charlotte/521763/; Emily DeRuy and Janie Boschma, "Where Children Rarely Escape Poverty," *The Atlantic*, March 7, 2016, www.theatlantic.com/education/archive/2016/03/poor-children-rarely-escape-poverty-here/472002/; Gareth Cook, "The Economist Who Would Fix the American Dream," *The Atlantic*, August 2019, www.theatlantic.com/magazine/archive/2019/08/raj-chettys-american-dream/592804/.

64. During the 2010s, spatial disparities were becoming even more stark. "Concentrations of poverty spread dramatically through Mecklenburg County in the last decade. In 2000 most distressed neighborhoods were centered in an area just north of uptown. Recently released census data from 2008 through 2012, though, show that distressed neighborhoods have extended south to Pineville and eastward to Harrisburg and Mint Hill"—a "crescent" across the center of the county. "Poverty Spreads across Mecklenburg," *CO*, August 3, 2014.

65. A summary of local news coverage in the days immediately following the shooting: "Killing of Keith Lamont Scott," Wikipedia, accessed May 7, 2024, https://en.wikipedia.org/wiki/Killing_of_Keith_Lamont_Scott.

66. "Charlotte Clergy Plan Shift from Marches to Long-Term Action on Race," *CO*, September 23, 2016.

67. Newsome continued to speak out about systemic racism in housing: "NC Black Leaders Say 2020 Is Time to Start Ending Racism," *RNO*, July 17, 2020; "The Woman Who Took Down the Confederate Flag on What Came Next," *New York Times*, June 14, 2020.

68. "A Look Back at the Protest Movement Born after Keith Scott Killing," WFAE, September 19, 2017, www.wfae.org/politics/2017-09-19/a-look-back-at-the-protest-movement-born-after-keith-scott-killing; "I'm Worried That Charlotte Has Not Been 'Transformed,'" *CO*, September 18, 2017; "Who's Who on Charlotte's Streets: Shooting Protests Merge Old and New," *CO*, September 28, 2016.

69. "Speaker IDs Changing City, a Neglected Root of Protests," *CO*, October 2, 2016.
70. "Local Advocacy, Help for Displaced Lake Arbor Residents," *Charlotte Post*, August 21, 2019, www.thecharlottepost.com/news/2019/08/21/local-state/local-advocacy-help-for-displaced-lake-arbor-apartments-residents/.
71. Dorsey, "Fight for Progress in the 'New South'"; Greg Lacour, "Black Charlotte Is Frustrated—and That's by Design," *The Nation*, September 26, 2016; C. Smith, "Desegregation and Resegregation of Charlotte's Schools."
72. "Keith Lamont Scott Shooting Sparks Calls to Fix Charlotte Affordable Housing Shortage," *CO*, February 2, 2017.
73. "Council OKs Police Review and Help with Housing, Jobs," *CO*, October 11, 2016; "Low-Income Housing: City Council's Priority Might Change," *CO*, October 17, 2016. And following up: "City Claims Victory on Affordable Housing Goal," *CO*, July 21, 2019. The 5,000 units were already being planned before the Keith Lamont Scott shooting. Committing to deliver in three years was impressive, nonetheless. It nearly equaled the amount built over the previous *fourteen* years.
74. "Every U.S. County Has an Affordable Housing Crisis," Bloomberg CityLab, April 27, 2017, www.bloomberg.com/news/articles/2017-04-27/a-county-map-of-the-american-affordable-housing-crisis. Here's the study: Liza Getsinger, Lily Posey, Graham MacDonald, and Josh Leopold, *The Housing Affordability Gap for Extremely Low-Income Renters in 2014*, Urban Institute, April 2017, www.urban.org/sites/default/files/publication/89921/gap_map_report.pdf. And the accompanying interactive map: https://apps.urban.org/features/rental-housing-crisis-map/.
75. Urban historians had long written about processes such as redlining and FHA-endorsed housing discrimination. But it took Rothstein's passionate, skilled prose—in the context of the highly publicized shootings of Black people during 2015–17—to bring the history to wide public attention. "A 'Forgotten History' of How the U.S. Government Segregated America," *Fresh Air*, May 3, 2017, https://freshairarchive.org/segments/forgotten-history-how-us-government-segregated-america. Also featured on *All Things Considered* that same month: "'The Color of Law' Details How U.S. Housing Policies Created Segregation," NPR, May 17, 2017, www.npr.org/2017/05/17/528822128/the-color-of-law-details-how-u-s-housing-policies-created-segregation. Local commentator Justin Perry wrote opinion pieces on *The Color of Law* in the *CO*: "A Disease We Refuse to Treat," *CO*, April 9, 2018; "We Still Keep Whites Separate in Charlotte," *CO*, January 22, 2019. Former Urban League CEO Patrick Graham brought the message to the Black newspaper the *Charlotte Post*: "Housing Crisis for Black Americans Is a 'De Jure' Issue," *Charlotte Post*, October 25, 2018.
76. Journalist Mary Newsom and UNC Charlotte's Urban Institute brought Desmond to town for a public discussion in September 2017. Mary Newsom, "Evictions: 'This Is a Symptom of a Greater Problem,'" UNC Charlotte Urban Institute, September 28, 2017, https://ui.charlotte.edu/story/evictions-e28098-symptom-greater-probleme28099/.
77. Greg Lacour, "The New Breed: Charlotte's Millennial Politicians," *Charlotte Magazine*, July 23, 2018, www.charlottemagazine.com/the-new-breed-charlottes-millennial-politicians/; "McColl, Winston, and the Investment We All Need to Make," *CO*, January 2, 2018. The council and Winston got much national attention, including Alter, *Ones We've Been Waiting For.*

78. "Leaders Issue 'Call to Action' to Address Charlotte's Racial Disparities," *CO*, February 7, 2018.
79. "Vi Lyles's $50 Million Housing Trust Fund? That's Not Bold Enough," *CO*, April 30, 2018.
80. The exact wording: "Ensure that each publicly funded development includes at least 20 percent of units for households earning 30 percent of the Area Median Income. A priority waitlist for an additional 10 percent of units will target extremely low-income tenants with rental subsidies or vouchers, where possible." City of Charlotte Office of Housing and Neighborhood Services, *Housing Charlotte*, 8.
81. "Death of a Neighborhood: Alvin C. Jacobs, Jr., and the Gantt Center Capture Destruction and Displacement in Brookhill Village," Creative Loafing Charlotte, September 6, 2018, https://issuu.com/creativeloafingcharlotte/docs/_2018_29_final_low.
82. "Charlotte City Council Backs New Low-Income Housing, but Vote Reveals Deep Divide," *CO*, April 23, updated April 24, 2018.
83. "Millions Go to Housing, but Poor Can't Afford It," *CO*, October 21, 2018.
84. "Millions Go to Housing, but Poor Can't Afford It."
85. "Charlotte Bonds for Housing, Neighborhoods and Streets Cruise to Easy Victory," *CO*, November 3, 2020.
86. "Private Donations for Affordable Housing in Charlotte Exceed Goals," *CO*, September 6, 2019.
87. "Charlotte Talks: The Color of Law Community Read," WFAE 90.7 public radio, January 23, 2019. OneMECK pushed Charlotteans to look holistically at issues of opportunity, critiquing public school pupil assignment policies and also urging a higher minimum wage. "Charlotte Living Wage Would Help Affordable Housing," *CO*, October 27, 2019; "Why Questions Remain about Affordable Housing," *CO*, March 30, 2019.
88. "From Brooklyn to Ballantyne: The Story behind Charlotte's Affordable Housing Crisis," *CO*, June 17, 2019. Kelley also published *Money Rock*, an empathetic book tracing the life and times of a cocaine dealer in the Piedmont Courts public housing project.
89. "Ballantyne Developers Reveal Town Center Details: More Housing and Retail," *CO*, July 31, 2019.
90. Grace Emmanuel Village Apartments, 704–728 N. Caldwell Street, Charlotte 28202; Allen Street Apartments / Central Square Apartments, 1015 E. 16th Street, Charlotte 28205. A summary of projects already on the drawing board: "Low-Income Housing: No Tax Credits for Weddington Road Project," *CO*, September 1, 2015.
91. Mezzanine at Freedom Apartments, 2635 Freedom Drive, Charlotte 28208; "Freedom Drive Project Hailed as New Model for Affordable Housing," WFAE, December 11, 2018, www.wfae.org/local-news/2018-12-11/freedom-drive-project-hailed-as-new-model-for-affordable-housing; Paul McFadden Jr., "Charlotte Church to Invest $2 Million in Mixed-Income Housing Development," Qcity Metro, September 12, 2017, https://qcitymetro.com/2017/09/12/charlotte-church-to-invest-2-million-in-mixed-income-housing-development/. *Charlotte Magazine* honored Covenant Presbyterian Church as a "Charlottean of the Year" in recognition of the Mezzanine initiative. "Charlotteans of the Year 2017: Covenant Presbyterian Church," *Charlotte Magazine*, November 21, 2017, www.charlottemagazine.com/charlotteans-of-the-year-2017-covenant-presbyterian-church/.

92. "950 Affordable Housing Units across the City Could Be Coming Soon," *CO*, July 9, 2019; "Charlotte City Council Approves Nine Affordable Housing Projects: Where They'll Go," *CO*, April 28, 2020. The 2020 projects made up the largest-ever one-year building boom for low-rent housing in Charlotte's history.
93. "Why Questions Remain about Affordable Housing," *CO*, March 30, 2019; "Charlotte Leaders Discuss Priorities at Retreat," *CO*, January 30, 2019. On the Local Initiatives Support Corporation nationally: von Hoffman, "Past, Present, and Future of Community Development."
94. "To Keep Affordable Apartments from Disappearing, City Commits $1M More," *CO*, July 20, 2021.
95. The Pines on Wendover Apartments, 628 N. Wendover Road, Charlotte 28211; "To Keep Affordable Apartments from Disappearing, City Commits $1M More." It was the second such purchase for the company, after Lake Mist Apartments. Ascent's work sparked national interest. "Charlotte May Have Cracked the Code on Affordable Housing. Here's How," *Fast Company*, January 25, 2021, www.fastcompany.com/90597128/charlotte-may-have-cracked-the-code-on-affordable-housing-heres-how.
96. "$58 Million Fund Will Buy, Preserve Affordable Housing," *CO*, November 4, 2020. Ascent's investments included a joint venture with Roof Above, the nonprofit provider of housing for Charlotte's homeless, to buy HillRock Estates, "a 341-unit apartment complex in east Charlotte for income-based affordable housing and permanent supportive housing for people who are chronically homeless." The hospital corporation Atrium Health invested in the deal, as well, so that some of its employees could rent in the complex. "Roof Above Buys Apartment Complex for Affordable Housing," WFAE, September 1, 2020, www.wfae.org/local-news/2020-09-01/roof-above-buys-apartment-complex-for-affordable-housing. See also "Charlotte Apartment Residents Wary as New Affordable Housing Deal Moves Forward," *CO*, April 29, 2019; "Charlotte May Use Property Taxes to Fund More Rent Vouchers," *CO*, November 3, 2021.
97. The 23,060 figure is only for households at 30 percent AMI. "Former Charlotte Hotel a Vehicle to Aid Chronic Homelessness," *Charlotte Post*, October 1, 2021; "Charlotte's Been Funding Affordable Housing This Way for 20 Years: Is It Working?," *CO*, January 29, 2022.
98. "1000 People Lined Up for 129 New Affordable Housing Units on Freedom Drive on Monday," Axios Charlotte, January 27, 2020, https://charlotte.axios.com/194059/1000-people-lined-up-for-129-new-affordable-housing-units-on-freedom-drive-on-monday/.

Epilogue

1. Elizabeth Renter, "First-Time Homebuyers Priced Out in Major Metros, Even before Pandemic," NerdWallet, May 20, 2020, NASDAQ.com, www.nasdaq.com/articles/first-time-home-buyers-priced-out-in-major-metros-even-before-pandemic-2020-05-20. "Even before 2020, the U.S. faced an acute housing affordability crisis. The COVID-19 pandemic made it a whole lot worse." Schwartz and McClure, "Why Building More Homes Won't Solve the Affordable Housing Problem." Schwartz and McClure took issue with analysts who tagged low supplies of new housing as the key factor in the rising prices. They pointed to markets where there is vacant housing—and yet prices have still risen. An example: "Home Prices Rise, Building Surges: Costs Push Starter Homes Out

of Reach of Many Memphis Residents," *Commercial Appeal*, February 2, 2020.
2. Peter Miller, "Mortgage Rate History: Chart and Trends over Time," Mortgage Reports, October 10, 2024, https://themortgagereports.com/61853/30-year-mortgage-rates-chart#loan-purpose; "Mortgage Rates Are Falling Again, but Does It Matter?," *San Francisco Examiner*, March 11, 2020.
3. "Will Real Estate Ever Be Normal Again? In Austin, Texas, and Cities around the Country, Prices Are Skyrocketing," *New York Times*, November 12, 2021; "U.S. Housing Market Has Doubled in Value since the Great Recession, Gaining $69 Trillion in 2021," Zillow, January 27, 2022, www.zillow.com/research/us-housing-market-total-value-2021-30615/; "Investors Bought $1.4B in Homes in Charlotte in Q3: Here's How That Stacks Up Nationally," *Charlotte Business Journal*, December 6, 2021; "Mecklenburg's Housing Report Released: Average Home Price Now $471k," Charlotte Stories, January 20, 2022, www.charlottestories.com/mecklenburgs-housing-report-released-avg-home-price-now-471k-with-record-low-inventory/.
4. The citywide average increase was 28.1 percent, with higher rates in particular areas. "Charlotte Rent Prices Increased by as Much as 65 Percent in One Year," Axios Charlotte, June 29, 2022, https://charlotte.axios.com/301450/charlotte-rent-prices-increased-by-as-much-as-65-in-one-year/; "Rent for $1,000 or Less: It's a Needle in a Haystack in Charlotte," *CO*, January 28, 2022.
5. Tent camps had long existed, usually hidden in wooded areas. The I277 tent city, existing from mid-2020 through February 2021, was much more visible. "Homelessness Special Report: The Last Days of 'Tent City,'" Axios Charlotte, February 22, 2021, https://charlotte.axios.com/248762/special-report-the-last-days-of-tent-city/.
6. "Charlotte May Use Property Taxes to Fund More Rent Vouchers," *CO*, November 3, 2021.
7. "'Our Homes Have Been Stolen from Us': Uptown Development Stirs Debate on Reparations," *CO*, August 2, 2019; "How Bulldozing Brooklyn Cost Black Charlotteans Millions in Generational Wealth," Axios Charlotte, June 27, 2022, www.axios.com/local/charlotte/2022/06/27/how-bulldozing-brooklyn-cost-black-charlotteans-millions-in-generational-wealth-300420.
8. "Insana: Signs of Slowing Inflation Now Emerge," CNBC.com, December 23, 2022, www.cnbc.com/2022/12/23/signs-of-slowing-inflation-emerge-and-the-fed-now-risks-doing-too-much.html.
9. See, for instance, Hackworth, *Neoliberal City*; and Jacobs, *Neoliberal Housing Policy*. Contrast with the more historically grounded work by von Hoffman, "Calling upon the Genius of Private Enterprise."
10. Szymanski, "In Charlotte Housing Debate, Let's Look at Underlying Factors."
11. "The Brooks Sandwich House Brothers Just Donated Family Land to Help Charlotte's Affordable Housing Crisis," Axios Charlotte, June 24, 2019, https://charlotte.axios.com/168750/the-brooks-sandwich-house-brothers-just-donated-family-land-to-help-charlottes-affordable-housing-crisis/.
12. The Cisneros quote came from a lengthy exploration of affordable housing issues that used Charlotte as its case study. Jason DeParle, "Slamming the Door," *New York Times Magazine*, October 20, 1996. DeParle concluded, "The point isn't that [Washington] has done nothing. The point is that it hasn't done enough. . . . It doesn't do nearly as much for the needy as it does for those with means."

13. "Charlotte's Been Funding Affordable Housing This Way for 20 Years. Is It Working?," *CO*, January 29, 2022.
14. "Charlotte's Been Funding."
15. "Charlotte's Been Funding."
16. "Charlotte Still Isn't Building Enough Affordable Housing for the Poor," Axios Charlotte, January 31, 2022, https://charlotte.axios.com/285908/charlotte-isnt-building-enough-affordable-homes-for-the-poor/; "Map: Where Affordable Housing Is Being Built in Charlotte, and Where It Isn't," Axios Charlotte, January 31, 2022, https://charlotte.axios.com/286199/map-where-affordable-housing-is-being-built-in-charlotte-and-where-it-isnt/.
17. Sources vary on total LIHTC allocation annually. For instance, $8 billion: "Low-Income Housing Tax Credit," Office of Policy Development and Research, HUD User, 2020, www.huduser.gov/portal/datasets/lihtc.html. Or $10.9 billion: "An Introduction to the Low-Income Housing Tax Credit, updated January 26, 2021," Congressional Research Service, 2021, https://fas.org/sgp/crs/misc/RS22389.pdf.
18. "Andrew Yang's Universal Basic Income Earned Him Fans. But Can He Win Votes?," *New Yorker*, January 23, 2021.
19. Rina Torchinsky, "Target Is Raising Its Minimum Wage to as Much as $24 per Hour," NPR, March 1, 2022, www.npr.org/2022/03/01/1083720431/target-minimum-wage; "Retailers' Wage Increases to Attract Workers Aren't Yet Denting Profits," *Wall Street Journal*, February 28, 2022.
20. Schwartz, *Housing Policy*, 252–58, 371–72.

BIBLIOGRAPHY

Archives
Baker Library, Harvard University
    HBS Entrepreneurs Oral History Collection
Charlotte Mecklenburg Library, Charlotte, NC
    Robinson-Spangler Carolina Room
City of Charlotte, NC
    [City Council] Meeting Minutes 1936–1978, www.charlottenc.gov/City-Government/City-Codes-Ordinances/Meeting-Minutes
Cornell University Library, Ithaca, NY
    Rare and Manuscript Collections
        John Nolen Papers
Franklin Delano Roosevelt Presidential Library and Museum, Hyde Park, NY
    Master Speech File, 1898–1945
J. Murrey Atkins Library Special Collections and University Archives, University of North Carolina at Charlotte
    Manuscript Collections
        Fred D. Alexander Papers
        Charlotte Redevelopment Commission Records
        W. Thomas Ray Papers
        Beaumert Whitton Papers
Mecklenburg County Register of Deeds Office, Charlotte, NC
Wilson Special Collections Library, University of North Carolina at Chapel Hill
    Southern Historical Collection
        Southern Oral History Program Collection

Interviews by the Author
Nelo Alford, November 27, 2020.
Laura Belcher, July 18, 2019.
Don Carroll, July 13, 2021.
Kevin Davis, December 1, 2020.
Ted Fillette, May 12, 2019, and April 9, 2021.
Annetta Watkins Foard, February 10, 2022.
Pat Garrett, August 24, 2019, and July 20, 2022.
Paul Leonard, March 2, 2020.
Vi Alexander Lyles, August 10, 2022.
Fulton Meachem, June 22, 2022.
Betty Chafin Rash, January 23, 2018.
Maggie Ray, April 20, 2021.
Pam Syfert, March 28, 2022.
Mel Watt, January 21, 2020.
Charles Woodyard, June 28, 2021, July 28, 2021, and August 23, 2021.

304 ■ Bibliography

Periodicals and Websites

Affordable Housing Finance
American Banker
Architectural Forum
Asheville Citizen
The Assembly
Atlanta Constitution
The Atlantic
Axios Charlotte
Bensenville (IL) Register
Bloomberg
Bloomberg Businessweek
Bloomberg CityLab
Boston Globe
Carolina Alumni Review
Carolina Public Press
Charlotte Business Journal
Charlotte Chronicle
Charlotte Magazine
Charlotte News
Charlotte Observer
Charlotte Post
Charlotte Stories
Chatham Record (Siler City, NC)
Chicago Tribune
CNBC.com
Commercial Appeal (Memphis)
Creative Loafing Charlotte
Curbed.com
Daily Independent (Concord, NH)
Decatur (IN) Daily Democrat
The Economist
Fast Company
Fortune
Greensboro News and Record
Harvard Crimson
House and Home
Los Angeles Times
MacLean's
Marmoneck (NY) Daily Times
Miami Herald
Minneapolis Star
Minneapolis Star-Tribune
Minneapolis Tribune
Multi-Housing News
Naples (FL) Daily News
Nashville (NC) Graphic
The Nation
NC Insight
New Yorker
New York Times
New York Times Magazine
NPR.org
Oakland Tribune
Philanthropy Journal
Politico
Public Health Reports
Queen City Nerve (Charlotte)
Raleigh News and Observer
Robesonian (Lumberton, NC)
Rocky Mount (NC) Telegram
San Francisco Examiner
Saturday Evening Post
Shopping Center World
The State (Columbia, SC)
Statesville (NC) Daily Record
St. Louis Post-Dispatch
Tampa Bay Times
Time
Village Free Press (Proviso Township, IL)
Wall Street Journal
Washington Post
Wilmington (DE) Morning News
WRAL TechWire

Books, Journal Articles, On-Line Reports, Theses, and Dissertations

Abt Associates Inc., Linda B. Fosburg, Susan J. Popkin, and Gretchen P. Locke. *An Historical and Baseline Assessment of HOPE VI: Volume I, Cross-Site Report*. Washington, DC: US Department of Housing and Urban Development, 1996. www.huduser.gov/publications/pdf/hopevi_vol1.pdf.

Adams, Thomas. *Regional Plan of New York and Its Environs*. Volume 2, *Building the City*. New York: Committee on the Regional Plan of New York and Its Environs, 1931.

Alter, Charlotte. *The Ones We've Been Waiting For: How a New Generation of Leaders Will Transform America*. New York: Viking, 2020.
Anderson, Bridget, with assistance from Shanika Jerger Butts. *Charlotte–Mecklenburg: 2020 State of Housing Instability and Homelessness Report*. UNC Charlotte Urban Institute, September 2020. https://z4b66d.p3cdn1.secureserver.net/wp-content/uploads/2020/09/2020-SoHIH-Report_FINAL.pdf.
Baker, Lindsay A., et al. "Grandparents Raising Grandchildren in the United States: Changing Family Forms, Stagnant Social Policies." *Journal of Societal and Social Policy* 7 (2008): 53–69.
Beard, Mary. *Women's Work in Municipalities*. New York: Appleton, 1915.
Birch, Eugenie Ladner. "From Civic Worker to City Planner: Women and Planning, 1890–1980." In *The American Planner: Biographies and Recollections*, edited by Donald A. Kruekeberg, 396–427. New York: Methuen, 1983.
Bishir, Catherine, and Tom Hanchett. "Houser, William H. (circa 1841–1912)." *North Carolina Architects and Builders: A Biographical Dictionary*. Accessed April 14, 2024. https://ncarchitects.lib.ncsu.edu/people/P000611.
Blain, Karen G. *The Clubwoman as Feminist: True Womanhood Redefined, 1868–1914*. New York: Holmes and Meier, 1980.
Blevins, Allen, and Tom Hanchett. *The Bank That Built: The Story of Bank of America and Charlotte*. Charlotte: Bank of America, 2019.
Boger, Mary Snead. *Charlotte 23*. Charlotte: Bassett Printing, 1972.
Bostic, Raphael W., and Arthur Acolin. "Affirmatively Furthering Fair Housing." In *The Fight for Fair Housing: Causes, Consequences and Future Implications of the 1968 Fair Housing Act*, edited by Gregory D. Squires, 189–206. New York: Routledge, 2018.
Bratt, Rachel G. "The Quadruple Bottom Line and Nonprofit Housing Organizations in the United States." In *The Affordable Housing Reader*, 2nd ed., edited by Elizabeth J. Mueller and J. Rosie Tighe, 196–211. New York: Routledge, 2022.
Brockenbrough, Martha. *Unpresidented: A Biography of Donald Trump*. New York: Feiwel and Friends, 2018.
Brown, Don P. "Taxability of Unincorporated Medical Associations—The Kintner Regulations." *Western Reserve Law Review* 12, no. 4 (1961): 777–91. https://scholarlycommons.law.case.edu/caselrev/vol12/iss4/9.
Buder, Stanley. *Visionaries and Planners: The Garden City Movement and the Modern Community*. New York: Oxford University Press, 1990.
Burnstein, Joseph. "New Techniques in Public Housing." *Law and Contemporary Problems* 32, no. 3 (summer 1967): 528–49. https://scholarship.law.duke.edu/cgi/viewcontent.cgi?article=3170&context=lcp.
Catz, Robert S. "Historical and Political Background of Federal Housing Programs." *North Dakota Law Review* 50, no. 1 (1973): 25–43. https://commons.und.edu/cgi/viewcontent.cgi?article=3258&context=ndlr.
"CDBG: A 25-Year History." *Journal of Housing and Community Development* 56, no. 4 (1999): 20–25.
Charlotte–Mecklenburg Historic Landmarks Commission. *Myrtle Square Apartments: Survey and Research Report*. 2006. http://landmarkscommission.org/wp-content/uploads/2016/12/Myrtle-Square-SR.pdf.
Chase, Charles E., Katie E. Horak, and Steven R. Keylon (Architectural Resources Group).

Garden Apartments of Los Angeles: Historic Context Statement. Los Angeles Conservancy, October 2012. www.laconservancy.org/wp-content/uploads/2022/11/Garden-Apartment-Context-Statement.pdf.

Chetty, Raj, et al. "Where Is the Land of Opportunity? The Geography of Intergenerational Mobility in the United States." *Quarterly Journal of Economics* 129, no. 4 (November 2014): 1553–623. https://academic.oup.com/qje/article/129/4/1553/1853754.

Childress Klein Center for Real Estate, UNC Charlotte. *The State of Housing in Charlotte Report.* 2019. https://realestate.charlotte.edu/wp-content/uploads/sites/1233/2024/08/State-of-Housing-in-Charlotte-Report-2019_FINAL.pdf.

Chu, Yongqiang. "State of Housing and Jobs." Charlotte City Council Housing and Jobs Summit, January 9, 2023. https://issuu.com/belkcollege/docs/soh_2023_final_report_1_.

Cisneros, Henry G. "Legacy for a Reinvented HUD: Charting a New Course in Changing and Demanding Times." *Cityscape: A Journal of Housing Policy and Research* 1, no. 3 (September 1995): 145–52.

City of Charlotte Office of Housing and Neighborhood Services. *Housing Charlotte: A Framework for Building and Expanding Access to Opportunity through Housing Investments.* Prepared in partnership with Enterprise Community Services, Inc. August 27, 2018. https://charlotte.uli.org/wp-content/uploads/sites/21/2018/08/Housing-Charlotte-Framework.pdf.

Congressional Research Service. *An Overview of the Section 8 Housing Programs: Housing Choice Vouchers and Project-Based Rental Assistance.* Congressional Research Service Report. EveryCRSReport.com, last updated February 7, 2014. www.everycrsreport.com/reports/RL32284.html.

Connolly, N. D. B. *A World More Concrete: Real Estate and the Remaking of Jim Crow South Florida.* Chicago: University of Chicago Press, 2014.

Covington, Howard E., Jr., and Marion A. Ellis. *The Story of NationsBank: Changing the Face of American Banking.* Chapel Hill: University of North Carolina Press, 1993.

Crawford, Margaret. *Building the Workingman's Paradise: The Design of American Company Towns.* New York: Verso, 1995.

Delmelle, Elizabeth C., Isabelle Nilsson, and Johanna Claire Schuch. "Rail Transit, Residential Mobility, and Income Segregation." UNC Charlotte Urban Institute, September 2021. https://pages.charlotte.edu/lightrailstudy/findings/.

Desmond, Matthew. *Poverty, by America.* New York: Crown, 2023.

———. "Unaffordable America: Poverty, Housing and Eviction." *Fast Focus*, March 2015. www.irp.wisc.edu/publications/fastfocus/pdfs/FF22-2015.pdf.

Dorsey, Sherrell. "A Fight for Progress in the 'New South.'" Bloomberg.com, October 7, 2016. www.bloomberg.com/news/articles/2016-10-07/a-fight-for-progress-in-the-new-south.

Douglas, Davison M. *Reading, Writing, and Race: The Desegregation of the Charlotte Schools.* Chapel Hill: University of North Carolina Press, 1995.

Edson, Charles L. "Affordable Housing—An Intimate History." *Journal of Affordable Housing and Community Development Law* 20, no. 2 (Winter 2011): 193–213. https://pdf4pro.com/view/affordable-housing-1-an-intimate-history-3c8526.html.

Fairbanks, Robert B. "From Better Dwellings to Better Neighborhoods: The Rise and Fall of the First National Housing Movement." In *From Tenements to the Taylor Homes: In Search of an Urban Housing Policy in Twentieth-Century America*, edited by John F.

Bauman, Roger Biles, and Kristin M. Szylvian, 21–42. University Park: Pennsylvania State University Press, 2000.

———. *The War on Slums in the Southwest: Public Housing and Slum Clearance in Texas, Arizona, and New Mexico, 1935–1965*. Philadelphia: Temple University Press, 2014.

Farmer, Scott. "Testimony of Scott Farmer, Executive Director, North Carolina Housing Finance Agency, before the Subcommittee on Transportation, Housing and Urban Development and Related Agencies, Committee on Appropriations, United States House of Representatives: Stakeholder Perspectives: Affordable Housing Production." Congress.gov, March 7, 2019. www.congress.gov/116/meeting/house/109012/witnesses/HHRG-116-AP20-Wstate-FarmerS-20190307.pdf.

Feins, Judith D. *Solving Crime Problems in Residential Neighborhoods: Comprehensive Changes in Design, Management and Use*. Washington, DC: US Department of Justice, 1997.

Feldman, Justin. "Gentrification, Urban Displacement and Affordable Housing: Overview and Research Roundup." *Journalist's Resource*, August 15, 2014. https://journalistsresource.org/economics/gentrification-urban-displacement-affordable-housing-overview-research-roundup/.

"FHA's Impact on the Financing and Design of Apartments." *Architectural Forum* 92, no. 1 (January 1950): 97–108. https://usmodernist.org/AF/AF-1950-01.pdf.

FHA Investigation: Hearings before the Committee on Banking and Currency. US Senate, 83rd Cong., June 28–July 30, 1954, Parts 1 and 2. Washington, DC: US Government Printing Office, 1954. https://books.google.com/books?id=xWS3nzPgMEQC.

FHA Investigation: Report of the Senate Committee on Banking and Currency, Pursuant to S. Resolution 229. Washington, DC: US Government Printing Office, 1955. www.washingtonpost.com/wp-stat/graphics/politics/trump-archive/docs/fha-investigation-report-by-senate-banking-comm.pdf.

FHA. *Planning Rental Housing Projects*. Revised. Washington, DC: Federal Housing Administration, 1947.

———. *Sixteenth Annual Report of the Federal Housing Administration, 1949*. Washington, DC: US Government Printing Office, 1950. www.huduser.gov/portal/sites/default/files/pdf/Sixteenth-Annual-Report-of-the-Federal-Housing-Administration.pdf.

Fillette, Ted. "North Carolina Residential Rental Agreements Act: New Developments for Contract and Tort Liability in Landlord-Tenant Relations." *North Carolina Law Review* 56, no. 5 (1978): 785–806.

Flanigan, Maureen A. "Gender and Urban Political Reform: The City Club and the Woman's City Club of Chicago in the Progressive Era." *American Historical Review* 95, no. 4 (October 1990): 1032–50.

Florida, Richard. "How Poor Americans Get Exploited by Their Landlords: American Landlords Derive More Profit from Renters in Low-Income Neighborhoods, Researchers Matthew Desmond and Nathan Wilmers Find." Bloomberg.com, March 21, 2019. www.citylab.com/equity/2019/03/housing-rent-landlords-poverty-desmond-inequality-research/585265/.

Freemark, Yonah. "Myth #5: Public Housing's Failures Led to a Natural Death." In *Public Housing Myths: Perception, Reality, and Social Policy*, edited by Nicholas Dagen Bloom, Fritz Umbach, and Lawrence J. Vale, 121–38. Ithaca, NY: Cornell University Press, 2015.

Friedman, Lawrence J., and James E. Krier. "A New Lease on Life: Section 23 Housing and the Poor." *University of Pennsylvania Law Review* 116, no. 4 (February 1968): 611–47. https://scholarship.law.upenn.edu/cgi/viewcontent.cgi?article=6136&context=penn_law_review.

Fullilove, Mindy Thompson. *Root Shock: How Tearing Up City Neighborhoods Hurts America, and What We Can Do about It*. 2nd ed. New York: NYU Press/New Village Press, 2016.

Fulwood, Sam, III. "The Costs of Segregation and the Benefits of Fair Housing." In *The Fight for Fair Housing: Causes, Consequences and Future Implications of the 1968 Fair Housing Act*, edited by Gregory D. Squires, 40–56. New York: Routledge, 2018.

Gaillard, Frye. *The Dream Long Deferred: The Landmark Struggle for Desegregation in Charlotte, North Carolina*. 3rd ed. Columbia: University of South Carolina Press, 2006.

———. *If I Were a Carpenter: Twenty Years of Habitat for Humanity*. Winston-Salem, NC: John F. Blair, 1996.

Galster, George, Anna M. Santiago, Robin E. Smith, and Peter A. Tatian, with Mary Cunningham and Charlene Y. Wilson. *Assessing Property Value Impacts of Dispersed Housing Subsidy Programs*. Washington, DC: Urban Institute, March 1999.

Garner, John S. "The Garden City and Planned Industrial Suburbs: Housing and Planning on the Eve of World War II." In *From Tenements to the Taylor Homes: In Search of an Urban Housing Policy in Twentieth-Century America*, edited by John F. Bauman, Roger Biles, and Kristin M. Szylvian, 43–59. University Park: Pennsylvania State University Press, 2000.

Gilmore, Glenda. *Gender and Jim Crow: Women and the Politics of White Supremacy in North Carolina, 1896–1920*. 2nd ed. Chapel Hill: University of North Carolina Press, 2019.

Goetz, Edward G. *New Deal Ruins: Race, Economic Justice, and Public Housing Policy*. Ithaca, NY: Cornell University Press, 2013.

Gordon, Roger H., James R. Hines Jr., and Lawrence H. Summers. "Notes on the Tax Treatment of Structures." In *The Effects of Taxation on Capital Accumulation*, edited by Martin Feldstein, 223–58. Chicago: University of Chicago Press, 1987. www.nber.org/books-and-chapters/effects-taxation-capital-accumulation/notes-tax-treatment-structures.

Gotham, Kevin Fox. "Separate and Unequal: The Housing Act of 1968 and the Section 235." *Sociological Forum* 15, no. 1 (March 2000): 13–37.

Gravelle, Jane. *Depreciation and the Taxation of Real Estate*. Congressional Research Service, October 25, 2000. www.everycrsreport.com/reports/RL30163.html.

Gress, Taryn, Seungjon Cho, and Mark Joseph. *HOPE VI Data Compilation and Analysis*. National Initiative on Mixed-Income Communities, Case Western Reserve University, September 2016. www.huduser.gov/portal/sites/default/files/pdf/HOPE-VI-Data-Compilation-and-Analysis.pdf.

Griffin, Nathan. "Single-Family Construction Once Dominated Mecklenburg, but That's Changed." UNC Charlotte Urban Institute, December 4, 2019. https://ui.charlotte.edu/story/single-family-construction-once-dominated-mecklenburg-e28099s-changed/.

Hackworth, Jason. *The Neoliberal City: Governance, Ideology, and Development in American Urbanism*. Ithaca, NY: Cornell University Press, 2014.

Hanchett, Thomas W. "Financing Suburbia: Prudential Insurance and the Post–World

War II Transformation of the American City." *Journal of Urban History* 26, no. 3 (March 2000): 312–28.

———. "The Other 'Subsidized Housing': Federal Aid to Suburbanization, 1940s–1960s." In *From Tenements to the Taylor Homes: In Search of an Urban Housing Policy in Twentieth-Century America*, edited by John F. Bauman, Roger Biles, and Kristin M. Szylvian, 163–79. University Park: Pennsylvania State University Press, 2000.

———. "Roots of the 'Renaissance': Federal Incentives to Urban Planning, 1941 to 1948." In *Planning the Twentieth-Century American City*, edited by Mary Corbin Sies and Christopher Silver, 283–304. Baltimore: Johns Hopkins University Press, 1996.

———. *Sorting Out the New South City: Race, Class, and Urban Development in Charlotte, 1875–1975*. 2nd ed. Chapel Hill: University of North Carolina Press, 2020.

———. "U.S. Tax Policy and the Shopping Center Boom of the 1950s and 1960s." *American Historical Review* 101, no. 4 (October 1996): 1082–110.

Hayden, Delores. *Building Suburbia: Green Fields and Urban Growth, 1820–2000*. New York: Pantheon, 2003.

Heycke, Hannah. "A New Approach to Housing Choice Voucher Implementation for Durham, North Carolina." Master's thesis, Duke University Sanford School of Public Policy, 2020. https://dukespace.lib.duke.edu/dspace/bitstream/handle/10161/20745/Heycke.Hanna.ConfFinalMP.pdf?sequence=1.

Hirsch, Arnold. *Making the Second Ghetto: Race and Housing in Chicago*. Enlarged ed. Chicago: University of Chicago Press, 2021.

"History of Changes to the Minimum Wage Law." *U.S. Department of Labor, Wage and Hour Division* website, www.dol.gov/agencies/whd/minimum-wage/history.

Hogan, James H. *Scattered-Site Housing: Characteristics and Consequences*. US Department of Housing and Urban Development, 1996. www.huduser.gov/portal/publications/pubasst/scatter.html.

Hostetter, Ellen. "The Emotions of Public Housing Policy: A Critical Humanist Exploration of HOPE VI." PhD diss., University of Kentucky, 2008.

Howard, Christopher. *The Hidden Welfare State: Tax Expenditures and Social Policy in the United States*. Princeton, NJ: Princeton University Press, 1997.

Hutchins, Nan, with J. W. York and Smedes York. *Cameron Village: A History, 1949–1999*. Raleigh: Spirit Press, 2001.

Inlivian. "Inlivian 2021 Moving to Work Annual Plan." Draft document. Accessed November 6, 2024. www.inlivian.com/wp-content/uploads/2020/10/FY2021MTWPlan_PublicCommentDraft-1.pdf.

Izard, Kathy. *The Hundred Story Home: A Journey of Homelessness, Hope, and Healing*. Charlotte: Grace Press, 2016.

Jackson, Kenneth. *Crabgrass Frontier: The Suburbanization of the United States*. New York: Columbia University Press, 1985.

Jacobs, Keith. *Neoliberal Housing Policy: An International Perspective*. New York: Routledge, 2019.

Jenkins, Destin. *The Bonds of Inequality: Debt and the Making of the American City*. Chicago: University of Chicago Press, 2021.

Johnson, Lyndon B. "Special Message to Congress on the Nation's Cities," March 2, 1965.

In *Public Papers of the Presidents of the United States: Lyndon B. Johnson, 1965*, 231–40. Washington, DC: US Government Printing Office, 1966.

Johnston, Steve. "A Charlotte Housing Tour: Programs and Preferences of Government." *NC Insight*, August 1982, 22–26. https://nccppr.org/wp-content/uploads/2017/02/A_Charlotte_Housing_Tour.pdf.

Joint Center for Housing Studies of Harvard University. "Rental Housing Affordability." In *America's Rental Housing: Evolving Markets and Needs*, Joint Center for Housing Studies of Harvard University, 2013. www.jchs.harvard.edu/sites/jchs.harvard.edu/files/ahr2013_05-affordability.pdf.

Katznelson, Ira. *When Affirmative Action Was White: An Untold History of Racial Inequality in Twentieth-Century America*. New York: Norton, 2005.

Kelley, Pam. *Money Rock: A Family's Story of Cocaine, Race, and Ambition in the New South*. New York: New Press, 2018.

Kroessler, Jeffrey A. *Sunnyside Gardens: Planning and Preservation in a Historic Garden Suburb*. New York: Fordham University Press, 2021.

Leonard, Christopher. *The Lords of Easy Money: How the Federal Reserve Broke the American Economy*. New York: Simon and Schuster, 2022.

Leonard, Paul. *Music of a Thousand Hammers: Inside Habitat for Humanity*. New York: Continuum International Publishing Group, 2006.

———. *Where Is Church? One Man's Quest*. Davidson, NC: Lorimer Press, 2012.

Leuchtenburg, William. *Roosevelt and the New Deal, 1932–1940*. New York: Harper Perennial, 2009.

Logan, John, and Harvey Molotch. *Urban Fortunes: The Political Economy of Place*. Berkeley: University of California Press, 2007.

Lord, J. Dennis, and George S. Rent. "Residential Satisfaction in Scattered-Site Public Housing Projects." *Social Science Journal* 24, no. 3 (1987): 287–302. www.sciencedirect.com/science/article/abs/pii/0362331987900772.

Love, Rose Leary. *Plum Thickets and Field Daisies*. Charlotte: Public Library of Charlotte and Mecklenburg County, 1996.

Mason, Joseph B. *History of Housing in the U.S., 1930–1980*. Houston: Gulf Publishing, 1982.

Massey, Douglas S., and Nancy A. Denton. *America Apartheid: Segregation and the Making of the Underclass*. Cambridge, MA: Harvard University Press, 1993.

McCarty, Maggie. *Introduction to Public Housing*. Congressional Research Service, January 3, 2014. https://fas.org/sgp/crs/misc/R41654.pdf.

McClaughry, John, and Charles H. Percy. "The Troubled Dream: The Life and Times of Section 235 of the National Housing Act." *Loyola University Chicago Law Journal* 6, no. 1 (Winter 1975): 1–45. https://lawecommons.luc.edu/cgi/viewcontent.cgi?article=2347&context=luclj.

McClure, Kirk. "What Should Be the Future of the Low-Income Housing Tax Credit Program?" *Housing Policy Debate* 29, no. 1 (January 2019): 65–81.

McDonald, John F. "Public Housing Construction and the Cities, 1937–1967." *Urban Studies Research* vol. 2011, article ID 985264. www.hindawi.com/journals/usr/2011/985264/.

Milgram, Grace. *A Chronology of Housing Legislation and Selected Executive Actions, 1892–2003: A Report by the Congressional Research Service*. Washington, DC: US Government Printing Office, 2003.

Morrill, Dan L. *Reconnaissance Survey of Superblock Apartment Projects in Charlotte-Mecklenburg.* Charlotte-Mecklenburg Historic Landmarks Commission, 2006. http://landmarkscommission.org/wp-content/uploads/2016/02/Reconnaissance-Survey-Of-Superblocks-In-Charlotte-Mecklenburg.pdf.

———. *Survey and Research Report on the Barringer Hotel.* Charlotte-Mecklenburg Historic Landmarks Commission, 2007, updated 2009. http://landmarkscommission.org/wp-content/uploads/2017/06/Barringer-Hotel-SR.pdf.

Mueller, Elizabeth J., and J. Rosie Tighe, eds. *The Affordable Housing Reader.* 2nd ed. New York: Routledge, 2022.

Muhonen, Elmer W. *Report on Audit—Section 236 Multifamily Housing Program.* US Department of Housing and Urban Development, January 1972. www.huduser.gov/portal/sites/default/files/pdf/Section-236-Multifamily-Program.pdf.

Naparstek, Arthur J., et al. *HOPE VI: Community-Building Makes a Difference.* Washington, DC: US Department of Housing and Urban Development, 2000. www.huduser.gov/publications/pdf/hope_vi.pdf.

National Park Service. "Modern Apartment Complexes in Georgia, 1936–1954." National Register of Historic Places, 2003. https://gadnr.org/sites/default/files/hpd/pdf/Ga_Modern_Apartments_Context_0.pdf.

"Neighborhoods and Violent Crime." *Evidence Matters* (newsletter of the HUD Office of Policy Development and Research), Summer 2016. www.huduser.gov/portal/periodicals/em/summer16/highlight2.html.

Nelson, Robert K., et al. "Charlotte," HOLC map, 1937, linked to scans of HOLC "Area Description" forms. "Mapping Inequality: Redlining in New Deal America." Edited by Robert K. Nelson and Edward L. Ayers. *American Panorama: An Atlas of United States History*, 2023. https://dsl.richmond.edu/panorama/redlining/#loc=12/35.218/-80.91&city=charlotte-nc&area=C2&adview=full&adimage=3/80.253/-152.754.

Newkirk, Vann R. "The Development of the National Association for the Advancement of Colored People in Metropolitan Charlotte, North Carolina, 1919–1965." PhD diss., Howard University, 2002.

Novogradac and Company. "LIHTC Properties in North Carolina's 9th District (Dan Bishop–R) through 2018." Novogradac. Accessed November 6, 2024. www.novoco.com/public-media/documents/north-carolina-lihtc-properties-nc9-102020.pdf.

———. "LIHTC Properties in North Carolina's 12th District (Alma Adams–D) through 2015." Novogradac, 2018. Accessed November 6, 2024. https://www.novoco.com/public-media/documents/nc12_2018_lihtc_properties.pdf.

———. "LIHTC Properties in North Carolina's 12th District (Alma Adams–D) through 2018," Novogradac. Accessed November 6, 2024. www.novoco.com/public-media/documents/north-carolina-lihtc-properties-nc12-102020.pdf.

Ogle, Maureen. *All the Modern Conveniences: American Household Plumbing, 1840–1890.* Baltimore: Johns Hopkins University Press, 1996.

Oliveri, Rigel C. "The Legislative Battle for the Fair Housing Act, 1966–1968." In *The Fight for Fair Housing: Causes, Consequences and Future Implications of the 1968 Fair Housing Act*, edited by Gregory D. Squires, 28–39. New York: Routledge, 2018.

Orlebeke, Charles. "The Evolution of Low-Income Housing Policy, 1949 to 1999." In *The Affordable Housing Reader*, 2nd ed., edited by Elizabeth J. Mueller and J. Rosie Tighe, 21–40. New York: Routledge, 2022.

Pastor, Manuel, et al. *Regions That Work: How Cities and Suburbs Can Work Together*. Minneapolis: University of Minnesota Press, 2000.

Peeler, Kirsten, Christine Heidenrich, Katherine E. Grandine, and Dean A. Doerrfeld. *Housing an Air Force and a Navy: The Wherry and Capehart Era Solutions to the Postwar Family Housing Shortage (1949–1962)*. Volume 3, *Appendices B through M*. The Digital Archaeological Record, Digital Antiquity, 2007. doi:10.48512/XCV8457950.

Plunz, Richard. *A History of Housing in New York*. Rev. ed. New York: Columbia University Press, 2016.

Polikoff, Alexander. *Housing the Poor: The Case for Heroism*. Cambridge, MA: Ballinger Publishing, 1978.

———. *Waiting for Gautreaux: A Story of Segregation, Housing, and the Black Ghetto*. Chicago: Northwestern University Press, 2006.

Popkin, Susan J., Bruce Katz, Mary K. Cunningham, Karen D. Brown, Jeremy Gustafson, and Margery Austin Turner. *A Decade of HOPE VI: Research Findings and Policy Challenges*. Washington, DC: Urban Institute and Brookings Institution, 2004.

Porter, Douglas R. *Engaging the Private Sector in HOPE VI*. Washington, DC: Urban Land Institute, 2002.

Radford, Gail. "The Federal Government and Housing during the Great Depression." In *From Tenements to the Taylor Homes: In Search of an Urban Housing Policy in Twentieth-Century America*, edited by John F. Bauman, Roger Biles, and Kristin M. Szylvian, 102–20. University Park: Pennsylvania State University Press, 2000.

Ritter, Luke. "The Discriminating Priority of Integration: Open Housing Activism in St. Louis County, 1968–1977." *Journal of the Illinois State Historical Society* 106, no. 2 (Summer 2013): 224–42.

Roessner, Jane. *A Decent Place to Live: From Columbia Point to Harbor Point—A Community History*. 2nd ed. Boston: Calf Pasteur Press, 2000.

Rohe, William M., et al. *Boulevard Homes HOPE VI: Interim Report*. Prepared by the Center for Urban and Regional Studies, UNC Chapel Hill, for the Charlotte Housing Authority, May 7, 2013, 22–24.

Romer, Christina D., and David H. Romer. "A Narrative Analysis of Postwar Tax Changes." University of California, Berkeley, June 2009. https://eml.berkeley.edu/~dromer/papers/nadraft609.pdf.

Rosen, Eva. *The Voucher Promise: "Section 8" and the Fate of an American Neighborhood*. Princeton: Princeton University Press, 2020.

Rothstein, Richard. *The Color of Law: A Forgotten History of How Our Government Segregated America*. New York: Liveright, 2017.

Rubinowitz, Leonard S., and James E. Rosenbaum. *Crossing the Class and Color Lines: From Public Housing to White Suburbia*. Chicago: University of Chicago Press, 2000.

Ryskamp, Dani Alexis. "Life in 'The Simpsons' Is No Longer Attainable." *The Atlantic*, December 29, 2020.

Schexnider, Alvin J. *Saving Black Colleges: Leading Change in a Complex Organization*. London: Palgrave Macmillan, 2013.

Schiesl, Martin J. *The Politics of Efficiency: Municipal Reform in the Progressive Era, 1880–1920*. Berkeley: University of California Press, 1977.

Schill, Michael H. "Distressed Public Housing: Where Do We Go from Here?" *University of Chicago Law Review* 60, no. 2 (Spring 1993): 497–554.

Schwartz, Alex F. *Housing Policy in the United States*. 4th ed. New York: Routledge, 2021.

Schwartz, Alex F., and Kirk McClure. "Why Building More Homes Won't Solve the Affordable Housing Problem." The Conversation, November 12, 2021. https://theconversation.com/why-building-more-homes-wont-solve-the-affordable-housing-problem-for-the-millions-of-people-who-need-it-most-171100.

Scott, Anne Firor. *The Southern Lady: From Pedestal to Politics, 1830–1930*. Chicago: University of Chicago Press, 1972.

"Section 608 Projects—Prevailing Wage Violations." In *FHA Investigation: Report of the Senate Committee on Banking and Currency, Pursuant to S. Resolution 229*, 92–93. Washington, DC: US Government Printing Office, 1954.

Smith, Clint. "The Desegregation and Resegregation of Charlotte's Schools." *New Yorker*, October 7, 2016.

Smith, Heather Brown, and William Graves. "The Corporate (Re)Construction of a New South City: Great Banks Need Great Cities." *Southeastern Geographer* 43, no. 2 (November 2003): 213–34.

Smith, Perry Rowan. "Federal Tax Aspects of a Section 236 Limited Dividend Development Entity." *Urban Lawyer* 4, no. 2 (Spring 1972): 315–17. https://www.jstor.org/stable/27892839.

Smith, Stephen Samuel. *Boom for Whom? Education, Desegregation, and Development in Charlotte*. Albany: State University of New York Press, 2004.

Sperbeck, William. "Suburban Multifamily Vacancy Rates and Federal Income Tax Policies." *Professional Geographer* 30, no. 3 (August 1978): 270–77.

Staats, Elmer B. *Section 236 Rental Housing: An Evaluation with Lessons for the Future*. Report to the Congress by the Comptroller General of the United States, January 1978. www.gao.gov/assets/130/121049.pdf.

Stack, Carol B. *All Our Kin: Strategies for Survival in a Black Community*. New York: Basic Books, 1983.

Stephenson, R. Bruce. *John Nolen: Landscape Architect and City Planner*. Amherst: University of Massachusetts Press, 2015.

Stuart, Guy. *Discriminating Risk: The U.S. Mortgage Lending Industry in the Twentieth Century*. Ithaca, NY: Cornell University Press, 2003.

Surrey, Stanley S. *Pathways to Tax Reform: The Concept of Tax Expenditures*. Cambridge, MA: Harvard University Press, 1973.

———. "Tax Assistance for Housing and Its Implications for the Federal Tax Structure and the Federal Budget." Fifth Annual Development Forum, Urban America, Berkeley, California, October 28, 1968.

Szymanski, Ken. "Can We Revive Real Meaning of 'Affordable Housing'?" UNC Charlotte Urban Institute, August 1, 2018. https://ui.charlotte.edu/story/can-we-revive-real-meaning-e28098affordable-housinge28099-0/.

———. "In Charlotte Housing Debate, Let's Look at Underlying Factors." UNC Charlotte Urban Institute, February 2, 2016. https://ui.charlotte.edu/story/charlotte-housing-debate-lete28099s-look-underlying-factors/.

Taylor, Keeanga-Yamahtta. *Race for Profit: How Banks and the Real Estate Industry Undermined Black Homeownership*. Chapel Hill: University of North Carolina Press, 2019.

Thomas, M. Lori, principal investigator. *Housing First Charlotte-Mecklenburg Research and Evaluation Project*. Process Evaluation Final Report, September 2020. UNC Charlotte

Urban Institute. https://z4b66d.p3cdn1.secureserver.net/wp-content/uploads/2020/09/HFCM-Final-Process-Evaluation-Report-2020-Final-9-2-20v3.pdf.

Tracy, James. "HOPE VI Mixed-Income Housing Projects Displace Poor People." *Race, Poverty and the Environment* 15, no. 1 (Spring 2008): 26–29.

Trounstine, Jessica. *Segregation by Design: Local Politics and Inequality in American Cities.* New York: Cambridge University Press, 2018.

Truman, Harry. "Special Message to Congress on Housing," February 23, 1948. American Presidency Project. www.presidency.ucsb.edu/documents/special-message-the-congress-housing.

United States. *Tax Incentives to Encourage Housing in Urban Poverty Areas: Hearings before the Committee on Finance, Ninetieth Congress, first session, on S. 2100 . . . September 14, 15, and 16, 1967.* Washington, DC: Government Printing Office, 1967. www.google.com/books/edition/Tax_Incentives_to_Encourage_Housing_in_U/9TV6SEXPXY4C.

US Census Bureau. "Quarterly Residential Vacancies and Homeownership, Third Quarter 2019." Release no. CB19-157. Census.gov, October 29, 2019. www.census.gov/housing/hvs/files/qtr319/Q319press.pdf.

US Congress. House. *Reauthorization of the HOPE VI Program: Hearing before the Subcommittee on Housing and Community Opportunity of the Committee on Financial Services, US House of Representatives.* 110th Cong., 1st Sess., June 21, 2007. Serial No. 110-44. Washington, DC: US Government Printing Office, 2007. https://fraser.stlouisfed.org/title/reauthorization-hope-vi-program-5075.

US Department of Housing and Urban Development. *Charlotte Housing Authority FY 2018 Moving Forward / MTW Plan.* Revised March 12, 2018. www.hud.gov/sites/dfiles/PIH/documents/CHAFY18PLANAppendices.pdf.

US Department of Housing and Urban Development. *A Guide to Public Housing Repositioning: Medium and Large Public Housing Authorities.* March 2021. www.hud.gov/sites/dfiles/PIH/documents/Guide_Repositioning_Medium_Large_PHAs.pdf.

Vale, Lawrence J. *After the Projects: Public Housing and the Governance of the Poorest Americans.* New York: Oxford University Press, 2019.

———. "The Future of Planned Poverty: Redeveloping America's Most Distressed Public Housing Projects." *Netherlands Journal of Housing and the Built Environment* 14, no. 1 (1999): 13–31. www.jstor.org/stable/41107778.

Vale, Lawrence J., and Yonah Freemark. "From Public Housing to Public-Private Housing: Seventy-Five Years of American Social Experimentation." *Journal of the American Planning Association* 78, no. 4 (2012): 379–402. www.tandfonline.com/doi/abs/10.1080/01944363.2012.737985.

Vandell, Kerry D. "FHA Restructuring Proposals: Alternatives and Implications." *Housing Policy Debate* 6, no. 2 (1995): 299–394.

Vann, Andre D., and Beverly Washington Jones. *Durham's Haiti.* Charleston, SC: Arcadia Publishing, 1999.

Verdier, James M. *Background Paper: Real Estate Tax Shelter Subsidies and Direct Subsidy Alternatives.* Congressional Budget Office, May 1977. www.cbo.gov/publication/21338.

von Hoffman, Alexander. "Calling upon the Genius of Private Enterprise: The Housing and Urban Development Act of 1968 and the Liberal Turn to Public-Private Partnerships."

Studies in American Political Development 27, no. 2 (October 2013): 165–94. doi:10.1017/S0898588X13000102.

———. *House by House, Block by Block: The Rebirth of America's Urban Neighborhoods*. New York: Oxford University Press, 2003.

———. "Into the Wild Blue Yonder: The Urban Crisis, Rocket Science, and the Pursuit of Transformation Housing Policy in the Great Society, Part Two." Joint Center for Housing Studies, Harvard University, March 2011. www.jchs.harvard.edu/sites/default/files/media/imp/w11-3_von_hoffman.pdf.

———. "The Lost History of Urban Renewal." *Journal of International Research on Placemaking and Urban Sustainability* 1, no. 3 (November 2008): 281–301.

———. "The Past, Present, and Future of Community Development in the United States." In *Investing in What Works for America's Communities*, edited by Nancy O. Andrews et al., 10–54. San Francisco: Federal Reserve Bank of San Francisco, 2012. http://whatworksforamerica.org/pdf/whatworks_fullbook.pdf.

———. "Why They Built Pruitt-Igoe." In *From Tenements to the Taylor Homes: In Search of an Urban Housing Policy in Twentieth-Century America*, edited by John F. Bauman, Roger Biles, and Kristin M. Szylvian, 180–205. University Park: Pennsylvania State University Press, 2000.

Watt, Jason N. "The East Independence Plaza Building, Charlotte 1973–1994: Reflections on the Meaning of Progress." Undergraduate thesis, Yale University, April 1995.

Webb, Michael D., and Timica Melvin. "Appendix C: Evaluating Moving to Work Compliance and Progress toward Statutory Goals." December 2022. In *Inlivian, Moving to Work Annual Report 2022*, 72–106. May 18, 2023. www.hud.gov/sites/dfiles/PIH/documents/CharlotteFY22Report.pdf.

Weber, Bret A., and Amanda Wallace. "Revealing the Empowerment Revolution: A Literature Review of the Model Cities Program." *Journal of Urban History* 38, no. 1 (January 2012): 173–92.

Wheaton, William L. C. "The Housing Act of 1949." *Journal of the American Institute of Planners*, 1949. Reprinted in *The Affordable Housing Reader*, 2nd ed., edited by Elizabeth J. Mueller and J. Rosie Tighe, 16–20. New York: Routledge, 2022.

Whiting, Sarah. "Super!" *Log*, no. 16 (Spring–Summer 2009): 19–26.

Wiese, Andrew. *Places of Their Own: African American Suburbanization in the Twentieth Century*. Chicago: University of Chicago Press, 2004.

Williams, Sabrina L. "From HOPE VI to HOPE Sick?" Dollars and Sense: Real World Economics, 2003. www.dollarsandsense.org/archives/2003/0703williams.html.

Wilson, William Julius. *The Truly Disadvantaged: The Inner City, the Underclass, and Public Policy*. Chicago: University of Chicago Press, 1987.

Winnick, Louis. *Rental Housing Opportunities for Private Investment*. New York: McGraw-Hill, 1958.

Woo, Andrew. "How Have Rents Changed since 1960?" ApartmentList.com, June 14, 2016. www.apartmentlist.com/research/rent-growth-since-1960.

Woods, Louis Lee, III. "Almost 'No Negro Veteran . . . Could Get a Loan': African Americans, the G.I. Bill and the NAACP Campaign against Residential Segregation, 1917–1960." *Journal of African American History* 98, no. 3 (Summer 2013): 392–417.

Wright, Gwendolyn. *Building the Dream: A Social History of Housing in America*. Cambridge, MA: MIT Press, 1983.
Yockey, Ross. *The Builder: The Croslands and How They Shaped a Region*. Seattle: Abecedary Press, 2004.
York, Smedes, with John Lawrence Sharpe. *Growing Up with Raleigh*. Raleigh: Lulu Publishing, 2014.

INDEX

202. *See* Section 202
207. *See* Section 207
221(d)(3). *See* Section 221(d)(3)
235. *See* Section 235
236. *See* Section 236
603. *See* FHA 603
608. *See* FHA 608

absentee landlords, 78, 83, 127
accelerated depreciation, 87–100, 104–5, 151, 223, 229; criticized, 89–91
Addams, Jane, 27
Addison Apartments, 112, 114
affordable housing: defined, 9–10, 146; named, 9; shortages after World War II, 49, 60; shortages in the urban renewal era, 69, 83–84, 120, 140; shortfall today, 1, 2, 6, 8, 207, 212–17, 222
Afro-American Mutual Insurance, 78, 79, 84
Alexander family, 56–57; Fred Alexander, 56–62, 80, 85, 109, 120, 133, 188; Kelly Alexander Sr., 45, 57, 80–85, 120
Alford, Ernest, 102–3
Alson Court, 36–38, 44
Anita Stroud Homes, 184
apartment boom in 1960s–1970s, 92–94, 100, 259n2
Arbor Glen, 110, 169, 181–83, 194, 230
Area Median Income (AMI): defined, 2; 30 percent AMI (extremely low income), 1, 2, 6, 8, 207, 212–17, 222
Arteaga, Stefania, 215
Ascent Housing, 221
Ashley Square, 137, 170, 184, 188, 190–92, 195, 202, 214; Springcroft at Ashley Park, 191
Atlanta, 41, 185, 281n20

Ballantyne neighborhood, 192, 217, 220
Baltimore, 76, 150
banks, 4, 159; First Union (becomes Wachovia 2001, merges into Wells Fargo 2008), 63, 159–60; NCNB (becomes Nationsbank 1991, then Bank of America 1998), 4, 55, 63, 160, 202; NCNB CDC (becomes Bank of America CDC 1998), 172, 173, 184, 186–87, 190
Bao Le, Cat, 215
Barringer Hotel (Cavalier Inn), 131, 139, 198, 200, 202
bathrooms, 39–40, 69–77, 86. *See also* privy toilet
Baxter, Herbert, 72
Beach Haven (New York City), 64
Beatties Ford Road corridor, 98, 102, 181, 184. *See also* Biddleville
Belk, John, 121
Belmont neighborhood, 33, 220
Belvedere Homes, 46, 186
Biddleville, 127–28, 138, 156, 209
Blankenship, A.V., 61
boardinghouse, 15, 43
bonds. *See* housing bonds
Booth Gardens (renamed Poplar Grove 2024), 10, 124, 139, 172
Boston, 126, 159, 170–74, 203. *See also* Massachusetts Housing Partnership
Boulevard Homes, 88, 105–8, 110, 111, 113; replaced by Renaissance West under HOPE VI, 170, 179, 184–85
Boyer, Martin, 41
Brightwalk, 2, 10, 59, 66, 160, 192, 230; construction and financing of, 170, 188–90
Brooke Amendment, 167, 293n32

318 ■ Index

Brookhill Village, 47, 67, 193; construction and financing of, 58–60, 106; initial rents at, 61; struggles over displacement, 216, 223–25
Brooklyn neighborhood of Charlotte: early history of, 20–22, 33–34, 44, 75; demolition of, 44–45, 77–86, 107, 122, 127, 161, 217; proposed re-redevelopment of, as Brooklyn Village, 228
Brookshire, Stan, 109
Bruns Avenue, 160–63
building codes, 6, 28, 145; resistance to, 69–77, 85–86, 140–42
busing. *See Swann v. Charlotte-Mecklenburg Board of Education*

Caldwell, Ralphine. *See* Local Initiatives Support Corporation
Cameron Village, Raleigh, NC, 65
Camp Greene, 70
Canada, Geoffrey, 185
Cannon, James, 93
Carroll, Don, 119, 124–25, 127, 134, 141, 147
Carter, Jimmy and Rosalynn, 152
Carver, George Washington, 106
Casey, Hugh, 118–20, 134
Cavalier Inn. *See* Barringer Hotel
Cedar Knoll, 123, 137
Centre South. *See* Strawn Apartments
CHA. *See* Charlotte Housing Authority
Chambers, Julius, 109, 115, 117–18, 134, 195
Charlotte, NC, affordable housing background, 1, 4–6, 210
Charlotte Housing Authority (CHA), 8, 10, 74, 131, 144, 154, 159, 168, 191, 193,; begun, 41; builds scattered-site housing, 123, 127, 129, 134, 137–38; business-minded approach, 198–206; desegregation of, 107; early public housing, 41–46, 67, 76, 84–85; HOPE VI projects, 173–86; Horizon subsidiaries, 198, 200, 201, 205, 290n8–9; *McKnight* lawsuit and consent decree, 118–22; renamed Inlivian, 8, 197, 205–6, 207–9, 233; takes over projects built by others, 98, 104–5, 109, 113–14

Charlotte Housing Trust Fund. *See* housing bonds
Charlotte-Mecklenburg Housing Partnership (CMHP), 10, 144, 165, 168, 173, 181, 219, 220; beginning, 158–60; Brightwalk, 188–91; Genesis Park, 182, 285n62; Park at Oaklawn, 182–84; renamed DreamKey Partners, 10; Seversville project, 160–63
Charlotte-Mecklenburg Schools, 5, 58, 59, 117–19, 121, 161, 178, 185
Charlottetown Terrace, 112, 114, 131, 139
Charlotte Uprising, 197, 215
cheap money, 101, 197, 199, 228, 290n6. *See also* low-interest loans
Cherry Community Organization (CCO), 127, 200–201
Cherry neighborhood, 127, 137, 195, 198, 200–202
Chetty, Raj, 213–14, 233
Chicago, 28, 29, 31, 51, 116, 133
churches: AME Zion, 20, 45, 57, 78–79, 98, 106, 111; Baptist, 58, 118, 217, 220; Methodist, 216; Presbyterian, 132, 220; United House of Prayer, 178, 220
Cisneros, Henry, 174
Civilian Conservation Corps, 32
Claiborne, Jack, 123, 134
Claremont Apartments, 137
Clasen-Kelly, Fred, 217
Clawson Village, 102, 153
Clay, James W., 150
Clemmons, Mr. and Mrs. J.C., 58
CMHP. *See* Charlotte-Mecklenburg Housing Partnership
Coble, Henry L., 107, 111
"coddling" the poor, 180, 203, 204
code enforcement. *See* building codes
Colean, Miles, 35
Coliseum Drive Apartments, 128, 137
Color of Law, The, 6, 34, 216–17
Columbia, SC, 57, 218
Columbia Point, Boston, 170–71, 173. *See also* Harbor Point, Boston
Community Development Block Grants (CDBG), 122, 127–28, 160

community development corporation (CDC), 172, 173, 184, 186–87, 190
community organizing, 124–28, 162, 179; in battles over siting of subsidized housing, 109, 157–58, 192; in Cherry, 200; after Keith Lamont Scott shooting, 217; in Seversville, 162; in switch from at-large to district elections, 124–26; in Third Ward and Fourth Ward, 172
Community Reinvestment Act (CRA), 159, 162, 172, 277n61, 281n14
Connelly, Charles W., 37, 41, 53
consent decree. See *McKnight v. Romney*
Cooper, Jack, 98
Corcoran Mullins Jennison, 170, 280n3
Cotswold Village, 66
COVID, 227
CRA. *See* Community Reinvestment Act
crescent and wedge, 5–6, 214
Crisis Assistance Ministry, 149
Crosland, John, 52, 62, 149, 150, 190, 200; building market-rate apartments, 92–93, 132; employing Paul Leonard, 103, 132–33; and executive Dionne Nelson, 185; and executive Judd Little, 185, 200; with Habitat for Humanity, 152–53; HOPE VI, development under, 160, 181, 183–84; Low-Income Housing Tax Credit, use of, 154, 156–58; Section 8 Project-Based projects, 132–33, 139; Section 221(d)(3) and Section 236 projects, 101, 102–3; and state-level leadership, 143–44, 146–48
Crutchfield, Edward, 62–63

Dalton Village, 88, 105–8, 111, 113; replaced by Arbor Glen under HOPE VI, 110, 169, 181–83, 194
Daly, George, 120, 126, 134
Davis, Mildred Baxter, 172
deed restrictions, 20
depreciation. *See* accelerated depreciation
Desmond, Matthew, 216
Dillehay, Harold, 67, 68
Dillehay Courts, 67, 68, 105, 106, 111, 113
Dilworth neighborhood, 33, 36, 55, 85, 114, 220

district elections, shift from at-large, 123–26, 127
Double Oaks: financing and construction of, 48, 55–61, 64–66, 83, 106; renovation of, 133; replaced by Brightwalk, 188–89
Douglas, Ben, 39, 41
Dove's Nest, 187
DreamKey Partners, 10, 138, 144, 170, 189, 224, 230. *See also* Charlotte–Mecklenburg Housing Partnership

Earle Village, 84, 113, 169, 170; remade as First Ward Place, 172–79, 205
Eastover neighborhood, 36–37
Eccles, Marriner, 35–36
ecology, 171
Edwin Towers, 84, 112, 114, 124
ELI. *See* extremely low-income (ELI) households
Elizabeth neighborhood, 18–19, 33–34, 55, 124
Ervin, Charles, 52, 101
Etheridge, Mark, 221
eviction, 27, 141, 216, 266n7
extremely low-income (ELI) households, 1, 2, 6, 8–9, 212–17, 220–22, 298n80; defined, 9, 215; incomes of Brooklyn residents, 83–84; incomes of FHA 608 tenants, 56–61

Faircloth, Lauch, 170, 180
Faircloth Amendment, 170, 178, 180, 205, 230
Fair Housing Act, 117, 120, 129, 134, 207
Fair Labor Standards Act, 26
Fairmarket Plaza, 133, 139, 156
Fairmarket Square, 154, 156–58, 166
Fairview Homes, 57–58, 229; financing and construction of, 25, 41–46, 72, 106, 139; replaced by Park at Oaklawn under HOPE VI, 160, 169, 179, 182–84
Federal Housing Administration (FHA), 18, 25, 32–33, 35–38, 47–68; aid to middle-class apartments, 32–38, 52–54, 62–63; FHA plan book, *Planning Rental Housing*, 52.

Federal Housing Administration (*cont.*)
  See also FHA 603; FHA 608; Section 202; Section 207, Section 221(d)(3); Section 235; Section 236
Federal Reserve, 101, 197, 199, 227–28, 290n6
Ferguson, Abner, 49
FHA. *See* Federal Housing Administration
FHA 202. *See* Section 202
FHA 207. *See* Section 207
FHA 221(d)(3). *See* Section 221(d)(3)
FHA 235. *See* Section 235
FHA 236. *See* Section 236
FHA 603, 50–51
FHA 608, 6–7, 47–68, 83, 86
fifty-unit cap, 121, 123, 136, 148, 169
Fillette, Ted, 75, 120, 126–29, 134, 140–42, 160, 217
financial literacy classes. *See* self-sufficiency training
First Union Bank, 63, 159–60
First Ward Place. *See* Earle Village
FMK Architects, 174
food desert, 110, 158
Forest Hills Gardens, 30
Foundation for Cooperative Housing, 102, 111
Freedom Drive, 222
Frye, Henry, 141
Fuller, Millard, 152–53
Fullilove, Mindy Thompson. *See* helping networks
Furman, David, 178

Gables senior apartments, 188, 194–95
Gantt, Harvey, 5, 98, 124–27, 134, 136, 140–41, 150, 172
garden apartments, 29–31, 36–37, 53, 65
garden city idea, 28–31, 37
Garrett, Patricia "Pat," 160–63, 184, 188–90
Gautreaux v Chicago Housing Authority, 116–17, 120, 133
Genesis Park neighborhood, 182, 188
gentrification, 1, 11, 128, 163, 197, 206, 209–13, 215–17, 220, 299n1; and K-shaped economy, 199

Ginnie Mae (Government National Mortgage Association), 98, 100, 131
Gladedale, 128–30, 137, 229
Glen Cove, 156, 166
Goode, Alson Lloyd, 37–38
Government National Mortgage Association. *See* Ginnie Mae
Grace Emmanuel Apartments, 220
Great Depression, 6, 23–43 *passim*, 49, 78, 144
Greenhaven Apartments, 102–3, 112, 113, 132
Greenville neighborhood, 102–3, 120, 127, 160, 161, 182, 188
Grier Heights neighborhood, 139, 148, 154
Grubb, Clay, 200, 216

habitable housing requirement, 140–42. *See also* building codes
Habitat for Humanity, 2, 103, 146, 152–53, 207–8
Hackberry Place, 172
Hall, Pat, 105, 121
Hampshire Hills neighborhood, 157–58
Harbor Point, Boston, 170–71, 173
Harris, Cora, 39, 71, 246n29
Harris, Patricia, 9
Harris and Kannon v. HUD, 120, 122, 126, 128, 267n15
Hawkins, Reginald, 98, 107, 111, 266n9
Heath, Kathryn, 159–60, 219
Helms, Parks, 141
helping networks, 76, 174, 179, 230
Hicks, Fred, 128
Hillcrest Apartments, 132, 139
Hoagland, Sandy, 177
Hogan, James B., 134–35
homeless shelters, 2
Home Owners' Loan Corporation (HOLC), 32–34
Honeycreek Senior Apartments, 186, 194
Hoover, Herbert, 27
Hoovervilles (tent camps), 27
HOPE VI, 169–70, 173–86, 230; causing loss of lowest-income housing, 177, 193, 210; and mixed-income ideal, 170–71, 173,

177–78, 180; off-site apartment construction, use of, 181, 182, 184–85; and one-for-one replacement, 177, 186, 205
Horizon Development. *See* Charlotte Housing Authority
Hoskins Mill, 154, 165
Housing Act: of 1934, 32; Wagner-Stegall of 1937; of 1949, 69; of 1954, 260n16
Housing and Urban Development (HUD), 9, 87, 98, 102–14 *passim*, 117, 123, 129–34 *passim*, 170, 180, 229, 233; funding cutbacks, 190, 204; lawsuits against, 117–22 *passim*, 126, 155. *See also* HOPE VI; Rental Assistance Demonstration; Section 8 vouchers
housing bonds: defined, 146; North Carolina Housing Trust Fund, 143, 149–51. *See also* Housing Trust Fund, Charlotte
housing code, 140. *See also* building codes
Housing Justice Coalition, 215
Housing Trust Fund, Charlotte, 8, 144, 208, 217, 234; recent growth of, 217, 219–21; spun off from Innovative Housing Fund, 155–56, 186–87
Housing Trust Fund, North Carolina, 149–51, 156–57, 160, 162, 164, 224, 230
Howard, Ebenezer. *See* garden city idea
Howell, Lisa Stockton, 216
Hunter Apartments, 18–19

income stagnation in 2000–2020, 176–77, 210–12
Independence Boulevard, 80
Inlivian, 197–206. *See also* Charlotte Housing Authority
Innovative Housing Fund. *See* housing bonds
Internal Revenue Service (IRS), 65, 88, 89, 122, 153–54
investor-owned subsidized housing, 10, 20–22, 31, 87–114. *See also* Low-Income Housing Tax Credit
investors buying up homes, 213

Jacobs, Alvin C., 216–17, 222, 224–25
Jacobs, Jane, 171

Jacobs, Rosalyn Allison, 217
Johnson, Lyndon B. (LBJ), 89, 116, 117, 133–34, 167
Johnson C. Smith University (JCSU), 63, 127, 156, 181, 209
Johnston Mill, 154, 166
Jones, Edwin, 41, 74, 76, 124

Kelley, Pam, 217, 220
Kelly, Mary and Pete, 217
King, Martin Luther, Jr., 115, 116, 117, 120, 126, 134
K-shaped economy, 197, 199, 209, 212, 227, 232, 289n6
Kucab, Bob, 148
Kuralt, Charles, 62

Lanham Act, 46
Lanning, James A., 117–18
Laurel Street, 144, 185, 220
Leafcrest, 123, 137
Leake, George, 98, 106–7, 118–22, 185
Lee, Howard, 146–47
Legal Aid, 118, 126, 127, 129, 142
Leonard, Paul, 102–3, 132–33, 134, 146, 153
Levittown, 51
LIHTC. *See* Low-Income Housing Tax Credit
limited-dividend financing, 28–29, 32, 35, 39, 221, 260n20
limited liability corporation (LLC), 89, 92–93, 132, 157, 204–5, 259n3; encouraged by IRS rule, 89
limited partnership. *See* limited liability corporation
LISC. *See* Local Initiatives Support Corporation
Little, Jud, 185, 200
Little Rock Homes, 98, 102, 106–7, 109–13, 118–22, 185, 194
LLC. *See* limited liability corporation
Local Initiatives Support Corporation (LISC), 220, 225
Loftis, V. P., 64, 66

low-income households: definitions, 7, 9, 43, 99, 167–68, 230. *See also* extremely low-income (ELI) households
Low-Income Housing Tax Credit (LIHTC), 6–7, 68, 186–96, 200, 217, 220, 230–31; acquisition and rehab, 154; defined, 151, 153–54, 230; incomes of residents eligible for, 167–68, 230; as part of HOPE VI, 173, 181, 184, 186; as part of RAD, 204–5; program created, 143, 145, 148, 151–69; plusses and minuses of, 164–65, 230–31
low-interest loans, 40, 131, 132, 172, 197, 199, 290n6; in Section 202, 113–14; in Section 221(d)(3), 95; in Section 236, 101; in trust fund projects, 145–46, 162; ultra-low interest rates set by Federal Reserve, 199, 227–28. *See also* cheap money
Lyles, Bissett, Carlisle and Wolff, 57, 59, 61
Lyles, Vi Alexander: actions as mayor, 197–98, 216, 217, 218–19; actions prior to mayoralty 156, 181, 186–87, 215, 218–19
Lynch, Phyllis, 126, 127
Lynx light rail, 184, 212–13, 231

Mack, Corrine, 216
Macon, Richard, 118, 120, 122
Marsh, Lex, 60, 66–67, 220
Massachusetts Housing Partnership, 159
Maulden, Julia, 152–53
McAlpine Terrace, 156, 166
McColl, Hugh, 62–63, 159, 172, 178
McCreesh Place. *See* supportive housing
McKinnon, Ray, 216, 220, 224
McKnight v. Romney, 109–10, 118, 120–21, 155; consent decree, 121–22, 123, 155, 267n21
McMillan, James, 117–19, 121–22, 124, 126–29, 134
McNeel, Luciel, 126, 129, 188, 195
Meachem, Fulton, 200–203, 205–6, 207–9
Meadow Oaks, 123–24, 137
Merino, Oliver, 215
Mezzanine, 220, 222
Michigan Boulevard Apartments. *See* Rosenwald Homes

minimum wage, 26, 64, 210, 235
mixed income / mixed use: commonplace before mid-twentieth century, 12–19, 75–76; considered state-of-the-art in 2010s, 8, 188–92, 200–203, 206, 220, 224, 23; desirability of, 8, 99, 171, 172, 186–87, 193, 231; encouraged under HOPE VI, 170, 173, 177–78, 184, 185, 230; forbidden by deed restrictions, 20; punished by HOLC, 33
Moore, W. Marshall, 53, 54, 66
Moore Place, 187. *See also* supportive housing
Morningside Apartments, 61, 64, 66, 97
Morris Field Homes, 45–46
mortgages: amortized, 32, 35; before federal involvement, 18, 32; interest deduction for homeowners, 3; long-term, federally insured, 18, 29, 32–33, 35, 72; mortgaging out, 51–52, 64–65; re-sold to Ginnie Mae, 100, 131. *See also* low-interest loans
MOTION, 102–3
Mott, Seward, 66
Myers Park neighborhood, 53, 55, 60, 216, 268n27; early rental housing in 18–19; and FHA 608, 53, 55, 60, 61; and redlining, 33–34; teardowns in, 206
Myrtle Apartments, 36–38, 41, 44, 53, 94

National Association for the Advancement of Colored People (NAACP), 45, 57, 80–85, 117, 120, 216
NationsBank. *See* banks
naturally occurring affordable housing (NOAH), 6, 90, 124, 232, 237; defined, 10; before government involvement, 3, 7, 11–23, 69; preservation of, 221, 234; recent losses of, 197–98, 206, 209–13, 220–22; systemic problems in, 140–42
NCNB. *See* banks
Neighboring Concepts architects, 201
Nelson, Dionne. *See* Laurel Street
New Deal, 24–27, 32–43 passim, 71; New Deal consensus, 27, 36, 144
Newland Road Apartments, 57, 58, 66

neoliberalism, 7, 229
Newsome, Bree, 215
Nguyen, Tin, 215
Nia Point, 105, 181
Nixon, Richard, 89, 91, 122, 148, 160; freezes housing funds in 1973, 103, 110, 160
NOAH. *See* naturally occurring affordable housing
NoDa neighborhood, 33–34, 43, 154
Nolen, John, 31
North Carolina Housing Finance Agency (NCHFA), 143, 145–54, 156–57, 162, 164, 230, 231
North Carolina Housing Trust Fund, 149–51, 164
North Clarkson Street Apartments, 128, 137

Obama, Barack, 203
Olmsted, Frederick Law, 29–30
one-for-one replacement, 180–82, 184
OneMECK, 217
Optimist Park neighborhood, 152, 213
Orchard Park Apartments, 102–3, 112, 113, 132, 154, 165
outhouse toilet. *See* privy toilet

Pappas, Peter, 190, 231
Park at Oaklawn, 46, 170, 182–84, 194
Parker Heights Apartments, 98, 107, 111, 154, 165
parking, 53, 174
Park Towne Terrace, 112, 114, 131, 139
Perry, Justin, 217
Phillips, Dwight, 61, 66, 97–98, 107, 111
Phillips Place, 190
Piedmont Courts, 25, 41–46, 72, 106, 168, 170, 179; redeveloped as Seigle Point under HOPE VI, 46, 170, 184–85, 195, 230
Pine Valley, 110
Pitts Drive Apartments, 104–5, 111, 113
Plaza Terrace Apartments, 47–48, 60, 64, 66–67, 193
political will, 122–29, 133–34, 213–22, 230, 232

Portillo, Ely, 203, 215
Pressley Ridge. *See* Roseland
privy toilet, 70, 72. *See also* bathrooms
project-based programs, 6; Section 8 Project-Based, 6, 114, 116, 129–35, 139, 149, 156, 163, 188; Section 8 Project-Based as part of RAD, 204. *See also* FHA 608; Section 221(d)(3); Section 236; Turnkey programs
Project-Based Voucher, 205
property values, 134–35
Prudential Insurance, 36
Pruitt, Wallace, 162
Pruitt-Igoe, 7, 115, 171
public housing, 6, 9–10, 39–46, 118, 121, 179, 205; defined, 10, 39, 113, 205; desegregation in, 107; Earle Village, 84, 113, 169, 170, 172–78, 179; employment requirements, 174–77; Fairview Homes and Piedmont Courts, 39–46; financing, 39–40, 290n32; opposition to, 8, 99, 109, 135–36, 192, 202, 232; Rental Assistance Demonstration (RAD), 197, 203–5; senior citizen projects (section 202), 112–14, 123, 131, 133, 156, 191, 192, 198; seniors projects as part of HOPE VI, 176, 184; Southside Homes and Belvedere Homes, 45–46. *See also* scattered-site program
Purpose Built Communities, Atlanta, 185

Quality Housing and Work Responsibility Act of 1998, 180

racial intermingling: barred by suburban deed restrictions, 20; common at start of twentieth century, 15–16, 71; punished by HOLC, 33
racial segregation. *See* segregation: racial
RAD. *See* Rental Assistance Demonstration
Radburn, 29–30, 35, 41, 53
Raleigh, NC, 65
Rash, Betty Chafin, 124, 127, 143, 149–50, 158–60, 172, 219
Rash, Dennis, 172
Ray, Tom, 118–21, 133–34

Reagan, Ronald, 6, 143–45, 149–50, 151, 155, 167, 198, 229, 230; Reagan consensus, 36, 144
Realtors' Standard House Ordinance, 72–77, 140, 236
Red Carpet Inn, 131, 139
Redevelopment Commission, 78–85
redlining, 33–34, 78, 80, 93, 116, 159, 172
Renaissance West, 110, 170, 179, 184–85, 195–96, 230, 233. *See also* Boulevard Homes
Renaissance West Community Initiative, 185
Rental Assistance Demonstration (RAD), 197, 203–5
Residential Rental Agreements Act, 141
Restorative Justice CLT, 228
revenue sharing, 116, 122–23, 127, 128, 155, 229
role models, 45, 75, 171–72, 191
Romney, George, 109, 118
Roosevelt, Franklin Delano (FDR), 24–27, 32, 37, 39, 144. *See also* New Deal
Root Shock. *See* helping networks
Roseland (becomes Pressley Southend, then Pressley Ridge), 97, 107, 111, 154
Rosenwald Homes, 29, 31, 35, 37, 221
Rothstein, Richard. See *Color of Law, The*
Rouse, James, 159

Salvation Army, 10, 139, 172
Sawyer, Vernon, 83, 122
scattered-site program, 6–8, 103, 110, 115–38, 169, 229, 231; Charlotte as national leader, 133–34; and consent decree, 121–22, 267n21; continued long-term use, 190, 193, 200, 214, 229, 231; end of, 155; fifty-unit cap, 121, 123, 136, 148, 169; impact of political will on, 122–29, 133–34
schools. See *Swann v. Charlotte-Mecklenburg Board of Education*
Schwartz, Alex F., 99, 205, 238, 248n1, 258n1, 299n1
Scotland Colony Apartments, 47, 53–56, 60, 66
Scott, Keith Lamont, 197, 214–17, 219, 224

Section 202, 113–14, 184
Section 207, 35
Section 221(d)(3), 87, 95–99, 103, 106, 111, 154, 229
Section 235, 102, 110–11, 122
Section 236, 87, 95–103, 107, 132, 145, 154, 229
Section 603. *See* FHA 603
Section 608. *See* FHA 608
Section 8 Project-Based, 6, 114, 116, 129–35, 139, 143, 149, 156, 163, 188; as part of the RAD program, 204
Section 8 vouchers, 6–8 *passim*, 10, 148–49, 163, 182; and source-of-income discrimination, 207–9
segregation: economic, 5–6, 75–76, 106, 121, 213–14, 233; "open housing" desegregation efforts, 116–21; racial, 6, 34, 41–42, 46, 56, 77–85, 107, 109, 157
Seigle Point, 46, 170, 184–85, 195, 230
self-sufficiency training, 174, 176, 185
Sellars, Stony, 200–201
Sellers, Louise, 127–28
Selwyn-Queens Apartments, 66
Selwyn Village, 47, 61–63, 67
set-apart (location ideal), 7–8
Seversville neighborhood, 160–63, 166; gentrification in, 209–10
sewer and water. *See* building codes
Shannon, Harrison, 174, 181, 198
shortages of affordable housing: shortfall today, 1, 2, 6, 8, 207, 212–17, 222; in the urban renewal era, 69, 83–84, 120, 140; after World War II, 49, 60
slum clearance. *See* urban renewal
Source of Income Discrimination (SOID), 207–9
SouthPark Mall, 2, 128, 131, 137, 170, 188, 190–91, 202
Southside Homes, 10, 46, 58, 106, 187, 193
Spangler, C. D., 52, 55–67, 83, 106, 133, 139, 160, 188; ownership in Brookhill Village, 58–60, 223–25; utilizes FHA 608, 55–67
Springcroft at Ashley Park, 191
Stein, Clarence, 29–30
Stevenson Apartments, 188

Stonewall Jackson Homes, 45–46
St. Paul Baptist Church, 58, 220
Strawn Apartments, 85, 112, 114, 196, 198; redeveloped as Centre South, 200–203
subsidized housing, 3, 36, 47, 63, 68, 69, 115, 145, and *passim*; subsidies to the wealthy, 3, 36, 53, 90–92, 143, 169
Summers, Cam, 107
Sunridge, 123, 137
superblock. *See* garden city idea
supportive housing, 187, 192
Surrey, Stanley, 90
Swann v. Charlotte-Mecklenburg Board of Education, 5, 117–19, 128, 134, 152
Syfert, Pam, 186, 218–19
Szymanski, Ken, 9, 230

Tall Oaks, 127, 137, 198, 200–202
Tarlton Hills, 128, 138
tax credits. *See* Low-Income Housing Tax Credit
tax shelters, 7, 87–105, 107, 132, 145, 150, 151–53. *See also* accelerated depreciation; Low-Income Housing Tax Credit
teardowns, 206–7, 209–10, 213
Techwood Homes in Atlanta, 41
Ten 05 West Trade, 186–87, 194, 219
Tenement Law, 28
tent camps, 27, 227–28
Tomlinson, Tommy, 62
Treloar House, 12–17, 33, 75
Truman, Harry, 46, 49
Trump, Fred and Donald, 64
trust fund. *See* housing bonds
Tryon Hills, 55–56, 58, 60, 61, 66, 106, 133
Turnkey programs: abuses under, 103–11, 229; defined, 103–5, 229; Turnkey I, 10, 87, 95, 98, 103–11, 181; Turnkey II, 104; Turnkey III, 98; Turnkey Leasing, 10, 87, 95, 98, 103–5

Unified Development Ordinance (UDO), 19, 243n3
United States Housing Authority (USHA), 39–41, 44

Urban Development Systems Corporation. *See* Westinghouse Corporation
urban growth machine (Logan and Molotch), 4
Urban Land Institute, 174, 202
urban renewal, 6, 44, 69–70, 140, 171, 217, 254n1; in Brooklyn neighborhood, 77–86, 131, 228; and displacement, long-term effects of, 106, 107, 126–27, 179, 210; ended, 122; in Greenville neighborhood, 102, 120, 127, 160, 161, 182, 188;

Vinroot, Richard, 158
Vinson, E. L., 106
vouchers. *See* Section 8

Wachovia Bank, 148, 162, 188
Wagner-Steagall Act, 39
Wards: First Ward, 2, 10, 12–17, 33, 84, 220; First Ward and HOPE VI, 169, 172–78, 205, 230; Second Ward (*see* Brooklyn); Third Ward, 2, 128, 172; Fourth Ward, 2, 10, 33, 84, 102, 114; Fourth Ward revitalization; 124, 150, 172
wartime housing, 31, 45–46
Watt, Mel, 150, 172; one-for-one replacement, 178, 180
Weaver, Robert C., 104
West Boulevard, 105–10, 118–21
Westinghouse Corporation, 98, 102, 106
Westminster Corporation, 131–32, 139, 148
westside neighborhoods. *See* Beatties Ford Road corridor; Biddleville; West Boulevard
Westwood Apartments, 61, 67, 133, 139
Weyerhaeuser, 132, 148
Weyland Homes, 47, 60, 61, 67
Wiese, Andrew, 34
Wilkinson Boulevard, 47, 60, 139
Wilson, William Julius, 171
Windsong, 110
Winner, Leslie, 130
women's club, 39, 43, 70–72
Woods, Ricky, 217, 220, 294n46

Woodyard, Charles, 177, 179, 181–82, 185, 190, 198, 200; cost-center accounting, 290n11
workforce housing, 66, 85, 99, 197, 206, 292n21
working poor, 155, 165, 168, 193
Works Progress Administration (WPA), 32, 40, 41, 57, 72

Yonkers, NY, 133
Younts, Paul, 60, 66, 67
YWCA, 10

zoning, 76, 80, 84, 109, 118; begins in Charlotte, 72, 80; inclusionary zoning, 236